South Asia: Crisis of Development

SOUTH ASIA
CRISIS OF DEVELOPMENT

The Case of Bangladesh

Moudud Ahmed

Ⓤ The University Press Limited

The University Press Limited
Red Crescent House
61 Motijheel C/A
P.O. Box 2611
Dhaka 1000
Bangladesh

Fax: (8802) 9565443
E-mail: upl@bttb.net.bd
Website: www.uplbooks.com

First published 2002
Third impression 2005

Copyright © Moudud Ahmed 2002

All rights are reserved. No part of this publication may be reproduced or transmitted in any form or by any means without prior permission in writing from the publisher. Any person who does any unauthorized act in relation to this publication may be liable to criminal prosecution and civil claims for damages.

Cover design by Ashraful Hassan Arif

ISBN 984 05 1653 1

Published by Mohiuddin Ahmed, The University Press Limited, Dhaka. This book has been set in Times New Roman. Designer: Babul Chandra Dhar and printed at Elora Art Publicity, 635 North Shahjahanpur, Dhaka, Bangladesh.

*Dedicated to
my wife Hasna, our son Aman, daughter Ana
and
Emily MacFarquhar, a friend*

Contents

List of Tables	ix
Acknowledgement	xi
Preface	xiii

Chapter 1   **South Asia as a Socio-political Unit**   1
               In Search of Identity   1
               The Movement for Pakistan and the Partition of India   8

Chapter 2   **Internal Problems and Performances**   19
               India   20
               Pakistan   30
               Sri Lanka   38
               Nepal   42
               Bhutan   47
               The Maldives   48
               Bangladesh   48
               Ethnic Conflicts: The Chittagong Hill Tracts   60

Chapter 3   **Inter-state Conflicts**   93
               India and Pakistan   94
               Kashmir   95
               The Military and the Effect of Nuclearization   110
               India and Sri Lanka   138
               India and Nepal   143
               India and Bhutan   144
               India and the Maldives   145
               Nepal and Bhutan   145

viii South Asia: Crisis of Development

	Bangladesh and Pakistan	145
	India and Bangladesh	147
	The Friendship Treaty	152
	Water Sharing and Farakka	157
	Other Conflicting Interests	186
Chapter 4	**Economy: South and South-East Asia**	191
	South Asia	191
	South-East Asia	192
Chapter 5	**The South Asian Association for Regional Co-operation (SAARC)**	217
Chapter 6	**Politics and State Management in South Asia: Some Characteristics**	231
	Assassination and Killing of Leaders	231
	Democracy within Parties	233
	Corruption and Patronage	235
	The Rule of Law	236
	The Bureaucracy and Governance: Policy Planning and the Policy-making Process	240
Chapter 7	**Bangladesh as a Test Case: Some Special Features**	247
	Quality of Elections	247
	Constitutional Recognition of an Interim Government	291
	Politics of Boycott and Resignation	298
	Political Victimisation and Repression of Opposition	300
	Polarisation and the Political Divide	302
Chapter 8	**The Future of South Asia: Issues and Options: The Case of Bangladesh**	305
	Role of Bangladesh	314
	Conclusion	323
Index		331

List of Tables

1.1	*Population, surface area and density of South Asian countries*	1
2.1	*Ethnic distribution of population of the CHT*	60
2.2	*Tribal household and population in Bandarban, Khagrachari and Rangamati Zilas, 1991 and 1981*	65
2.3	*Names and population of tribes*	71
3.1	*China, India and Pakistan: Military strength*	137
3.2	*Pakistan and India: The rival nuclear arsenals*	137
3.3	*Arrangement to share the Ganga as per the ad hoc agreement, 1975*	161
3.4	*Water sharing under the agreement of November 1977*	165
3.5	*Water sharing under the agreement of December 1996*	171
3.6	*Comparison of the quantity of water to be received according to the treaties signed in 1977 and 1996*	178
4.1	*Economy, wealth and poverty: South Asia*	193
4.2	*Social sector: South Asia*	194
4.3	*Military spending: South Asia*	195
4.4	*Population, surface area and density: South-East Asia*	200
4.5	*Economy, wealth and poverty: South-East Asia (Group 1)*	200
4.6	*Social sector: South-East Asia (Group 1)*	201
4.7	*Economy, wealth and poverty: South-East Asia (Group 2)*	201
4.8	*Social sector: South-East Asia (Group 2)*	202
4.9	*Structural change: Korea*	202
4.10	*Average welfare indicators: Korea*	202
4.11	*Economy, wealth and poverty: South Asia and Korea*	203
4.12	*Social sectors: South Asia and Korea*	204
4.13	*Economy, wealth and poverty: Cambodia and Vietnam*	206
4.14	*Social sector: Cambodia, Laos and Vietnam*	206
4.15	*Population, surface area and density: China, India and Korea*	206
4.16	*Economy, wealth and poverty: China, India and Korea*	207
4.17	*Economy, wealth and poverty: India and China*	209

4.18	*Military spending: India and China*	210
5.1	*Intra-SAARC trade in relation to world trade*	225
5.2	*Major export markets of SAARC member countries, 1991*	225
5.3	*Major import markets of SAARC member countries, 1991*	226
5.4	*Structure of production, 1991*	226

Acknowledgement

I would first like to thank the Frederick Ebert Stiftung to arrange for me once again a fellowship in 1996 at the South Asian Institute of Heidelberg University to start writing this book. I am grateful to Professor Dietmar Rothermund and Dr. Dieter Conrad for their support at the Institute. I am grateful to Professor Harry Harding, Dean of the Elliott School of International Affairs at The George Washington University for inviting me as a Visiting Professor in 1997, which again gave me an opportunity to work further on this book. I am also grateful to the Ford Foundation, New York, to provide the necessary fund for the Fellowship at the Asia Center at Harvard in 1998. I am grateful to Dr. Gowher Rizvi, now the head of the Ford Foundation, New Delhi for his assistance in this regard and for helping me in identifying some of the issues I needed to address in this study. Finally I must acknowledge with deep appreciation the warm friendship, support and inspiration I received from Emily and Professor Roderick MacFarquhar all the years particularly since my defeat in the election and for my assignment at the George Washington University and all the facilities they provided for me at Harvard. I am grateful to Mr. Mamun-Ur-Rashid for giving so much time to go through the manuscript and make the book ready for publication. I am grateful to Mr. Mohiuddin Ahmed, Managing Director of the University Press Limited, for taking a keen interest in publishing this book. Finally thanks to my secretary Mr. Ashok Bhattacharya for typing the manuscript several times over the years I have been working on the book.

If there are any factual mistakes in this book, I shall appreciate if readers come forward to have them corrected so that the second edition can be improved.

Preface

This is the first book I have written, as a free citizen. It has taken a longer time to finish. The initial manuscripts for the earlier books, written in long hand, could be finished without interruption while I had been in jail at different times for political reasons. But the circumstances were different this time. Having lost the elections in both seats in June 1996 and the by-election in September 1996, I started thinking that I should now seek the wilderness and retire from politics. Seclusion could be the only refuge for a defeated politician like me. Thanks to the Frederick Ebert Stiftung, I was provided a Fellowship to go once again to Heidelberg University. While overlooking the Necker river and the Castle on the hill, I decided to concentrate on writing on a topic I had desired for a long time. The books I have so far written mainly touched issues on Bangladesh. This time I wanted to look beyond.

In recent years, the more I thought of the future of Bangladesh, the more I was drawn into searching the problems associated with our development efforts. My mind was agitated with various questions. Why was Bangladesh not making progress to the extent it should have? Why, despite all the advantages the sub-continent has, it is lagging behind the South East Asian countries? What has gone wrong with us?

Why has India, the largest and the most dominant state in South Asia, not been able to lead this region to prosperity? Having inherited from the British a strong system of administration, an organised military structure, a thriving class of entrepreneurs, a proven judicial system, English as a language for an immediate international exposure in trade, business and diplomacy and an elite class of highly articulate political leaders, South Asia remains one of the poorest regions of the world. With a contiguous landmass of over

4.488 million sq. kilometres and a population of over 1.3 billion, South Asia is endowed with vast natural resources together with access to important sea lanes on its three sides, but has not been able to achieve an economic break-through like many of the countries in the South East and East Asian regions.

In education, health care, housing and other basic human needs the achievements in some of the South East Asian countries are phenomenal. So too is their achievements in economic development, and in creating national wealth, savings and investment. Their productions in agriculture, manufacturing and the level of human productivity in these countries are much higher than any of the countries in South Asia. Even though countries like Vietnam, Laos and Cambodia, still have vestiges of communism, they are performing better than India, Pakistan, Bangladesh or Sri Lanka. In the 1950s and even till the early 1960s, the per capita income of the people of East Pakistan, now Bangladesh, and that of Korea was around US $70. But today, in an astonishing surge in economic growth accomplished by South Korea, its per capita income has risen to almost US $10,000. Compare this to India which is still saddled with $360, Pakistan $420, Sri Lanka $430 and Bangladesh at $340. Why has India not been able to lead South Asia? It could have done so by being friendly to her neighbours and evolving a dynamic growth model for economic development. Why has SAARC not been able to help in developing a collective growth pattern as ASEAN has done?

I must confess that, although by culture and tradition, I belong to South Asia — but until a few years ago I only had a notional view about the countries that surround us. I have now tried to understand our neighbours, particularly India and Pakistan, in order to determine the role Bangladesh can play in this region and our own future in the fast changing world.

The work was partially done at Heidelberg in 1996. The next opportunity to work on the manuscript came in 1997. I was then at the Elliott School of International Affairs of The George Washington University teaching two post-graduate courses on development issues as a Visiting Professor. Finally, in 1998 at the Asia Centre at Harvard, again as a visiting Fellow, I could finish this manuscript.

It has taken almost four years of work on this manuscript including revisions, corrections and editing to make it ready for publication.

The readers may find that I have not adequately addressed all the questions raised in this study, which may have been so due to my constraints as a practicing lawyer and politician. However, I wish to leave those with our scholars and academics to deal with.

The views expressed in this book are exclusively mine. It is an academic exercise and has no connection with the political party to which I belong. I have always been optimistic about the potential of our country to improve the quality of life for our people and I have tried to reflect my own vision of South Asia and Bangladesh. I alone remain responsible for the contents of this book and the views expressed therein.

Dhaka 31 July, 2002 *Moudud Ahmed*

Chapter 1

South Asia as a Socio-political Unit

In Search of Identity

South Asia, a region of ancient civilisations, today contains more than 1.3 billion people or about one-fifth of the world's population. Its vastness, diversity, location and natural surroundings make it the most attractive peninsula on earth. It is commonly referred to, in the geo-political context, as a sub-continent stretching from the Indian Ocean in the south to the world's highest range of mountains, the 2,600 kilometres long Himalayas, in the north. The major countries of this region — namely, India, Pakistan and Bangladesh, de-colonised from the British rule in 1947, and Sri Lanka in 1948 — have inherited some advantageous institutional features such as an administrative structure and a democratic tradition. Each country of the region, rich in its own heritage and culture, is a unique component of a shared glorious past.

Table 1.1 Population, surface area and density of South Asian countries

Country	Population (millions)	Surface area (000 square km)	Density per square km
India	987	3,288	330
Pakistan	131	796	171
Bangladesh	128	144	965
Nepal	24	147	160
Sri Lanka	19	66	290
Bhutan	1.7	47.02	16
Maldives	0.28	0.03	8.74

Source: *Human Development in South Asia 1999* (Dhaka: The University Press Limited).

The history of India as a subcontinent is not a cohesive one. From its very origin, it has been extremely divergent, as the area comprises of various races, languages and cultures, and has suffered many wars and conflicts. Because of the topography, geology and the ecological system, rivers have played an important role in dividing the land and the people. The changes in the courses of rivers have caused frequent changes in the country's history. Just as the civilisations grew on the banks of the vast rivers and their basins, so also they disappeared with the shifts in the river systems. Until the nineteenth century, geographical conditions divided the history of India into three broad, but well-marked compartments[1]; the northern plains comprising the basins of the Indus and the Ganges; the Deccan plateau south of the Narvada but to the north of the Krishna and Tengubhadra rivers; and the far south, comprising of the lands beyond those rivers south of Krishna and comprising the Tamil states. Even within these compartments were numerous states and kingdoms, tribes and divisions. Although they became a part of the Indian Empire in the nineteenth century, the Burmese territories have their own history. Similarly, Sri Lanka has had a distinct political existence of its own.

The northern plains, rich and alluvial and the seat of many of the early civilisations, always attracted foreign invaders, and provided access to the new breed of rulers and creation of their kingdoms. Along with the conquerors like Alexander the Great in the fourth century B.C came streams of Chinese scholars and pilgrims, as the region was then known as the Holy Land of Buddhism. Fa-Hsien and Hiuen Tsang in the fifth and seventh centuries A.D were the most prominent of these scholars. In more recent times, Central Asian and Arab scholars such as Al Beruni and Ibn Batuta have recorded their travels to India. While the rulers of the north have on number of occasion transgressed south into the Deccan area and beyond, the southern rulers hardly ever crossed into the north.

The unity of India or the governance of India as a sovereign unit has always been the desire of many conquerors and rulers of India. It has hardly ever come true. In such a diversified and divided land, the Mauryas, who could hold parts of modern Afghanistan as far as

---

[1] Vincent A. Smith. *The Oxford History of India*, edited by Percival Spear, fourth edition, p 1.

Hindukush, had to be content with their control extending south up to the northern parts of Mysore. The empires of the Kushans and Guptas were confined to the northern plains and even the Emperor Ashoka did not attempt to bring the Tamil states under his sovereignty. In accounts of the rule of the Mughal Emperor Akbar, Tamils are not mentioned. This has led historians to believe that even at the peak of his rule the southern kingdoms of India were not part of his scheme of territorial expansion.[2] Only during the rule of Emperor Aurangzeb could India be described, in a federal sense, as united largely under one domain.

In the sixteenth century, European invaders who came by sea and waterways, mostly for trade and commerce, visited India. The Portuguese, Dutch, followed by Vasco da Gama's arrival at Calicut in 1498. French merchants and adventurers who established settlements mainly in the coastal areas with commercial and exploitative motives were ousted by the most successful of the "trading companies", the British East India Company. With the growth of Bombay, Karachi and Calcutta as navigable ports during the British rule, the Indian subcontinent emerged as a place of great attraction for colonial aspirants. By the time of Warren Hastings in the eighteenth century, the process of political unification had seriously begun.

India can claim to be a region of wide diversity in religion, race, culture and language. Megasthenis, the ambassador of the Greek ruler (Satrap) Selukas Nikata, recorded 118 known kingdoms in India in the fourth century BC. India was enormously varied not only in the politically territorial sense, its climate, represents a great diversity in altitudes, temperature and rainfall and is subject to brutal extended droughts. Its vast luscious, green land adjoins arid deserts; from low alluvial plains rise the highest mountains in the world. Although with the advancement of technology, the earlier geographic barriers created by rivers and mountains have gradually disappeared, the Indian subcontinent has sustained hundreds of distinct languages and dialects, states and kingdoms.

At different stages of its history, the subcontinent has given birth to and nurtured numerous religions, cults and practices of worship of

---

[2] *Ibid.*, p. 6.

deities of various origins. Of these, Buddhism was the most prominent religious development, which expanded its influence beyond the subcontinent. Then came Christianity and Islam. The rise and rapid spread of Islam was of historical significance. The impact of the old Persian civilisation and language was based on the scripture Avesta. Christianity did not take root except at the southern tip of the subcontinent until the arrival of the British rule on Indian soil. However, Islam came as a powerful force inspiring a large section of the population. As a new religion, it was more modern, searching and invigorating. Saints and Sufis preached it as a way of life and it had a great immediate impact. Not the Muslim conquerors but the Sufis and saints that attracted the people of the sub-continent to the principles of Islam and the concept of the unity of God.

The rapid spread of Islam was almost a miracle. Soon after the death of the Prophet, his followers took his message outside Arabia and quickly converted other nations to the revolutionary and dynamic socio-political thoughts of the new religion. The domain of Islam very rapidly spread over Persia, Syria, Turkey and Egypt, and along the coast of North Africa up to Spain in the west. In the east, it swept through India and the Far East to the land known as Indonesia. The saints, leaders and military commanders of Arabia, left by the Prophet, formed a united and free nation inspired by Islam. They moved out of Arabia to accomplish their missions as ordained by Islam. The Arabs touched the coast of Makran as early as 642 A.D. The teenager soldier-commander, Mohammad bin Qasim, conquered Sind in 712 A.D. Sultan Mahmud of Ghazni marched up to the coast of Gujarat in 1020 and was followed by Muhammad of Ghor in the twelfth century. From then for the next eight hundred years, until the beginning of British rule in the eighteenth century, Muslims were the predominant rulers of the subcontinent.

The golden period of Muslim rule was that of the Great Mughals. With the ascendancy of Babar, the process of incorporating extensive territories into the empire began. Humayun, Akbar, Jahangir and Shahjahan all ruled over that empire and finally Aurangazeb was able to bring, for the first time in history, almost the whole of the Indian sub-continent under one empire. If Muslim rule in India, stretching nearly 800 years, had been oppressive or dogmatic, or fanatical rule of Islamic zealots, the outcome would have been different. Instead, the religious tolerance of the rulers, inspired by the basic tenets of forbearance preached by Islam towards other religions and showing honour and respect to other beliefs as embedded in the Koran was amply manifested. It allowed all other religious communities to coexist with considerable freedom. Some of the emperors, notably Akbar, earned the reputation of being largely secular monarchs.

However, of all the religions of the subcontinent, the most ancient is Hinduism; it propagates the worship of deities of various forms and nature. It is a religion practised from the prehistoric period. Hinduism developed through different phases but has overall retained its ancient form, and has survived primarily in India. Unlike Islam and Christianity, which predominate in many countries and under many types of governments, Hinduism is confined to India and, by extension, to Nepal. In the absence of any systematic account of its growth, it is difficult to develop a chronological history of its development. Subsequent to the prehistoric period came the development of Indo-Aryan institutions in the north together with the Brahmanical cult and culture. This strengthened Hinduism over the whole of India, although in the Dravidian culture and tradition in the south and east some prehistoric forms of worship and practices continued to survive. With the rise of Indo-Aryan and Brahmanical institutions and despotism of the Brahmin culture, the influence of the Mongolian institutions, which had developed around the tribes racially allied to the Tibetan, Gurkha and other Himalayan nations gradually waned and had come close to extinction. The predominance of Indo-Aryan and Brahmin authoritarianism led to the caste system being developed from an early stage. Caste as a hierarchical social system was the invention of the Brahmanical institution. It created a superior class and race to dominate other classes that were considered inferior, by their very birth, and were relegated to the lower classes.

The institution of Indo-Aryan Hinduism, based on the Vedic literature, had further solidified its hold over the years. The Vedas contained the traditional source of knowledge and it is claimed to have been received as an inspired revelation known as *Sruti*, which again is supplemented by traditional learning through *Sriti*. Therefore, the Vedic literature composed by the Rishis and its cultural manifestations constituted an important period of Indo-Aryan history and civilisation. The Vedas are divided into three or four parts and are known as 'Puranas'. They constituted the basic tenets of prayers, which were supplemented by the Brahmans and Upanishads. Together they, at a subsequent stage, provided the foundation for the Vedanta philosophy at a more sophisticated level. The Rig Veda, the oldest and the most important part of the Vedas, and the Samhita, the essential part of each of the Vedas as arranged in a series of books and treatises, created the fundamental basis for the development of the Hindu religion.

Hinduism is an old and ancient religion. The roots of Hinduism go back to the Rig Vedic age and even further to the Harappa culture.[3] In the face of the challenges of other religions and despite the invasions of multitudes of races, languages, culture and civilisations, Hinduism has survived. Hinduism has, nonetheless, gone through transformation at various stages of Indian history, but its basic tenets have remained the same — largely because of its language and literature, which were accepted universally by its followers. Besides, the Vedic literature, the Brahmanas and the Upanishads, epitomised in Vedanta, it was the emergence of Sanskrit as a fully fledged script language that established a new bridge between the Vedic period of literature and the later period when two epics, Ramayana and Mahabharata, were composed. These epics brought fresh life and quality to the literature, lyrics and writings in terms of grammar, vocabulary and style. The Ramayana, a single long narrative poem, authored by Valmiki, the legendary poet, is believed to have been composed in the early part of the sixth century BC. The Mahabharata, a collection of compositions by various authors was formulated sometime between 400 BC and AD 200. The Bhagavat Gita, a philosophical poem of eighteen discourses in classical Sanskrit, was added at a later stage to the Mahabharata.

The Vedic concept of worshipping nature had also undergone changes under the cult of Brahma, Vishnu and Siva, bringing in new gods and goddesses to symbolise power, fate, water and strength. New gods known as Ganesh and Parvati were introduced. Despite all the transformation that Hinduism had undergone, however, its core philosophy remained intact. And amidst all the diversity of races,

---

[3] *Ibid.*, p. 52.

languages, cultures and sects, all the wars and conquests, internal feuds and fights between the Aryans and Dravidians, the Hindu religion survived as a source of unity among its believers throughout India.

The political unity of India has always been the aspiration of Hinduism, and the concept of a universal sovereign based on Hinduism runs through the Sanskrit literature. The belief that all the Indian peoples, from the north to the extreme south, are bound by Hindu culture is emphasised in many inscriptions made by rulers at various stages of history and described in Mahabharata[4]. In the History of the Sikhs (1853, p. 283), Joseph Cunningham, while describing the Sikh fears of British aggression in 1845, recorded that 'Hindostan, moreover, from Caubul to the valley of Assam, and the island of Ceylon, is regarded as one country ... with the predominance of one monarch or one race'. Therefore, the ideal of political unity in India existed for more than 2,000 years. The continuous pursuit of that ideal explains the long acquiescence of India under British rule and the rapid growth of the All India National Congress under the leadership of Mahatma Gandhi.[5]

The political unity of India — named the Indian Empire — developed and nurtured for nearly 200 years during British rule. Although the British achieved their colonial mission of ruling the territory, they did so with the strong support and collaboration of the Hindu elite communities. When the British decided to colonise India, they had to fight and take power from the Muslim rulers. In order to retain power they acquired the support of the other community, the Hindus, which was larger in numbers than the Muslims. The British pursued a 'divide and rule policy' between the Muslims and Hindus until their last day in India.

Nonetheless, in spite of the emergence of all the diverse peoples, races, languages, sects and cultures of India, and despite the dominance of Islam for over 800 years, the fundamental unity of Hinduism was not eroded in the mainland of India. It developed into a civilisation of its own, different from any other existing religion anywhere else in the world. The influence and authority of the Brahmins, the

---

[4] *Ibid.*, p. 6.

[5] *Ibid.*, p. 7.

institution of the caste system created by the Brahmins and accepted and practised by Hindus, and their veneration of the cow, create an underlying unity amongst Hindus. Almost all Hindus respect Sanskrit as a sacred language and recognise the authority of Vedas and other ancient scriptures. The great gods like Vishnu and Siva are worshipped all over India. The pilgrimages to the holy places and the seven sacred cities from north to south, the cult of rivers and ceremonial bathing in the Ganges, the passionate attraction of the tales of Ramayana and Mahabharata — all speak of the single underlying theme of Hinduism in India.

In his introductory chapter to *The Oxford History of India*, Vincent A. Smith writes: 'India beyond all doubt possesses a deep underlying fundamental unity, far more profound than that produced either by geographical isolation or by political suzerainty. That unity transcends the innumerable diversities of blood, colour, language, dress, manners and sect.'

It is necessary to know the background of Hinduism and Hindu India, not from any communal point of view, but to understand the country and the people better in the political and global context. When we discuss South Asia, a region where India not only covers the largest area but also is dominant in both population and military power, it will assume greater importance still — the future of South Asia largely depends on the future of India. The erosion of the dominant role of the Congress Party and the rise of the Bharatiya Janata Party (BJP) to the central stage of Indian national politics is only one indicator of the importance of this religious unity. On the other hand, the constitutional pronouncement of secularism and its practice by great leaders like Mahatma Gandhi and Pandit Jawaharlal Nehru will always earn a commendable recognition in history. However, the fact that India is primarily a Hindu state, the land of Brahmans[6], cannot be ignored, as is manifested in Indian politics today.

The Movement for Pakistan and the Partition of India

From the beginning of British rule to it demise in 1947, the Muslims suffered as a minority community. In education, employment, wealth

---

[6] *Ibid.*, p. 7.

and business they were underprivileged compared to the Hindu majority community, who were taken into confidence by the colonial rulers for their own vested interests. When the movement for independence started, the Indian leaders of the National Congress represented India as a whole, irrespective of the race, caste or religion. Nevertheless, their underlying expectation was that the new unified India would be a Hindu India.

The Muslims, having realised that they would continue to be economically exploited and suppressed as a minority after the British granted independence to India, raised the demand for a separate homeland of their own as a distinct nation. The Muslims of Bengal, who began mobilising for a Muslim homeland simultaneously while the independence movement in India was developing, played the leading role. Their demand took formal shape when the historic Lahore Resolution was passed at the Annual Conference of the All-India Muslim League in 1940, which the Muslim delegates of all the provinces of India attended. The resolution not only envisaged 'autonomous and sovereign states', but also declared how the rights of minorities would be safeguarded in the future constitution. A.K. Fazlul Huq, a Bengali leader, moved the resolution as follows:

> *That it is the considered view of this session of the All-India Muslim League that no constitutional plan would be workable in this country or acceptable to the Muslim unless it is designed on the following basic principles, viz. that geographically contiguous units are demarcated into regions which should be so constituted with such territorial adjustments as may be necessary, that the area in which the Muslims are numerically in a majority, as in the North-Western and Eastern Zones of India, should be grouped to constitute independent States in which the constituted units shall be autonomous and sovereign.*
>
> *That adequate, effective and mandatory safeguards should be specifically provided in the Constitution for minorities in the units and in the regions for the protection of their religious, cultural, economic, political, administrative and other rights and interests in consultation with them.*
>
> *That this session further authorizes the Working Committee to frame a scheme of Constitution in accordance with these basic principles, providing for the assumption finally by the respective*

> *regions of all powers such as defence, external affairs, communications, customs and such other matters as may be necessary.*

There has been a lot of controversy over the interpretation of the Lahore Resolution because of its somewhat peculiar wording. The fact however, is that the Muslims of India—particularly those of Bengal, without whose support the cause of dividing India on religious lines could not have gained its momentum—had to be united, and only a resolution to that effect could achieve the necessary unity. As far as the intentions of the Muslim leaders were concerned, it was clear, beyond any doubt, from the third paragraph of the resolution that completely autonomous and sovereign states were contemplated. What was actually meant by 'independent States' or 'autonomous and sovereign' in the first paragraph and the word 'finally' in the third paragraph may provide scope for interpretation. However, if the resolution is read as a whole and considered in the geo-political context of the circumstances then prevailing the intention of the authors is clear.

It is quite probable that the spirit of the Lahore Resolution inspired both the Cripps Mission and the Cabinet Mission, which recommended complete autonomy for the provinces. The fact that the Muslim League did not oppose this part of their recommendations further substantiated the aspirations of the Muslims in India. The Muslim League's main objection was to the creation of 'one India'. It feared that in such a set of circumstances Muslims would ultimately be subjugated by the Hindu majority in the federal structure and the whole purpose of creating a 'homeland' for Muslims would be frustrated.

The Lahore Resolution was, however, subsequently side-tracked when another resolution was passed in a meeting of the elected representatives of the Muslim League in the federal and provincial legislatures on 9 April 1946, it read:

> *The Convention of the Muslim League Legislators of India, Central and Provincial, after careful consideration hereby declares that the Muslim nation will never submit to any Constitution for a United India and will never participate in any single constitution-making machinery set up for the purpose, and that any formula devised by the British Government for transferring power from the British to the people of India, which does not conform to*

> *the following just and equitable principles calculated to maintain internal peace and tranquility in the country, will not contribute to the solution of the Indian problem. That the zones comprising Bengal and Assam in the north-east and the Punjab, North-West Frontier Province, Sind and Baluchistan in the north-west of India, namely, Pakistan zones where the Muslims are a dominant majority, be constituted into a sovereign independent state and that an unequivocal undertaking be given to implement the establishment of Pakistan without delay.*

It is evident from the above that the Lahore Resolution was neither amended nor repealed. The ruling elite of the Muslim League of Pakistan's early days, who mainly came from India and the Punjab, had now realised that 'independent States' for the Muslims in India would not be realistic and held that there should be one state for all the Muslims in India. According to them, the Lahore Resolution was a mistake and should have been ignored completely. The fact was that the elections of 1945-46 were now over and the Muslims had given their overwhelming support to the proposal for the creation of Pakistan. Thus, they would have achieved their main purpose of having a 'homeland'. Having discovered that Bengal and the Punjab were going to be divided, the undisputed leader of the Muslim League, Mohammad Ali Jinnah thought that smaller regions like East Bengal could not survive as sovereign states, and therefore the Muslim majority areas should constitute 'one sovereign independent state'. The Muslim League leaders also felt that their demand for one Pakistan would put further pressure on the British and lead them to appreciate the strength of the aspirations of the Muslim. But none of these arguments was tenable in view of the fact that the resolution of April 1946, which amended the Resolution of 1940, was passed even before the Cabinet Mission had arrived in India. It was obvious that some persons within the Muslim League had decided that there would be one state for the Muslims and the attempt was to pre-empt the possibility of more than one Muslim state emerging when the British left India. Moreover, Muslims had already demonstrated their unity through the elections, and once the British accepted the concept of Pakistan, it was an internal matter for Muslims to decide how they would govern their own regions.

The validity of the 1946 resolution was challenged on the ground that the Lahore Resolution passed by the general body of the Muslim League could not be amended or modified by a resolution of a mere parliamentary body. It is true that the Lahore Resolution was not a law nor that it could not be altered or changed. However the validity of the Lahore Resolution has to be seen in the context of the subsequent resolution in April 1946. The fact remained, nonetheless, that there was a consensus amongst the Muslim that the different regions, because of their deep-rooted diverse characteristics, were to be autonomous.

It was the desire of almost all the people of all the regions of the Indian subcontinent, notwithstanding their religious affiliation, that considerable political independence should be guaranteed to the respective regions. The whole basis of the Pakistan movement was that the Muslims of different regions would have a homeland where they would be able to improve their conditions, which otherwise would not be possible because of Hindu exploitation. The Muslims required a place of their own where they could practice their own culture and ideology in an environment free from Hindu domination. Muslims were the majority in the whole of Bengal and they supported the cause of Pakistan without considering whether all or part of Bengal would become part of Pakistan, as long as they could manage to control their own affairs and retain their own culture and ideology.

It was the Muslims of Bengal and the Bengal Muslim League who strengthened the cause of Pakistan. While the Bengali Muslims lent full support to the creation of Pakistan, the other regions in the northwest, including the Punjab, were still sceptical about the whole scheme. It was only from 1946 onwards that the Punjab offered real support to the movement for Pakistan. Ironically, although Bengal was the heart of the struggle for Pakistan, the leadership of the Muslim League gradually concentrated in the hands of the Muslim landlords, the Muslim businessmen and the civil servants none of whom were from Bengal. When Pakistan was at last achieved in 1947, these classes of people constituted its ruling elite and almost all of them were either already in West Pakistan or migrated from India to West Pakistan. This helped West Pakistan to gain all the economic and political advantages of the 'promised land'. The neglect of East Bengal

Pakistan) started from that very first day. The few Bengali Muslim landlords who could occupy significant positions in the new government either identified themselves with the new ruling elite of Pakistan or were ineffective because of their lack of commitment to the development of the region to which they belonged[7].

During the later part of British rule, when the demand for decentralisation became acute, the House of Commons provided a legal foundation for a federal structure of government. The Government of India Act (1935) proclaimed India as a 'Federation of Provinces and States' (Article 5) and outlined the jurisdictions of the federal and provincial governments.

The Indian National Congress, led by Mahatma Gandhi and Jawaharlal Nehru, strove from the start for an undivided India and endeavoured until the end to achieve it. They claimed that the Muslim League did not represent all the Muslims in India and had used the Lahore Resolution to apply pressure on the British government. Because of the influence that the Indian National Congress leaders had on the last Viceroy and particularly the close personal relationship that had developed between Nehru and the Mountbatten family, they were confident, until the end, that they would be able to secure a united India. However, to the Muslim League leaders this meant nothing but a Hindu India and was therefore unacceptable.

During the three last years of the British rule and particularly after the Lahore Resolution in 1940 and the end of the Second World War in 1945 various negotiation took place between the parties and the leaders in which a number of proposals and counter proposals were considered. However, in the elections held in 1945-46 both for the central and provincial legislature, the Muslim cast their votes overwhelmingly in favour of the Muslim League. This changed the political scenario further by strengthening the hands of the Muslim League leaders. It was now established that the Muslim League represented the wishes of Muslims as much as the Indian National Congress did for the Hindus, giving rise to a clear dividing line between the two peoples. In the key province of the Punjab, the

---

[7] For the purpose of this study a detail discussion on the British rule and policies pursued by the British with regard to the two communities of Hindus and Muslims and the background of the movement and partition is not necessary.

Unionist government supported by the Congress could not survive for long after the wishes of the Muslims were so explicitly announced.

The broad principle of the proposed division of India was that the Muslim majority areas would constitute Pakistan and the Hindu majority areas would constitute the new state of India. The Indian National Congress, although it claimed to represent the whole of India including the Muslims and based its movement on the slogan of Indian nationalism, was essentially representing the interests of the Hindu landlords, big business and upper and middle-class Hindus. The emergence of the Muslim League and the demand for a separate homeland for the Muslims as a nation distinct from the Hindus, occurred largely as a reaction to the emergence of the Indian National Congress as representing primarily the vested interests of the Hindu community[8]. When the movement for partition intensified, the Congress shifted its formal position from secular nationalism to a communal platform by demanding the partition of the Punjab and Bengal along with the partition of India. At this point the actual intention of the Indian National Congress was exposed through an exchange of letters between Gandhi and Sarat Bose, in which the latter wrote: 'It grieves me to find that Congress which was once a great national organisation is fast becoming an organisation of Hindus only'[9].

The Cabinet Mission led by Lord Pethwick Lawrence arrived in India in April 1946 with Sir Stafford Cripps as a member of his team. A new proposal on the model of an earlier one suggested by the Cripps Mission was put forward in May, which envisaged a kind of a confederation that aimed to satisfy both Congress and the League. Under this scheme, the powers of the federal government were reduced and individual provinces were given the right to form a union or federation of provinces and to decide for themselves the powers they would exercise outside of federal governance. The federal union was, however, to control defence, foreign affairs and communication. It would ensure full Muslim autonomy in the Muslim-dominated provinces. On this basis, a National Constituent Assembly

---

[8] Quoted from Badruddin Umar: Pakistan and the Minority Muslim; *Weekly Holiday*, Dhaka, August 14, 1998.

[9] *Ibid.*

would be convened and an interim national government would formed.

The proposal, too, was unacceptable since the Congress would not acknowledge the League's principle of parity in representation. Later, when the Viceroy's Council was formed with the Congress alone, the Muslim League called for a 'Direct Action Day' on 16 August, resulting in a violent riot all over the major provinces. Hindus were massacred in Calcutta, and so were Muslims in Bihar, and the carnage continued in the Punjab, United Provinces and East Bengal. During this entire period, suspicion and mistrust between the parties involved deepened further, each side putting the blame on the other. The Muslim League also became suspicious of British intentions, as did the Congress. The mistrust engendered during this process between the Muslim and Hindu leaders escalated further.

The British government was in acute economic and political crisis at home and perhaps realising that they were about to lose control over the law and order situation in India, were now in a hurry to leave the subcontinent. Lord Wavel who was the Viceroy in 1946 was recalled by Prime Minister Atlee and was replaced by Lord Mountbatten who was given explicit instruction that the British Rule in India had to be brought to a close by June 1948. With Jinnah's declaration that 'the Muslim League will not yield an inch in its demand for Pakistan', Mountbatten and Nehru found that the dream of a united India was no longer realisable. With creation of Pakistan a looming reality, the Congress leaders themselves now proposed the partition of both Punjab and Bengal.

On 3 June 1947, Lord Mountbatten announced the decision of the British government that 'India will be partitioned on the basis of the demands made by the League and the Congress leaders and the frontiers will be marked in the contentious provinces of the Punjab, Bengal and Assam on the recommendation of a Boundary Commission and the independence will be effective from 14 August 1947.' The Congress and the League accepted the same, each with their respective reservations. The Sikhs, under the leadership of Baldev Singh were fighting for freedom themselves and remained extremely dissatisfied with the arrangement made by the British to please the two major communities. Following the enactment of the Indian Independence

Act on 18 July 1947, the Indian Empire was dismantled and two independent states were created. While Jinnah became the Governor-General of Pakistan, Lord Mountbatten was left to become the first Governor-General of the independent India on 15 August 1947.

The Independence Act made provisions for setting up two independent dominions: Union of India and Pakistan. The regions were demarcated to constitute the dominion based on Muslim and Hindu majority areas, and in the process, Bengal and the Punjab were divided. By Section 3(1) of the Act, the province of Bengal as constituted under the Government of India Act (1935) ceased to exist and in lieu thereof two new provinces were constituted, known as East Bengal and West Bengal. Similarly, by Section 4(1), the province of the Punjab ceased to exist and in lieu thereof two new provinces, namely East Punjab and West Punjab, were constituted. East Bengal now became a full province, as did West Punjab, within the new state of Pakistan. By virtue of a referendum, the district of Sylhet of the province of Assam also decided to join Pakistan and became a part of the province of East Bengal under Section 3(3) of the Independence Act.

This ended British rule in India and brought to a close the long struggle for self-determination of the people of India. It also began a process of de-colonisation at a global level. While the chapter of partition was resolved, the problems it left were innumerable and some were so deep rooted that their consequences still prevail in the psycho-politics of the subcontinent.

All parties resented the recommendations of Sir Cyril Radcliff's Boundary Commission. In particular, the exclusion of Calcutta from East Bengal was seriously opposed by Pakistan. Even more significant was the way the Punjab was divided which produced far-reaching effect in the geopolitics of the new states. The allocation of half of the Muslim majority Gurdaspur district to India was in clear violation of the principles of allocating Muslim majority districts to Pakistan. This deviation from the principle gave India land access to Kashmir and was seen as an antagonistic act towards Pakistan. Radcliff in collusion with Lord Mountbatten made the award to favour India and Nehru. The Sikhs, led by Master Tara Singh, were most aggrieved, as they had not only failed to secure any substantial autonomy but had found their land divided down the middle. They have a distinct culture of their own based on their ethnic language and religion and thus felt they had been let down. This unhealed wound only festered which became evident in the long years of post-independence history.

The attack on the Golden Temple by the Indian army on the orders of Indira Gandhi to crush the Khalistan independence movement, and the consequent assassination of Mrs.Gandhi, is something Indian leaders would not forget.

Besides the boundary demarcation, the immediate fall-out of the partition was an un-precedent large-scale cross-migration, affecting millions of people and causing untold misery. The loss of life was estimated at around half a million, and the migration of more than 5 million people each way led to massive ethnic and refugee settlements in the north-western sector. This created phenomenal socio-economic and political problems in both countries. On the eastern side, the same situation arose when Hindus from East Pakistan crossed into India and Muslims from Bihar and West Bengal crossed into East Pakistan, in approximately equal numbers. The settlement of all these refugees preoccupied both governments for many years, giving rise to a permanent source of socio-political conflict and ethnic tension in both countries.

Then came the question of annexation. The British left hundreds of princely states and satellites, mostly propped up, created and nurtured to maintain and perpetuate colonial rule over the subcontinent. About 562 such states with their rulers and princes were left to the mercy of the two giant states. Most of them fell within the territory of the Union of India. Soon after 14 August 1947 and in some cases even before that date most of the smaller states opted to merge into the new India. While many were bullied into accepting Indian sovereignty by the threat of economic and political seclusion, others were inducted into India with promises of special privilege and honours, material rewards and financial guarantees. Once merged or annexed, they were integrated into different provinces according to their respective proximity of culture and language.

Of these, three states Junagarh, Hyderabad and Kashmir posed immediate concern to India and Pakistan. Junagarh, a small seaport state in Kathiawar, had a Hindu majority with a Muslim ruler. The Nawab opted for Pakistan, but as Junagarh was surrounded by Indian territory Indian troops marched into it and forced a plebiscite to decide whether the people wanted to join the Indian Union. Hyderabad was a much larger state with Nizam as the ruler and a vast population, of which nearly 80 percent were Hindus. Nizam was wealthy and powerful and wanted time to take his decision. However, India did not allow that. In the summer of 1948, Indian troops went into action and took over the state of Hyderabad.

Kashmir, situated in the northwestern foothills of the Himalayas and known for its scenic beauty and natural wealth was another problem because of its geographical location. The state is of strategic interest to Russia, China, Pakistan and India, although the land is mainly contiguous with Pakistan. It was of particular strategic interest to Pakistan because of its traditional economic links and its irrigation network was based on rivers, which originated in Kashmir[10].

---

[10]For detail discussion on Kashmir, see pp. 95-110.

Chapter 2

Internal Problems and Performances

In order to appreciate the prospects and potential of South Asia as a regional unit, a realistic assessment of the conditions within each society and their relations with others is essential. It is only natural that each country will have its own historical links, culture, religion and social and political constraints. Furthermore, each has its own stage of economic development with which to determine its objective conditions for coping with both internal and external problems. Despite all such divergence, some are deeply conflicting and contradictory in nature, the urge to achieve faster economic growth for the well being of the people drives the leaders and governments to seek greater co-operation and closer relationships with their neighbours to achieve that common goal.

South Asia contains 1.3 billion people, in a land of 4.4 million square kilometres, but its level of economic development is minimal. Almost 50 percent of the world's poor and illiterate people live in this region. It shares a very small proportion of the world trade, less than 2 percent. In 1992 its share of exports was only 0.89 percent and of imports 1.07 percent[1], whereas military spending rose in the region by 12 percent between 1984 and 1994 compared to less than 2 percent growth in the ASEAN region. Defence spending increased from 2.6 percent to 3.6 percent of GDP in India and from 5.2 percent to 6.6 percent in Pakistan.[2]

---

[1] Sabbir Ahmed, SAARC Preferential Trading Arrangement: A Preliminary Analysis, Reference BIISS Journal, Vol. 16 No. 2 1995, p. 170.

[2] *Human Development Report 1997* (Oxford: Oxford University Press/World Bank).

India

India is the largest state of South Asia[3] with a population of just over a billion within 3288 thousand square kilometres. Its population is seven times bigger than that of Pakistan or Bangladesh, 59 times that of Sri Lanka and 40 times than Nepal. The population of Bhutan and the Maldives are too tiny to even deserve to comparison. In size and population, it is overwhelmingly dominant in terms of both its economy and its military power. Like all other states in South Asia, India suffers from acute economic problems, and it is considered one of the poorest countries in the world. More than 328 million people (35 percent) live below the poverty line, 346 million (37 percent) have no access to safe water, 665 million (70 percent) are without access to sanitation, 292 million adult males (27 percent) are illiterate, 182 million adult females (62 percent) are illiterate and 53 percent of children under the age of 5 suffer from malnutrition. On the other hand, India has, to its credit, raised 500 million people above the poverty line and has managed to maintain the economic and political structure of a vastly divergent federal, multicultural, multinational and multilingual state that can only be compared with the USA. With a middle class of 200 million people, India today is one of the largest markets in the world for trade and business.

The primary success of India is that it has been able to sustain a democratic system without any interruption and, despite being one of the poorest countries, has established the largest democracy on earth. Unlike Pakistan, India pursued a democratic approach to governance and established a parliamentary system of government similar to that of Britain. Jawaharlal Nehru, a student of Harrow and Cambridge was deeply influenced by British values. As the architect of India's participatory political system, he led the new state and ensured that the roots of democracy were properly nourished. Changes of government since 1947 have taken place with the consent of the people and the press has enjoyed total freedom.[4] So has the judiciary. These three

---

[3] South Asian States are India, Pakistan, Bangladesh, Sri Lanka, Nepal, Bhutan and the Maldives. Although meagre compared to the world, among the South Asian countries India has more than 90% of the coal and crude petroleum, major portions of production of Uranium, copper, iron and lead ores. Only one half of South Asian land is arable of which 81% belongs to India.

[4] Except when Mrs. Gandhi imposed emergency in 1977.

essential instruments have contributed to the emergence of a strong civil society, which is now firmly established. The basic institutions for holding election as fairly as possible within the framework of existing laws have been strengthened by making the Election Commission as an independent organisation as is the judiciary. Despite all the fears and apprehensions, democracy in India has survived its acid test even after the demise of the Nehru dynasty and the upheavals of the emergency period instituted by Indira Gandhi.

There was considerable turmoil and uncertainty, dislocation and bloodshed following the partition of India, but its leaders moved quickly to frame the constitution for the new Union. In less than two years a commendable democratic constitution had been framed and passed by the Constituent Assembly. It became effective from 25 January 1950 and established a bicameral legislature to suit the needs of a federal state. The state contained minorities of all kinds, the largest of whom were the Muslim. They constituted about 13% of the population. Although the country had a predominantly Hindu populace, the constitutional declaration that it would be a secular state was seen as offering security for all the communities. All the human rights enshrined in the charter of the UN were embodied as fundamental rights in the Constitution and independence of the judiciary was ensured. There have been subsequent legal conflicts between the executive and the judiciary, leading to a series of amendments, but the Constitution has remained supreme. The Supreme Court of India has played an increasingly crucial role in upholding the basic structure of the Constitution and on many occasions has not hesitated to enlarge its jurisdiction, and where the executive has failed to effectively discharge its duties, to expound law to safeguard the rights of citizens and ensure the immediate implementation of laws.

Internally, India has monumental problems. It has conflicts of an insurmountable nature — ethnic, religious, territorial, inter-state and between the states and the federal government. Communal riots are a routine phenomenon: some years have seen an average of one riot per day. The aspiration of the Tamils in the south to link with those in Sri Lanka across the sea, the movement for an independent Khalistan of the Sikhs in the Punjab, which led Mrs. Gandhi to send troops to the Golden Temple, the struggle of the Kashmiris for freedom and the insurgencies in the seven north-eastern states of India, all aspiring for independence, have kept the administration of the country under constant strain. The intensified movements of the tribal guerrilla organisations of the northeast areas mostly neglected, oppressed and inaccessible — led by different groups in the states of Assam, Meghalaya, Tripura, Manipur, Mizoram, Nagaland and Arunachal, have forced India to deploy about 250,000 soldiers in these hilly states and about 600,000 soldiers in Kashmir to guard the country's territorial integrity. This has caused a huge rise in military spending for over a decade now. In each of these northeastern states, underground organisations supported by their aboveground fronts, sometimes working in collaboration with each other, are gaining in strength. According to the reports published in Indian newspapers, the principal organisations operating in the region are the NSCN, the Himar People's Convention (HPC) and the Bodo Security Force, Assam, which are actively engaged in Assam; the All Tripura Tribal Force (ATTF) in Tripura; the PLA, PREPAK and KCP in Manipur; the A'chick Liberation Front (ALF), the Hyunitrep Volunteers Council and KSU-FKJGP in Meghalaya; and the United Liberation Volunteers in Arunachal. The organisations have also agreed amongst themselves to operate in all the seven states,[5] the ULFA are now perhaps the most active underground organisation of the region with around 3000 trained cadres.[6] As its military operations are almost always brutal and repressive, known for indiscriminate killings, arson, rape and torture of those in custody, India is constantly embarrassed before the world community on the question of human rights in Kashmir, the Punjab and the northeastern states.[7] There is also the enormous economic cost and the loss of life and property of any military operation. On the other hand, India cannot ignore the sensitive issues and territories involved for the sake of its own security and national sovereignty. In containing some of these ethnic and religious issues, India has sacrificed a number of very valuable lives such as that of Mrs. Indira Gandhi at the hand of a Sikh bodyguard and her son Rajiv Gandhi at the hand of a rebel Tamil suicide bomber.

---

[5] *The Statesman*, October 12, 1992.

[6] *India Today*, August 10, 1998.

[7] ATTF: All Tripura Tribal Force, ALF: A'chik Liberation Front, HVC: Hyunitrep Volunteers Council.

With the demise of the Nehru dynasty and, with that, the loss of one single national party to govern the country, national politics in India has gone through dramatic changes. The provincial, parochial, ethnic and linguistic parties scattered all over India are gaining strength based on local considerations not related to the national issues of India. In the last five years, India has seen a succession of five coalition governments, and since the death of Rajiv Gandhi there has not been any single-party government. Narshima Rao, despite being the Prime Minister representing the Congress, could govern only with the support of others, including CPM.

A scenario that is widely expected to continue for many years to come with the weakening of the central government is that the state governments will demand devolution of authority and power from central government and seek greater autonomy. This will lead to a fundamental change in the basic structure of Indian politics and administration. The Indian establishment in New Delhi is already concerned about the lack of command and direction in national politics, and those who believe in the concept of "greater" India and India emerging as a global power are beset with frustration and looking for alternatives. The focus of politics around the Nehru family, the ideological stance of secularism at the national and international levels, and the leadership of the Congress held India together for many years. Now a strong section in the Delhi establishment sees an alternative in the rise and perpetuation of the rule of Hindu fundamentalism. The rise to power of Shiv Sena and the BJP in a 'secular India' has to be seen from this perspective. The fast ascendancy of the BJP into the power spectrum demonstrates a new and changing dimension in Indian politics. They had only two seats in Parliament in 1984, which increased to 80 seats in 1989, and this was enlarged to 182 seats in 1998 again in 1999. Whether in power or in opposition, the BJP and Hindu fundamentalism have come to stay in India as a strong political force.[8]

---

[8] In the month-long general elections held in October 1999, third in four years, 360 million voted to elect 538 Members of Parliament from among 4648 Candidates at a cost of US$ 200 million. Despite the fact that BJP was forced out of power, in the election it was however able to retain the same number of 182 seats which they held in 1998. Although BJP did not increase its number but all other parties in the alliance benefited from the overall popularity of BJP and increased their respective seats. Vajpayee's National Democratic Alliance was able to raise the

This fundamentalist element has always existed in India. Hinduism one of the ancient religions on earth, has not changed much. Since India is virtually the only land where it is practiced, its people have sustained deep historical roots derived from the literature of the Vedas and the rule of Ashoka. As discussed earlier that although the Indian National Congress wanted to use 'Indian nationalism' to achieve a single united India, it was the Hindu merchant class and the Brahmin elite who provided the guiding spirit for the freedom movement It was at their insistence that the Punjab and Bengal were partitioned and Kashmir was conquered. Mahatma Gandhi, Nehru and others educated in England with a secular taste, might have been honest in their intentions, but the people they represented were united because of the spirit of Hinduism enunciated and inspired by the Vedas, Bhagabat Gita and the epics in Ramayana and Mahabharata. A large section of people in India — and they may even be a majority — still loathes fundamentalism. But in the vacuum that exists today in India, due to a lack of farsightedness on the part of their leaders, they have been demoted to the role of mere onlookers.

The assassination of Mahatma Gandhi at the hand of Nathuram Godse, a Hindu fanatic linked with the RSS soon after independence only demonstrated how deep-rooted the force of fundamentalism was, even during those euphoric years. Although Nathuram and Narayan Ate were condemned to death and none came forward to defend their action, the killing was always regarded a political act. Nathuram, his brother Gopal Godse, who was sentenced to life imprisonment in the trial, and their other associates Madanlal Pahva and Vishnu Karkare, were all articulate political activists in Pune. They firmly believed in an *Akhanda Bharat* or undivided Hindustan. While he was editor of Hindu Rashtra, Nathuram had written fierce articles criticising the Mahatma and the leaders of the Congress for betraying the cause of the people by agreeing to the partition of India. When Mahatma announced on 12 January 1948 that he was going on a fast in protest against the non-payment of Rs. 55 crores to Pakistan[9] as compensation from the division of financial assets between the two new countries,

---

combined number of seats in the Parliament to 296 compared to 253 in 1998 to return to power once again. *Time and India Today, October 18, 1999.*

[9] *India Today*, August 3, 1998.

Nathuram and Narayan came to the conclusion that Gandhi must die. Within eighteen days, Gandhi was dead when three bullets had pierced through his chest.

Inspired by Hindutva, Nathuram cherished the glory of a united India and in his deposition in court he asserted that Gandhi 'had no right to vivisect the country, the image of our worship'.[10] Although he confirmed the death penalty, Justice G.D. Khosla, one of the three judges of the Court of Appeal wrote later that 'women could be seen sobbing after Godse's deposition ... I have no doubt that had the audience of that day been constituted into a jury they would have brought in a verdict of "not guilty" by an overwhelming majority'.[11] Gopal Godse said 'they did not want the truth to emerge'. When Gopal Godse was released from prison in 1962 and published "Gandhi's Murder and After" in 1965, the book was banned by the Congress government, but this ban was overruled by the Bombay High Court in 1968.

Nathuram knew he was representing a strong public sentiment and he faced the trial to justify his action. On 15 November 1950 when he was taken to the gallows with a map of an undivided India clutched in his hand for his final departure, he asked his brother to have his ashes sunk in the holy Sindhu river 'when she will again flow freely under the aegis of the flag of Hindustan. It hardly matters even if it takes a couple of generation to realise my wish. Preserve the ashes till then'.

What Nahuram Godse did was a gruesome and highly criminal act for which he was tried, convicted and hanged. He took the life of one of the greatest leaders of the twentieth century and a man who has left behind a philosophy to be cherished for all time. However, Nathuram is now once again reincarnated with great enthusiasm. The Shiv Senas still hold him as a symbol of a cause. His ashes, which were collected soon after the authority had dropped them in the Ganges river and not in the Sindhu as he desired, are maintained in a silver urn in a residential flat in Pune,[12] where 15 November is

---

[10] The Congress Government banned the publication of the depositions, "May it please your honour".

[11] The information described in these paragraphs is based on the cover story published in *India Today* on August 3, 1998.

[12] *Ibid.*

observed as a 'Martyr Day'. They still pledge to realise Nathuram's dream of a united India by saying 'It took the Jews 1600 years to recover Jerusalem', implying that they will also wait for as many years to achieve their goal.

The ghost of Nathuram Godse still haunts India. Pradeep Dalvi wrote the play "Mai Nathuram Godse Boltey", based on the life of Nathuram Godse, in 1984. It portrays Nathuram as both as martyr and a murderer, and reveals his character and convictions. The Security Board finally cleared the play after 14 years for open performance following the installation of a Shiv Sena/BJP government in Maharashtra and Delhi. It created a storm and tickets were sold on the black market. Although the performance was immediately prohibited on the advice of the central government, it is understood that BJP only did this because it was eager to maintain a mild image to stay in power and to avoid any confrontation with the opposition. However, this has pleased neither the people nor the regular members of Shiv Sena and the BJP. If the prohibition is challenged in court, the ban was likely to be overruled and the performance would then begin again with much more enthusiasm, having received so much publicity. Moreover, the Deputy Chief Minister of Maharashtra, Gopinath Mande, belonging to the same school of thought, only reconfirmed the sentiment by saying, "Stopping the play does not mean that Godse's ideology will be barred".[13]

The apparent resurgence of the ideology of Nathuram Godse in recent years has presented a challenge concerning its national character and disposition not only to the Hindu nationalist government of the BJP, but to India as a whole. With the decline of the Congress and the rise of Hindu fundamentalism in India in the last decade, the minorities have felt increasingly insecure. This is particularly true of the Muslims, the largest group, numbering 120 million people, who are the innocent victims of a sense of vengeance and enmity felt by Hindu fundamentalists against Pakistan, a Muslim neighbour. In December 1992, led by L. K. Advani and Bal Thackaray, militant Hindu volunteers of Jana Sangha and Shiv Sena — the grassroots organisation of

---

[13] Gopal Godse, a Hindu fundamentalist, brother of Nathuram Godse who assassinated Mahatma Gandhi on 30 June, 1948 remained in jail for 18 years. He told the Time Correspondent "Gandhi's principle was bogus". *Time*, 21 February 2000.

BJP, which now leads the central government in Delhi — stormed
462-year-old Babri Mosque at Ayodha, which had been built by
Great Mughals. In spite of a High Court injunction, they tore it
art in broad daylight, while the police looked on. Horror at their
tion electrified the sentiments of Muslims all over the subcontinent.
hen the Muslims in Bombay, now called Mumbai, reacted, a major
t broke out in the city and the surrounding areas. The Shiv Senas
taliated by massacring hundreds of Muslims, including women and
ildren in 1992-93.

The Congress government of Narshima Rao failed to take any clear
and. On the contrary, it gave a public impression of compromising
ith the forces of communalism. This was clearly against the
owed political philosophy of the Congress inherited from Gandhi
d Nehru. In the face of rising Hindu nationalism, the Congress
vernment failed to protect the minorities. As is usually the case, a
dicial commission was constituted to take the steam out of the
tuation. Justice B. N. Sri Krishna of the Bombay High Court
eaded it. Before the commission could complete its work, however,
Shiv Sena/BJP government came to power in Maharashtra in January
996 and immediately stopped the inquiry. In April 1996, the Commission
as again restored with an enlarged mandate to report on the
Mumbai bomb blast of March 1993 by the time the Commission
ubmitted its report in February 1998, the BJP had taken control of
e central government again, and the same Maharashtra government
at had scrapped the Commission was ruling the state.

Although it took about five years for the Commission to submit
he 800-page report, it was acclaimed as a bold and courageous
ocument that clearly identified those responsible for the massacre
f innocent minority Muslims. Known as the Sri Krishna report, it
eld Sena activists responsible for such 'vigilantism'. It singled out
Bal Thackaray, one of the most influential leaders of the day and the
hief of Shiv Sena, who 'like a veteran general' commanded his
oyal Shiv Sainiks to retaliate with organised attacks against the
Muslims'.[14] Immediately demands were raised all over India to take
stern action against those responsible for the killings. The Naib

---

[14]*India Today*, August 17, 1998.

Imam of Delhi, Jame Masjid, called upon all the leaders of Congr[ess] and other parties to demand the arrest and punishment of Bal Thackar[ay]. Jyoti Basu, the Chief Minister of West Bengal, also demanded le[gal] action against Bal Thackaray.

However, nothing happened. It was not Bal Thackaray alone, but the leaders of the Maharashtra government including the Ch[ief] Minister and the State Home Minister, who were involved in t[he] killing. Although BJP was in the government, again they lacked t[he] courage to take action based on the Commission report. So t[he] Maharastra government on the ground that it was 'biased and an[ti] Hindu', rejected the report of the Commission. Acceptance [or] rejection of a public inquiry report became less relevant than t[he] ideological politics that dominates India today. Sri Krish[na] Commission report had only shown how deeply Hindu fanaticis[m] had cut through the central theme of Indian national politics and ho[w] divided India now was. Since February 2002, the Hindu fanatics l[ed] by the BJP-affiliates known as the Shiv Senas have perpetrated [a] planned ethnic cleansing operation, a form of genocide, killing mo[re] then 1000 Muslims, including pregnant women, children, rapin[g] hundreds of women and making more then 100,000 homeless in t[he] state of Gujarat. While the BJP-led central government of Atal Biha[ri] Vajpayee stood by and watched, its cohorts in the BJP sta[te] government of Gujarat led by Chief Minister Narendra Modi, apparently patronised the wicked carnage for months at an end.

The Delhi establishment and their think tanks, which do not belon[g] to any particular political party, are also divided. Rising Hind[u] nationalism and its consolidation in the political power structure replacing a declining Congress, may not be able to hold India togethe[r] in the face of numerous conflicts and contradictions, and the divergen[t] forces operating within the country. Without a strong and stable government, India would neither remain united nor be able to attain it[s] cherished goal of playing a global role in the new millennium. The present constitution and system of government is no longer appropriat[e] for the changing needs of India. Having developed a strong civil society India now needs to move forward. It is feared that, if the presen[t]

---

[15]See *India Today* May 13 and 20, 2002.

...tem of governance continues for many years, with a weak and ...ided central government in the form of coalitions, India will be ...ble to contain the internal situation or achieve its external ambitions. The Indian political system is not fully democratic and the ...vernment is not in a position to adopt reforms to alleviate poverty ...d pursue the kind of economic policies to bring about the ...eakthrough achieved by some of the South-East Asian countries. ...e present parliamentary system, the state-centre relationship, the ...pointment of governors, presidential rule, the Supreme Court's ...wer of judicial review and the appointment of judges are cited as ...eas where radical changes are needed as early as possible.[16] To ...ve effect to this major transformation, a meeting of all the major ...litical parties could be convened. If a consensus on the issue is ...ached, it could be referred to a referendum to adopt a new ...nstitution for India.[17]

India is a country of vast resources. It has almost all the raw ...aterials required to emerge as an industrial power. With abundant ...tural resources, a strong middle class, trained and skilled managerial ...rsonnel, cheap labour and a large market of over a billion people, ...potential and prospects are unlimited. It has an experienced ...reaucracy, a resilient and enterprising business community and a ...ilitary establishment of long tradition. In certain areas, it has also ...hieved significant progress. In the production of food, the most ...sential item for mankind's survival, India is not only self-sufficient ...it can maintain a reasonable buffer stock in its godowns.[18]

Yet, India is still in a state of underdevelopment. Poverty and ...alnutrition are widespread, and there is a lack of primary health ...re, drinking water and sanitation. The country is still considered ...e of the poorest in the world with a per capita income of US$ 360. ...ountries in South-East Asia, which were in a far less advantageous

---

In the book: India at the cross roads: Does India need a New Constitution, Justice B.L. Hansari, a judge of the Supreme Court gives his views. Unfortunately he died just before the book was published. Eastern Law House, 1998. See also the recent debate for political reforms sparked by the Indian Prime Minister in January 2000. *India Today*, January 31, 2000.

If the changes are brought by way of amendment the Supreme Court may strike them down on the ground of being violative of the basic structure of the constitution.

See Table No. 41, p. 46, Statistical Outline of India, 2001-2002. Tata Services Limited, Mumbai, December 2001.

position than India in terms of economy, infrastructure, institutio[ns], business, bureaucracy and exposure to the outside world, h[as] marched forward and have achieved far more economic progr[ess] than India.[19] In education, health care and land reforms, In[dia] continues to lag way behind.[20] It has failed to set a model of grov[th] for other countries to follow in South Asia.

For more than 40 years since independence, India has follow[ed] an economic policy initiated by its founding leader, Nehru, inspi[red] by the Fabian theory of a welfare state. Overwhelmed by [the] idealism of socialist theories, the Indian leaders followed restricti[ve] policies in which their own industrial base grew under governme[nt] protection and regulations, and the state played the pivotal role [in] achieving economic growth. The banks, insurance compani[es,] communication sector, energy, steel and petrochemicals all remain[ed] in the public sector. Along with the largest democracy, India a[lso] developed the largest government on earth.

Only since 1980-90, has India shifted from the old policy structu[re] to a new regime and gradually opened its market to external inve[st]ment and competition. The economic reforms introduced have n[ot] yet been fully implemented; nor have they yielded any substant[ial] result. In the Cold War era, India pursued a non-aligned forei[gn] policy that brought it closer to the Soviet Union. With a social[ist] bias, India followed a kind of mixed economy and received mor[e] political, economic, technological and military assistance from t[he] Soviet Union. It will need careful analysis to determine whether a[nd] to what extent India has benefited from the kind of policies that we[re] pursued during that period. Moreover, whether India's failure [to] match the growth of the South-East Asian countries or to develop [an] economic model of its own was the result of the policies that [its] leaders had followed for more than 40 years.

Pakistan

After its creation in 1947, Pakistan moved in a different directi[on] from India, in terms of both administration and economic policie[s.]

---

[19] See Table No. 4.6 and 4.8.
[20] See Table No. 4.1.

Its two parts were separated by about 1,600 kilometres, with India in the middle, Pakistan was faced with an abnormal situation in governing the country. All those in the central leadership of the Muslim League were Urdu-speaking upper class Muslims identified with the western part of Pakistan. The influential bureaucrats and business class who had migrated from India joined them. Dominated by the powerful politicians and bureaucrats, almost all belonging to the western part, Pakistan adopted a centralised administration using Islam as the uniting bond between the two parts of its territory. With the death of Mohammad Ali Jinnah in 1948, however, it suffered a severe vacuum in political leadership and the country fell into the hands of politicians and bureaucrats largely belonging to Pakistan's dominant province, the Punjab.

Besides differences of language and culture, and the distance between the two parts of Pakistan, there were already some imbalances in the socio-economic structures of the two regions. The eastern part had a larger population and less land, whereas the western part had more land and a smaller population. Although the western part comprised of four distinct provinces, they were not all equally developed and the Punjab, being both larger in terms of population and economic development, it dominated the politics of Pakistan. A combination of politicians, big business and bureaucracy constituted the ruling elite in Pakistan, who determined the course of politics of the new country. The Lahore Resolution, which galvanised the cause of Pakistan amongst the Muslims, was no longer on the agenda; nor was there any political will and leadership to give the new nation a democratic structure.[21]

It took Pakistan nine years to frame a constitution. This constitution made the country a federal state under a parliamentary system of government based on a principle of parity; that is, an equal representation in the National Assembly from East and West Pakistan as two 'units'. The President was given certain important prerogative powers. The degree of autonomy given to the two units was limited, and the most important powers were retained by the central government.[22]

---

[21] See for detail, Moudud Ahmed, *Constitutional Quest for Autonomy*, pp. 1- 44.
[22] *Ibid.*, pp. 45-63 on the constitution making process of 1956.

Even then, this constitution did not last more than 30 months. A general election was scheduled for February 1959 but on 7 October 1958 the military intervened and Ayub Khan, the Chief of Army Staff, took over control of the state. After the army had administered the country for four years under martial law, a tailored constitution was introduced in 1962 under which elections to the National Assembly were to be held based on an indirect vote. Ayub believed that this 'basic democracy' would better suit the genius of the people. Under the 1962 constitution, powers were more concentrated in the hands of the President, administration was centralised and the military was strengthened. Ayub ruled for eleven years until he was forced to step down in the face of a mass uprising in March 1969.[23] He handed over power to his Chief of Army Staff, Yahya Khan, who again proclaimed martial law, which continued until the break-up of Pakistan.[24]

Ayub's ruthless centralised administration created new economic and political disparities between the two wings of Pakistan. By depriving the Bengalis who were the majority of the population, from taking part in the administration of the country and not allocating resources on a democratic basis led to the intensification of the struggle of the Bengalis to establish the 'right to live' in a fair and equitable autonomous state. After Ayub was overthrown, the first ever general elections were held in Pakistan in December 1970 — January 1971 under a Legal Framework Order of Martial Law. In the elections, held on a 'one person, one vote' basis under a universal adult franchise, the Awami League, representing the aspirations of Bengalis, secured 167 out of 169 seats in the 300-member National Assembly. Thereby, with an absolute majority, the Awami League gained the mandate of the people to govern the whole of Pakistan.

However, Pakistan's elite class, ruled and dominated by the military, would not accept the verdict of the people. With Zulfikar Ali Bhutto on their side — he being keener to fulfil his own ambitions, having secured a majority in West Pakistan for his Pakistan People's Party (PPP) — the army decided to crack down on the majority Bengalis to frustrate the verdict of the people. The legitimate right of the

---

[23]*Ibid.*, pp. 64-187.

[24]*Ibid.*, p. 183.

Bengalis, earned through a peaceful election, was denied. This led to an armed struggle, in which the Bengalis under the umbrella of the Awami League were supported by India and received help in terms of logistics, sanctuary, finance and training. They earned their independence when the Pakistan army garrison in the east finally surrendered to the joint command of India and Bangladesh at the Dhaka Race Course on 16 December 1971,[25] while the Bangladesh government-in-exile was still stationed in Calcutta.

After its defeat and humiliation, the military in Pakistan returned to barracks and Zulfikar Ali Bhutto,[26] the majority leader of West Pakistan, now became the President of Pakistan charged with recovering and steering a truncated nation. In 1973, Pakistan received its third constitution. It was now designed as a federal state with autonomous status being given to the four states of Sind, Baluchistan, North-West Frontier Province (NWFP) and the Punjab under the framework of a parliamentary system of government. After the elections in 1973, Bhutto returned to the post of Prime Minister and Pakistan for the first time enjoyed a constitutionally elected, democratic regime. Although Bhutto hailed from Sind, the Punjab continued to be the bastion of power.

Before the civil society in Pakistan could take root, the brief period of democracy that Pakistan enjoyed was again subverted when the Pakistan army intervened and Bhutto's own Chief of Army Staff, Ziaul Huq, removed him from the elected post, proclaimed martial law and assumed the supreme authority of the state in July 1977. As usual, the failure and corruption of the politicians were blamed to justify the army takeover. Ziaul Huq not only hanged Bhutto on the charge of having committed a political murder, but also ruled for nearly thirteen years. He died, along with the US Ambassador, in a C-130 aircraft crash reportedly caused by a bomb concealed in a fruit basket. This was reportedly part of a conspiracy to assassinate the military dictator at a time when an intense political movement was already raging in the country under the leadership of Bhutto's daughter, Benazir.

---

[25] See for more detail Moudud Ahmed: *Constitutional Quest for Autonomy*, pp. 187-248.

[26] See for the role of Bhutto during the critical months prior to the break-up of Pakistan. *Ibid.*, pp. 214-232.

After the death of Ziaul Huq and in the face of public agitation against military rule, a general election was held in Pakistan in 1990. Since then Pakistan had returned to a democratic order but within two years of Benazir Bhutto's election, President Ghulam Ishaq Khan dismissed her on charge of corruption, economic mismanagement and incompetence. Mohammad Nawaz Sharif of the Pakistan Muslim League replaced her as Prime Minister. Soon the two offices of the Prime Minister and President faced a conflict of power and authority, which led the same President to remove Nawaz Sharif from the elected office. This time on being challenged the Supreme Court held the President to have removed the Prime Minister illegally and Nawaz Sharif was reinstated. As another general election was due, a demand for a neutral government to conduct the elections was accepted.

Moinuddin Ahmad Qureshi, a former World Bank Executive Vice-President and a distinguished economist, was appointed to head an interim government supported by the West and the military. In this election, Benazir Bhutto again returned to the office of Prime Minister in October 1993. However, well before she could complete her tenure, the man whom she had nominated and her party elected to the office of the President Sardar Farook Ahmad Khan Leghari— dismissed her from office on the same charges of corruption and inefficiency, and ordered for a fresh election. Bhutto went to court, but the Supreme Court this time upheld the action of the President.

This dismissal of an elected Prime Minister by the arbitrary authority of a President under a parliamentary form of government, inconceivable in India or Britain, only shows how fragile the institution of democracy was in Pakistan. One of the reasons was that, although the army had returned to barracks, military leaders continued to play a dominant role in Pakistan politics.

In the national election held on 3 February 1997, Nawaz Sharif swept the polls and returned to Parliament with more than a two-thirds majority. Benazir Bhutto, having had two opportunities to govern the country, became the Leader of the Opposition with only 18 out of 237 seats in the National Assembly. Although the people had elected Nawaz Sharif, he knew he had to contain the army by forming a National Security Council with military generals. This demonstrated that the army could not be totally excluded from the political power in Pakistan. Sharif, however, with his overwhelming majority in Parliament, changed the constitution to remove the President's prerogative of dismissing any elected government, and thereby reduced the office of President to that of a mere titular head. To give Pakistan an Islamic face, the government of Nawaz Sharif also presented a bill in Parliament to make Sharia law the Supreme Code of justice and administration.

Nevertheless, these changes did not help Nawaz Sharif. Less than three months after the retreat from Kargil incursion and two weeks from the end of his time as Chief of the Army, General Pervez Musharraf, the chief of the Pakistan army staged a bloodless *coup d'etat* against the elected government of Nawaz Sharif, enabling the military to take over state power in Pakistan once again. This was a most unusual takeover by a general who, earlier in the day while on a Pakistan International Airlines flight from Colombo to Karachi on 12 October 1999 was informed that the Prime Minister had dismissed him in his absence. The rank and file rallied around the Chief of the Army who took over power, proclaimed a state of emergency and designated himself as the Chief Executive of the country without any reference to law, not even by any proclamation of martial law. As usual, the new ruler promised that he would restore 'real democracy' in the country, wipe out corruption and restore the collapsing economy for the welfare of the people. After eleven years of democracy, Pakistan once again starts a new journey under military rule.

Unlike India, where democracy has flourished and become institutionalised, Pakistan has experienced an extremely chequered course. It is doubtful whether the institutions of democracy in Pakistan can ever take root and provide the country with a sound and stable democratic system. While civil society in India, with unqualified freedom of the press and judiciary, has developed into an agile and strong force, in Pakistan it is fragile and yet to mature.

In foreign policy, Pakistan from its inception, in contrast to and in competition with India, has leaned towards the USA. During the entire Cold War period, Pakistan received as much support, both economic and military, from the USA and the West as India did from the Soviet Union. Pakistan was always considered a trusted ally of the West. While Pakistan signed military pacts with the South-East Asia Treaty Organisation (SEATO) and the Central Treaty Organisation (CENTO) in the 1950s, India signed a Friendship and Co-operation Treaty with the Soviet Union in 1971, for the same reasons of national security. The respective geopolitical relationships of India and Pakistan with the two superpowers had sharpened their conflict in terms of their foreign policies. While India lent support to the Soviet Union after it had, with 40,000 troops[27], invaded Afghanistan on 27 December 1979, Pakistan received an aid package of $3.2 billion to contain communism as it was considered a front-line state of the West.[28] Since the loss of Bangladesh, Pakistan has been attempting, for both economic and military purposes, to assume, in combination with other Muslim countries, as active role in Central Asia.

In economic policy, Pakistan did not follow the Fabian philosophy. Because of its early ambition to achieve an economic breakthrough, it relied more on a capitalist framework. In order to develop business and investment it relied more on the West, which eventually led it to depend heavily on aid and foreign assistance. The two long periods of military rule under Ayub Khan and Ziaul Huq helped to increase wealth and per capita income,[29] but due to lack of political direction and stability, and repeated political upheavals leading to the break-up of Pakistan, the economic goals could not be achieved. In the absence of accountability of the successive governments under military regimes, corruption and concentration of wealth in the hands of the few distorted the development of the social sectors.[30]

Lack of leadership in formulating policies and of transparency in the administration caused the failure to achieve the desired results. In its obsession with Kashmir and perceived threats from India, the involvement of the military in politics and their demand for increased budget allocation, their failure to develop a mature political leadership had led Pakistan into the poverty trap and it remains one of the

---

[27] Bhabani Sen Gupta: India's Support of Soviet Invasion of Afghanistan Gains and Losses, *Dhaka Courier*, September 5, 1979.

[28] Afghanistan is considered to belong to Central Asia than South Asian region.

[29] US$ 420 compared to US$ 360 in India.

[30] In Pakistan 22 families controlled more than half of banking and industrial business.

poorest countries in the world.[31] A different policy from India was pursued but it also failed to evolve a model for development in South Asia. In addition, because of its emphasis on religious dogmas and its reluctance to pursue any population control policy, its population has increased quickly to nearly 130 million, exceeding that of Bangladesh which in 1971 had 75 million compared to Pakistan population of around 60 million.

There have been some important economic achievements. In food production, for example, Pakistan is not only self-sufficient, but is also an exporter of foodgrain. However, the economy of Pakistan today is in very bad shape. With the end of the Cold War and Soviet withdrawal of troops from Afghanistan, Pakistan's strategic importance has drastically reduced. Since the cut in US aid in 1990 over its nuclear programme, Pakistan has not made any substantial economic headway. Although the interim government of Moin Quereshi infused some hope by introducing certain useful economic reforms, its constant drainage of resources in military spending, corruption and political instability has led Pakistan to a perilous state of near-bankruptcy. With $30 billion in debts, Pakistan's macro-economic structure is on the verge of collapse.[32] Gross domestic savings, investment and growth have declined in recent years. The average annual GNP growth rate in 1996/97 dropped to 0.0 percent.[33]

In the social sectors, too, the performance has been poor.[34] In Pakistan 41 million people (34%) live below poverty line, 56 million (40%) are without access to safe water, 98 million (70%) have no access to sanitation, 49 million adult males (62%) are illiterate 28 million female adults (76%) are illiterate and 38% of children below the age of 5 suffer from malnutrition.[35] The austerity measures and economic reforms recently introduced are yet to yield results.

---

[31] Pakistan's defence expenditure as percentage of GNP in 1995 was 5.2% compared to India's 2.8% and the defence as percentage of education and health expenditure was 12.5% compared to India's 6.5% Mahbub-ul Haq and Khadija Haq, *Human Development in South Asia 1998*, The University Press Limited, Dhaka, p. 184.

[32] See *Human Development in South Asia 1999*, p. 203, The University Press Limited, Dhaka.

[33] *Ibid.*, p. 195.

[34] *Human Development in South Asia 1999*, p. 196, The University Press Limited, Dhaka.

[35] *Ibid.*

The religious, ethnic and tribal conflicts in Pakistan continue to be a source of strain and instability. The intractable conflicts between the Shia and Sunni communities — both are Muslims and believe in Islam — are on the increase. Pakistan has moved more towards Islam and shows its strong affinity towards the Muslim world in order to contain growing fundamentalism. However, the flow of arms from Afghanistan as well as Iran also imports Islamic militancy into Pakistan, causing a great threat to internal security. The question of effective rule and stability in Pakistan still hinges on the issue of what kind of relationship the provinces should have with the central government. The question of autonomy and the quality of governance will determine how strong Pakistan can be as a state.

The country has not yet, after 50 years of independence, addressed some of its basic, crucial issues. The inter-ethnic problems within the provinces, like the Baluchi-pashtu in Baluchistan and the Pashtu and non-Pashtu communities in NWFP, are threatening the social stability of these regions. A most alarming conflict has arisen in Sind between the Muhajirs — the Muslim refugees from India — and the local ethnic Sindhis, which frequently paralyses Karachi their largest commercial city. The growth of gangsters and private armies in this city creates a sense of great insecurity to the life and property of both rich and poor, and constantly threatens the prospect of any improvement in Pakistan. The Muhajir Quami Mahaz (MQM), a powerful, local front of refugees, now plays an important political role both at the center and in the Province, which makes it even more difficult to bring the situation in Karachi under control.

Sri Lanka

Sri Lanka is a vibrant and resilient nation, an island of immense natural beauty. Like India, it has practiced uninterrupted democracy since gaining independence in 1948 excepting a failed coup attempt in 1962, with elected governments, freedom of the press and judiciary, and a well-developed civil society. Through years of institutional growth, democracy in Sri Lanka has taken healthy root, and the country is considered the most literate nation of South Asia.

Sri Lanka began with a parliamentary system of government that continued for nearly 30 years. It adopted its first republican constitution in 1972, and six years later, in order to ensure a more centralised administration for quick economic growth, it adopted a second republican constitution. This constitution changed the system of government from a parliamentary to a presidential form, retaining the democratic structures of other institutions and rights as they were before. After about eighteen years of the presidential system, the country again returned to a parliamentary form of government in 1995. Only recently the country has again returned to a presidential system of government. Every change of government in Sri Lanka under both the systems has taken place through a democratic process. It had general elections in 1947, 1952, 1956, 1960 (twice), 1965, 1970, 1977, 1988 and 1994. To its credit, Sri Lanka has a high level of participatory politics compared to other countries of the region.[36]

Sri Lanka is a multi-ethnic society. According to the 1981 census, the population is Sinhalese 74.6 percent[37], Sri Lankan Tamils 17.6 percent, Indian Tamils 5.5 percent and Muslims 7.4 percent. The Sinhalese are the dominant group overwhelmingly Buddhist. They constitute the elite class and have been governing the country from the beginning. Tamils are Hindu and speak Tamil. If all the Tamils are taken together — Sri Lankan, Indian and Muslim Tamils — they constitute more than 20 percent of the population. The Tamil concentration is in the northern and north-eastern part of the country close to the Indian shore across the Palk strait, where 50 million Tamils live in the Indian state of Tamil Nadu. Tamil minorities have resisted being dominated by the Sinhalese for many years and after independence, no serious effort was made to safeguard their interests.

The problems of ethnic conflict were aggravated by the centralised nature of administration practiced in Sri Lanka throughout the last 50 years. The presidential system, in particular, led to the centralisation of power and domination by the Sinhalese, making the minority Tamils feel more neglected as they continued to be deprived of any access to real power. This led to the issue of devolution of powers, autonomy to the regions and the relationship of the regions to the central government.

---

[36]Shelton U. Kodikara. *The Security of South Asia in the 1990s*, BIISS Journal. V.13 No. 2, 1992, p. 168.

[37]*Devolution and Development in Sri Lanka*, edited by Sunil Bastian, International Centre for Ethnic Studies, Colombo, Sri Lanka 1994, p. 153.

Sri Lanka, being a unitary republic with a single 225-seat Parliament, faced great difficulties in accommodating the demands of the minorities in the north, particularly when the majority of the population, the Sinhalese, was opposed to this. But when the demand for decentralisation and devolution of power started to take violent forms, the constitution was amended (Thirteenth Amendment) in November 1987 pursuant to the Peace Accord signed with India in order to create Provincial Councils with certain limited powers. In order to implement the law, the Provincial Public Service Commission, Finance Commission, Police Commission and Land Commission were constituted.

When the elections to the Provincial Council were held, the ruling United National Party won all the seats. However, the principal opposition party, the Sri Lanka Freedom Party, did not participate, which rendered the election almost meaningless. It did not serve the purpose of the amendments made to the constitution. In the North-East, the most volatile of all places, one of the Tamil groups, the Eelam People's Revolutionary Liberation Front (EPRLF), accepted the system and won the election in the North-East Provincial Council. However, the most important and active militant organisation, the Liberation Tigers of Tamil Eelam (LTTE), not only rejected the structure envisaged in the amendment, but also boycotted the polls. The elections were held and the Councils were formed under the physical supervision of the Indian Peace Keeping Force. This made the elections more farcical and unacceptable to the majority of the Tamil.

None of the constitutional measures taken, including the elections, was sufficient to contain the situation. In the absence of any effective devolution of authority in the form of either a federation or finally a separate state, which the Tamils demanded, this constitutional exercise was bound to fail. The North-East Council, established in 1987, was dissolved by the central government in March 1990.[38] The Provincial Council in the south did not take off either, due to lack of enthusiasm amongst the local leaders.[39]

---

[38] *Ibid.*, p. 3.

[39] There are 8 Provincial Councils, see Shelton U. Kodikara, *The Security of South Asia in the 1990s* p. 168.

The Tamil movement in the northeast surrounding Jaffna, the provincial town, gradually took an extremely violent turn, causing a colossal loss of life and property. The LTTE turned into a regular underground organisation equipped with trained guerrillas and sophisticated weapons, and had sufficient strength to confront the Sinhalese soldiers. Every time the Tamils from their hideouts attacked the official troops, reprisals were conducted with venom against the Tamil civilians who were arrested, detained, harassed and repressed.

In the 1980s, the armed conflict took a bitter turn despite India's attempt at mediation. As the Sri Lankan government, dominated by the Sinhalese Buddhist elite, opted for a military solution to the crisis, the army was deployed to crush the movement. However, as the years went by, it did not achieve any success. This ultimately led the government of Sri Lanka to invite India to provide a military solution. Pursuant to a Peace Accord signed with India in July 1987, the Indian Peace Keeping Force (IPKF) landed in Sri Lanka to crush the Tamil militants.

This only aggravated the situation further. The peacekeeping force was seen as foreign troops on the soil of Sri Lanka. When the Indian troops went into operation they acted ruthlessly, creating more resentment amongst the ordinary people, both Sinhalese and Tamils. The Sinhalese army felt undermined as the Indian troops took over the operation, while the Tamils called them a 'foreign occupation army'. Tamils demand for an independent state became more intensified than ever before. Finally, the crisis deepened further when the Sri Lankan government found that the IPKF was not making much progress in the war, it wanted the Indian troops to withdraw and India refused to comply. The relationship between the two countries sank to its lowest level.

This ethnic armed conflict still continues and has cost 55,000 lives since 1983.[40] It has crippled an otherwise extremely high-potential nation of South Asia. Had there been no Tamil conflict, Sri Lanka would have been the first South Asian country to match the NICs of South-East Asia and become a member of the ASEAN. Even today,

---

[40]*New York Times*, 2 October 1998 and the report relating to the 3-day battle over taking the control of a highway with 1200 dead. The war for secession in Sri Lanka continues as LTTE faces 120 thousand strong Sri Lankan army. *India Today*, 22 November 1999.

if the Sri Lankan government could bring about an effective political solution, since no military option will work, the country could make great headway economically.[41] It could save about 4.5 percent of the GDP, equivalent to about Rs. 33 billion in resources, for its development projects. The conflict has not only increased the involvement of the army, with their continuously growing military budget, but also slowed down the development process of the country.

Still, Sri Lanka's literacy rate is the highest in South Asia at nearly 95 percent. Its per capita GNP is $430, which is higher than Pakistan's $420 and India's $360. Sri Lanka provides free education from the primary level to the universities. Women take an active part in all spheres of life. Because of its high literacy rate, Sri Lanka faces two acute problems. There is an elevated level of unemployment among the educated youth, who are not able to use their talent or education for any productive purpose. This leads to widespread frustration and disappointment. Young Tamils are then easily persuaded to join the armed cadre of the liberation forces. The lack of sufficient university places and facilities for research in high technology deprives a large number of talented youths of the chance to obtain higher education and seek jobs at home and abroad.

In games, sports and culture, Sri Lankans excel at every level. Besides their rich cultural heritage the country has a high standard of intellectual activity, which has always attracted international admiration. In cricket, although a comparatively small country, Sri Lanka has presented the best team in the World for at least the last three years and has the honour of being the champion of the World Cup.

Nepal

Nepal, a land-locked kingdom at the foothills of the panoramic peaks of the Himalayas, is a freedom loving independent state surrounded by India, China, Bhutan and Bangladesh. With a population of

---

[41] In Sri Lanka President Chandrika Kumaratunga presented a bill to amend the Constitution. These were to bring some fundamental changes establishing a quasi-federal system. It would ensure that Tamil dominated regions could merge and gain administrative autonomy. Although this was not what would fulfil the real LTTE demands, it was indeed a step in the right direction. But as the President's party did not have the required number of votes to pass the amendment bill in a 225-member Lower House and the bill, in the end, had to be withdrawn. *India Today*, 21 August 2000.

4 million, it is a multi ethnic, multi linguistic kingdom. Although it is described as a Hindu State, under its constitution the state does not discriminate against any citizen on ground of religion, race, caste, sex or ideology. Although it is still a constitutional monarchy, but till about a decade ago the king used to run the state as the Chief Executive, and the legislature and the government the kingdom had were to function in his name and under his command.

Historically, Nepal has always maintained its independent identity based on its own hilly culture. Because of being surrounded by the major countries like India, China and now Bangladesh with divergent culture, religions and political overtones, Nepal has always been eager to maintain a posture of neutrality. As Nepal is a small and locked country surrounded by the giant state of India, the King faced great difficulties in pursuing an independent and neutral foreign policy. Nepal's economy and politics continued to be influenced by and largely dependent on India for many years because of its geographical location and traditional religious and business links, its trade and commerce, export and import, and for access to the sea.

A series of agreements signed between Nepal and India in the early 1950s regulates their relationship in almost every sphere of the economy. The most significant and important of all are (1) The Treaty of Peace and Friendship and (2) The Trade and Transit Treaty signed in 1950 between the two countries, the latter being renewable every ten years. Despite these agreements, Nepal has always looked for alternative in its trade and business transactions. Although over the years Nepal trade dependence on India has decreased, in essence Nepal relies on India for the import of all its essential goods.[42] Transit of Nepali goods through India to Bhutan needs India's permission, as for any other country. Nepal signed a Trade and Transit Agreement with Bangladesh in 1980, but the agreement could not be implemented until 1988 because of a delay in the signing of an agreement between India and Bhutan to provide the necessary transit facilities. Thereafter India withheld permission for Nepal to use its territory to enter Bangladesh. India also strongly

---

[42] Sabbir Ahmed BIISS, Vol. 16, No. 2 of 1995.

promoted its proposal to implement a free trade zone with Nepal on the eastern border.

Nepal's resources include timber, rocks, limestone and tourism. With its total U.S.$4.9 billion in GDP, an average annual GDP growth rate of 4.2 percent and a per capita income of U.S.$220, it has 53 percent of its population living below poverty line and is one of the poorest countries of the world.[43]

A crisis with India over the renewal of the Trade and Transit Agreement in 1989, led to a mass movement initiated and organised by the Nepal Congress Party, which forced the King to forgo many of his powers and accept a new constitution for Nepal. This new constitution, adopted in November 1990, replaced the earlier *Panchayat* system — a kind of indirect and nominated government under the direct control of the King — with a parliamentary system of government elected under the universal adult franchise. This led to a radical change in the constitutional structure of the country. The constitution was drafted along the same lines as other constitutions of the subcontinent. Federal in nature, it provides for a bicameral system, consisting of a House of Representatives of 205 members directly elected by people and a 60-member National Assembly. Of these 60 members, the House elects 35, the King nominates 10 and 15 are elected by an electoral college representing the various Development Regions into which the country is divided.

The constitution guarantees all the fundamental rights, justifiable and enforceable, including equality before law and freedom of thought, assembly and association, as enshrined in the Charter of the United Nations. Freedom of the press and independence of the judiciary are also secured under the constitution. Although Nepal has been declared a Hindu kingdom, the right to practice other religions is guaranteed, and there is no discrimination on grounds of religion, race, caste or sex.

The Prime Minister, who is the Chief Executive and is collectively responsible to the House, heads the government. As long as the Prime Minister enjoys the confidence of the majority of Members of Parliament, he runs the government. The King continues to be the symbol of the Nepali nation and the 'unity of the Nepalese people',

---

[43] See *World Development Report 2000*, Oxford: Oxford University Press and Table No. 4.1.

and the constitution has not disturbed the right of succession to the throne according to the royal custom and tradition.

Following the elections under the constitution, for the first time held directly under a multi-party system, the Congress formed the government with the Nepal Communist Party as the principal opposition in the House of Representatives. Since the introduction of the new constitution there has been a number of changes in the government of Nepal, but on each occasion the change was effected peacefully on the basis of the parliamentary rules. However, it will obviously take time for Nepal to develop effective democratic institutions.

Like other countries in the region, Nepal suffers from ethnic problems. There is the conflict between the aboriginal Nepalese or hill Nepalese and the Nepalese of Indian origin; the latter dominates the economy and politics of Nepal, which is resented by the hill Nepalese. While the Nepalese of Indian origin in the southern part of the country are demanding autonomy, the hill Nepalese wants them out of their territory. The Gurkhas of Nepal, known to be great warriors and ferocious fighters, aspire to have a Gurkha-land of their own in the southern approaches of the Himalayas. Armed conflicts between the Nepalese force an extreme Maoist insurgent in a number of Nepalese provinces continue unabated.[44] However, none of these conflicts has reached the level of destabilising the Nepalese society or country.

In order to maintain its policy of achieving some kind of balance and neutrality, Nepal has proposed that their country should be declared a zone of peace. The Nepalese monarchy has made persistent efforts to maintain the identity of Nepal as an independent state.[45] It has tried to improve its relations with China to the extent of signing a friendship treaty with them.[46] Both countries signed a boundary agreement in order to ensure peace. Nepal has also secured military assistance by purchasing arms from China to the annoyance of the government of India.

---

[44] Robin Raphael's Testimony to Congress on South Asia, March 12, 1997.

[45] Derived from the author's experience in dealing with Nepal on the question of Water Sharing of the river Ganges.

[46] M. Abdul Hafiz, Regional problems and prospects for Cooperation in South Asia, BIISS Journal, Vol. 8, No. 4, 1997, p. 400.

Bhutan

Bhutan, the land of the thunder-dragon, is a small land-locked monarchy on the southern slopes of the Himalayas. It is surrounded by India in the south and China to the north, with a population of 1. million.[47] A vast largely barren and hilly land of around 47,000 square kilometres,[48] the country has been ruled by the present dynasty of kings since 1907. On the sudden death of his father, the present King Jigme Singhe Wanchuk, called back from his school in England, and was enthroned in 1974 when he was only nineteen.[49]

The King reigns as the absolute ruler of Bhutan. But traditionally the Bhutanese monarchy has ruled with compassion, tolerance and a liberal mind. As followers of Tantric Buddhism, they are docile in nature and prefer to live a secluded life of their own culture and environment. As far back as 1953, King Jigme Singye Dorji, the father of the present king, initiated a democratic process to make his rule more accountable, but it received no response from the kingdom's oligarchy. Then in 1968 the King again made some serious propositions to restructure the monarchy to include some democratic values. He surrendered his right to veto the bills passed by the National Assembly and made provision for passing no-confidence motions in the Assembly against the King. He also established the first High Court of Bhutan and introduced the idea of a Council of Ministers.[50] However, the reforms were not pursued with the right determination. The gradual exposure of Bhutan to the outside world through education and technology has been so extensive that the kingdom can no longer remain isolated. It has to keep pace with the changing environment of globalisation and the demands raised by its own citizens, who now have more knowledge of civil rights and democratic systems of governance.

Bhutan has a 150-member National Assembly, of which 105 are indirectly elected by heads of families, the King nominates 35 and 10

---

[47] *Human Development in South Asia 1999*, The University Press Limited, Dhaka, p. 195.

[48] *World Development Report 1999-2000*, Oxford: Oxford University Press, p. 272.

[49] Harun-ur Rashid, Bhutan: Welcome changes in the political system, *The Daily Star*, July 22, 1998.

[50] Mahendra P. Lama: Can Reforms in Bhutan consolidate the democratic process? *The Daily Star*, August 8, 1998.

nominated to represent the clergy. The assembly has neither any control over the executive nor any effective role in policy making. Its main function is consultative in nature.

The King has recently introduced some reforms through a *kasho* — an edict or proclamation — to democratise the country. The proposed changes are (1) the election of Cabinet ministers by the Assembly; (2) the role and responsibilities of the Cabinet to be decided by the Assembly; (3) the adoption of a mechanism to move a vote of no confidence against the King. The King has further suggested some measures introducing checks and balances between the three organs of the state: the legislature, executive and judiciary. But these reforms have not been well received by those who are in the Assembly or by those demanding more democracy. Members of the National Assembly are reluctant to accept any change. They are happy with the way the King runs the country now. According to them, any kind of electoral process for induction into the Cabinet will immediately result in partiality, squabbles, vested interests and corruption, which may not ultimately produce suitable candidates.[51] The India-based leader of the United Front for Democracy in Bhutan has rejected the reforms, as he wants direct elections to the National Assembly. The other opposition leaders and parties, although small and fragmented, have raised similar voices. The Nepali-speaking minorities, however, have welcomed the changes. The National Assembly of Bhutan has debated the proposals intensively and it will take time before any substantive devolution of power takes root, but it can be said that the process of democratisation will eventually take a definite shape in Bhutan.

Bhutan, too, is not free of ethnic conflicts, nor is it free from the influence of insurgencies in neighbouring countries. It is under constant pressure from the underground insurgents of the northeastern states of India, particularly Arunachal and Assam. The country also has a perceived security problem in accommodating or accepting the section of people who came originally from Nepal and are not considered to be Bhutias or the original inhabitants of Bhutan. About 96,000 Bhutanese — allegedly of Nepali origin — have crossed into Nepal

---

[51] *Ibid.*, Mahendra P. Lama.

as refugees, which have created tension between Bhutan and Nepal. This large population of Nepali origin is the main cause of ethnic conflicts within Bhutan.

Soon after the partition in 1947, Bhutan signed a treaty with India in 1949 whereby it regained its monarchy and the status of an independent state, but its defence and external affairs were to be controlled by India. Because of the size of its economy and a free trade agreement with India, Bhutan's economic development is totally dependent on India. Its only transit route is through India and in order to do business with any other country, such as Nepal, Bangladesh or China, it has to seek India's permission.

Bhutan nevertheless desires to maintain its independent status as far as possible. It maintains a Permanent Mission at the UN with offices in New York and Geneva and embassies in India, Bangladesh and Nepal. Though Bhutan's very existence is linked to India because of its geographical location, their deeper desire is to maintain a neutral position by striking a balance between India and China. However, the earlier agreements signed with India bind the country in almost all spheres of its sovereignty, and due to a lack of political leadership and any strong civil society in the country, it does not have the courage to revise or rescind these agreements. Bhutan nevertheless wishes to pursue a more multilateral approach and to widen its sovereign authority it supports Nepal's proposal for a zone of peace.

The Maldives

The Maldives is a small country with a population of 0.28 million, comprising hundreds of tiny islands in the Indian Ocean. It has a one-party rule with Abdul Mamun Gayum as the President. Its main source of wealth is fish and tourism. It is, in the international context, a vulnerable state because of its size and location.

Bangladesh

Born out of a bloody Liberation War with Pakistan in 1971, Bangladesh emerged as an influential state in South Asia in spite of its small size. Because of the resilience of its people and their history of struggle, the independence of Bangladesh ushered in a new hope for the inhabitants of this region. During the British rule, the overwhelmingly Muslim population of Bengal had voted for the creation of Pakistan based on a resolution passed by the All India Muslim League at Lahore in 1940. It was hoped that the territory first known as East Bengal and later renamed East Pakistan would enjoy full autonomy within the framework of Pakistan.

But after its foundation, Pakistan moved in a different direction. When the new country needed more understanding and cohesion between the regions, the ruling elite in Pakistan, mostly dominated by the leaders from the western part, undermined the dynamics of statecraft. The country already represented two broad national entities, not only in language, culture and distance between the two wings of the state, but also in terms of economy and ecology. Prudence and leadership demanded an immediate democratic order and an effective autonomous status for all the regions to allow Pakistan to grow into a strong modern state.

However, the country began without any basic law of its own, under the umbrella of the Indian Independence Act of 1947. Then came the perilous attempt to impose Urdu, a language of only 3.5 percent of the population, who were mostly upper-class migrants to Pakistan from India, as the only national language of the country. Since this was not the language of most people in East Pakistan, the Bengalis vehemently opposed it. This sparked the beginning of a nationalist movement in East Pakistan. The Bengalis, who constituted the majority in Pakistan, were denied their democratic rights to govern the country, to take part in policy planning or to allocate the resources of the state. On the contrary, they continued to be economically exploited. The sale of raw materials from East Pakistan earned about 70 percent of Pakistan's foreign exchange, but this was used for the development of industries and establishments, including the military, in West Pakistan. The political and economic deprivations of the Bengalis encouraged a nationalist movement of grave magnitude.

A constitution introduced in 1956 was not allowed to function because of the imposition of military rule in 1958, which continued until the break-up of Pakistan. A violent mass uprising, demanding full autonomy based on a six-point formula, brought the fall of the first military regime in March 1969. The subsequent military regime failed to comply with a popular mandate, established through the only general election held in Pakistan's history, in December 1970.[52] The ruthless crackdown on the Bengalis in March 1971 plunged the country into a bloody War for Independence.[53]

Awami League's victory in the general election held in 1970-71, gave it the right to represent the cause of the Bengalis. When the people entered into an armed struggle against the Pakistan army crackdown, the League assumed the formal leadership in the War of Independence. A government-in-exile was formed and was based in Calcutta. With the active and direct support of India the War continued for nine months. A middle-of-the road bourgeois political party, the Awami League, relied totally on India, supported by the Soviet Union on the international plane, to achieve independence. In the process, a deep and solid tie developed between the Awami League, the government of India and its elite establishment in New Delhi. Finally, when the Pakistan army surrendered on 16 December 1971 at the Dhaka Race Course, the Awami League was installed in power in an independent Bangladesh.[54] India, because of its direct involvement in the War of Independence, continued to have a deep-rooted influence in the politics of Bangladesh. The aspirations of the Bengalis to have a free and independent country of their own coincided with the design and purpose of India to weaken its principal enemy in the region. This combination of mutual interest led to the break-up of Pakistan.

Within a year of the end of the war, the Constituent Assembly of Bangladesh, comprising members elected to the Provincial and National Assemblies of Pakistan in 1970-71, had adopted one of the finest constitutions in South Asia. The constitution was passed on 4 November 1972 and made effective from 16 December 1972, commemorating the day of victory.[55] A parliamentary system of government in the Westminster style was introduced with a well-defined preamble,

---

[52] Due to the devastating cyclone in November 1970, elections in about 16 coastal constituencies were postponed and held in January 1971.

[53] For the entire background leading to the break-up of Pakistan read Moudud Ahmed: *Constitutional Quest for Autonomy*.

[54] See Moudud Ahmed *Ibid*.

[55] See Moudud Ahmed: *Era of Sheikh Mujibur Rahman*, pp. 108-161.

state principles, enforceable fundamental rights as enshrined in the Charter of the UN and an independent judiciary. The first elections under the constitution were held in 1973 and the Awami League secured 293 seats out of 300.[56]

However, despite the Awami League's popularity and command over the country, in September 1973, Article 33 of the constitution was amended to provide laws for preventive detention and a new Part IXA was incorporated to include emergency provisions in the constitution. In February 1974 the Special Powers Act was enacted, a repressive black law which provided for preventive detention without trial and to deal with other social and economic offences. On 28 December 1974 a state of emergency was proclaimed under the new provision made in the constitution,[57] and on 25 January 1975, about two years after the enactment of the constitution, further amendments were introduced and passed to change the basic structure of governance from a multi-party parliamentary democracy to a one-party monolithic system of government.

Sheikh Mujibur Rahman, the founding father, who was the Prime Minister now became the President of the Republic and assumed all the powers of the state. All the existing political parties were banned and only one political party – BAKSAL – created and led by him, was allowed to function. All the newspapers were closed except four, which were under government control; fundamental rights were suspended and the judiciary was made subservient to the executive. Civil servants and military officials were to be members of the single political party.[58] The provisions for elected local governments were deleted from the constitution and instead the country was divided into 64 districts, each to have a Governor responsible for their administration, who was appointed by the President.[59]

---

[56] The Awami League would have won the election in any case, but they still rigged the elections in at least 30 constituencies. See Moudud Ahmed: *Era of Sheikh Mujibur Rahman*, pp. 168-174.

[57] In the early morning of 29 December the author who was then the secretary of the most active civil rights organisation, Committee for Civil Liberties and Legal Aid, was the first person to be arrested under the Special Powers Act and kept in jail for about 3 months without any trial.

[58] For detail about the Awami League Rule from 1972-75 read Moudud Ahmed: *Era of Sheikh Mujibur Rahman*.

[59] The Fourth Amendment under which the one-party rule was established deleted Article 59 and 60 of the Constitution.

In the early hours of 15 August 1975, Mujib was brutally killed along with the members of his family and close relatives by some young army personnel, mostly retired freedom fighters. Khandaker Moshtaque Ahmed, the most senior minister and a leader of Mujib' party, became the President. But it did not end there. There was coup and then a counter-coup within the army in the first week of November 1975. During these events four senior Awami League leaders, known as rivals of Khandaker Moshtaque, were killed inside the Dhaka Central Jail where they had been held in captivity, by almost the same set of army officers.

On 7 November 1975, in an uprising of the *jawans* and masses Ziaur Rahman, the Chief of Army Staff and a war hero, was released from house arrest and installed in power. By the second week of November, the army, as young as the country itself, took complete control of the affairs of the state. With the death of Sheikh Mujib the entire perspective of Bangladesh politics changed. Its foreign policy shifted from the Indo-Soviet axis to the Sino-American Islamic block. Saudi Arabia, Pakistan and China were the first countries to give recognition to the new government.[60]

Most important of all, besides a change in economic policies and a tilt in foreign relations, there was a reversal in the social and political trends of the country. The 'collaborators' and the religion-based political parties who were supporting Pakistan and had opposed the independence of Bangladesh were rehabilitated and given the opportunity to participate in national politics.

Bangladesh then had two long spells of military rule. Ziaur Rahman a popular and charismatic general, ruled from 7 November 1975 to 30 May 1981 when some freedom fighters army officers stationed in Chittagong, killed him. Zia reversed the one-party rule and introduced a multi-party system. He restored the fundamental rights, the independence of the judiciary and the freedom of press, and held national elections, which was contested by all the political parties including the Awami League. He strengthened the military from 26,500 to 77,000 personnel, restored their institutional status and prestige, increased the defence budget and was enormously popular amongst the *jawans*.

---

[60]See for detail, Moudud Ahmed, *Era of Sheikh Mujibur Rahman*, pp. 306-307.

Internal Problems and Performances   53

and yet his own men shot him down after he had survived about seventeen previous coup attempts.[61]

After the death of Zia, the 78-year old Vice President Sattar, a former judge was taken from his bed at Dhaka's Combined Military Hospital to Bangabhaban, where he was administered the oath, to assume the office of President. The country survived the vacuum left by Zia and the continuity of constitutional rule was well maintained. Under the constitution, election for the office of President was to be held within 180 days. In the election held on 15 November 1981, Sattar as a nominee of the Bangladesh Nationalist Party (BNP), which had been created by Zia with an Islamic ideological bias, was elected in a direct poll as the first civilian President. He defeated Dr. Kamal Hossain, who had been nominated by the Awami League.

The army hierarchy played an important role in selecting Sattar as a presidential candidate. While supporting constitutional rule, they needed him also to restore discipline in the barracks and hold trials under the Army rules for the rebellion that had killed Zia. As a result of the court martial, twelve officers were hanged and seventy removed from service, almost all of them were freedom fighters. Once the chain of command was fully restored, General H. M. Ershad, as the Chief of Army Staff, then demanded a constitutional role for the military in the administration of the country. In an interview with the Guardian of London before the presidential election and with the BBC afterwards, Ershad's statements had already raised apprehension about the renewed ambition of the military. Only one day after Sattar announced his Council of Ministers and less than thirteen days after the new elected President was sworn in, the General issued a statement on 28 November 1981 spelling out the role of military in Bangladesh and demanding a formal position for the army in the decision-making affairs of the state.[62]

Finally, in the early hours of 24 March 1982, 128 days after the presidential election and 270 days after Zia's death, the army led by General H. M. Ershad again seized power in Bangladesh. The President was removed, Parliament was dissolved, the constitution was suspended

---

[1] See for detail about the rule of Zia. Moudud Ahmed: *Democracy and the Challenge of Development*, pp. 1-158.

[2] See for detail Moudud Ahmed: *Democracy and the Challenge of Development*, pp. 144-253.

and political activities were banned. The country was run once again under a Martial Law Proclamation. Ershad adopted the same route of civilianisation as Zia but in spite of holding a meaningful election in which all the political parties would participate, Ershad was not able to earn, till the end of his rule, any legitimacy. Unlike Zia, Ershad faced great opposition to his rule from the major political parties. Each time he attempted to legitimise his regime, Ershad encountered resistance. In February 1984, after two failed attempts, Ershad barely managed to hold the local elections at the Upazila level — new subdivisions created as a part of his reforms for decentralisation of the administration — and in March 1985 a referendum, held under the stringent cover of martial law, endorsed him to run the country as the President. In March 1986, Ershad held a general election in the midst of widespread violence and vote rigging, in which only the Awami League, one of the two major political parties, participated. The election ultimately suffered from a lack of credibility and was rejected by the people in general. In October 1986, when Ershad held the election to the office of President, no major political party put up a candidate and it turned out to be a farce. In 1988 when he called for another general election, all the major political parties boycotted it.

Ershad ruled for nearly nine years, but throughout his rule he faced political resistance and his regime lacked the legitimacy to rule. Finally, in the face of a rebellious mass movement led primarily by the BNP and the Awami League, Ershad was over thrown. On 6 December 1990, according to the demands of the opposition, Ershad resigned and handed over power to Chief Justice Shahabuddin Ahmed who would lead the nation as the head of a caretaker non-partisan government on a new journey in search of democracy.[63] With this came the fall of Ershad as well as the end of army rule.[64]

In the first nineteen years of its history, Bangladesh suffered military rule for nearly fifteen years and the experience of democracy was of little substance. After the first three years, it saw a spell of

---

[63] Author resigned from the office of Vice-President to enable Ershad to appoint Chief Justice Shahabuddin as the Vice-President, who then entered into the office of President after Ershad had resigned on the same day.

[64] For detail of Ershad and a comparative study of the two military regimes, read Moudud Ahmed *Democracy and the Challenge of Development*, pp. 211-248.

one-party rule. This was followed by two long periods of rule under absolute martial law — a little less than four years under Zia and a little more than four years under Ershad. There was an intervening period of civilian rule by Sattar for ten months and, prior to Zia, the rule of Moshtaque for three months under martial law proclaimed by him in August 1975.

After the election held under a non-partisan caretaker government, which set an unprecedented example in constitutional history, the BNP emerged as the single majority party and Begum Khaleda Zia, widow of President Ziaur Rahman, assumed the office of Prime Minister under the existing presidential system. Pursuant to the pledge made before the election, the BNP government introduced a major constitutional change in the Twelfth Amendment to return the country to the parliamentary system. The entire nation was united again, the amendment to the constitution was passed unanimously in the newly elected Parliament and the Constitution of 1972 was restored.

The opposition parties in Parliament demanded that all future elections be held under a non-partisan caretaker government and on this issue led a countrywide movement for nearly two years. On 15 February 1996, the BNP government held a general election in which no opposition party took part, thus rendering the polls meaningless. This only aggravated the anti-government agitation, which reached its climax in March 1996 and forced the BNP to introduce the Thirteenth Amendment to the constitution. This provided a permanent arrangement for a neutral caretaker government to take oath of office three months prior to the holding of every general election. Since then Bangladesh has held another election, under a neutral non-partisan caretaker government in June 1996. The Awami League secured the highest number of seats, though not an absolute majority, and Sheikh Hasina, the daughter of Sheikh Mujibur Rahman, assumed the office of Prime Minister after being in opposition for 21 years. In the next election held on October 1, 2001, again under a neutral caretaker government, the BNP- led 4 Party Alliance returned to power with a two-thirds majority in the Parliament.

Although military interventions have taken place in Bangladesh in the past, it is thought unlikely that these will recur in the future for various reasons. One of the cogent reasons for this is the lack of international support in the present global situation with the end of the Cold War and the cessation of ideological conflict between the two superpowers. Military intervention to contain communism or to balance the influence of the rival superpowers in a particular region is no longer necessary. Moreover, there is a fear that western countries, particularly the USA, may cut off aid to a country where the military overthrows an elected civilian government.[65]

So democracy in Bangladesh appears to have come to stay. The emergence of two strong political parties and the holding of general elections under a neutral caretaker government are the two significant factors that provide Bangladesh with a unique opportunity to sustain a healthy growth of democracy.

In the structure of the economy, Bangladesh has gone through changes as radical as those in the political sphere. As early as in March 1972, the Awami League government, in order to implement its plan for socialist transformation, nationalised 80-85 percent of the nation's industrial, banking and insurance assets and business, bringing them under direct control of the state. In the economic policies pursued during that period, the state was given the principal role in driving the country ahead, and private and foreign investments were not encouraged. The Planning Commission prepared the first Five Year Plan with objectives derived from the philosophy of socialism. Large public corporations were set up and workers were promised shares in the industries to increase productivity. The bureaucracy and the political leadership took control of the economy.

After the death of Mujib and the end of the Awami-BAKSAL rule, the policies were revised. Zia began the process of privatisation, but

---

[65] The recent military take-over in Pakistan and the mild attitude demonstrated by the US towards it may however encourage a new trend for re-emergence of military rule in other parts of the world. On October 12, 1999 General Pervez Musharraf on his return from an official visit to Sri Lanka assumed the office of the Chief Executive in a military coup. When he was on the plane Nawaz Sharif, the Prime Minister, dismissed him and allegedly tried to divert the Pakistan International Airlines plane carrying Pervez Musharraf by not allowing it to land at Karachi. As soon as the news of his dismissal reached the Cantonment, the Commanding Officers of the core units of Pakistan Army decided to intervene. Soldiers seized the T.V. Station and took over the airport in Karachi where the General landed with only 5 minutes of fuel left in the plane. Seven hours later he announced the overthrowing of the elected government. The following day the Constitution was suspended and the whole of Pakistan was brought under the control of the armed forces.

took time to set the macro-economic policies on the right track. It needed an overall reorientation of the entire bureaucratic machine, which had developed a vested interest in the state enterprises. The unexpired Five-Year Plan had to be totally recast and it took time for the new government to change the laws to create conditions conducive to let the private sector playing the desired role.

When Ershad took over, he adopted bolder steps. He denationalised industries and returned the jute and textile mills to their Bangladeshi owners, moving fast to privatise large and medium-sized industries by outright sale to the public. These actions brought new confidence in the private sector and Bangladesh gradually embarked upon a free market economy. This pattern of development was initially followed in Pakistan and with these changes the Bangladesh economy started to depend heavily on foreign aid and assistance.

During Ershad's time, infrastructural development in the energy and communication sectors required a heavy infusion of capital borrowed from the multilateral agencies, increasing the proportion of foreign debt. The dependence on foreign aid in the implementation of the development budget rose to almost 100 percent. The revenue expenditures exceeded the revenue receipts. National savings and investment declined and the economy at the macro-level took a downward turn.

The BNP government, having received the mandate of the people in 1991, spent its first two years restoring discipline in economic management and succeeded in stabilising the macro-economic indicators in the country. A surge in revenue income obtained by adopting economic and fiscal reforms, helped to bring a change in the overall economy. Bangladesh became an active participant in global integration by adopting principles of liberalisation, which critics argued were 'too fast too soon'. In the budget that the BNP presented for 1995/96, the dependence on aid in the development budget was reduced from 100 percent to 57 percent and the national contribution of resources for development increased to 43 percent. The next government of the Awami League pursued the same macro-economic policies and the avowed policy of the government based on the market economy continued to hold ground. But because of its internal over-borrowing, general fiscal mismanagement and failure to effect any large-scale privatisation due to their earlier belief of "socialist transformation", the Awami League government could no make any substantial progress in economic reforms.

Bangladesh has set an example of completely reversing a economy from almost a state of total nationalisation to a market economy within a short span of time, which not many Third World countries have been able to achieve. The painful and difficult task of denationalisation faced by each government from Ziaur Rahman t Begum Zia, with Ershad and Sheikh Hasina in between, was no easy to sustain politically in the existing socio-economic conditions The surge in exports of ready-made garments, all in the privat sector, beginning primarily during Ershad's time, has been phenomenal. The volume has increased by about 25 percent in the last several years, raising the export earnings in this sector to over $ billion. Due to this industry, women today play a dominant role in the manufacturing sector and their employment in these industries ha infused new confidence and awareness about their role in society as a whole. The two giant national non-government organisations Grameen Bank and the BRAC, have earned a worldwide reputation for their contribution to the empowerment of women in Bangladesh in both self-employment and education.

Except for unforeseen calamities, Bangladesh can claim to have achieved for a population of 130 million a near self-sufficiency in food production. Bangladesh started with a population growth rate of around 3 percent, but the control programme framed by each successive government has brought it down to 1.4 percent. Child immunisation has covered almost 90 percent, and the supply of acceptable drinking water reaches about 95 percent of the rural population. The increased number of females, more than males in percentage terms, attending schools all over Bangladesh indicates a future avenue for women to take a participatory role in the nation-building programmes of the country. The institution of Upazila, initiated by Ershad but abandoned by the first BNP government of Begum Zia, was set as a model for decentralisation of the administration and is now followed in some parts of India. Once re-established, as pledged by the present government, the system will have a profound impact on the rural economy and employment. The engagement of the Bangladesh army in the operation of international peacekeeping forces besides being a good source of foreign exchange has earned considerable goodwill abroad.

But Bangladesh's economy remains small and poor. The per capita income is about $340. Its GDP growth rate moves between 4.5 and 5.5 percent on average, although the budgetary target is set above 6 percent. Calamities come in cycles of ten years or so and they sweep away some of its achievements. In 1996-97 its gross domestic investment as a percentage of GDP stood at 21 percent, national domestic savings at 15 percent and exports at 14 percent. The number of people living below the poverty line is estimated at 48 percent, those without sanitation at 65 percent and health services at 55 percent, and illiteracy levels at 62 percent. Despite following the World Bank and IMF prescriptions and a liberal economic policy for the last two decades, achievement has not been up to the expectation in terms of alleviating poverty and improving the quality of life. Bangladesh remains one of the poorest countries in the world.[66] The hangover from the socialist economy practiced in the first few years after independence still looks alternative to many politicians, economists, planners and bureaucrats. Some 40 percent of industrial business is still in the hands of the state causing heavy losses, to the tune of $1 billion annually, at the cost of the taxpayers.

With the on going liberalisation programme in hand, Bangladesh economy is in transition. Due to a lack of resources and weak capital growth in the private sector, an economic breakthrough has not yet been possible. If any economic leap forward is to be achieved, it has to come through the private sector, which is inexperienced and still needs to grow. On the other hand, the major advantage that Bangladesh enjoys over most of the South Asian countries is its homogeneity. It is a compact, homogeneous and truly unitary state. Almost everybody speaks the same language, eats the same kind of food and pursues the same culture. Except the religious minorities of not more than 10-12 percent, the entire population is Muslim. The ethnic tribes are very small in number, about half a million. Their largest concentration is in the Chittagong Hill Tracts. With all these advantages and having followed the ground rules of liberalization for

---

[66] See Tables 4.1 and 4.2.

development, Bangladesh should have achieved much more than it has today.[67]

Ethnic Conflicts: The Chittagong Hill Tracts

Despite the homogeneity of the state and the fact that the tribal community is small, Bangladesh is not free from ethnic conflicts. These conflicts mainly concern the tribes residing in the Chittagong Hill Tracts (CHT) areas, northeast of the port city of Chittagong, bordering India and Myanmar.

Table 2.1 Ethnic distribution of population of the CHT

Name of ethnic group	Total	Percentage of population[a]
Bangalee[b]	470,000	50
Chakma	240,000	24
Marma (Magh)	143,000	14
Tripura	61,000	6
Murung	22,000	2.2
Tanchangya	19,000	1.9
Bom	7,000	0.7
Mro (Kuki)	5,000–8,000	0.5–0.8
Punkho	3,500	0.35
Chak	2,000	0.20
Kheng	2,000	0.20
Khumi	1,200	0.12
Lushai	700	0.07

Source: *Preliminary Report of Population Census*, Bangladesh Bureau of Statistics, Dhaka, 1991.

Notes: [a]Showing the population of 1991 in rounded figures. [b]20 per cent of the total Bangalee population in CHT are temporary settlers belonging mainly to different law-enforcing groups (i.e. military or police), plus traders.

CHT is a vast area of about 13,150 square kilometres or one-tenth of the entire country. It has a population of only about one million people including the Bengali settlers. About half of CHT is covered with tropical evergreen rain forests with valuable species of hard wood and plants.[68] Besides its enormous resources of land and forest,

---

[67]The reasons of these failures are stated at different stages of this study.

[68]Mohammad Abdur Rob: Resource Potentials of CHT, *Weekend Independent*, 9 May 1997.

It has great potential in minerals in the form of gas, oil, hard rocks, limestone and coal. It already generates hydro-electricity. Because of its scenic beauty and secluded mountainous location with facilities for water skiing, yachting, fishing and angling, it could be turned into the most attractive area for the tourism industry in the country.

On 15 February 1972, Manabendra Narayan Larma a prominent tribal leader met the then Prime Minister, Sheikh Mujibur Rahman and submitted a four point demand as follows:

a. Autonomy for CHT and establishment of a special legislative body.
b. Retention of regulation 1 of 1900 in the Bangladesh Constitution.
c. Continuity of the institution of tribal chiefs.
d. A constitutional guarantee restricting any amendment of the Regulation of 1900 in the constitution and imposing a ban on Bengali settlement in CHT.[69]

But Mujib turned him down and refused to accept any of his proposals when the constitution was adopted in November 1972, which termed every citizen as "Bangalee" (Bengali). Larma as a Member of the Constituent Assembly refused to vote for it as he claimed that he was not a Bengali. He declared that 'a Chakma can never be a Bangali ... our main worry is that our culture is threatened with extinction. But we want to live with our separate identity'.

Having failed to persuade Sheikh Mujib to accept his proposal, Larma on 15 February 1972 formed a political front called Parbattya Chattagram Jana Sanghati Sangha (PCJSS) under his own leadership, in which he included the leaders of the Rangamati Communist Party. As a consequence, an armed wing of the Jana Sanghati, named *Shanti Bahini*, was established on 7 January 1973.[70]

The issue of CHT has been the focus of international attention for a long time. The demand for self-rule by the indigenous people of that region has been a source of embarrassment to every government. It has led to armed rebellion, confrontation, reprisals, military action

---

[69] Mizanur Rahman Shelley: *CHT: The Untold Story*, Center for Development Research, Dhaka, p. 110.
[70] *Ibid.*, p.11.

and escape to India across the border, where the tribesmen are trained in insurgency. This has been going on for years at a great cost in terms of lives and resources. Insurgency in the region has produced many deaths, both civil and military, but it has not achieved its goal. Rather the problem has become a permanent threat to the security of the state.

The decision of Mujib's government to allow families from the over-crowded lowlands to settle in the thinly inhabited, secluded highlands of the tribes in order to establish national integrity and homogeneity amongst the people of one 'Bengali nation' proved to be not only wrong but disastrous. The tribesmen, around 500,000 in number, have been living in that mountainous terrain in a sheltered culture for decades. The intrusion of outsiders into their life and land gave them the immediate reason to reiterate their demand for an autonomous state. They declined to be part of 'Bengali' culture which was alien to them, and were not willing to be called 'Bengali' as the constitution of 1972 had decreed. The lowland settlers (around 470,000 in number) had not only disturbed their traditional way of life, but also destroyed their age-old system of *jhoom* or "slash and burn" cultivation. They were allotted or allowed to grab land belonging to the tribesmen, dislodged them from their homes, took away their business and injured their cultural pride.[71]

The tribesmen had to retaliate for their own survival. Some ambitious, politically motivated tribal leaders were emboldened and organised guerrilla warfare under various names. The broad-based association Jana Sanghati, with its armed wing called *Shanti Bahini*, started murdering the settlers. The Bangladesh army intervened to save the settlers and killed some insurgents, which led to reprisals on both sides. Eventually, the settlers were placed in designated camps to be guarded by the army, and some of the tribesmen crossed into India for refuge, shelter and guerrilla training.

The picturesque hills and lakes of CHT had become a forbidden land, completely under army control, with tourists and outsiders debarred from visiting most of the area. Clearly, the original aim of sending the settlers to integrate the tribesmen into a homogenous Bengali

---

[71] For distribution of population in CHT, see Table 2.1.

...tion has been totally frustrated. The settlers now live in camps, ...eir freedom of movement is restricted, they have no land to cultivate, ...e is insecure and they are entirely dependent on government handouts, ...using a strain on the national resources. Similar conditions apply ...those tribesmen who have been uprooted by the settlers, and to the ...uerrillas, who have returned from India where they had fled as ...fugees and are now in camps under army security, being fed by the ...overnment.

That the issue is a political one has been known for a long time ...ut the question was how to deal with it. Almost all the army commanding ...fficers stationed in Chittagong had recommended a political ...olution to the issue. General Manzur had, with considerable ...oresight, clearly advised the authorities to abandon the military ...ption and advocated a political solution to the crisis. Rather, it was ...he politicians who failed to take a clear decision. So the crisis ...ngered causing increased bitterness between the two neighbouring ...ountries.

After Zia had consolidated his authority, a massive programme ...or the development of CHT was undertaken, aiming at the improvement ...f roads and bridges, educational institutions and medical care at an ...nitial cost of Tk. 250 crores. But on the questions of the integration ...f the tribes into the mainstream population, the same policy was ...ursued and in the process military involvement increased in order ...o contain the insurgency in the region.

During the first three years of Ershad's military regime, the policy ...owards CHT remained unchanged. One of the earliest economic ...neasures taken by Ershad, in line with the policy of development ...dopted by Zia, was to declare CHT a Special Economic Area in order ...o provide special facilities for tribal people and to generate economic ...ctivities and employment opportunities. Under this programme, the ...ncentives provided were: (1) tax relief for small and cottage ...ndustries; (2) exemption from fees for importing capital machinery ...nd spares; (3) only 5 percent interest on money borrowed for projects, ...ayable in ten annual instalments from the day the project began ...operation; (4) reduction of interest on bank loans for commercial ...urposes to 5 percent; (6) tax holiday for twelve years; (7) exemption of all cinemas from payment of excise and amusement taxes.

In order to integrate the tribal people into the central administration, 5 percent of all government employment was now reserved for them. In addition, the government decided to fill more than 180 vacancies in various government departments and state scheduled banks with tribal people of the country. In educational institutions also there were reservations for the tribal population and the qualifying grade for admission was reduced to 40 percent instead of 45-60 percent required by others. Moreover, to encourage business activities in CHT, all work on development project costing more than Tk. 200,000 was reserved for tribal contractors. A further incentive was that 10 percent of the total development projects undertaken in the area were reserved for tribal contractors. The tribal contractor could, in addition bid for work through open competition for the rest 90%. A special Five Year Development Plan was undertaken for CHT in 1984-85 at an approximate cost of Tk. 265 crores. This was in addition to the direct allocation made for the Upazila Parishad from the central budget.

When Ershad finally realised that the military option would not work, he made serious attempts to arrive at a political solution. A high-powered national committee, headed by Air Vice Marshal (Rtd.) A.K. Khandakar assisted by the Area Commanding Officer General Abdus Salam, entered into protracted negotiations with the belligerent leaders, which continued for about eighteen months. The two sides arrived at a consensus and a written understanding was drawn up on how to bring about a structural change for maximum self-rule within the framework of a sovereign Bangladesh. The arrangement enabled the tribesmen to retain their own culture and heritage and at the same time to look after their own administrative affairs. This understanding was then codified, with the approval of the cabinet, into three separate laws enacted for the local governments at Rangamati, Bandarban and Khagrachari districts.

The scheme was to have a 31-member Local Government Council in each district, the Chairman and Members of which would be directly elected by the people in such a manner that both the tribes and settlers would be represented in proportion to their population but under all circumstances the Chairman and the majority Members would be from among the tribesmen. Besides education, health, riculture, livestock and other subjects, the two most crucial areas r the tribesmen to retain control, were the right to land and law and der. The tribesmen were very sensitive about their land being taken ver by outsiders by purchase or lease, and their internal security stem failing to provide adequate guarantee for their safety. The w provided that no land in the district could change hands without e authority of the elected council, all the personnel up to the level f Sub-Inspector of Police would be recruited locally, and the police ould function under the control of the Council.

Table 2.2 Tribal household and population in Bandarban, Khagrachari and Rangamati Zilas, 1991 and 1981

Zila	Household						
	Census 1991			Census 1981		
	Total	Tribal	Non-tribal	Total	Tribal	Non-tribal
Bandarban	45,944	21,517	24,427	31,055	15,981	15,074
Khagrachari	71,249	33,369	37,880	47,574	29,753	17,821
Rangamati	78,008	42,271	35,737	52,070	29,280	22,750
Total	**195,201**	**97,157**	**98,044**	**130,699**	**75,014**	**55,685**

	Population						
	Census 1991			Census 1981		
	Total	Tribal	Non-tribal	Total	Tribal	Non-tribal
Bandarban	229,612	108,473	121,139	161,987	89,503	72,484
Khagrachari	340,095	164,799	175,295	265,590	172,880	92,710
Rangamati	397,713	225,323	172,390	280,879	177,075	103,804
Total	**967,420**	**498,595**	**468,825**	**708,456**	**439,458**	**268,998**

Source: Based on PRPC, 1991.

With a tribesman as the elected Chairman, enjoying the status of Deputy Minister and a huge administrative set-up of his own, staffed by senior officers such as the Deputy Commissioner, a new feeling of confidence and importance prevailed among the tribal population. It had undoubtedly opened up a new chapter for the peaceful political settlement of a problem that had haunted the nation for a long time. If sustained, there was hope for the peaceful co-existence of the tribal and non-tribal people, which would allow the tribesmen to preserve their own life and culture.

The three laws were identical for three districts of CHT, but completely different from the laws made for the Upazilas or for any other part of the country. The salient features of these laws were as follows:

1. The District Councils were named Local Government Councils. The tribal population was guaranteed a two-thirds majority in each Council, and the Chairman and Members were to be elected directly under universal adult franchise.

2. Proportional representation was guaranteed to all the existing tribes to ensure their participation.

3. The Chairman, who had to be from among the tribal members, was to be Chief Executive of the Local Government Council. The tribal chiefs of each district i.e. the Chakma Chief of Rangamati, the Mong Chief of Khagrachari and the Boman Chief of Bandarban could attend meetings of the Council.

4. The Deputy Commissioner of the district was to act as the Secretary of the Council.

5. The Council could create new posts, appoint different classes of official and make rules of conduct for them.

6. The Council would have a budget for a development plan of its own for each financial year, which would be conceived, prepared and implemented by the Council covering all the areas assigned to their authority under the law.

7. The Council was empowered to levy taxes, rates, tolls, etc. and to evolve a machinery to realise the same.

8. The Council was empowered to make rules to conduct its own business and also with regard to all the matters that fell within its jurisdiction (for which 29 areas were identified in the law itself).

9. As far as the power and functions of the Local Government Council were concerned, a separate schedule was annexed to the law under Section 22 of the Act giving the Council total responsibility for the following subjects: maintenance of law and order, co-ordination of the development activities of the entire district and support and assistance for this purpose, education, health and family planning, public health, agriculture and forestry, livestock,

fisheries, co-operatives, industry and commerce, social welfare, culture, construction of roads and bridges, maintenance and control of ferries, implementation of development projects assigned by the central government, communication, irrigation and water supply and all measures necessary for the uplifting improvement of the tribal areas.

The most significant of all the powers that the law provided for he local government are the following:

a. All police personnel from the rank of Assistant Sub-Inspector downwards were to be appointed by the Council and transferred and removed according to the rules framed by the Council itself. The Council would also be responsible for determining the terms and conditions of service, training, recruitment and uniform. The Chief of Police would immediately report any offence or incident in the district to the Chairman of the Council, on whose instruction the police would be bound to act.

b. No land in the district could be transferred or settled in any form without the prior approval of the Council, and no land could be sold or transferred without the prior approval of the Council to any person who was not a permanent resident of the district — excepting those that were already under the control of the central government or which it decided to transfer in the greater national interest.

c. If any dispute arose between the members of the tribal area in connection with any social, cultural or tribal matters, the issue was to be raised with the local headman, who would adjudicate and settle the matter in accordance with the tradition and custom of the tribes concerned. An appeal from such a settlement would lie with the respective chiefs of the districts, for which the Council would frame the rules and procedures. In the same month, Parliament passed another bill relating to the tribal areas of CHT to maintain certain special provisions, laws, regulations, customs, traditions and tribal value. The old law, known as the Chittagong Hill Tracts Regulations, enacted in 1900, was now repealed. A new law was made to ensure that the tribal population could maintain their own life and culture. By this law, all the earlier provisions relating to the area's social and economic structure and cultural traditions were restored and guaranteed. The provisions relating to the office of the Chakma Chief Bomang Chief and Mong Chief were re-established with their corresponding jurisdiction, facilities and privileges. The existing chief was to continue in their offices. Similar provisions were made with regard to the headmen of the tribes for realisation of land development tax with the power of a Tahsil. No headman could, however, be removed without consultation with the Chief of the district.

d. The traditional *jhoom* cultivation would continue under the supervision and control of the Deputy Commissioner. *Jhoom* tax could also be imposed and the law laid down how the taxes would be realised and how they would be divided amongst the headman and the headmen and the Chief after being apportioned by the government.

e. The system of *jhoom* tarsi was to continue, whereby the Chief was to supervise the activities of the headman. Tribal people were allowed to cut and use for domestic purposes the special kind of thick grass grown in CHT without paying a fee. The use of grazing land for the animals would continue at the existing rate and system. Any tribal person could, with the approval of the headman, take possession of land not exceeding 30 decimals outside the municipal area without any settlement for the purpose of building a homestead.

Any political arrangement of this nature would take time to yield permanent results. That some insurgents would continue to pursue their goal of a separate homeland was not difficult to understand and the general sense of insecurity was yet to fully subside. Tribesmen who started returning from India had to take refuge in camps in their own land rather than live freely as they had done before. The army was still in control of the security of CHT. Nevertheless, the participation of the tribesmen in their own socio-political and development activities, and the opportunity to establish their own leadership could eventually lead to a successful solution of the problem. If the idea of governing the area by force was abandoned by future governments and the tribesmen were allowed to maintain their own way of life, as conceived by the new legislation, the insurgency would subside through lack of public support. The area and the people of CHT would then be a harmoniously integrated part of a sovereign Bangladesh.

The largest religious minority in Bangladesh are the Hindus. At the time of the partition of India and thereafter at different stages, most of the affluent and educated Hindus have migrated to India, leaving the poorer and disadvantaged ones behind. These people constitute about 10 percent of the total population. Unlike India, communal riots and tensions in Bangladesh have been an extremely rare occurrence. Normally all the communities in the country live in peace and harmony. Only on occasions when a big communal incident occurring in India — such as the demolition of Babri Mosque in 1992 — ripples in Bangladesh as a reaction, which in any case always subsides quickly. Although Ershad incorporated Islam as a state religion into the constitution, it has not made any difference to the relationship between the Muslims and others, as the communities in this region have lived together for centuries in harmony and mutual tolerance. The constitution also guarantees the fundamental rights, including the right to practice religion, to all citizens and the right of equality against any form of discrimination, protected and effectively enforceable by courts of law.

The political arrangement, achieved after a long and arduous negotiation with the tribal leaders during Ershad's time, could have yielded a positive result if the laws made for the three newly created Local Government Councils had been implemented in true earnestness and if the process of participation in the management of their own affairs, based on a concept of self-rule, had been given sufficient time and opportunity. One of the best possible ways of achieving this, the laws envisaged, was to have regular elections to the Local Government Councils, which could have strengthened and consolidated participatory politics as well as the process of integration amongst the people in the region. The laws guaranteed the tribal population the biggest role in running the administration, including control of the police force and the Councils, which were to be headed by tribal representatives. If there had been regular elections and if the Council headed by tribal leaders had been able to function effectively for while, the extremists could have been isolated. The people who ha fled to India would have started to return and resettled in their homeland and taken part in the development of the area.

Although a section of the *Shanti Bahini* opposed the peace process, the government went ahead with the implementation of th agreement that it had arrived at through the formal negotiations wit the Jana Sanghati. The laws were passed in February 1989 and four months later, in June of the same year, the first free elections wer held in the three districts under the new laws. Despite the threats and intimidation of the Shanti Bahini dissidents, the elections were hel successfully with a voter turnout of more than 50 percent. The elections were watched and reported on by more than 3 international media representatives from all over the world. The three administrative bodies of CHT, headed by three tribal leader elected by the people, started functioning from 2 July 1989.[72]

In July 1990 the government established a separate ministry fo CHT, named as the Ministry of Special Affairs. In order to attach due importance to it and to ensure the implementation of the laws which required co-ordination amongst various ministries, the ministry was placed under the Vice-President of the country. After the election in 1991 it was placed under the Prime Minister's Secretariat.

It is obvious that no political arrangement, after such a long period of deprivation and hostility, could satisfy all sections of the people at once. Thus a section of the Jana Sanghati and Shant Bahini continued to pursue their old demand of complete autonomy leading to independence, and continued with their terrorist activities These would have gradually subsided if the local governments of the region could have ensured a healthy democratic development of its own administration and secured the existence of their own values tradition and culture without any interference from the centra government.

---

[72]Mizanur Rahman Shelley, *CHT: The Untold Story*, Centre for Development Research, Dhaka pp. 146-147.

A peaceful political process of establishing an autonomous status for CHT had begun not only to give recognition to the larger tribes, such as the Chakma, Murma and Tripura, but also to offer a participatory role for the ten smaller disadvantaged groups as well, who had always been ignored in the past. Almost all the subjects listed in the laws, including primary education, agriculture, health and population planning, were now transferred to the elected Councils. Between April 1980 and September 1989, 2294 insurgents surrendered and between 1987 and 1990 more than 30,000 tribe members had returned from the camps across the border.[73]

Table 2.3 Names and population of tribes (estimates from 1991 Census)

Sl. no.	Name of tribe	Bandarban	Rangamati	Khagrachari	Total
1	Bawm	6,429	549	–	6,978
2	Chak	1,681	319	–	2,000
3	Chakma	4,163	157,385	77,869	239,417
4	Khumi	1,150	91	–	1,241
5	Khyang	1,425	525	–	1,950
6	Lushai	226	436	–	662
7	Marma	59,288	40,868	42,178	142,334
8	Murong	21,963	38	40	22,041
9	Pankho	99	3,128	–	3,227
10	Tanchangya	5,493	13,718	–	19,211
11	Tripura	8,187	5,865	47,077	61,129
12	Mro	–	126	–	126
13	Rakhain	–	70	–	70
14	Shaotal	–	–	253	253
15	Others	229	174	102	505
Total		**110,333**	**223,292**	**167,519**	**501,144**

On the other hand, the non-tribal citizens of all three districts raised serious objections against the discriminatory provisions depriving them of their right of equality and equal protection under the law, as laid down in the constitution. According to them, besides the right to property and profession, the electoral system, which discriminated against them and guaranteed that tribe members were

---

[73] *Ibid.*, p. 147.

always to be Chairman of the Councils, was against many of the fundamental rights guaranteed in the constitution. Despite the fact that these grievances were genuine, however, the government was able to pacify the non-tribal citizens for the time being, pleading the greater interest of the nation.

For some unknown reason, the BNP government refrained from giving full effect to the laws. Most disappointing was that the elections to the Local Government Councils were repeatedly postponed by extending the terms of the existing Councils and each time the tenure was extended by amending the laws. Despite the directions given by the Supreme Court in their judgement that Local Government Councils must be elective bodies and that election to all such bodies must be held within a specified time, the BNP government held no elections in the Chittagong Hill Tract district during its entire five-year rule.[74]

In May 1992, when Begum Khaleda Zia visited Delhi, the matter was taken up with her counterpart in India, Mr. Narshima Rao. As a result the Jana Sanghati announced a ceasefire, which ceased the negotiations for the return of the remaining refugees in India. After this meeting with the Indian Prime Minister, the government constituted a nine-member Parliamentary Committee in July 1992 headed by Col. (Rtd.) Oli Ahmad, the Communication Minister, to negotiate with the tribal leaders. As a result of the subsequent negotiations, the return of the refugees began on 15 February 1994. When a final agreement on the outstanding issues was almost in sight, a movement to paralyse the government was initiated by the Awami League. Taking advantage of the situation, and in order to destroy the progress made in the negotiations, Upendra Lal Chakma the leader of the armed cadres of the *Shanti Bahini* raised certain demands including seeking independence outside the structure of the constitution, which the BNP government declined to accept.

The government, without holding the elections, had entered into fresh negotiations with Jana Sanghati, the front organisation of the Shanti Bahini, in July 1992. The stand of the BNP government, like the one taken by all previous governments, was that the demands, which would infringe the basic structure of the constitution, could

---

[74] 44 DLR AD 319.

not be accommodated, but it was ready to concede any proposal short of infringing the constitution. In other words, any arrangement to be arrived at would have to be within the framework of the Bangladesh constitution. The tribal leaders could see the logic behind this position and accepted it. But it is suspected that pressure from some quarters in India, which was instrumental in giving training and sanctuary to *Shanti Bahini*, did not allow them to come to any arrangement with the BNP government. It has always been realised by all previous governments that had entered into negotiations with the Jana Sanghati that the Sanghati's political moves were under the total control of the Indian authorities. In any case, before any conclusion could be reached, the BNP government got into political trouble with the opposition in Parliament, leading to general elections held in February and June 1996.

With the change of the government in Bangladesh after the June elections, and with the Awami League having always been aligned to India, the environment for fruitful negotiations improved. A special Parliamentary Committee on CHT was constituted with the parliamentary Chief Whip as the Convener to negotiate the issue with the Jana Shanghati, officially represented by its President, Jotirinda Bodhpriya Larma, known as Shantu Larma, the leader of the Shanti Bahini. The negotiations supported by India, came to a conclusion much earlier than expected. The terms of the agreement were kept extremely secret and in the absence of participation by the opposition members of Parliament, the negotiations took on the character of a partisan matter between the Awami League government and the Sanghati inspired by India. It was as though they had nothing to do with the nation. The proposals were not discussed in any forum — neither within the Awami League itself nor in any meeting of its parliamentary party. Even the media were not allowed any access to them. The proposed terms of the agreement were not placed before either the parliamentary party or the Cabinet. The nation was deprived of an opportunity to hold any debate on a subject that was so central to the security of Bangladesh.

Based on the negotiations completed by the Parliamentary Committee, represented solely by the members of the Awami League, an agreement was signed between the Convener of the Committee and the President of the Jana Sanghati on 2 December 1997.[75] Once it was signed, the terms of the agreement came to the knowledge of public. The agreement already having been concluded, ministers were then taken into confidence and the Cabinet endorsed the instrument on 22 December, twenty days after it had been formally signed.

The agreement provoked sharp and critical reaction amongst the people. Not that it was unwelcome as a peace accord in the interest of the nation. There has always been a national consensus that there should be a political solution to the issue of CHT, an area of great strategic importance in terms of both the security and economy of the country. Restoration of a normal peaceful life in the area has always been the desire of the whole nation. There has always been unanimity amongst all political parties that the fourteen tribes must be given the right to live in their own way with their own culture, tradition and characteristics. Their right to land and the *jhoom* culture must be preserved. But the hostile reactions concerned on substantive points of sovereignty, which according to critics, violated the basic structure of the constitution.

The procedures followed in signing this agreement, which was of the highest national importance, were bitterly criticised on the ground that the government had not taken the nation into confidence. It was not a matter for the government alone to decide. It should have been a bipartisan national document arrived at through a consensus after a full debate at national forums and in the media. The reason why the agreement was signed even before the Cabinet had seen or approved it continues to be a mystery. This secret method followed by the government in a matter of high national priority only aroused suspicion in the minds of the people as to what had actually happened behind the scenes. This feeling led to numerous questions that remain unanswered.[76]

Subsequently, in order to implement the agreement, the government introduced four bills on 12 April 1998: three in the form of amendments to the Acts passed in 1989 and one new bill called

---

[75] The opposition members in the Committee abstained from taking part in the negotiations.

[76] See numerous press reports published where Shantu Larma complains that the agreement was yet to be implemented affirming opposing suspicion about acceptance of some possible secret understanding between the parties and the silence of the government over such allegation.

the CHT Regional Council Bill for the foundation of a separate Council for the whole of CHT, comprising all three districts. Despite their reservations, the BNP could not ignore the importance of the issues involved and demanded a general debate on the subject before the formal discussion of the bills began. This was agreed upon in a meeting of the Advisory Committee of Parliament presided over by the Speaker.[77] In the Parliamentary Special Committee meeting on 16 and 27 April 1998, BNP members actively participated and submitted their views on each section of the four bills, which were surprisingly found not to have been included in the proceedings of the meetings. So on the day the report of the Special Committee was submitted before the House, the BNP walked out of Parliament in protest.[78]

During this period, from 26 April, just prior to the debate on the bills, the live broadcast of parliamentary proceedings, which was a long-time practice, was suddenly stopped simply to ensure that the views of the opposition did not reach the public.

On the morning of 3 May, the legislative programme, which is normally distributed by the Parliament Secretariat to MPs the previous evening, did not include any other items, not even the question hour, other than these bills on the CHT districts. That day all the bills were placed before the House for consideration. The BNP Members of Parliament submitted 4,365 amendments to the three bills, and under the Rules of Procedure each member had a right to speak on his amendment. However, the Speaker gave the ruling, supported by the Leader of the House and the Prime Minister, that only eight BNP MPs would be allowed to speak, and all the bills being identical in nature, they would be taken up together for consideration.[79]

The BNP raised serious objections in Parliament, but the Speaker, unlike in other Parliament, took a partisan stand to every objection put forward by the opposition. He had earned a reputation for acting in this way from the very beginning. The ruling party or the Speaker would not have been disadvantaged if discussions had been allowed

---

[77] Statement by the Leader of the Opposition in Parliament on April 12, 1998.

[78] See the statement made by Begum Zia in the Press Conference held on May 5, 1998.

[79] Ibid.

to take place, since the scope of discussion on amendments is normally very limited under the Rules of Procedure. Generally a minute or so in given to each MP and then the Speaker can regulate repetition and allow one member to speak only once on all his amendments. It would have taken perhaps an additional two weeks or so to complete the passage of the bills. If they had done so, the ruling party could at least have claimed that the bills had been passed with the participation of the opposition. In protest at such an undemocratic and arbitrary action on the part of the Speaker and the Prime Minister, the BNP walked out of the House and the bills were passed on the same night without any opposition involvement.

This incident, when the bills were passed so hurriedly without allowing any deliberation by the opposition in Parliament, only reaffirmed the suspicion and apprehension in the minds of the people about the agreement itself. The BNP and many other parties and professional groups took the stand that neither the agreement signed earlier nor the laws relating to CHT were acceptable to the people on the principal ground that the implementation of such an agreement would be detrimental to the national sovereignty and territorial integrity of Bangladesh. They asserted that this agreement would not bring any peace to the area; rather it would endanger peace for the whole of Bangladesh.

It was argued by the opposition that these laws had changed the fundamental structure of the constitution and thereby the character and nature of the state. If implemented, they would encourage parochialism, divisiveness, provincialism and separatism amongst the people in CHT and elsewhere in the country. They would encourage the tribal extremists to struggle further to secede the region from the rest of the country, thus threatening the very integrity of the state. These laws would only serve to inspire those who are deeply committed to destabilising the state and prosperity of Bangladesh. The opposition alleged that such actions were only manifestations of a deep-rooted conspiracy against the national interest of the country, and that the laws in their present form, if implemented, would seriously threaten the country's sovereignty and territorial integrity.

The opposition further argued that the Awami League government had signed the agreement with the separatists to serve the geo-political interest of India connected with the insurgencies that was going on in its northeastern states. It would throw open a large territorial area of Bangladesh for the use of Indian forces and the citizens of the neighbouring states, turning the place into a hot-bed of civil war in the region. Instead of achieving peace, Bangladesh would be pushed into a situation similar to Lebanon, Sri Lanka and Bosnia, and caused it to divert its scarce resources into containing the situation in the CHT, thereby permanently disabling Bangladesh from making any economic headway. The entire thrust of economic priorities of Bangladesh would be totally frustrated. Moreover, signing an agreement with Shantu Larma, who had no representative status of any kind, could lead to the collapse of the agreement in future in the face of further insurgency in the area.

The claims, allegations and apprehensions of the opposition were based on the following:

- The creation of the Local Government Councils in each of the three districts came within the purview of Articles 59 and 60 of the constitution. This being one of the basic features of the Republic that all Local Government Councils must be elective and perform such functions as laid down in the constitution. But in the amendments, the words 'Local Government' were deleted, so the amendments not only changed the fundamental character of the original law and the structure of those Councils, but also excluded these Councils from the structure of the constitution itself. Being extra-constitutional, this amendment not only violated one of the basic features of the constitution but also would strengthen the demand for an independent state in course of time.

- In the amendments, two distinct classes of citizen were created, namely tribal and non-tribal, in each district. With rights, privileges and obligations different from each other. The laws therefore discriminate between citizens of the same country, violating the fundamental law of equality enshrined in the constitution (Articles 27 and 31).

- Section 6e(vi) and 11 of the amended laws imposed special conditions on non-tribal citizens for them to be eligible as voters and candidates in any election. The effect of the law was that for a non-tribal person to be a voter, he had to be a permanent resident of CHT. Permanent residents would only be those who owned a homestead and cultivable land, whereas in order to own or transfer any land, prior permission of the tribal authorities would be required. To be a candidate in an election, a non-tribal person, even if he is the owner of land and a homestead, will need a certificate from the tribal Circle Chief. The practical effect of such laws is that no non-tribal citizen can be a voter or contest any election in CHT whereas he has the right to do so anywhere in Bangladesh under the constitution. This removed the region from the rest of the country and created a distinct territorial identity for it in direct violation not only of the fundamental rights guaranteed in the constitution but also of the principles of sovereign structure of a constitutionally defined state.

- Under the amended Section 64(1)(a) no land belonging to the state can be awarded for lease, settlement, purchase, sale or transfer without the prior approval of the Council of the particular district, which violates Articles 36 and 42 of the constitution.

By restricting the state in dealing with land, the sovereign power of the state, protected by the constitution and exercised by the central government, has been seriously compromised, eroding its jurisdiction and authority over CHT as an integral part of the state. For example:

- Under Para 8, the authority of the government exercised through the office of the Commissioner has been withdrawn. The Councils, by way of framing rules, will now decide who that authority will be.
- Under paras 17 and 28, the authority of the government has been withdrawn.
- Under Para 26, the authority of the tribal minister has been placed above that of the government itself.
- Under the amended Section 64(1)(b), any land under the jurisdiction of the Councils in the district cannot be acquired

or transferred even by the government without consultation with or approval of the Council concerned. The restriction on the government is also a violation of Article 144 of the constitution.

- Under Para 29 of the amended law, the power of the government to realise the land development tax by Acts of Parliament has been transferred to the Councils in violation of the provisions of the constitution relating to taxation, which is an exclusive jurisdiction of Parliament.

- Under the amended Section 68(a)(i) the government will not frame any Rules without consulting the Council, but even then under Section 68(b)(ii) if any Rules framed by the government appear to be 'difficult or objectionable', the Council may apply for reconsideration, amendment, repeal or relaxation and the government would take the necessary decision in this regard.

- Under the amended Section 69(a)(i), the government's approval would not be necessary to frame the Regulations for the Councils.

- Under the First Schedule, as amended by Para 35, the power and authority to supervise and improve law and order, including control of the police is now vested with the Council instead of the Government.

- Under the Second Schedule, as amended by Para 36, the Councils would be entitled to a royalty and not the government, in the contracts for exploration and production of mineral resources.

The most significant development of all is the creation of a Regional Council under a new and independent law called the Chittagong Hill Tracts Regional Council Act. Although the purpose of the Council, as described in the preamble, is to co-ordinate the three districts of CHT and all their work, the law is a comprehensive one. The Regional Council will function as a higher executive authority over the entire CHT. acting as a single administrative and political unit. It will have its own offices in the districts. Such a concept directly violates Article 1 of the constitution. It is argued that once the provisions of this law relating to jurisdiction, powers and functions are analysed, it will be evident that the government has in effect created a state within a state, in violation of the basic structure of the constitution. Some of the main features of the Act are as follows:

- Parliament is elected by the people for the whole of Bangladesh and it is the supreme law-making body for the entire country, but its sovereign authority has been restricted to the extent that if the government takes any initiative to make a law relating to the Regional Council or the District Councils of CHT, it has to consult the Regional Council and the relevant District Council, and frame the law after considering the advice and suggestions of the Councils. In a situation of emergency or war, or in making laws relating to the security or economy of the state, if Parliament must wait for a District Council or the Regional Council to give its opinion and suggestions, only dangerous consequences will follow.

- Under Section 22(d), the regional Council will be responsible for supervision and co-ordination of the general administration, law and order, and the development of the entire region. Under Section 22(f), it will be the license-issuing authority for heavy industries in the region. It can be argued that an authority to issue or not to issue licenses for heavy industry in the region directly involves the question of the security of the state, which cannot be surrendered to the Regional Council.[80]

- Under Section 26, the Regional Council has been given an unjustified authority to sign any treaty or contract, and the Council under regulations framed by it will determine the method and procedure of signing such a treaty. This provision is considered to be a violation of Articles 144 and 145 of the constitution, which state that all contracts and documents will be drawn up and concluded by the authority of the Chief Executive of the State.

---

[80]The discussion on the laws on CHT is based on the statement made by Begum Zia at a Press Conference held on May 5, 1998 and the statement made by H.M. Ershad on behalf of Jatiya Party on 3rd May 1998 in the Parliament.

- The powers given to the Regional Council relating to land, property and employment, similar to those given to the District Councils, violate the constitutional right of equality.
- Besides all these laws, certain provisions of the agreement signed with the Jana Sanghati that involve the security of the state, but which for obvious reasons could not be incorporated into the law, have been undertaken by the government to be implemented by executive orders, posing a more dangerous threat to the sovereignty of the state. For example:
  - Even if a member of Jana Sanghati had killed or raped someone during the insurgency, he could not be punished or held for trial; nor could such a member be arrested, punished or prosecuted in future.
  - Within a specified time after the agreement was signed, all the camps of the Army, Ansar and Village Defence Party spread all over CHT had to be withdrawn and confined to their headquarters. This left the security and defence of the entire region without any safeguard or control by the state. As a result, according to newspaper reports, at least 200,000 foreign citizens from the neighbouring states of India have already entered Bangladesh to settle.[81]
  - Moreover, the deployment of army in any deteriorating law and order situation or at a time of natural calamity, or for any other work, can only be done to assist the civil administration of the Council, and the Council may refuse to request such assistance. It is argued that this restriction on the deployment of its own armed forces within its own territory limits the exercise of sovereign authority by the state, and removes CHT, which constitutes one-tenth of the total national territory, from the command and control of the central government.

In answer to the point raised that Article 28(4) of the constitution empowers the state to make special provisions for women or children,

---

[81] Based on the reports published in *The Daily Ittefaq* on March 26, 1998 and other newspapers during 1998-99.

or for the advancement of backward sections of the population, it can be argued that such provisions are desirable as well as acceptable, as long as they do not violate the basic structure of the constitution and threaten the sovereignty and territorial integrity of the state. Besides since 1975 successive governments have made special provisions for the improvement of CHT, introducing special development plan worth billions of Takas to open up opportunities for employment, business and education in the region.

In substance, the opposition argues that some of the provisions of the agreement signed between the Awami League government and the PCJSS, and the consequent changes in the three District Council Acts and the creation of the Regional Council: (1) are a threat to the sovereignty and territorial integrity of Bangladesh endangering the peace and prosperity of the entire country; (2) are a violation of the basic structure of the constitution (3) will encourage the insurgents in CHT to demand a separate state, foster parochialism and provincialism in other parts of the country and thereby advance the disintegration of the state; (4) will lead to a loss of command and control over one tenth of the country's territory, thus threatening the security of the state; and (5) are done more to secure the geo-political interest of India and to help India to contain its belligerent states in the north-east and ultimately the People's Republic of China, than in the interest of Bangladesh.

The opposition very much favours a peace agreement, but demands that the agreement signed should be revised to safeguard the constitution and territorial integrity of the state. An agreement of this nature must be backed by a national consensus so that the entire nation stands behind it.

On constitutional and legal issues, the opposition has relied on the judgement delivered by the Appellate Division of the Supreme Court on the Eighth Amendment of the constitution. This related to the bifurcation of the High Court Division introduced by Ershad for the decentralization of the administration of justice.[82] The issue involved in this case related to the creation of permanent Benches of the High Court Division at Rangpur, Jessore, Comilla, Chittagong, Sylhet and

---

[82]Reported in 1989 BLD (Special), p. 1.

Barisal. By amending Article 100 of the constitution on 9 June 1988 the President was authorised to fix the territorial jurisdiction of the permanent Benches by notification, and thereby curtail the exclusive territorial jurisdiction of the permanent seat of the High Court Division at Dhaka.

In their judgement, declared by a majority of three to one (Justice A.T.M. Afzal dissenting), the judges of the highest court in the country[83] touched upon many important constitutional issues.[84] Of these, three inter-connected points are very significant and highly relevant to the laws made for CHT: (1) the scope and extent of the amending power of Parliament; (2) whether any basic structure or essential feature of the constitution can be altered or changed by Parliament under any law or under the amending power given by Article 143; and (3) the concept of the unitary character of the state.

On the issue of the amending power of Parliament, Justice Badrul Haider Chowdhury in his judgement stated: "Necessarily, the amendment passed by Parliament is to be tested as against Article 7, because the amending power is but a power given by the constitution to Parliament, it is a higher power given than any other given by the constitution to parliament, but nevertheless it is a power within and not outside the constitution".

On the issue of the basic structure of the constitution, Justice Chowdhury said: 'Some of the features are basic features of the constitution and they are not amendable by the amending power of Parliament. In the scheme of Article 7 and therefore of the constitution the structural pillars of Parliament and judiciary are basic and fundamental ... the constitutional scheme if followed carefully reveals that these basic features are un-amendable and unalterable'.

On the issue of the unitary character of the state, Justice Chowdhury concluded: The amendment purports to create territorial units which eventually may claim the status of federating units, thereby destroying the very fabric of a unitary Republic. In other words, by sowing the seeds of regionalism, the next step can be dismantling the fabric of the Republic.

---

[83] The author does not agree with the majority views on restricting the amending power of the Parliament on an issue like this and agrees with the views taken by Justice A T M Afzal.

[84] 1989 BLD (Spl) 1.

On the issues of the amending power of Parliament and the basic structure of the constitution, Justice Shahabuddin, who later became the Chief Justice and at the time of writing is the President of the Republic, held in his judgement as follows:

> There is no dispute that the constitution stands on certain fundamental principles, which are its structural pillars and if those pillars are demolished or damaged the whole constitutional edifice will fall down. It is by construing the constitutional provisions that these pillars are to be identified. Implied limitations on the amending power are also to be gathered from the constitution itself including its preamble .... Amendment is subject to the retention of the basic structures. The court therefore has power to undo an amendment if it transgresses its limit and alters a basic structure of the constitution.

On the issue of the unitary character of the state, Justice Shahabuddin said:

> Nor is it permissible to create a separate High Court under the Supreme Court as it will run counter to the unitary character of the state, opening a door for the ultimate disintegration of the state .... As to the unitary character of the state, it is clear that in view of the homogeneity of her people, having the same language, culture, tradition and way of life, within a small territory the state has been so organized as a unitary state by its founding fathers leaving no scope for devolution of the executive, legislative and judicial powers in different regions to turn into provinces ultimately.

On the amending power of Parliament, Justice Mohammad Habibur Rahman in his judgement expressed similar views, saying: 'when Parliament cannot by itself amend the preamble, it cannot indirectly by amending a provision of the constitution impair or destroy the fundamental aim of our society.

On the issue of the unitary character of the state, Justice Rahman, in Para 484 of his judgement, said: 'It has been repeatedly pointed out before us that because of the unitary character of our Republic the constitution makers devised only one Court for the whole of Bangladesh in the Supreme Court of Bangladesh .... Our founding fathers devised a composite Supreme Court to emphasise the oneness of the country'.

Based on this judgement, which had struck down not an ordinary law passed by a majority but an amendment to the constitution passed by two-thirds of the Members of Parliament, the opposition argued that the amendments and the new law for creating a Regional Council were ultra vires. There is no scope for creating regionalism, provincialism or special areas in Bangladesh under Article 1 of its constitution, which reads as follows:

> Article 1: Bangladesh is a unitary independent sovereign Republic to be known as the People's Republic of Bangladesh.[85]

Besides the unitary character of the state, the other basic features of the constitution that have allegedly been impaired, damaged or destroyed by such laws are as follows:

1. The territorial integrity of the state. Article 2 of the constitution reads:

    a. The territories, which immediately before the proclamation of independence on the 26th day of March 1971 constituted East Pakistan [and the territories referred to as included territories in the Constitution (Third Amendment) Act, 1974, but excluding the territories referred to as excluded territories in that Act; and]

    b. Such other territories as may become included in Bangladesh.

2. Supremacy of the constitution and people as the only source of power. Article 7 reads as follows:

    (1) All powers in the Republic belong to the people, and their exercise on behalf of the people shall be effected only under, and by the authority of, this Constitution.

    (2) This Constitution is, as the solemn expression of the will of the people, the supreme law of the Republic, and if any other law is inconsistent with this Constitution that other law shall, to the extent of the inconsistency, be void.

3. Democracy of the Republic. Article 11 reads as follows:

    The Republic shall be a democracy in which fundamental human rights and freedoms and respect for the dignity and worth of

---

[85] 1989 DLR AD, p. 165.

the human person shall be guaranteed, and in which effective participation by the people through their elected representatives in administration at all levels shall be ensured.

4. Equal opportunities for all the citizens. Article 19 reads as follows:

   (1) The state shall endeavour to ensure equality of opportunity to all citizens.

   (2) The state shall adopt effective measures to remove social and economic inequality between man and man and to ensure the equitable distribution of wealth among citizens, and of opportunities in order to attain a uniform level of economic development throughout the Republic.

5. Equality before the law for all the citizens. Article 27 reads as follows:

   - All citizens are equal before the law and are entitled to equal protection of the law.

6. Equal protection of the law for all the citizens. Article 31 reads as follows:

   - To enjoy the protection of the law, and to be treated in accordance with law, and only in accordance with law, is the inalienable right of every citizen, wherever he may be, and of every other person for the time being within Bangladesh, and in particular no action detrimental to the life, liberty, body, reputation or property of any person shall be taken except in accordance with law.'

7. The right of citizens to move freely within Bangladesh and settle anywhere they wish. Article 36 reads as follows:

   - Subject to any reasonable restrictions imposed by law in the public interest, every citizen shall have the right to move freely throughout Bangladesh, to reside and settle in any place therein and to leave and re-enter Bangladesh.

8. The right to property. Article 42(1) of the constitution reads as follows:

   - Subject to any restrictions imposed by law, every citizen shall have the right to acquire, hold, transfer or otherwise dispose

of property, and no property shall be compulsorily acquired, nationalised or requisitioned save by authority of law.
9. The sovereignty of Parliament and its absolute power to make laws for the entire country.

The opposition took these matters as far as the President, expecting that when the bills were sent to him for his assent — one of the few powers the President still enjoys under the constitution — they would be examined based on the principles he himself had enunciated in his judgement on the Eighth Amendment.[86] Hundreds of telegrams reached his office from lawyers all over the country, urging him to defend the constitution, which he was obliged to do under the oath he had taken on assuming the office of President. But Justice Shahabuddin, who had so painstakingly discouraged any kind of provincialism or regionalism in his judgment, finally assented to the bills.

The Awami League considered the peace accord with the tribal insurgents a major political achievement for Bangladesh. The government took credit that, for the first time in the last 25 years, Bangladesh had been able to achieve a great diplomatic success in bringing the ethnic conflict in CHT to a close, which no government in the past could do. Within a very short period after its assumption of power, the Awami League government was able to convince India to stop giving training and sanctuary to the insurgents and persuade the insurgent leaders to enter into negotiations for a peaceful settlement. This had now ended a 25-year-old war that had cost thousands of human lives, both civil and military, and a colossal amount of national resources. Military spending in the region will now fall drastically and the resources thus saved can now be used for other priority sectors. The government maintained that none of the laws, the terms of the agreement with the PCJJS or the creation of the Regional Council, violated any provision of the constitution or any of its basic structures. With the peace agreement concluded, the surrender of arms by the insurgents took place on 10 February 1998. It was acclaimed all over the world and it was hoped that the nation

---

[86] 1989 DLR AD, p. 165.

would now be able to concentrate more on its economic development. A long-standing issue of conflict with India had been resolved to the mutual benefit of both the countries.

The agreement has not satisfied all the people in CHT. There is extreme unhappiness among the Bengali settlers; at the same time the tribal people also have their reservations. A section of the insurgents had already rejected the agreement, claiming that their leaders compromised their demands. The points they make are as follows:

1. Shantu Larma, a Chakma, has no elective representational position. He cannot therefore represent all the tribes.
2. The tribes, other than the Chakmas, who constitute more than half of the tribal population, have their own conflicting interests, which have not been resolved.
3. Within the Chakmas there are also groups, sub-groups and leadership rivalries.
4. They demand recognition for CHT as a distinct national entity in the constitution.

The Pahari Chatra Parishad (Hill Students Forum), the Hill Women's Federation and the Pahari Gono Parishad, who are known to be vocal opponents of the agreement, further argued that the agreement had been concluded hurriedly and represented a denial of the rights of the Hill people. In their view, full autonomy for the Hill people, their recognition as a distinct nationality, and ultimately their independence was the only answer, and this required the expulsion of all the Bengali settlers from CHT. They collectively term all the ethnic nationalists who want 'constitutional recognition of their national identity and right of self-determination' as 'Jumma'.[87] The dissenting forces further demand the total demilitarisation of CHT. All military cantonments should be withdrawn from CHT, and trials should be held of those who had committed atrocities against members of Jana Sanghati. According to them, 'without justice peace cannot reign in that area'.

The Chittagong Hill Tracts Commission, which has an international network, is also critical of the agreement. According to the Commission,

---

[87] *Ibid.*, Statement of Dipti Shunder Chakma, President of the Pahari Chatra Parishad.

he agreement has failed to resolve some of the basic issues needed to ensure peace in the region, such as: (1) resettlement of the Bengali settlers outside CHT, without which the agreement would be meaningless; (2) the crucial issue of land under jumma cultivation and the return of such land to the original owners on determination of such ownership within a specified time; (3) international monitoring and supervision of elections for the District Councils; and (4) past human rights violations, publication of the inquiry reports into the massacres in Logang in 1992 and Naniarchar in 1993 and the trial of those responsible for such atrocities.

The dissenting insurgents at the field level continue to strive for full independence of the region. More intriguing is the fact that neither Shantu Larma and his group nor the Awami League government and its agencies took any action against those who openly agitate for full independence of CHT; nor did they discourage them from so doing.

On the other hand, Shantu Larma and others who led the signing of the agreement are not happy either with its implementation. According to them, some of the vital terms of the agreement have not been reflected in the laws of the District Councils or the Regional Council. Shantu Larma's comrades have also disputed his appointment as the Chairman of the Regional Council. Due to all these contradictions and pressures from within,[88] the entire peace accord may fall through. Indeed, it is widely apprehended that Shantu Larma has signed the agreement as a stopgap arrangement in order to achieve the ultimate goal of independence, and that he could change his stand at any stage in the future.

It can be argued that an agreement to resolve an armed conflict of this nature is better than not having any agreement at all. There has

---

[88] For several months after his appointment, Shantu Larma did not take the oath of his office. He still maintains that the government has not implemented all the terms of the agreement and threatened in a speech made at Bandarban on 30 October 2000 that he will call upon his people to take up arms once again for the realisation of their demands. Although the Prime Minister has refuted his allegation, Shantu Larma continues to keep his options open. He has also admitted that, since the signing of the peace agreement, 23 members of Jana Sanghati Samity have been killed, armed terrorists opposed to the agreement have abducted 55 and the situation in CHT is getting worse everyday. It is true that hostility between the extremist groups and between tribesmen and non-tribesmen continues in CHT. See *The Independent*, 3 and 4 November 2000, and the *Daily Ittefaq*, 6 November 2000. See also the *Daily Dinkal*, 6 November 2000.

been a ceasefire and surrender of arms, however unsatisfactory the quantum might have been, and at least a temporary peace has been achieved. Full implementation of the agreement and achieving complete peace may take time, but at least a positive peace process has begun. This much credit the Awami League government would certainly deserve.

The question is: what has been the cost? Its significance, implications, fallout and consequences cannot be assessed at this stage. This agreement will keep the mind of the nation agitated for many future governments. If the matter had been resolved in a bipartisan manner, taking the entire nation into confidence and by trying to achieve a national consensus, the risk of such an agreement could have been consciously shared by everyone. Its success would have belonged to the people and its failure would have belonged to the political leadership collectively.

Awami League government's unilateral approach both in concluding the agreement and in passing the laws for its implementation has divided the nation on this critical issue. To many, a solution will not be found unless a national consensus is achieved. The ultimate resolution of the conflict, or the success of the present agreement, would depend on the following issues:

1. How will the rights, obligations and future status of Bengali settlers in CHT be determined?
2. With the change of government in Bangladesh, will the other parties uphold the agreement?
3. With the change of government in Bangladesh, will India still have the same policy as it had towards Bangladesh?
4. Since this kind of agreement is not legally enforceable, will it fall apart on any excuse and will Shantu Larma then return to insurgency once again?
5. As long as the agreement exists, how will the government exercise control over the vast territory and prevent foreign infiltration from endangering the sovereignty and security of the state?
6. How should the government deal with the insurgents who still continue with their operations?

7. Will the future of CHT depend on the relationship between India and Bangladesh or India's policy towards Bangladesh?
8. Even if the agreement is fully implemented, will the insurgency stop, will the demand for independence be given up and will peace prevail, no matter what kind of government there is in Bangladesh?

Nothing can be predicted in the implementation of such an agreement, which is directly linked to the relationship between Bangladesh and India. However the issues raised need thorough brainstorming and a collective bipartisan consensus involving the entire nation. No single political party can take this responsibility. Ethnic and religious conflicts have raged in Northern Ireland for 30 years; many minority issues concerning Indians and Hispanics still remain unresolved in the USA; ethnic conflicts with the Tamil Tigers in Sri Lanka have continued for more than two decades. So it is in Bosnia, Chechnya and Turkey, Pakistan and Afghanistan and even more so in India, where, besides the conflicts in the Punjab and Kashmir, the ethnic insurgencies and conflicts in the seven northeastern states have occupied the central authorities attention for decades, with separatists demanding independence and a separate homeland. The central governments in all of these countries are keen to resolve their crises, but in each case the fundamental issue of sovereignty and territorial integrity overrides all other considerations in the negotiations for a settlement. It is not known what motivated the Awami League government to rush to conclude such an agreement.

Chapter 3

Inter-state Conflicts

In South Asia, India is so overwhelming in size and population that it can almost claim to be the region by itself. But there are at least six neighbouring countries, which, together with India, constitute today's South Asia. As India is large and strong, one might have expected it to develop a broad vision of the entire region, acting as a model state for peace, development and prosperity. But it could not do so. It could set itself up neither as a model for economic development or as a nation that was friendly, cordial and generous towards its neighbours.

From its independence in 1947, India's policy towards its neighbours was guided mostly by negative considerations. It was reluctant to accept the principle of sovereign equality in its dealings with her neighbours. One of the major psychological factors that motivated its leaders to adopt such an attitude was the partition of the subcontinent and the creation of Pakistan. They were never willing to accept Pakistan as a sovereign state, as they thought that neither the creation nor the existence of Pakistan had any rational basis. Thus instead of accepting the reality of the situation, domination, hegemony and hostility became the predominant psychosis of Indian policy-makers towards their neighbours. A sense of territorial aggrandisement, if not arrogance, dominated the minds of the Indian ruling elite, which had far-reaching consequences for India's relations with its neighbours, and ultimately for its own future as a formidable regional power.

Immediately after independence, India first consolidated its territorial position. It militarily took over the princely states of Junagarh and Hyderabad, conquered the Portuguese enclave of Goa and turned Sikkim into a protectorate. By signing a treaty with Bhutan in 1949, it removed the latter's foreign policy options, trade and business freedom; and a similar treaty with Nepal removed Nepal's entire economic leverage. After occupying the Muslim majority state of Kashmir, India had to fight a war with Pakistan as early as in 1948. So the wound of partition was by no means healed in 1947.

Secondly, India followed a principle of bilateralism in its policy towards its neighbours, which in effect discouraged any initiative to resolve regional issues collectively by soliciting the co-operation of any third country. India's persistent refusal to involve Nepal, not to mention China, in the augmentation and sharing of the Ganges water is a clear example. India has followed the same principle even within the framework of SAARC.

Thirdly, India pursued the ambition of playing a global role beyond the region of South Asia. This aspiration was driven by India's possession of a vast land and population, huge potential wealth, rich ancient history and status as the largest democracy in the world.

India and Pakistan

India's psychosis vis-à-vis Pakistan and vice versa is widely known. We have already discussed the background to the relationship between the two countries. The core issue that guides and motivates both the countries in their relationship with each other today is the status of Kashmir, a territory overwhelmingly inhabited by Muslims who are now engaged in an armed struggle to establish their right of self-determination. While Pakistan insists that, pursuant to the UN resolution of April 1948, a plebiscite is to be held to determine the future of Kashmir according to the wishes of its people, India asserts that Kashmir is now an integral part of India and it will not allow any third party to interfere in the matter. It is, however, willing to discuss the issue with Pakistan on a bilateral basis. A series of discussions have taken place at various levels, both nationally and internationally, but without any result.

A new situation has now emerged because of the nuclear tests conducted by India on 12 and 13 May and by Pakistan on 28 and 29 May 1998. These tests have changed the entire geopolitical perspective, not only concerning the relations between the two countries, but also involving the whole of South Asia and beyond. We will discuss both these issues but it is sufficient to say at this stage that the conflict between India and Pakistan emanates from roots much deeper than the issue of Kashmir alone. It originates from the birth of Pakistan as a Muslim state; a state that India has refused to accept. When we discuss the future of South Asia, we will find that this issue between the two dominant states stands as an impediment to any collective effort to develop the region. The security threats now arising from the possession of nuclear bombs by the two neighbours are more real than ever before, and concern not only the states of South Asia but also the world as a whole.

Kashmir

In ancient times before it emerged as a single political unit, Kashmir comprised a number of small states and provinces ruled by different kings. It had been conquered and ruled by different races over the millennium. From the eleventh century, with the invasion of Mahmud of Ghazni, for nearly 800 years Kashmir remained under the influence of the Muslims. Kashmir was ruled by Muslim dynasties beginning in the fourteenth century, with Sultan Shamsuddin as the monarch and ending with the Mughals. In 1819 Kashmir came under the rule of the Sikhs and about 30 years later it was ceded to the British. But after the British signed the Treaty of Amritsar in March 1846 the valley was transferred back to the Sikhs for a sum of Rs.75,00,000 (75 lacs). The Muslim Governor, Sheikh Imamuddin, who mobilised forces to oppose the Dogras led by Gulab Singh, did not accept this treaty. British forces suppressed his rebellion. At the time of the independence of India, Hari Singh of the Dogra dynasty was the ruler of Kashmir, a state where 80 per cent of inhabitants were Muslims.[1]

For centuries, Kashmir, now known as Jammu and Kashmir, has been close to the territories now known as Pakistan. Its economy was closely linked with Pakistan. The countries are contiguous by land and because of Kashmir's terrain, the entire trade and commerce of Kashmir was transacted through Pakistan. Pakistan is the principal

---

[1] Masood Hasan, 'Incomplete Partition Process: Kashmir and Self-Determination', *South Asian Studies*, Vol. 12, No. 2, 1995, p. 65, Table 2. This demography has, however, changed since the annexation of the state by India. Out of 45 Tahsils Muslims were the majority in 35, Hindus in 9 and Buddhists in 1.

market for Kashmiri timber and all its major imports come through Pakistan using its network of roads, rail and waterways.[2] Politically the long-cherished dream of the Kashmiris was to have a state of their own. But because of its weak political leadership, the outsiders have always ruled the territory. From ancient times Kashmir has attracted foreign invaders, travellers and exploiters. Although some great leaders of the subcontinent descended from the valley of Kashmir, they were few in number and were not interested in becoming leaders of a small state. Both Nehru and Allama Iqbal came originally from Kashmir. While Pandit Nehru in 1929 called for complete independence of India from Britain, at the Lahore session of the Indian National Congress, Allama Iqbal declared at the session of the All India Muslim League that the Muslims constituted a distinct nation in the subcontinent. So it fell to Sheikh Mohammad Abdullah, another illustrious son of the valley, to follow the cause of the Kashmiris. But as ruler of Kashmir, Abdullah despite all his efforts always faced difficulties and in the end he was unable to fulfil the people's aspiration for independence and existence as a separate state.

Abdullah was a schoolteacher who came to prominence in 1931 after his arrest for mobilising the Kashmiris for a mass revolt against the ruler of Kashmir. Martial law was declared and British troops were called in to bring the situation under control. This adventure earned him the title 'Tiger of Kashmir'. Soon after his release, Abdullah called a convention and formed the All Jammu and Kashmir Muslim Conference in Srinagar, the first political platform of its kind for the self-rule of Kashmir. The Kashmir movement was then given a formal shape.

Abdullah, although a devout Muslim, was a liberal politician. In the wake of the national movement led by the Congress, he came close to Nehru and took a more secular stand. In 1938 he dropped the word 'Muslim' from the name of the movement and renamed it as the Jammu and Kashmir National Conference, which enabled Hindus to join. When Abdullah sought the admission of the National Conference to the All India State's People's Conference, which was an affiliate of the Indian National Congress, he was immediately

---

[2] Salman Khurshid, *Beyond Terrorism: New Hope for Kashmir* (New Delhi: UBSPD, 1994), p. 44.

considered by the Muslim leaders to be an ally of the Congress. This resulted in the break-up of the National Conference and the revival of the Jammu and Kashmir Muslim Conference, which then started working in close liaison with the Muslim League. The political position taken by Abdullah had considerably weakened his standing among the Kashmiris, although it made him acceptable to the Congress as a national leader.

In the meantime, when the All India Muslim League passed the Lahore Resolution in 1940, with an unequivocal declaration in favour of establishing independent states for the Muslims, Abdullah's position became more tenuous. Having found that he was losing support within his own state, he was desperate to return to mainstream politics. On the hundredth anniversary of the Treaty of Amritsar in 1946, Abdullah launched a 'Quit Kashmir' movement against the Maharaja Dogra's rule. This was seen by Mohammad Ali Jinnah, who was then the undisputed leader of the Muslims of India, as a divisive course. It was a move neither directly against the British nor in favour of the Muslims of India or even Kashmir. Consequently, neither the Muslim League nor the Muslim Conference lent support to this programme. However, this movement led to the arrest of Abdullah and restored his popularity in the valley quite considerably. While Abdullah was in prison, the National Conference boycotted the elections held in January 1947 and the Muslim Conference, having won 16 out of 21 seats reserved for Muslims, claimed the leadership of the Kashmiris in the valley.

In political terms, Kashmir was now divided into two camps, one led by Abdullah and the other by the Muslim Conference. The aims of both remained the same — a free and independent Kashmir. Because of Abdullah's close link with the Congress and the Indian leaders, he suffered setbacks in his struggle for an independent Kashmir. His political manoeuvring led to his spending some time in jail and some time in power, as will be evident from his role once India was partitioned in 1947.

In the case of Kashmir, an area with a large Muslim majority, India denied them same principle, which led them to independence from British rule to work for the Kashmiri people. It was expected that, if it were not totally independent, Kashmir would be part of

Pakistan or aligned to Pakistan. As soon as the people of Kashmir were found to be overwhelmingly in favour of being part of Pakistan or being aligned with it, the Indian leaders moved in a calculated manner to annex Kashmir. With a Hindu ruler of Kashmir at hand Lord Mountbatten as the Governor-General was ready to honour Nehru's sentimental attachment to Kashmir. It was now a question of showing some support from the masses to their idea of annexation. In a political manoeuvre before moving Indian troops to Kashmir Nehru sent Sarder Patel to Maharaja Hari Singh to release Abdullah from prison. On his release, Abdullah went to New Delhi in October 1947 to negotiate extended autonomy for Kashmir. Meanwhile, India sent its troops to invade the valley in violation of the principles laid down in the Partition Plan of 3 June 1947. Although Pakistan attempted to resist the Indian aggression, the British military commander of its troops who continued to receive instructions from New Delhi and Mountbatten hamstrung it.

Besides the Pakistani forces that had already entered Kashmir, the Indian troops landed at Bargam Airport in Srinagar on the morning of 27 October 1947. Hari Singh, the Hindu ruler, was forced to sign the Instrument of Accession in the same afternoon and wrote a letter to Mountbatten as the Governor-General of India seeking military assistance.[3] With the Instrument of Accession in its hand, India continued its invasion, and the war also continued to take its sad toll. Indian troops occupied the main valley of Jammu and Kashmir and have continued to do so to this day.

In a clever diplomatic manoeuvre, having already committed aggression against Kashmir and occupied the main valley, India rushed at the same time to the United Nations Security Council to resolve the dispute. After a long deliberation, the Security Council passed a basic resolution on 21 April 1948 calling for a plebiscite under the supervision of the United Nations to decide the future status of Jammu and Kashmir according to the wishes of its people. In order to implement this resolution, the most important step taken was the formation of the United Nations Commission for India and Pakistan (UNCIP), consisting of five members: the USA, Argentina,

---

[3] Masood Hasan, 'Incomplete Partition Process: Kashmir and Self-Determination', p. 65. *South Asian Studies*, Vol. 12, No. 2, 1995.

Belgium, Columbia and Czechoslovakia. After the UNCIP team visited Kashmir in July 1948, the official cease-fire in Kashmir became effective from 1 January 1949.[4] Although open hostilities came to an end, skirmishes continued between Indian and Pakistani forces. Since then the Commission and the Security Council have passed many resolutions at different stages calling for the determination of the status of Kashmir 'in accordance with the will of the people'.

While the resolutions of the United Nations were yet to be enforced and the dispute remained unresolved, India proceeded to implement its own plan. It took three different approaches from the day the Instrument of Accession was signed by Hari Singh against the wishes of the people of Kashmir. India claimed that, the accession being legally and constitutionally valid.[5] It had the right (1) to exercise all the powers given under the Instrument of Accession; (2) to adopt all legal and constitutional measures necessary to make Kashmir an integral part of India; and (3) to maintain the necessary diplomatic postures at the United Nations to safeguard its international image.

In the constitution completed in 1949 and made effective from 26 January 1950, India took its first formal step in deciding the future of Kashmir. Under Article 370 of the constitution, transitional provisions were made relating to Kashmir. Although this article imposed limitations on the power of the Indian Parliament to make laws for Kashmir, in order to keep in line with the Instrument of Accession, the central government of India retained the control of the three vital functions of the state: namely, defence, foreign affairs and communications. In 1951 elections were held in the Indian occupied Kashmir for a Constituent Assembly, and under the Delhi Agreement of 1952, fundamental rights guaranteed by the Indian constitution and the jurisdiction of the Indian Supreme Court were extended to Kashmir notwithstanding Article 370 of the Indian constitution.

In order to secure public support prior to the accession of the state by India, Hari Singh appointed Abdullah as Prime Minister. Although Abdullah still allegedly desired an independent Kashmir, he was reappointed after the farcical election in 1951. When Abdullah moved

---

[4] Ahmad Ejaz, 'Kashmir Dispute and US Security Concerns in South Asia', *South Asian Affairs*, Vol. 1, No. 1, September 1996, Lahore.

[5] Salman Khurshid, *Beyond Terrorism: New Hope for Kashmir* (New Delhi: UBSAD, 1994), p. 51

for greater autonomy and self-determination of the Kashmiris, his government was dismissed at the instance of the Indian central government. In August 1955 Abdullah was jailed where he was kept of and on for eleven years, by which time Kashmir had been totally integrated into India.

To facilitate the integration process further, Bakshi Ghulam Mohammad, a henchman of the Indian Congress, replaced Sheikh Abdullah as Prime Minister. In 1954 the custom barriers between India and Kashmir were removed and in the same year the jurisdiction of the Indian government was extended further to include all the subjects under the "Union list" of the Indian constitution. In 1956 the Indian constitution was amended to absorb Kashmir into India. In 1957 Kashmir was put in the same category as any other state or province of India in all financial matters, and in the following year the Central Service of India (AIS) and the Indian Election Commission were extended to Kashmir.

After the conflict with China in 1962, India took further steps to consolidate its position in Kashmir. In the face of growing discontent amongst the Kashmiris, Khawja Shamsuddin replaced Bakshi Ghulam Mohammad as Prime Minister, but he did not last long either. The public mood had turned violent by the end of 1963 and the demand for the release of Abdullah took the movement to the streets of Srinagar, leading to the burning of public buildings. In order to bring the situation under control, Abdullah was released from prison in April 1964 and Ghulam Mohammad Sadiq, a supporter of Abdullah, replaced the incumbent Prime Minister. Both the Indian Prime Minister, Pandit Nehru, and the Pakistan President, Ayub Khan, invited Abdullah to discuss the future of Kashmir, but the proposed talks never took place as in May 1964 Nehru died.

Lal Bahadur Shastri, the next Prime Minister of India, took the final steps to integrate Kashmir into India. He reinstated Bakshi, who had earlier helped to bring Kashmir close to India and who was likely to readily comply with the measures taken by the Indian central government. The titles of President and Prime Minister of Kashmir were downgraded to Governor and Chief Minister respectively. In line with other provinces, Members of Parliament from Kashmir were now to be directly elected by the people instead of by the Legislative Assembly. Articles 356 and 357 of the Indian constitution were also extended to Kashmir to enable the central government to take direct control of the government of Kashmir by imposing the President's rule.[6]

By all these actions India sought to reaffirm its position that Kashmir had become 'an integral part of India'. The cease-fire line determined after the war in 1948 and confirmed by a UN Security Council resolution in that year was to continue as the de facto international border or 'line of control' between India and Pakistan. On the other hand, Pakistan continued to rely on the resolution of the United Nations and the international commitment for a plebiscite to decide the future of Kashmir according to the wishes of its people.

When in December 1964 India abolished the special status of Kashmir, without any plebiscite and in violation of United Nations resolutions, turning it into a province of India, the Kashmiris reacted violently. Pakistan also took it as a serious threat to its security. Sheikh Abdullah was again taken to jail. Pakistan intensified its support for the Kashmiris and the tension between the two countries led to another fierce war in September 1965. This conflict, known as the Kashmir War, lasted about three weeks. As expected, it was a war without a victor, but caused colossal damage to both the countries. A cease-fire was agreed by the intervention of a United Nations Security Council resolution passed on 20 September 1965.[7]

In order to restore a harmonious relationship between India and Pakistan and create a congenial atmosphere for resolving their disputes by peaceful means, the Soviet Union took the initiative and brought together Ayub Khan and Lal Bahadur Shastri in Tashkent in January 1966. The Tashkent Declaration appeared to pave the way for a better relationship, raising the hope that the two neighbours in South Asia would move closer to each other and solve their outstanding problems peacefully. But although the agreement was a diplomatic success internationally and satisfied the domestic politics of both countries for the time being by saving the face of both countries'

---

[6] *Ibid.*, p. 54.

[7] Ahmad Ejaz, 'Kashmir Dispute and US Security Concerns in South Asia'. *South Asian Affairs*, Vol. 1, No. 1, September 1996, Lahore.

leaders, the core issue of Kashmir remained unresolved. Pakistan's assertion that the Kashmir issue should be resolved by a plebiscite pursuant to the UN resolution was counter-acted by India on the ground that Kashmir had since then become an integral part of India and no international or third party intervention was necessary.

Because of its strategic importance, Kashmir became a great national security concern for both India and Pakistan. In the regional context of Asia, the conflict between Pakistan and India over the issue could not be ignored by their powerful neighbour, China, or by the Soviet Union as an interested superpower. After the end of the Second World War and the partition of the subcontinent, India had taken an active role in the Non-aligned Movement, which was perceived as an international platform to vindicate the cause of the downtrodden Third World nations as opposed to the affluent societies of the West. During the 1950s and 1960s, however, the influence of Communism and the rising power of the Soviet Union over the emerging countries could not be underestimated.

In the global political context, the foreign policies of India and Pakistan took two different directions, influenced by their mutual mistrust and historical rivalry. Pakistan leaned more towards the West, whereas India, though it claimed to uphold the non-aligned philosophy, leaned towards the Soviet Union to maintain its superior influence in the subcontinent. In order to strengthen its own security position, Pakistan entered into two military pacts, the South-East Asia Treaty Organisation (SEATO) and the Central Treaty Organisation (CENTO), backed by the USA. India, as a result, continued to draw both military and diplomatic support from the Soviet Union in order to advance its plans to integrate Kashmir into India.

In the meantime when India and China entered into a war in 1962 over a piece of land on India's northern border, the geopolitical situation changed again. China was consequently brought to the forefront of the conflicts in South Asia, not only because of its own dispute with India, but also because of the dispute between India and Pakistan on the issue of Kashmir. The military aid given by the USA to India, in order to contain China during the Sino-Indian War, was seen by Pakistan as a betrayal of a long-standing friendship with the West, and led Pakistan to forge a new relationship with China.

With the war over, India much to the disappointment of the USA did not change its own foreign policy as far as the superpowers were concerned. In the process, China came closer to Pakistan and continued to be so, to contain Soviet as well as Indian influence in the region. Pakistan now found China a more dependable friend than the USA. Following the ideological rift between the Soviet Union and China and the war between China and India in 1962, the strategic importance of Kashmir increased further for all the three countries. As the Cold War and the politics of *détente* intensified in the region, the superpowers did not hesitate to take sides on the issue of Kashmir. At the same time, China, as a bordering state, could not ignore the issue either as it had a direct strategic interest in Kashmir's future.

The situation then changed again when Soviet troops invaded Afghanistan, raising a great security concern for the USA in South Asia and the Gulf region. Three million refugees crossed the border into Pakistan, which was considered a front-line state and under immediate threat. Consequently, it was felt necessary to strengthen Pakistan militarily to contain the Soviet Union.

A package of $3.2 billion economic and military aid, including modern weapons, was made by the USA to Pakistan, and this was seen by India as a threat to its own security. India's criticism of the UN resolution for the withdrawal of Soviet forces from Afghanistan, the return of Afghan refugees and the independence of Afghanistan, and the policy that India pursued throughout these years of condoning the Soviet invasion, brought China closer to both Pakistan and the USA on the issue In the third war between Pakistan and India in 1971, which divided Pakistan and created a new state of Bangladesh, Pakistan enjoyed the support of China and USA, while the Communist bloc under a Friendship and Co-operation Treaty signed with the Soviet Union directly supported India.[8].

Kashmir therefore turned out to be a point of contention not only for India and Pakistan, but also for the Cold War rivalry between the two superpowers, which took opposing sides[9] to retain their own sphere of influence in the region. As a result, because of the involvement of

---

[8] *Ibid.*

[9] The Soviet Union on at least two occasions exercised its right of veto in favour of India in the dispute between the two countries over Kashmir.

the Soviet Union and the USA and their divergent interests, the Kashmir issue could not be resolved on a permanent basis. In the process, however, India gained time to integrate Kashmir gradually as part of its dominion.

The Indian government for its own ends used Sheikh Abdullah, a patriot and a devout Kashmiri. Whenever there was a political uprising under his leadership, he was put to jail; whenever there was any crisis where his support was necessary, he was released from jail and given the lure of political office to overcome the situation. He was jailed and released, posted as the head of the government and overthrown again according to the strategy of the Indian government, the ultimate aim of which was to integrate Kashmir into India. Military force went unchallenged, reaffirming the old dictum of 'might is right' which was used to give India a spurious claim to legitimacy.

Kashmiris feared a similar fate to that which had befallen the inhabitants of Goa, a Portuguese colony overrun by Indian troops, and of Sikkim, a small kingdom to the north at the foothills of the Himalayas, which was turned into an Indian protectorate. All these actions on the part of India had sown deep roots of mistrust about its hegemonistic designs amongst all its neighbours. They were hindering the development of a healthy bilateral and regional relationship, which the growth and prosperity of all the peoples of the area required.

After the whole process of integration of Kashmir into India had been completed from the constitutional point of view, state elections were held alongside the general elections taking place all over India in February 1967. The election in Kashmir was held with Abdullah and all other leaders in jail and a Congress-backed government was formed. Once the government was established Abdullah was released, but his return gave the mass movement for self-rule in Kashmir a new momentum, so he was again put behind bars. Soon afterwards Abdullah was released again, but by that time he had lost the energy to fight for the independence of Kashmir. In 1975, now aged about 70 years of age and having suffered repeated imprisonment, Abdullah finally accepted the sovereignty of India over the valley of Kashmir by signing a six-point agreement, known as the Kashmir Accord, with Mrs Indira Gandhi. The dream for a free Kashmir nevertheless remained in the hearts of millions of Kashmiris.

As there was no other leader parallel to him in status, Abdullah enjoyed enormous respect and popularity in Kashmir. He became the Chief Minister again, receiving a popular mandate in the election held in 1977, and remained so until his death in 1982. His son, Dr Farooq Abdullah, succeeded him but soon fell from power due to his fight with the central leadership in New Delhi. Later on, he too compromised his position and, with the help of Rajiv Gandhi, the favourite son and heir apparent of Mrs Gandhi, he returned to the government following a thoroughly rigged election held in 1987, which was opposed and boycotted by the Muslim United Front.

All efforts to find a peaceful solution to the problem of Kashmir have so far failed. Every time Pakistan has taken the matter to the United Nations or to any world forum, India has raised constitutional and legal issues, asking everyone to look at the reality of the situation and claiming that Kashmir is a bilateral issue between India and Pakistan, in which the UN and other third parties have no role to play. When the governments of Pakistan and India meet on a bilateral basis, which they have done on numerous occasions at the levels of Secretaries, Ministers and Heads of Governments, India takes the resolute position that Kashmir is a part of India and a plebiscite is not on the agenda. It even argues that Pakistan is illegally occupying part of Kashmir, which it must surrender.[10] Pakistan, on the other hand, goes on lobbying the world community to prevail upon India to adhere to the resolutions of the United Nations. India may concede, as a final settlement, the existing cease-fire line as the permanent line of control and an international border between the two countries, but for Pakistan and the Kashmiris this solution remains impossible to accept.

Over the last 50 years at different levels and different stages, the issue has come up for discussion in international forum and resolutions have been passed. After the first war between India and Pakistan over Kashmir, the Security Council passed a resolution in April 1948 for an UN-supervised plebiscite to determine the wishes of the Kashmiri people, and the implementation of this resolution was pursued in various ways. The United Nations Commission for India and Pakistan (UNCIP), constituted for this purpose, conducted its

---

[10] Speech of the Indian Congress President N. S. Reddy published in the *Christian Science Monitor*, January 8, 1962.

affairs with sufficient interest, visited Kashmir and passed resolutions but it could not make much progress despite the direct and active support of the American administration. Similar UN Resolutions were passed in March 1951, January 1957 and December 1957.

At the bilateral level, numerous meetings were held between India and Pakistan on various issues, but no progress was made on the problem of Kashmir. In a meeting held in September 1959 between Ayub and Nehru, two agreements were signed to resolve the border disputes in the Eastern and Western Sectors. In September 1960, the two sides also resolved the Indus basin water dispute at the mediation of the World Bank. But when the Kashmir issue was raised nothing moved. When President Kennedy suggested that Ayub and Nehru come together to resolve the Kashmir issue, with the mediation of the World Bank President Eugene Black, Pakistan accepted the proposal but India rejected it.[11]

After the Kashmir War in September 1965, which led to the Tashkent Resolution sponsored by the Soviet Union, Ayub Khan and Lal Bahadur Shastri agreed to resolve all the outstanding disputes between the two countries by peaceful means. Within two months of the agreement, the two Foreign Ministers met in March 1966. But as India maintained its old position that Kashmir was an integral part of India, the talks collapsed without any result. At the end of the war in 1971, Mrs Indira Gandhi and Zulfiqar Ali Bhutto signed the Simla Agreement in 1972, again raising the hope of settling disputes, including that of Kashmir, by peaceful means. By the Simla Agreement both sides agreed to accept the cease-fire line as the line of control, 'without prejudice to the recognised position of either side'. They also agreed under Clause 6 of the agreement to discuss 'the modalities and arrangements for the establishment of durable peace and normalisation of relations, including the question of repatriation of prisoners of war and civilian internees, a final settlement of Jammu and Kashmir and the resumption of diplomatic relations'.[12]

However, the 'modalities' for the final settlement of the Kashmir issue could not be determined at any subsequent meeting, and so

---

[11] S.M. Burke, Pakistan Foreign Policy: A Historical Analysis 1973, Oxford, p. 237.
[12] See the Simla Agreement signed on July 2, 1972.

there was no progress on the core issue. On the contrary, by invoking and interpreting the provisions of Clause 1(11), wherein the two sides agreed to settle their differences by peaceful means through bilateral negotiations or by any other peaceful means mutually agreed upon between them, India demanded the withdrawal of the United Nations observers stationed in Kashmir since 1949.

With India bolstering its position in the region, following the break-up of Pakistan and its first nuclear test in 1974, no serious discussion has since taken place on Kashmir at either national or international level. As every year passed, India continued to integrate Kashmir into its own territory in a planned and calculated manner. India's position, that Kashmir is a part of India, is unshakeable and it was underscored again and again that India would not give away the sovereign authority that it claims over Kashmir. On the other hand, it is inconceivable that Pakistan can resolve the issue militarily in its favour, as Pakistan neither has the military power to subdue India nor is in a position to mobilise world opinion to launch a collective war on India through the UN over the issue of Kashmir.

But the burning desire of the Kashmiris to achieve their freedom could not be suppressed. The right of self-determination is an internationally recognised path to independence. Despite the failure of Pakistan to safeguard the Kashmiris' interests, India's diplomatic manoeuvres and coercive tactics, Sheikh Abdullah's failure and the subsequent surrender of Kashmir to India, the path towards freedom has now taken a different turn for the Kashmiris. In remote areas, at the foothills of the Himalayas, the otherwise simple people have in groups, without any known leaders of high stature, realised that their rights would not be established by peaceful means, and have thus taken up arms to achieve their own independence.

The movement for freedom and independence started intensifying in the late 1980s. The Muslim United Front was not allowed to take any effective role in the election held in 1987. The result was rigged on a massive scale and the Kashmiris were deprived of their right to vote. All the Kashmir activists were forced to go underground to escape the torture and repression of the Indian authorities. India started calling them separatists, miscreants and terrorists, claiming that Pakistan patronised them with the aim of destabilising India; the

Kashmiris called themselves *mujahidin*, the warriors of freedom. Although Pakistan denies having anything to do with the rise of the movement in Kashmir, it is a recognised fact that Pakistan supports the Kashmiris in their struggle for freedom for historical reasons and will perhaps continue to do so.

Since 1988 Kashmir has been under siege. There has hardly been any peaceful civil administration in Srinagar. This state of 12 million people is governed with the control and supervision of over 600,000 Indian troops. Indian as well as international news reports confirm that the armed struggle of the different liberation forces in Kashmir has led to serious clashes, causing colossal loss of life and property. In a popular armed uprising for independence, the struggle goes through different stages, and the conflicts take on different shapes and characters.[13] The repeated violations of human rights by Indian troops, behaving as an occupation army,[14] firing on civilians, burning indiscriminately, raping, torturing and killing, conducting extra-judicial executions and responsible for deaths in custody, have been widely reported.

The armed struggle of the Kashmiris and the Indian repression has brought the issue of Kashmir to the forefront of the world attention. After the collapse of the Soviet Union and emergence of the USA as the only superpower, the situation has changed again. Kashmir is now considered as an item for conflict resolution on the agenda of the USA. The initiatives and statements made by high officials of the USA, including the President, have brought Kashmir once again into prominence.[15] Moreover, the nuclear tests conducted by India and then by Pakistan have further highlighted the issue of Kashmir to the world community. Although India would like to call them terrorists, the organisations that continue to fight to establish the right of self-determination of Kashmir are reported to be well entrenched in the valley and commanding popular support. They are

---

[13] The detail of Bangladesh's struggle for independence and what the Pakistan army did to Bengalis in 1971 is contained in Moudud Ahmed, *Bangladesh: Constitutional Quest for Autonomy* and *Era of Sheikh Mujibur Rahman*.

[14] When the military are engaged in any operation, they move according to their own rules of game. They are not expected to care about the human sides.

[15] See Assistant Secretary of State Robin Ruphel's Statement in October 1991 and February 1994, and President Clinton's speech in the General Assembly in 1997.

the Jammu and Kashmir Liberation Front (JKLF), the Revolutionary Front of the Talu Party, the Kashmir Students League, the Muslim United Front and the Hizbul Mujahidin.

In early May 1999, an estimated 600 to 800 Kashmiri freedom fighters crossed over the line of control and entered Indian territory from Azad Kashmir, a part of Kashmir controlled by Pakistan. They took up a strategic position well into the territory of India in a remote mountainous region to the northeast of Srinagar, the capital of Kashmir, at various points from Kargil to Matayan, and from Drass to Kaksar.[16] The initial aim was to cut off Leh from Srinagar by taking over the vitally strategic highway. In the face of worldwide condemnation, particularly by the western countries and Japan, Pakistan was put into a defensive position and could not justify such an intrusion into Indian territory beyond the line of control dividing the state of Kashmir, as determined by the Simla Agreement of 1972. Although Pakistan initially denied having anything to do with the infiltrators, it soon became obvious that the Pakistan army was directly involved in the operation.

The objective of the Kargil operation was to focus world opinion on the high state of tension in Kashmir, to build a new international consensus and to put pressure on India to resolve the Kashmir issue. On 15 June 1999 the American President urged Nawaz Sharif to pull out from Kargil and in the last week of June he sent General Zinni to Islamabad to convey his message. The American President also sent an envoy to New Delhi, urging India to show restraint. On 28 June, Sharif visited China looking for support, but failed to gain any active endorsement. In the face of the world public opinion and strong

---

[16]Pakistan has a 3,000-kilometre border with India (*The Economist*, June 19, 1999). The War of Kargil broke out in the critical 510-kilometre Srinagar-Kargil-Leh highway. The 32-day war ended in the defeat of Pakistan, which ultimately led to the fall of the elected government of Nawaz Sharif. The main allegation of the Indian government was violation of the line of control by the infiltrators from the other side of the border (*India Today*, July 5, 1999).

Indian patrols first detected the infiltrators occupying 25 kilometres of Indian territory on the Indian side of the line of control between 8 and 15 May 1999. Indian air strikes started on May 26, 1999. Pakistan denied that it had any hand in the Kargil operation. Sharif went to China on June 28, and the USA on July 4, 1999, where he agreed to pull out the infiltrators. India recaptured the lost territory and on 11 July Pakistani infiltrators started returning. Nawaz Sharif addressed the nation on radio and television to explain the pullout. The Kargil War was fought at 4,150 m, climbing up to 5,490 m high in the mountains north of the Himalayas (*India Today*, July 26, 1999 and February 21, 2000).

retaliation from the Indian army, retreat was the only option for Pakistan. As a diplomatic device, Nawaz Sharif finally rushed to Washington on a self-sought invitation. In a joint statement issued after a meeting with the American President, Pakistan agreed to pull out and retreat from Kargil.

The conflict had in the meantime led to a full-fledged battle known as the Kargil War. It lasted for 74 days and covered an area of 150 square kilometres. India deployed 20,000 troops and used all the weapons at its disposal to fight 1,500 *mujahidin* at 5,000-5,500 m above sea level. India lost more than 400 soldiers with about 600 injured, and claimed to have killed 700 Pakistani 'infiltrators'.[17] By 14 July the Indian troops had taken control of their territory along the line of control and the Indian Prime Minister declared victory in the war.

This defeat in Kargil made the position of Nawaz Sharif more vulnerable. Although the army in Pakistan did not expressly disagree with Sharif's decision to pull back from Indian territory, the army in reality could not accept it so easily. The militant groups in Kashmir thought that the deal in Washington was a conspiracy against the freedom struggle of the people of Kashmir. The religious groups accused Sharif of having betrayed the nation. However, despite its retreat from the Kargil heights, Pakistan's purpose of bringing the issue of Kashmir into the limelight was well served. The American President gave an assurance that he would take personal interest in the matter and seek an early solution.[18]

The Military and the Effect of Nuclearization

What is ambition for India is a security threat for Pakistan. When India followed its victory over Pakistan in 1971 with its first nuclear test in 1974, once more demonstrating its supremacy in the region, Pakistan took it as a challenge for survival and pursued the development of its own 'Islamic bomb' more actively. Although both countries were eager to acquire the technology for such a weapon, the test in 1974 was a real turning point. Facilities for building nuclear capabilities were kept secret, but it was not unknown to the world community

---

[17] *India Today*, July 26, 1999.
[18] *Ibid.*

that India and Pakistan were striving in the same direction, although they did not admit it in public.

The devastating mass killing power of nuclear weapons is almost incomprehensible. The much smaller bomb that the USA dropped on Hiroshima and Nagasaki towards the end of the Second World War, which the world almost dreads to think of today, makes it clear that such warheads may wipe out the whole human race. Yet mankind who built them knowingly would now like to restrict their use and further production. Philosophically, it is a matter of destiny. You build a weapon knowing that it may destroy you and yet you feel compelled to make it. You achieve fast economic growth and at the same time create holes in the ozone layer to make your own existence on earth difficult, if not impossible. Again it is the genius of men to realise the destructive ills of such developments and strive for a cure. Bombs are not made not to be preserved in showcases but to be used, and most likely they will be used; how, when and where no one knows. This apprehension will always be there to haunt the human race until the weapons are totally destroyed by all those who have them — an unlikely event, at least in the near future.

So the consensus now is that, until nuclear weapons are or can be totally destroyed, their use should be restricted immediately. Inspired by this common aim of saving mankind from its own destruction, the focus is on stopping the proliferation of such weapons — their spread and further manufacture — and those who have the capability to make them must be required to stop any further nuclear tests. In order to contain the situation, two international treaties have been formulated: the Nuclear Non-Proliferation Treaty (NPT) and, more important and relevant now, the Comprehensive Test Ban Treaty (CTBT).

Nuclear weapons technology developed quickly during the Cold War era, leading to a ferocious arms race between the two superpowers. In pursuance of a self-articulated policy of deterrence, the two sides developed arsenals of nuclear weapons that, if used, could destroy the entire world. It was argued that in order to ensure peace, a balanced development of nuclear weapons was necessary, since a country's self-protection meant that its opponents would not use the weapons if by so doing it risked nuclear retaliation. The policy of deterrence, arising primarily out of mutual fear and apprehension, worked successfully for the last 50 years, but what would have happened if it had failed, say in the Cuban missile crisis? The unwritten rule of deterrence might have minimised the use of the weapons, but it could never abolish the possibility of their use completely. Instead it provided a rationale for building bombs without any restriction. Secondly, those who have the weapons may argue it that since the Soviet Union has collapsed and there is no Communist superpower to contain, the philosophy of deterrence has lost its force and the only logical course is to pursue total disarmament.

Why is it not done then? Will it ever be done? On the contrary, those countries that have the weapons are continuing with more tests. When Britain deployed nuclear submarines during the Falklands War in 1982, no protest was made. France resumed its nuclear tests at Mururoa Atoll in the South Pacific — a total of six tests in 1995 and 1996 — without much condemnation from other members of the world community, and when China conducted its last tests in 1996 on the ground that the tests made for improving the 'technology, reliability, safety and modernisation' of the existing stock, no one raised any question.[19] The USA has recently approved the building of a giant laser, the National Iquition Facility, to facilitate further nuclear explosions.[20]

All of these developments suggest that nuclear weapons are here to stay and that the advance of technology cannot be rolled back. If no effective steps can be taken towards the total destruction of the existing weapons, it is highly unlikely that a total ban on tests or non-proliferation of weapons can be achieved in the near future. So what we are actually talking about is weapon control and not a weapon-free regime. The world will have to live with the fear of the use of nuclear weapons and the hope that no country having these weapons will use them. This leaves the world with a highly uncertain future.

---

[19] It is argued that in the process China reduced its number of weapons, keeping its strength and capability the same. When the UK declared a 25 per cent reduction in its warheads, this did not mean that it was reducing its nuclear capacity. It was only replacing the Polaris missiles Trident-11 0-5 air and sea Cruise missiles, keeping the overall strength the same. See Masood Hasan, 'Incomplete Partition Process: Kashmir and Self-Determination', p. 56.

[20] *Ibid.*, p. 73, n. 89. In October 1999 the US Senate voted against ratification of the CTBT, causing a great setback for the US government, which puts pressure on other countries to sign the treaty.

However, it can be argued that the attempt to ban tests is better than nothing. It will at least ensure some discipline and control over any further proliferation.

The Nuclear Non-Proliferation Treaty[21] has been signed by most countries (140 by 1990), but these are mostly states that have neither the ambition nor the capacity to develop nuclear weapons. Elsewhere it has failed to achieve its goal, particularly due to the response of some very vital countries that are engaged in or have the capabilities of acquiring nuclear weapons. Among those prominent countries that did not sign the Treaty are India, Pakistan, North Korea and Israel. Although they have not signed the NPT, Brazil and Argentina have both signed a treaty for a nuclear weapons-free zone in Latin America. South Africa is the only country to develop nuclear weapons and then decided to dismantle them, which it did in 1991 mainly because the white minority rulers, before they surrendered to the majority, did not want the black rulers to have such weapons in their hands. Belarus, Kazakhstan and the Ukraine had huge arsenals of nuclear weapons at the time Soviet Union was collapsing in 1991. They have signed the NPT, but they are still in possession of these deadly weapons. Algeria, which has built a reactor capable of producing weapons-grade material, has signed the NPT.

Iran, Iraq and Libya although signatories to the NPT, are strongly believed not to have abandoned their projects and each is considered to be volatile in this respect. They are developing missiles with a range of between 150 and 500 kilometres. North Korea signed an agreement in 1994 with the USA to freeze its nuclear activity, in exchange for fuel, oil and two nuclear reactors. However, it is now threatening to go ahead with its programme[22] because the USA has defaulted on the delivery of its compensation payments, partly due to the reluctance of Congress to foot the cost. It is believed to have warhead missiles ranging up to 1,500 kilometres. Israel is known to have bombs and an arsenal of around 100 warheads with a missile range up to 1,500 kilometres. Arab–Israeli conflicts and the Middle East crisis will encourage Iraq, Iran and Libya to proceed with their

---

[21]NPT extended indefinitely in PAS.
[22]*Newsweek*, May 25, 1998.

nuclear programme as the West refuses to take any action against Israel, which has so far not signed the NPT.

Of the 44 countries that either have nuclear weapons or are capable of developing them, the states in Europe, Japan and Canada have signed the NPT because of the US nuclear umbrella they already enjoy and the US weapons stationed in their territories.[23] For the same reasons, Taiwan and South Korea signed the NPT in 1977 and 1975 respectively.

The best-known nuclear weapons states are the five members of the Security Council of the United Nations. The USA was the first country to have acquired the bomb, which it used in 1945, and it has so far conducted 1,030 tests, more than the rest of the world put together. It has 12,070 warheads and missiles with a range up to 13,000 kilometres, capable of reaching anywhere in the world. The Soviet Union (now Russia) was the next to develop a nuclear capability and has conducted 715 nuclear tests, the first in 1949. Although its arsenal is shrinking, it has 22,500 warheads with missiles ranging up to 11,000 kilometres. Britain conducted its first nuclear test in 1952 and has 380 warheads with missiles ranging up to 5,300 kilometres. France first tested in 1961 and has conducted 210 tests, including six as recently as 1995 and 1996. It has 500 warheads with missiles ranging up to 5,300 kilometres. China first tested nuclear weapons in 1964 and has 450 warheads with missiles ranging up to 11,000 kilometres. The last two countries, the first countries in the Third World to have tested bombs, in May 1998, are India and Pakistan, the two most powerful states in South Asia, which have fought three wars in last 50 years. Both countries have so far refused to sign the NPT, despite considerable pressure from the West.

India, the dominant state of South Asia and the largest democracy in the world, with a population of nearly 1 billion, has always cherished the ambition to reach the global stage, despite the acute poverty from which its people suffer. With Pakistan, an almost eternal enemy, as a neighbour; the fall of the Soviet Union, a trusted friend in the international power structure; the rise of China on the other side of the Himalayas as an economic and military giant in

---

[23]China signed the NPT in March 1992 and France did so in August 1992.

Asia; and a perception that the USA is giving more importance to China and Pakistan, India began to feel insecure and isolated. Internally it had a fragile coalition government of sixteen-odd parties[24] with divergent views and ideologies. The economic depression, the issue of the Punjab, the rising insurgencies in the seven northeastern states and the embattled valley of Kashmir have raised the question of India's security at a higher plane than ever before. India's security concerns and its feeling of being deprived of a global role, including a permanent seat in the Security Council, led them to believe that now was the time for it to prove that India must get the place in the international arena that it deserved. Both for domestic political reasons and for the purpose of international advancement, the Hindu nationalist government of India took the opportunity of staging the explosions to establish itself in the club of nuclear weapons states.[25]

Inspired by the ancient history of its Vedic culture, India's ambition to revive its glorious past was only natural. The partition of India was a wound that the country needed to heal by establishing its desired supremacy over South Asia, but also had to reach beyond in order to occupy a position in the centre-stage of world politics. To fulfil its own designs and to relieve its security concerns, largely from the regional point of view, India's first strategy was to create an industrial base, without which no military power could be achieved. It has a large amount of thorium, uranium and coal deposits, but not enough hydrocarbon deposits, whose availability is essential for industrial progress. So the use of nuclear energy to generate power for peaceful development purposes was a natural course for India to adopt. In the process, however, Indian strategists and scientists had access to technology to refine quality grade uranium and plutonium necessary to build nuclear bombs. India built Apsara, their first nuclear reactor, in 1956 and has continued to build many more reactors. It developed eight commercial power reactors in co-operation with others and another seven on its own. Its commercial nuclear power construction programme was known to be the largest in the

---

[24]The first coalition government of Atal Bihari Vajpayee formed after the election held in 1998.

[25]See the interview given by the Indian Prime Minister, *Newsweek*, May 25, 1998.

world after Japan.[26] India's quest for nuclear technology intensified further when China conducted its nuclear test in 1964.

In war, there is no morality. On the question of security, there is no scope for ethics. India, like other countries, used the civilian nuclear power and research programme as a cushion for generating nuclear weapons. It used the reactors and technology supplied for peaceful nuclear research to acquire plutonium for bombs. India received extensive outside assistance from a large number of countries. When India conducted its first test in 1974, termed as 'peaceful nuclear explosion' by Mrs Gandhi, it used plutonium produced in the Canadian-supplied Circus research reactor, which was made operable by heavy water supplied by the USA.[27] This plutonium was separated from Cirna spent fuel at a reprocessing plant constructed with the unannounced assistance of European companies and the US. India acquired the power reactors from the USA, Canada and Russia. Canada, China, Norway, Romania, the Soviet Union and West Germany supplied the heavy water needed to operate these plants. Canada, France, Switzerland and West Germany supplied heavy water plants that enabled India to produce its own heavy water for power and military production reactors.[28]

Although Zulfiqar Ali Bhutto pushed Pakistan into developing an 'Islamic bomb' in order to assume the role of nuclear leadership of the Muslim world, in essence it was a response to the security threats posed by a 'Hindu India'. The historical mistrust of Indian leaders generated during the entire period of British rule leading to the partition; the three wars that Pakistan had fought with India; the loss of Hyderabad and then Kashmir to the occupation of the Indian troops; the overrunning of Goa and Junagarh by India, and the turning of Sikkim into a protectorate; the integration of Kashmir into India in total disregard of the UN resolutions — all these events meant that Pakistan's scientists and military hawks could not sit idle.

---

[26] A. R. Siddiky, 'South Asian Security: The Nuclear Dimension', paper presented at the SAARC AAPSO conference, Colombo, November 26-29, 1993.

[27] Steven Dolley, Nuclear Control Institute, Washington, DC, June 9, 1998.

[28] The USA stopped the supply of enriched-uranium fuel for India's Tarapur Power Reactor in 1981 and so it continued to do even after the tests in 1974. See Masood Hasan, 'Incomplete Partition Process: Kashmir and Self-Determination', p. 60.

Pakistan felt insecure in the face of India's might and arrogance as a neighbour. It was seven times larger than Pakistan in population and size, and stronger both in economic terms and military power, with more than one million soldiers and the world's fourth largest conventional military establishment. The humiliating defeat of Pakistan's army in 1971, leading to the loss of East Pakistan, and the nuclear explosion in 1974 made Pakistan react to India's nuclear design.

In 1988 when India tested its *Prithvi* missile with a range up to 250 kilometres, Pakistan also started developing missiles of its own. India then developed the Agni missile with a range up to 2,500 kilometres, covering targets all over Pakistan. In response, Pakistan built the Ghauri missile with a range up to 1,500 kilometres. It was the fear that India, which had never accepted the creation of Pakistan, was determined to destroy it and turn the subcontinent into one united India that motivated Pakistan to develop its nuclear programme. It was more a question of security than pride or ambition that led Pakistan to react in the manner it did.

So Pakistan followed the same route as India, gradually building its own nuclear weapons programme. What India developed at Pokhran in Rajasthan, Pakistan did at Chagai Hills in Baluchistan. Because of its close ties with the West and particularly with the USA, Pakistan came under pressure not to pursue a nuclear policy and was subject to close scrutiny. At one stage the USA stalled all economic and military aid to Pakistan by invoking the Pressler Amendment in 1990. Although this was disastrous for Pakistan's overall development, it could not roll back its security programmes in the face of India's hegemonic design. So at the end of the Cold War, the discriminatory and contradictory policies of the USA towards Pakistan made its leaders more desperate. With the Afghan War over, the USA no longer needed it to contain the Soviet Union. Pakistan felt abandoned and isolated, and saw the US policy as a betrayal.[29] As a result it continued to pursue its nuclear programme. While the USA lost its influence over Pakistan, the latter saw nuclear capacity as the ultimate guarantor of its statehood.

---

[29] Senator Joseph R. Biden, 'A New Approach to South Asia', Carnegie Foundation for International Peace, July 9, 1998.

Pakistan, like India, used the civilian nuclear power and research programmes to develop its own nuclear devices. While India used reactors and technology to acquire plutonium for bombs, Pakistan developed a highly enriched uranium capability on the pretext that the uranium would be used to fuel its civilian reactors, which operate on natural enriched uranium.[30]

Pakistan relied almost entirely on China for its nuclear programme. It is believed that Pakistan developed its devices on a tested nuclear bomb design supplied by China in the early 1980s. The Khushab reactor, constructed with the assistance of China, was used to produce plutonium for weapons, which also used Chinese heavy water from the safeguarded Canadian-supplied Kanupp power reactor. Pakistan developed its ability to enrich uranium using a centrifugal design stolen from URENCO, a European consortium, in the 1970s.[31] France provided the components for reprocessing and Germany provided tritium, tritium-production technology and important machinery required to produce nuclear weapons.[32]

India persistently and quite justifiably refused to sign the NPT and also actively opposed it, both for psychological reasons and for more substantive, tactical ones. India considered the NPT a cover to allow the five members of the Security Council to enjoy the paramount privilege of having nuclear weapons and doing whatever they liked. These members wanted to restrict the nuclear club exclusively for themselves and to dictate to the rest of the world what to do and what not to do. The Indian government considered the treaty to be discriminatory, inequitable and one-sided.[33] It legitimised the weapons that the five countries already had and stipulated that no one else should have bombs. They would not make any public promise or agreement to destroy their own weapons, which would always give them an upper hand in deciding the destiny of the world. From India's point of view, therefore, the NPT is an instrument used by the West to maintain its own economic and military interests. They can go on

---

[30] Steven Dolly, Nuclear Control Institute, Washington, DC, June 9, 1998.

[31] *Ibid.*

[32] *Ibid.*

[33] K. Subrananium: Ways out of Race: edited by John Hassard, Tom Kible and Patricia Lews, World Scientific Preventing Proliferation of Nuclear Weapons: Forestalling 1995.

testing weapons, as France and China recently did, or if necessary use or threaten to use them, as Britain did in the Falklands War.

Pakistan supports the contention of India, although it would have signed the NPT if India had done so. But as long as India does not concede, Pakistan cannot do so, from the perception of its own security. So it takes the same stand as India in international forums and conferences. Both India and Pakistan have signed the Limited Test Ban Treaty (LTBT) of 1963 and both have been members of the International Atomic Energy Agency (IAEA) from its inception in 1959. At the UN and other international forums, both India and Pakistan continue to support resolutions calling for a comprehensive test ban, non-use of nuclear weapons and their total elimination.

The NPT is seen in the Third World as an unequal treaty. It discriminates between those who already have nuclear weapons and those who do not have them. It legalises the possession and proliferation of nuclear weapons by those five states and gives them a monopoly without requiring them to provide any undertaking that they will destroy such weapons. As a result, the nuclear weapons states have more advanced missiles and bombs today than they had in 1970 when the NPT was launched. There has been a great advance in nuclear submarines acquired by the nuclear weapons states in the last 28 years in spite of the NPT.

It is argued by the five original nuclear states that if all the countries capable of having nuclear weapons are allowed to have them, it may endanger security because such weapons may fall into the hands of irresponsible civil and military leaders. This argument is not taken seriously by the nuclear threshold countries, which maintain that Americans did not hesitate to use the bomb in Hiroshima, that Europeans used all the weapons they had in both world wars and that Hitler and Mussolini were not citizens of the Third World. The NPT curtails the sovereignty of the states that do not yet possess the weapons, in the absence of any guarantee from the five states that nuclear weapons will not be used against non-nuclear weapons states. Almost all the developed countries that have weapons or are members of the NPT have extensive nuclear power programmes to generate energy, but on the plea of dual-use technology a double standard is maintained by the London Suppliers Club between those who have signed the NPT and those who have not.

This double standard is also reflected in the behaviour pattern of the nuclear weapons states towards those who are capable of having such weapons. While Israel is known to have bombs and continues freely to export or buy nuclear-related technologies and maintain nuclear weapons facilities on its own soil, it still receives the largest amount of US economic and military aid even while the Pressler Amendment is in force. In Arab-Israeli conflicts, countries that have signed the NPT are penalised, while Israel, which is not a signatory, proceeds with impunity. According to India, Pakistan and many other countries — those that have and those that have not signed the NPT, and those that do not enjoy a nuclear umbrella — there is no guarantee that nuclear weapons will be 'safe' in the hands of the five.[34]

In refusing to join a restrictive treaty like NPT India, Pakistan and China have shown their respective perception of their security considerations and they have pursued their respective nuclear programmes in the face of the pressures by the Western powers. In the process, India, having a better economic margin, has suffered less. But Pakistan has suffered enormously in terms of economic and military aid. Pakistan is way behind in both technology and military strength and will perhaps remain so, but its determination to survive as a nation keeps her going in the programme.

India was the first to call the shots. After the test conducted in 1974, the world community knew that India had acquired the capability of producing nuclear weapons. With the *Prithvi* and Agni missiles tested successfully, it also acquired the technology to deliver the deadly weapon. Now the question was when India — the country of Mahatma Gandhi, liberated from the colonial rule of the British on an anchor sheet of non-violence — would openly declare that it possessed the most violent weapons ever invented for the destruction of mankind. With the end of the Cold War and the fall of the Soviet Union — a trusted friend who could otherwise have provided security cover — India could not ignore the fact that its long-standing enemy, Pakistan, had launched the Gouhri missile with the assistance of China. As a result of the emergence of Hindu fundamentalism in India, and the coming to power of a sixteen-party coalition government

---

[34] K. Subranamium, 'Regional Conflicts and Nuclear Powers', *Bulletin of the Atomic Scientist*, May 1984, p.16.

led by the Bharatiya Janata Party, advancing its own brand of nationalism, India wanted to be treated seriously by the world community. It was no longer willing to be left behind or ignored. It wanted to be a member of the exclusive club of rare privileges by becoming a nuclear weapons state.

In extreme secrecy, concealed from the powerful American satellite KH-011 and the CIA, which has the world's largest intelligence apparatus, India stunned the world by exploding three nuclear devices in five seconds at Pokhran, 100 kilometres from the Pakistan border at 3.45 p.m. on Monday, 11 May 1998. The explosions created a 100-metre-high dust cloud 'blossom like a lotus flower' in the sky.[35] When the rest of the world erupted in horror and condemnation, India blasted two more devices only two days later. It was the worst and most blatant act of proliferation in 24 years.

From President Clinton to Kofi Annan, from Britain to Japan, all in one voice condemned India. The USA was disappointed and President Clinton called India's move 'a fundamental mistake'; such 'action by India not only threatens the stability of the region, it directly challenges the firm international consensus to stop the proliferation of weapons of mass destruction'. Kofi Annan, the UN Secretary-General, described it as 'a step backward. The world needs fewer nuclear powers, not more of them.'[36] China also reacted strongly to the Indian explosion. It condemned the nuclear tests and called on the international community to pressure India to stop developing nuclear weapons. China feared that 'it will bring very serious results to peace and stability in the South Asian region, even in the world' and accused the Indian government of blatantly ignoring international opinion in choosing to push ahead with nuclear weapons development. While condemning India for conducting the tests, almost all the world leaders, knowing the relationship Pakistan had with India, urged Pakistan not to follow the suit. Pakistan hoped that if it refrained from reacting to the Indian explosions, the ban imposed earlier by the US government would be lifted and the F-16 fighters that Pakistan had purchased from the USA would finally be delivered.

---

[35] *Time*, May 25, 1998. The coded message used in the blast was 'White House has collapsed'. In 1974 it was 'Buddha has smiled'. *Newsweek*, May 25, 1998.

[36] *Ibid*.

Acting under its own laws, the USA immediately imposed sanctions on India, which meant the loss of $51.3 million in aid during 1998 and the blocking of $4 billion of projects pending at the US Export-Import Bank, $10.2 billion in financing from the Overseas Private Investment Corporation for US firms doing business in India, $20 million in farms and export credits, all military aid and the export of some defence items.[37] The USA suggested that it would force the International Monetary Fund to withhold loans to India worth $3 billion. Japan also reacted immediately, cancelling $30 million in aid and threatening to block another loan package of $1 billion. Germany put $168 million in development aid on hold and Denmark froze its $28 million.[38]

Inside India, the whole nation was euphoric. The streets were filled with people rejoicing and celebrating with glory and pride. The image of an otherwise weak government improved markedly, catching people's imagination. The political parties, politicians, business community, bureaucracy, military, farmers, industrial workers, media and professionals all over the country endorsed the tests. Atal Bihari Vajpayee, head of the six-week-old government, was greeted with jubilation and showered with millions of fresh petals everywhere he went, boastfully declaring that 'India is now a nuclear-weapons power'. India justified its tests purely from the security point of view, as Vajpayee explained in a letter to Clinton after the tests were conducted.

The immediate reaction of Pakistan was not difficult to understand. Obviously it was overwhelmed with both surprise and fear, particularly concerning the time selected for the detonations. According to Pakistan, with a Hindu chauvinist government in power in India, and fuelled by the historical distrust which is deeply rooted into the relationship between the two countries, India would immediately cast her attention on Kashmir, where armed Muslim militants had grown in strength to liberate Kashmir from the Indian occupation and rule. Secondly, Pakistan had always feared that India could launch a surprise attack on Pakistan, if not to conquer it, then to dismantle its nuclear facilities and other vital installations. 'The Indian leadership

---

[37] *Newsweek*, May 25, 1998.
[38] *Ibid.*

has gone berserk,' reacted the Pakistan Foreign Minister, but Balasaheb Thackaray, the right-wing leader of Shiv Sena, the power base of the Hindu majority government of India, said: 'It had to be done, we have to prove we are not eunuchs.'[39]

The USA took urgent initiatives to persuade Pakistan to gain the moral high ground by showing restraint. Nawaz Sharif, the popular Prime Minister of Pakistan, responded by saying, 'We don't want to madly do what the Indians have done. We want to show the world that we are a responsible nation.' However, Pakistan made it clear to the USA and others that it would wait to see how severe the sanctions were against India and how much the world community meant business. Pakistan wanted the Kashmir issue resolved under UN supervision and the repeal of the Pressler Amendment. But the sanctions imposed on India were not tough enough. Although US officials calculated it at $20 billion, Indian economists estimated it at only $2 billion, which India had the strength to bear.

In Pakistan, people of all shades of opinion across the country demanded retaliation and this sentiment could not be ignored. Pakistan had never hesitated to challenge Indian threats in the past. The scientists in Pakistan were eager to share their own success in the field. Abdul Quader Khan, the chief nuclear scientist in the country, said he was only waiting for the orders to come. Pakistan had to consider, amongst others, three vital factors based on some of their own presumptions:

1. *Internal condition:* The feeling was that restraint would win global goodwill, but that in reality would not mean anything. There was no positive indication that the Pressler Amendment would be repealed or the Kashmir issue placed on the world agenda. On the contrary, it was thought that the sanctions imposed on India were mild and that the West did not mean business. The condemnation of India was only in words. Russia, France and even Britain refused to impose any sanctions. Almost the whole of Europe remained aloof from the USA on this issue. On the other hand, public emotion at home was rising. Although any kind of sanction would hurt Pakistan in

---

[39] *Ibid.*

its present economic crisis, Pakistan had been under an economic and military embargo from the USA since 199... and had survived, so any new sanction would not make much difference. Pakistanis were ready to make sacrifices, but no... to accept the humiliation of India's monopolistic hegemony. So the public mood was that Pakistan should also go fo... nuclear explosions and prove that it also had the bombs.

2. *National security:* Pakistan also believed that restraint o... silence might be taken as a sign of weakness both at hom... and abroad. There might be a perception that Pakistan had n... bombs or was not in a position of devising or deploy one which would immediately encourage India to attack Pakista... and destroy its nuclear facilities thereby lead India to a... unquestionable position of superiority in the entire region... Kashmir would then be India's forever. If India attacke... Pakistan, it was believed that neither the USA nor Russi... would come to its aid, and in such a situation China woul... also hesitate to provide direct military support in order to avoid the prospect of a global war.

3. *International perspective:* Unless Pakistan proceeded with the tests, India's position would be further consolidated in the world arena. It would exercise a dominant influence in world politics. Despite the embargo, India could be inducted as nuclear weapons state, or at least gain the status[40] of one and may even acquire a permanent seat in the Security Council. On the other hand, if Pakistan proved its capability of exploding nuclear devices too, it would stand on the same footing as India and claim the same right and standing in the world community.

Pakistan finally opted to be at par with India. Pakistan's national security assumed more importance than any other consideration. For Pakistan, it became a question of its own existence and survival. India, having initiated the nuclear tests already, had taken the blame

---

[40] The status of nuclear-weapons state was made effective for those who had acquired nuclear weapons prior to 1968.

r it worldwide. Pakistan's explosion of nuclear devices would be en as only a reaction to that and earn lesser blame, given the ternationally recognised antagonism between the two countries.

Within fifteen days of the second Indian tests, on 28 May 1998 kistan exploded five nuclear devices underground in the Chagai ills of Baluchistan, close to the Afghanistan and Iranian border. In doing it claimed 'to have matched India'.[41] The test did not come a surprise to the world community. In his address to the nation, the akistan Prime Minister said that India's recent test of five nuclear vices 'vitally tilted the balance of power in the region. The testing mbined with the development of long-range missiles seriously reatened the security of Pakistan.' He alleged that Pakistan had ceived no offer of assistance or security guarantees from the rest of e world. On the contrary, the West's lacklustre attitude only emed 'to embolden India'.

The people of Pakistan immensely enjoyed the pride and thrill of ploding the nuclear devices. Their jubilation matched that of the dian people when India had exploded their nuclear device. The tire nation rallied behind the government on this issue. All Muslim untries were happy in Pakistan's achievements. Pakistan's neighbours ch as Bangladesh, Sri Lanka and Nepal, although refrained from elcoming the venture, at least breathed a sigh of relief for the time eing. For them it was better to have two countries rather than one ith nuclear weapons in the region — a peculiar psychological xpression in the circumstances. When Nawaz Sharif called for acrifice and support, the response from the Pakistani masses was verwhelming and spontaneous. People hugged each other, danced the streets and exchanged flowers and sweets with joy and a sense f pride.

As expected, the USA imposed similar sanctions on Pakistan as it ad on India. In order to withstand the impending economic hardship, akistan declared a state of emergency on 29 May, adopting all kinds f austerity and economic measures. These included the sale of the uxurious new mansion built for the offices of the Prime Minister. he next day, 30 May, Pakistan tested its sixth nuclear device,

---

[4] See Nawaz Sharif, address to the nation, May 28, 1998.

claiming it to have been 'a tit for tat' response to stay ahead of the India's five tests!

The nature of the tests: The Indian government claims to have tested three different designs on 11 May 1998: a fission bomb with yield of 12 kilotons (an explosive power equivalent to 12,000 tons of TNT); a thermonuclear device with a yield of 43 kilotons; and a low yield device. On 13 May, India tested two additional devices that produced a total yield of less than 1 kiloton.[42] All together the devices had three times more effect than the bomb that destroyed Hiroshima. As India insisted that it had not tested a boosted fission device, it is assumed that the thermonuclear device it tested was hydrogen bomb.[43]

Pakistan claimed to have detonated, on 28 May, five simultaneous nuclear explosions with boosted devices made with Highly Enriched Uranium (HEU), producing a total yield of about 40-45 kilotons. India, however, contended that they were in the range of only 10-1 kilotons. US intelligence, on the other hand, confirmed a recording of only two nuclear explosions on that day, with a yield of 6 kilotons. Pakistan claimed that the yield of the additional test conducted on 30 May was within a range of 15-20 kilotons, but US intelligence estimated it to be far less.[44] Although Pakistan has not built hydrogen bomb, it has the capability of doing so.

The nature of the bombs: India's nuclear bombs are fuelled by plutonium, a man-made by-product of fissioning uranium in nuclear reactors. At the end of 1995, India had 315-45 kilograms of weapons-grade plutonium, which would be enough to produce 63-6 bombs.[45]

Pakistan fuelled its bombs with Highly Enriched Uranium (HEU) and is in possession of 335-400 kilograms of weapon-grade uranium enough to have 16-20 bombs. If, however, as Pakistan claims, it is using boosted warhead designs, it could produce a larger number of bombs with the same amount of material. Pakistan's relatively new

---

[42]The bomb exploded in Hiroshima in 1945 had an estimated yield of 18 kilotons.

[43]Steven Dolley, Nuclear Control Institute, Washington, DC, June 9, 1998.

[44]*Ibid.*

[45]*Ibid.*

reactor at Khushab, built with Chinese assistance, can produce enough plutonium for at least three bombs a year.[46]

The delivery system: Both Pakistan and India are in possession of advanced aircrafts for delivering nuclear weapons. While India deploys Jaguar, Mirage 2000, MIGs 27 and 29, Pakistan has F-16 fighters among others.

Both countries have ballistic missiles. India's *Prithvi* has a range of 150-250 kilometres and the two-stage Agni missile, based on Soviet and German technology, has a range of 1,500-2,500 kilometres with an ability to hit targets anywhere in Pakistan. The Agni missile, if stationed in Assam, can hit many crucial targets in China as well. India has about 70 missiles.

On the other hand, Pakistan has about 30 nuclear-capable M-11 missiles supplied by China with a range of 280-300 kilometres. It recently developed the Ghauri missile, built with Chinese and North Korean assistance, which has a range of 1,500 kilometres.[47]

The same day that India exploded the nuclear devices, 11 May, the Indian army successfully test-fired a short-range Trishul (Trident) missile in the eastern state of Orissa, to test its surface-to-surface capabilities; the missile had a range of 50 kilometres. Pakistan had earlier developed two surface-to-surface Missiles, Haft-1 (80 km) and Haft-11 (300 km). These missiles reduce the warning time on both sides to nearly zero, making the prospect of a nuclear crisis extremely serious. India could hit targets in Pakistan in 4 minutes and Pakistan could hit India in less than 12 minutes.[48]

China Factor: China's engagement in the gigantic task of economic reform and its quest for economic growth have caused a great shift in its foreign policy both towards the neighbouring countries in Asia and towards the West. Since the time Deng Xiaoping launched the four-point modernisation programme in 1978,[49] China's priority has been to concentrate on economic growth, which has continued to bring great results for over a billion people in Asia. During the last

---

[46] *Ibid.*
[47] *Ibid.*
[48] *Ibid.*
[49] As a Bangladesh minister, in 1978 the author had a 90-minute meeting in the Great Hall with Deng Xiaoping, who explained in detail the future development strategies of China.

two decades China has therefore tried to avoid international confrontation and has emphasised peace and stability.

In its own national interest China has pursued a policy of amity and friendship with neighbouring countries. With a GDP growth rate of around 11 per cent, the highest in the world, for more than a decade, China has adopted a long-term view of international politics and its perceived role on the global stage. In order to keep pace with the economic miracle that the country has achieved in certain areas China is now interested more in technological development, reforming its banking system and restructuring and privatising industries than in entering into any contentious issues. Even in respect of Taiwan, which China claims as an integral part, a moderate policy has been pursued and business goes on even better than before.

Although China is seen by the West as likely to emerge as the most powerful economic and military power in the world in another 25-30 years, this does not distract China from its present priorities. Like any other ambitious country, China would obviously like to take advantage of the post-Cold War global economy — without, of course, compromising its doctrinaire stance in the management of its statecraft.

Pakistan continues to be a close friend of China, but the latter's policy towards South Asia basically reflects its priorities at home. These drive China towards having an improved relationship with India as well, with which it fought a war in 1962 over a chunk of disputed land on India's northern border. Although China continued to test its nuclear devices as late as 1996, reportedly having a yield of 200 kilotons, it immediately went for a voluntary moratorium on all nuclear tests after July 1996. China's bilateral relationship with India has improved considerably, particularly with the visit of Li Peng, the first Chinese Prime Minister to visit India since the war in 1962. Normalisation of relations with India has therefore been a major component of China's foreign policy in South Asia.

China is not only a signatory of both the NPT and the CTBT, but also plays an active role in international efforts to stop the proliferation of nuclear weapons. China has assured India that China's self-imposed moratorium on future nuclear tests and on the development of missiles was aimed at reducing the arms race in Asia. In pursuit of the same policy, China has not only improved its relationship with Russia, but continues to make efforts to forge stronger ties with the USA.

And yet India, at a time when the relationship between the two countries has normalised and improved, continues to focus on China as a security threat. In order to justify the nuclear tests and convince the West, India has pulled the 'China Factor' into the scene. Without any context or apparent reason, George Fernandez, a seasoned Indian politician and the new Defence Minister, described China as India's 'Potential No. 1 enemy'. In a letter to President Clinton soon after the detonations and in the face of the world's bitter criticism, the Indian Prime Minister pointed out that there existed an 'atmosphere of distrust' in India's relations with China, an 'overt nuclear weapons state on our borders, a state which committed an armed aggression against India in 1962'. Vajpayee admitted that relations with China had improved, but complained that 'an atmosphere of distrust persists mainly due to the unresolved border dispute'.[50] Aiming at Pakistan, Vajpayee wrote: 'To add to the distress, that country has materially helped another neighbour of ours to become a covert nuclear weapons state ... at the hands of this bitter neighbour we have suffered three 'acts of aggression' in the last 50 years.' In protest, China came out with a strong statement insisting that India was trying to make China the scapegoat, projecting it as a nuclear threat to justify its own ambition to dominate South Asia.

International Impact: The impact of the explosion of nuclear devices by India has been monumental worldwide. Mahatma Gandhi's non-violent India, a leader of the Non-aligned Movement, has now developed and tested the most deadly weapons of mass destruction, a move followed by Pakistan. The detonation of nuclear devices by the two inimical states of South Asia has had disastrous consequences. In the world context, it has been a severe blow to the movement for the disarmament and non-proliferation of nuclear weapons pursued by the world community. It has demonstrated the failure to stop proliferation. The existing nuclear weapons states were forced to accept the loss of their monopoly, following their failure to take effective steps towards a meaningful disarmament

---

[50] Press Trust of India, reported on May 13, 1998 and published in newspapers worldwide.

process. On the contrary, they took it as an exclusive privilege to continue with their tests as late as 1996, which was not only self-contradictory but also utterly hypocritical in not setting honest examples for genuine non-proliferation. The result, in the global context has been a severe setback to the movement for non-proliferation and the erosion of trust and confidence in past and future initiatives in this field. The indefinite extension of the NPT in 1995, the reopening of the CTBT scheduled for September 1999, the reduction of nuclear stocks under START-I and START-II, and the Co-operative Threat Reduction Programme to improve the safety and security of weapons in the former Soviet Union will all come under a cloud, at least for the time being.

The explosion of nuclear devices by India and Pakistan will also encourage other Third World countries to go nuclear, which will have far-reaching consequences for maintaining peace and stability from both regional and global perspectives. Once it is established that a country can build a nuclear bomb and get away with it, and that such a country then becomes a nuclear power or nuclear weapons state, whether or not it is party to the NPT, the entire human endeavour to achieve a nuclear-free world will be in great danger. If countries like Iran, Iraq, Libya, North Korea and Israel go nuclear, it will have devastating effects in the world scenario in the new millennium. If Israel goes nuclear, it will destabilise the entire peace process in the Middle East. If North Korea develops nuclear bombs, it will not only frustrate the agreement drawn up with the USA in 1994, but also destroy any prospect of the Korean unification. All these situations will lead to fierce arms races and precipitate security threats to all states, both those with and those without nuclear weapons.

In the regional context, besides the inevitable arms race between India and Pakistan, with increased budgets for their respective defences, the entire security perception of the region as a whole has changed dramatically. China will also have to react to the changing situation. The Indian Defence Minister's declaration that China is "the potential enemy no.1" will only escalate suspicion and mistrust between the two countries. If India installs the Agni missile, which has a range up to 2,500 kilometres, in Assam to reach targets in

China, it can only be expected that China will take precautionary measures of its own. This will lead to further nuclearization of Asia and escalate the intensity of the arms race between the two giants across the Himalayas. This may lead China to eventually withdraw from the NPT and CTBT, which will be disastrous for world peace. Relations between the two countries are not expected to improve and it will not be surprising if China cancels its export of enriched uranium to India for the generation of much-needed electricity.

In the South Asian context, with the nuclear explosions in India and Pakistan, the entire socio-economic, politico-military perspectives of the region have changed. If peace and security are the essential preconditions for progress and prosperity, and if stability is needed to contain social dynamics, the explosions at Pokhran and Chagai Hills have changed their dimensions altogether. They have altered the politics, geopolitics and security perceptions of all the countries of South Asia, and particularly those of the five smaller nations. India is already too large an economic and military power for its smaller neighbours to cope with. They have experienced extreme difficulties in laying the foundations of co-operation between these states neighbouring India under the guiding spirit of the SAARC, an organisation launched in Dhaka in 1985 to strengthen regional co-operation for peace and progress. The nuclearization of South Asia has now thrown the prospects of SAARC into great uncertainty, even threatening its existence.

South Asia is now in more danger than ever before. The impact of the nuclear tests has not only endangered the peace and security of the region, but has made bleak the prospects of future amity and co-operation between the states. Both India and Pakistan will have to increase their budgets for military spending at the cost of more important social and economic priorities. Domestically, because of the countries' limited resources, such a diversion of funds for expensive nuclear devices will give rise to social and political instability and unrest. They will have the bombs, but no beans to eat. As human security is more linked to the economy than to weapons, the entire region will continue to suffer from the present state of under-development. The dreams of achieving progress and prosperity through co-operation and peaceful means, as enshrined in the charter of SAARC, have been damaged if not totally destroyed. South Asia will have deprived itself of the chance to take advantage of the post-Cold War era.

The worst victims of the new situation are Bangladesh, Sri Lanka, Nepal, Bhutan and the Maldives, which aspire to remain independent and prosper in peace and harmony. Although collectively and psychologically these states may benefit from the nuclear balance of power between India and Pakistan, politically they will suffer the most. As nuclear arms are essentially part of a political-weapon system and military politics dominate economic considerations, both the sovereignty and security of the smaller states in South Asia will be permanently at stake.

The question arises, now that India and Pakistan have the bombs where and how are they going to use them? First, one has to take the issues of conflict between India and Pakistan into consideration. The most contentious issue between them is the status of Kashmir. India with the fourth largest military establishment in the world, does not need a nuclear bomb to defend Kashmir, a territory it has kept under its control for 50 years, and it cannot conceivably need or use a nuclear bomb to defeat the Kashmir liberation forces. Similarly, Pakistan cannot think of snatching away Kashmir from India by using a nuclear bomb; if it tried to do so, it would only kill the Kashmiri Muslims who are already fighting for their independence. The other neighbours of India are too small and weak, in both economic and military terms, to require the threat or use of Indian nuclear weapons. Whatever conflicting issues India may have with them, nuclear weapons will not be necessary to solve them.

Then comes the discord with China. The border dispute that India has with China centres on a small, barren, desolate and uninhabited land in the cold and pernicious slopes of the Himalayas. No military scientist will plead for the use of a nuclear bomb for such a piece of land. India would not use nuclear bombs to kill its own Hindu citizens in order to crush the insurgencies in the northeastern states. Nor should Chinese co-operation with the Burmese government raise any alarm that India might use such an option. On the other hand, given China's well-recognised economic priorities over any military ambition and the consequent shift in its foreign policy to avoid confrontation and strive for peaceful development, it is not going to use a nuclear bomb to crush the insurgents who are harboured in the adjacent Indian bases to return the Dalai Lama to the throne of Tibet. It is highly unlikely that India trains such insurgents, but in any case for China to think of using nuclear devices for such a purpose is out of question.

Why then have the bombs? Theoretically and on the face of it there is no good reason or justification particularly for poor countries like India and Pakistan to have the weapons. The case of Pakistan, because it followed India's lead to the nuclear club, it is understandable if not desirable or endorsable. If India had not pursued a nuclear policy, Pakistan might not have done so. But why India? Is it ego, pride, prestige, ambition, or just the desire to achieve the status of a nuclear weapons state and thereby play a role on the world stage? Or is it to prove the scientific and technical achievements of the nation? After pleading for total disarmament for nearly three decades and taking a leading role in the Non-aligned Movement, India has blasted the devices thus ignoring the universal opinion against nuclear proliferation. Although, after the blast, the Indian Prime Minister announced that India would not conduct any more tests, as did Pakistan, these announcements are almost routine utterances, do not mean anything substantial and are not taken seriously.

The stand taken by the five members of the Security Council, which are also the present nuclear-weapons states, is that neither India nor Pakistan will be given any recognition as nuclear-weapons states; only those who acquired nuclear weapons prior to 1968, before the NPT was drawn up, are so recognised. Moreover, if this stipulation is violated and they are recognised as nuclear-weapons states, the whole purpose of the movement for non-proliferation, the NPT and CTBT will be totally frustrated. It will also encourage others to explode nuclear weapons and achieve the same status. Consequently, India and Pakistan cannot expect to be recognised or admitted to the exclusive club of five nuclear-weapons states.

But whether India and Pakistan are officially recognised or not, and whether they are allowed to sit at the same table as the other five or not, the fact is that they have the proven capability of having nuclear devices. Vajpayee has already claimed 'we are a nuclear-weapon power',[51] 'India is now a nuclear-weapons state' and 'we have the capacity of a big bomb now'. Pakistan's Nawaz Sharif has echoed the same tone, saying 'we have matched India'.[52] Both countries now have the bombs and are capable of having more of the most effective apparatus of mass destruction man have ever invented.

As already stated, bombs made at such a colossal cost and risk are not to be put in showcases or window displays. They are produced for use. Vajpayee confirms it when he says, 'We will not use these weapons against anybody. But to defend ourselves, if need arises, we will not hesitate.'[53] Western military analysts, while confirming the view that the situation in South Asia is not such as to warrant any use of nuclear weapons — particularly so in the case of India's dispute with Pakistan or China — say that the most likely use of nuclear weapons would be as a 'pre-emptive first strike against the other side's nuclear forces'. This is the reality of the danger in South Asia. When former US President Clinton calls India's move 'a fundamental mistake';[54] it is only history that will tell us the magnitude of this mistake.

A section of the international community argues that, now that India and Pakistan have the bombs, it is better to accept the reality of the situation. To keep them outside the ring will be more dangerous than to bring them under some discipline and regulation. As the facilities in both countries are not safeguarded by any internationally recognised safety and security measures, the international community should persuade both countries to sign the CTBT and provide the technologies for a proven command and control system. However this view is strongly opposed on the ground that it will defeat the entire purpose and spirit of the movement for non-proliferation of nuclear weapons and encourage other countries to follow the South Asian examples. It is further argued that the international community must continue with full sanctions until these two countries

---

[51] *Newsweek*, May 25, 1998.

[52] Address to the nation, May 28, 1998.

[53] *Newsweek*, May 25, 1998.

[54] *Ibid*.

unconditionally ratify the CTBT,[55] freeze production of all military and civilian nuclear explosive material and agree to roll back their nuclear weapons programmes.[56]

Economic effects: The sanctions imposed on India may have had a cumulative effect of blocking around $20 billion in aid and investment. However, Indian economists felt that the country would be able to withstand their effects and that, in any event, their actual impact would not be more than $2 billion, which could partly be offset by increased remittances from the highly nationalistic Indians working abroad. Prime Minister Vajpayee thought that with India's large market now being opened for investment, Americans would put their own economic interests ahead of the nuclear issue, so the sanctions would not work. Nevertheless, if sanctions continued, India will find itself left behind in the economic progress the world is making. It will be in India's interests to restore a congenial environment for foreign investment in India and the credibility of the new government in the world community.

For Pakistan, with an overseas debt liability of $30 billion and an economy already under great strain since the withdrawal of US economic aid in 1990, the case was somewhat different. Although it had taken strong economic measures to withstand the storm, its economy still depended largely on the assistance of the World Bank and IMF. It also believed that international sanctions do not generally work but if the sanctions continued and the USA prevailed upon the IMF to take a restrictive attitude in providing necessary financial assistance, Pakistan would face further economic disaster. The emphatic support given by the people to their government at the time of the blast was not to last long in the face of economic hardships, lack of jobs and declining business. With the emergency situation already restricting normal life, opposition was becoming restive and agitating to take the people to the streets.

Led by the USA, the international community has already induced the two countries to enter into negotiation. During the United Nations

---

[55] The USA has signed but not yet ratified the CTBT. Ironically, as recently as October 13, 1999 the Senate refused to ratify the CTBT, which has weakened the US position in urging the threshold countries to sign the treaty.

[56] Steven Dolly, Nuclear Control Institute, Washington, D.C., June 9, 1998.

General Assembly session on 23 and 24 September 1998, Pakistan and then India gave assurances that they would sign the CTBT within a year when global discussion reopened in September 1999.[57] Both Prime Ministers said that negotiations were going on with the USA and expected that sanctions would be lifted.

The USA wants India and Pakistan to sign and ratify the CTBT unconditionally without being recognised as nuclear-weapons states, to freeze all facilities and testing, and to roll back their nuclear programmes, as Belarus, Kazakhstan, the Ukraine and South Africa have done. They will be required to strengthen export controls and fully comply with international arms control agreements.[58] Both countries may be in a position to sign the CTBT and may also agree to suspend testing, but it is almost unimaginable that either of the present governments in India and Pakistan will be in a position to freeze their respective nuclear facilities and roll back their nuclear programmes. Because of the inherent conflicts between the two states, neither would be in a position to withstand the political backlash such an action would induce, both at the domestic level and in international relations.

As far as the withdrawal of sanctions is concerned, it was not going to be an easy task. The US President cannot do anything on his own. Either he has to be authorised by the Congress to apply a waiver or the Congress may amend the law. The Congress, dominated by the Republicans, is reluctant to do this unless it is fully satisfied about the terms of the negotiated agreements.[59] So the whole matter will take time.

South Asia will therefore continue to be the centre of an arms race, and peace and stability in the region will remain under constant threat. In the absence of total global disarmament, which is not foreseen in

---

[57] Nothing has happened in September and no one has yet signed the treaty. On February 20, 1999 the Indian Prime Minister crossed the Punjab Customs Post in a bus to meet with his Pakistan counterpart, Nawaz Sharif, on the occasion of launching a regular service between Delhi, India's capital, and Lahore, the capital of the Punjab of Pakistan. After the bus ride the two leaders signed an agreement on February 21, 1999 called 'The Lahore Declaration', taking immediate steps to reduce the risk of accidental or unauthorised use of nuclear weapons. *The Economist*, May 22, 1999; *Independent* and *Daily Star*, February 23, 2000.

[58] *New York Times*, 24 and 25 September 1998.

[59] Sanctions since then have been partly waived by the US President, on October 1, 1999.

Table 3.1 China, India and Pakistan: Military strength

	China	India	Pakistan
Defence expenditure (1996)	$40 billion	$10.4 billion	$3.7 billion
Army	2,200,000	980,000	520,000
Tanks	8,500	3,314	2,120
Towed artillery	14,500	4,175	1,590
Air force	470,000	110,000	45,000
Combat aircraft	4,970	777	429
Navy	265,000	55,000	22,000
Submarines	61	17	9
Destroyers	18	6	3
Frigates	36	18	8

Sources: *Military Balance 1997-98*; *India Today*, 5 July 1999, *Holiday*, 12 June 1998. See also *India Today*, 7 January 2002 and *Time* 14 January 2002.

Table 3.2 Pakistan and India: The rival nuclear arsenals

Pakistan	India
Nuclear Warheads:	**Nuclear Warheads**
30 to 50	45 to 95
Ghauri (IRBM)	**Agni (IRBM)**
Range: 870 miles	Range: 1,500 miles
Payload: 1,500 lbs.	Payload: 2,200 lbs.
Nuclear capable	Nuclear capable
From Lahore:	From Golpalpur, Orissa:
to Delhi (283 miles), 3.2 mins	to Karachi (1,200 mls), 14 mins
to Bombay (880 mls), 10.2 mins	to Yunan, China (1,100 mls), 12.4 mins
HATF (SSM) range	*Prithvi* **(SSM)**
I – 50 miles (no guidance system)	Range: 90–220 miles
II – 185 miles (on drawing-board)	Payload: 1,000–2,000 lbs., nuclear
III – 370 mls (on drawing-board)	From Jalandhar, Punjab:
	to Islamabad (230 miles), 2.54 mins
	to Lahore (71 miles), 50 secs
Chinese M9, M11 (SSM)	Trishul (SSM)
Range: 190–370 miles	Range: 3–6 miles, nuclear capable
	unconfirmed
	Akash (SSM)
	Range: 15–18 miles
	Nag (anti-tank)
	Range: 2.5 miles

Notes: SSM: Surface-to-surface missile. IRBM: Intermediate-range ballistic missile.
Source: *Holiday*, Dhaka, 12 June 1998. See also *India Today*, 7 January 2002 and *Time*, 14 January 2002.

near future, fierce rivalry between India and Pakistan, and in the years to come between the two giants of Asia, India and China, will put the security of almost half of the world's population in great danger.[60]

Besides the nuclear issue, there are other intra-regional and inter-state conflicts that have retarded the progress of the region and held back the process of co-operation envisaged under the Charter of SAARC. Equally important are the internal conditions of individual states — their social, economic, cultural, intellectual and political environments — which affect their ability to achieve and sustain co-operation between countries for mutual benefit. Co-operation immediately implies mutual benefit. If two states opt for co-operation, it must benefit and advance the respective national interests of both countries. The benefits may not be equal and or identical. However, it is not the quantum but the quality of benefits that counts. Not every forum of co-operation yields benefits; some may even be harmful. So the purpose of co-operation must be clear and well defined.

India and Sri Lanka

India's relations with Sri Lanka have been better than those with Pakistan, but have not always been without stress. At times they have sunk to the lowest level. The ethnic Tamil-Sinhalese conflict in the north, which has seriously weakened an otherwise resilient Sri Lankan society, for two decades, is an issue at point. A strong section of Sri Lankan opinion blames the Indian authorities for initiating and encouraging the rise of ethnic regionalism in order to sustain their influence in that country.

Tamils are an independent group of people with their own language and culture, living largely in the Indian state of Tamil Nadu in the south, close to Sri Lanka but separated from it by the Palk Strait of the Indian Ocean. While the bulk of Tamils, around 50 million, live in India, a sizeable number live in Sri Lanka. Of Sri Lanka's 18 million population, about 18 per cent (12.6 per cent Sri Lankans and 5.5 per cent Indians)[61] are Tamils, constituting nearly one-fifth of the

---

[60] India has increased the defence budget by 28 per cent, the largest ever increase in a single year and it is a direct sign of intensifying the arms race in South Asia. See the Indian Budget, 2000-01.

[61] Sunil Bastian (ed.), *Devolution and Development of Sri Lanka: International Centre for Ethnic Studies*, Colombo, Sri Lanka, p. 153.

entire population. Most of these people live in the north of Sri Lanka across the strait from India. The bulk of Tamils belong to the Hindu religion, although their language bears more weight in their identity, which increases their number further compared to the Muslim and Christian Tamils.

Over time, as the Tamils grew in strength, their violent insurgencies, so long ignored by the Sinhalese — Buddhist ruling elite, were recognised by the government of Sri Lanka and attempts were made, mostly using military means, to bring the situation under control. The escalation of armed conflict threatened the security not only of Sri Lanka but also of India. The swelling number of refugees crossing into Indian territory raised fears in Indian minds that Sri Lanka might seek international support, leading to military assistance from the West. India hastened to take the lead and diplomatic negotiations between the two countries led to the conclusion of an agreement signed between India and Sri Lanka in July 1987.

Pursuant to this Indo-Sri Lanka Agreement,[62] in order to restore peace, India deployed 46,000 troops[63] and dispatched an Indian Peace Keeping Force (IPKF) to Sri Lanka. India established its own command over the territory, ignoring the authority of the Sri Lankan government and its military. On the other hand, Indian troops could not crush the Tamils either and no peace was at sight. The death toll on both sides only increased and Tamils gained a propaganda advantage from the fact that a foreign army of occupation was butchering them. The Sri Lankan military establishment felt utterly humiliated by the presence and command of the Indian army and its independent operations, conducted without regard to Sri Lankan priorities.

Finally, when the government of Sri Lanka wanted the Indian troops to withdraw, the government of Rajiv Gandhi refused to do so for security reasons, which led to a serious international crisis. As a reaction to India's stand, Sri Lanka not only boycotted but also withdrew from the SAARC Foreign Ministers' meeting in 1988.

Sri Lanka took the Indian action as a naked violation of her sovereignty and territorial integrity. Because of its growing involvement

---

[62] See Indo-Sri Lanka Agreement, Ministry of External Affairs, Government of India, New Delhi, 1987.

[63] *Bangladesh Observer*, Dhaka, 13 July 1989.

in the Tamil conflicts, Sri Lanka had been critical of India for many years, accusing India of not showing respect to another member country's independence and territorial integrity by refraining from acts of aggression, interference, violence and oppression.[64] Now India's refusal to leave the soil of Sri Lanka only confirmed Sri Lanka's view that India had a grand design to exercise hegemony and supra-national authority over neighbouring states. As a further protest at Indian aggression and the presence of Indian troops in Sri Lanka, the latter refused to attend the Council of Ministers' meeting scheduled to be held in Islamabad on 1 and 2 July 1989, which almost led to the collapse of the SAARC.

It shocked and surprised Sri Lanka that, despite its President's official call to withdraw the troops, India would not do so. President Ranasinghe Premadasa of Sri Lanka went to the extent of blaming India for creating chaos in his country and said, 'I do not expect Prime Minister Rajiv Gandhi to dictate terms to us and attract international condemnation of a big country bullying a small neighbour.'[65] Sri Lanka maintained that 'the only condition on which IPKF was invited to Sri Lanka and the only condition that should be satisfied for the withdrawal of the IPKF is the decision of the President of Sri Lanka'.[66] India rejected the Sri Lankan demand for a pullout by maintaining that the withdrawal of troops had to be conditional upon an improvement in the law and order situation and devolution of power by giving autonomy to the Provincial Council in the northeast region. This led to a dispute about the terms of the agreement and acrimonious statements between both countries.

The fact that India was deeply involved in the Tamil crisis from the very beginning of the ethnic conflict motivated Sri Lanka to come to terms with India when the ethnic conflict reached its peak in mid-1980s. Sri Lanka perceived that, as India was deeply involved in the issue and the insurgents were Tamils who had links with India, the latter could be effective in any mediation or negotiation to settle the issue. The peace accord was therefore signed with India rather

---

[64] The statement of the Sri Lankan Foreign Minister in the third session of the SAARC Council of Ministers, New Delhi, 1986.

[65] *Amrita Bazar Patrika*, 24 June 1989.

[66] *Amrita Bazar Patrika*, 16 June 1989.

than the Tamils. One of the primary objectives for this was to generate and enforce the cessation of hostilities by way of devolving power to the region and holding elections to enable the Tamils to participate in the development of their own region. But despite the presence and operations of the Indian army, the ethnic conflict only sharpened and took on a different dimension. Having found that the operations of the IPKF were highly counterproductive and the Tamil Tigers were keen to talk to the Sri Lankan authorities rather than the Indian generals, Sri Lanka decided to ask India to withdraw its troops.

With 46,000 troops on its soil and India refusing to withdraw them, the entire situation was aggravated further. It was a long and complex period for Sri Lanka. The presence of Indian troops, their commanding position over the island and their subsequent refusal to withdraw opened up many new dimensions in all fronts. Inside Sri Lanka a state of emergency had to be reimposed to bring the economic and the law and order situation under control. When the Sri Lankan government was about to conclude an agreement with the Tamils for the cessation of hostilities, the Eelam National Democratic Liberation Front urged India not to withdraw on the ground that the Sinhalese might take reprisals against the Tamils. A group started recruiting volunteers' brigades for training, assisted by the IPKF, to resist such reprisals.[67] In this unusual state of affairs, India started getting involved in the national politics of Sri Lanka, which created further uncertainties in the minds of all sections of the people and pushed the situation out of control.

The two armies, the Sri Lankan and Indian, started exchanging shots. The hostilities and mistrust only increased between Sinhalese and Tamil, Tamil and Tamil, the IPKF and LTTE, and the JVP and IPKF.[68] India's decision to stay in Sri Lanka to ensure the 'safety and security of the Tamils' ran counter to its earlier role of assisting the Tamil Tigers. It was ironic that India as of that day wanted to crush the Tigers, whom they had nurtured and actively encouraged for nearly two decades. This stand was seen as a plan for continuing with the Indian presence on the island for long-term strategic reasons.

---

[67] 'Sri Lankan Crisis over IPKF Withdrawal', *BIISS Journal*, Vol. 10, No. 3, 1989, p. 249. See also Iftekharuzzaman, 'Changing Global Scenario: Challenges for Bangladesh', *BIISS*, 10 June 1989.
[68] *Ibid.*

All through these events the opposition inside India was critical of the government. The BJP leader Vajpayee called it a blunder of major proportions to have trained, armed and financially assisted the LTTE and then to put all options on the group.[69] Rajiv Gandhi had to maintain a strong stand in view of the ensuing general elections in India. Having lost more than a thousand soldiers already, the withdrawal of Indian troops without achieving peace or crushing the Tamils would have caused a great electoral setback for the Indian Congress at home.

When the Sri Lankan government finally reached an agreement with the Tamil Tigers for a cessation of hostilities, the Indian authorities ignored it. They argued that the Tamils had made the agreement so that the Indian troops would leave Sri Lanka, and that once they had gone the Tamils would return to their operations.

It is true that successive governments in Sri Lanka had failed to contain and resolve the ethnic conflict due to their own lack of vision and incompetence. The intransigent position of the central government only helped the dissenting and secessionist forces to gather more strength and public support. As Sri Lankan governments did not have the courage to stand up to their giant neighbour, the Tamil issue slipped out of their hands. In the end they handed it over to India of their own volition, whatever compelling domestic reasons there might have been.

On the other hand, the good intentions of India in helping a neighbour to resolve its most crucial problem were marred by its subsequent decision to keep thousands of troops on another country's soil, despite repeated demands for their withdrawal by the host country. The IPKF, too, was unable to restore peace or resolve the Tamil crisis. India's best defence was that it had not deployed its troops on its own. On the contrary, it had done so on being invited by the Sri Lankan government pursuant to an international agreement under which they were obligated to carry out certain obligations and responsibilities. In the face of the ruthless operations of the Indian troops, the LTTE changed its strategy. In order to embarrass India and get its troops off the island, it came forward to settle the issue

---

[69] *The DAWN*, 13 June 1989.

with the Sri Lankan government, which obviously the Indian authorities did not like.

The episode came to an end with a face-saving device. The arrangement was made for a phased withdrawal of Indian troops on the basis of a jointly worked-out timetable, which of course was to be executed at the option of India. In its own interest, both for cost and security reasons, India did not want to station a permanent military force in Sri Lanka. Although the troops had to return to their own land and the Tamil problem had not been solved, the strategic gain for India was enormous. Its persistent refusal to withdraw the troops when they were asked to do so might have invoked international criticism and made its small neighbours fear for their own security in future, but India had achieved its goals. It had proved its role and strength as a regional power and demonstrated its will to establish its position on the global stage.

India and Nepal

The security and economy of Nepal has been tied to India, ever since the Treaty of Peace and Friendship was signed in July 1950. The Agreement on Commerce and Trade was also signed in the same year between the two countries. Subsequently, the two countries signed a number of other agreements during 1950's and 1960's. As a result, Nepal's desire to establish its own identity could not blossom, since its socio-economic development largely depended on India.

Landlocked between India and China, Nepal would like to maintain a balance between the two, which the former obviously does not like. The King of Nepal, who used to run the country as its Chief Executive, tried to pursue a policy of neutrality in the region, which led Nepal to sign a Friendship Treaty as well as a Boundary Treaty to ensure peace with its northern neighbour China. Nepal's declaration of the area as a zone of peace was also not liked by India. An arms deal with China, to the annoyance of India, led the Nepal Congress, an appendage of the Indian Congress, to strip the King of all his major executive powers and plunged Nepal into a serious economic crisis when the question of renewing the Agreement on

Commerce and Trade arose. India suddenly stopped all trade and business in Nepal.[70]

Nepal would like to rescind some of the treaties signed earlier, but does not have the courage to assert its position. In August 1980 it signed an agreement with Bangladesh for trade and transit facilities, but India did not give Nepal permission to pass through 19 kilometres of its land to get into the territory of Bangladesh. India wants Nepal to continue to primarily use Calcutta Port at a huge cost of money and time. Because India's consent is required for any kind of transit facility, Nepal has to rely totally on India for the import of all essential items. The currencies of India and Nepal are openly convertible and used as valid currency in each other's markets. As a result of its economic control of the kingdom, India maintains a great degree of influence in Nepal's internal politics, which is also dominated by the Nepalese of Indian origin.

India and Bhutan

Similar to Nepal, and perhaps in a more intrinsic manner, Bhutan is economically totally dependent on India. With a population of 1.7 million in an area of 47,000 square kilometres, Bhutan mainly relies on its resources being imported or exported by land through India. But strategically, like Nepal, Bhutan is important particularly to India, as India and China surround it. It is also close to the insurgent states of the northeast. Here, too, the King wants to pursue a neutral policy as far as China is concerned, but this is not possible. Bhutan's foreign policy is determined by India under an agreement signed in 1949 soon after the British had withdrawn from the subcontinent. Similarly, in economic policy, the only trade route for Bhutan is through India and for Bhutan to do any business even with its neighbours would require a transit permit from India.

Bhutan has a cross-country problem with India but it has to be very cautious not to annoy India. The issue of Bhutias living in Sikkim and the northern part of West Bengal has yet to be resolved. Bhutan is still in search of its own identity, but is not content with being totally

---

[70]Bangladesh helped Nepal by airlifting fuel/petrol during that time.

subjugated by India. It wants to revise some of its treaty obligations with India and diversify its trade and foreign relations. Bhutan supports Nepal's proposal of declaring the area a zone of peace.

India and the Maldives

The Maldives is a tiny state in the Indian Ocean. It is governed by one-party rule and is virtually under total Indian domination. Indian military intervention in the Maldives in 1988 demonstrated, as in Sri Lanka, India's position of 'superpower' in the region.

Nepal and Bhutan

The interstate conflict between Nepal and Bhutan arises from an exodus of nearly 96,000 Bhutanese of Nepali origin that were pushed into Nepal, creating for the latter an enormous socio-economic problem. These refugees, living in hundreds of shelters and camps, have brought a great economic strain on the country, besides causing disruption to law and order. The Bhutanese resent those of Nepalese origin in Bhutan who dominate the country's economy and politics. Diplomatic efforts have been going on for several years to resolve the issue, but India's inactivity is regarded as mysterious.

Bangladesh and Pakistan

Although Pakistan was divided after a long political conflict of 24 years, which ended in a bitter and bloody war in 1971, tension was eased after the Simla Agreement and the subsequent joint settlement offer by India to Pakistan of a three-way repatriation of its defeated soldiers held in India and the stranded citizens in Pakistan and Bangladesh. While the brutal attack of the Pakistan army on the Bengalis and the genocide it committed on them were still fresh in people's minds, hectic diplomatic efforts were made to bring the two Muslim countries closer again.

The final issues boiled down to the trial of 195 prisoners of war in Bangladesh and Pakistan's recognition of Bangladesh as a sovereign state. At the mediation of some eminent Muslim leaders, Sheikh Mujib traded the trial of the prisoners against receiving recognition from Pakistan.[71] On 22 February 1974, Pakistan formally accorded recognition to Bangladesh, as did Iran and Turkey. A good-will mission of the Islamic Summit came to Dhaka with an invitation for Mujib, and the next day an Algerian aircraft flew Mujib and his delegation on a historic flight to Lahore, where he was received by Bhutto at the airport, to the annoyance of many Indians. As his effigy was burned in Calcutta, Mujib termed Pakistan's recognition of Bangladesh a 'triumph of truth'.

Subsequent to the recognition and the Islamic Summit, the three countries met at New Delhi in April 1974 to formally drop the proposed trial of the 195 prisoners of war. The three-way repatriation that had already started in September 1973 continued until April 1974, but the issue of the repatriation of those non-Bengali-speaking citizens, known as 'Biharis', who owed allegiance to and opted for Pakistan remained unresolved. Their status had been determined by the International Red Cross and accepted by both Pakistan and Bangladesh. However, Pakistan tried to take the advantage of the ambiguity of the terms of repatriation and initially only agreed to take some of them on humanitarian grounds.

Pakistan does not deny that it will take back 500,000 Biharies living in miserable conditions and causing a constant strain on the economy and social order of Bangladesh. Every time Bangladesh takes it up with Pakistan, the latter makes a commitment, but it has not yet been carried out. Pakistan claims to need $400 million for their rehabilitation and seeks foreign assistance for this purpose. In Bangladesh this is seen as a deliberate attempt by Pakistan to obviate its international obligations, and it reminds the Bengalis of the old atrocities of 1971, which the people would otherwise like to forget.

Besides the question of the repatriation of the Pakistanis stranded in Bangladesh for the last 30 years, the issue of the countries' assets and liabilities as of 25 March 1971 has not yet been settled. Pakistan has never accepted that it owes anything to Bangladesh, but the matter remains unresolved. In the domestic politics of Bangladesh, political parties have often raised these issues, particularly the one relating to the Biharis, to remind the people of the past crimes that Pakistan

---

[71] See for detail Moudud Ahmed, *Era of Sheikh Mujibur Rahman*, pp. 231-44.

committed against the Bengalis. Although, through the passage of time, the issue of assets and liabilities has become diluted because of the inaction of successive Bangladeshi governments, both issues are still raised by parties who are ideologically opposed to Pakistan.

India and Bangladesh

At the time of its birth as an independent nation in 1971, it might have been thought that Bangladesh would be India's best and most friendly neighbour. The courageous role that India had played, even risking a global confrontation to assist and support the war of the Bengalis to liberate their country from the colonial rule of Pakistan, should have been the basis of a permanent and eternal friendship between the two countries. Bangladesh could look at India with a great amount of indebtedness for India's active support of Bangladesh's struggle, without which the independence could not have been achieved within such a short period. But then what went wrong? Why, in the last 30 years, have relations between the two states suffered so many setbacks? Why is it that the vast majority of people in Bangladesh do not consider India a friendly neighbour?

When the Pakistan army cracked down on the Bengalis on 25 March 1971, all the Awami League leaders except Mujib crossed the border kept open by India. With the assistance of the Indian government, the Awami League leaders formed a government-in-exile and the Indian government provided shelter, food, training, equipment, materials and the finance for the Bangladesh government to gain independence. Although the Indian government was cautious in helping anybody other than those who held allegiance to the leadership of the Awami League, many other political parties and nationalist cadres took part in the war and used India as a sanctuary.

When the war of independence broke out, India's desire to weaken its number one enemy coincided with the aspirations of the Bengali nationalist forces. India wanted to increase its influence and maintain its superiority in the subcontinent, and the Bengalis wanted to win the war and gain their independence. The alliance suited both sides, not least because two political parties of the same character and social classes represented the two governments. In the absence of Sheikh Mujib, the leadership of the Awami League was weak and submissive, which helped India to establish complete control over the government-in-exile.[72] In the course of the nine-month struggle, the bond between the Awami League and the Indian government grew stronger and they developed a deeper understanding. It was therefore only natural for India to want the 'armed struggle' to remain within its control and a government of its own liking to be installed in Bangladesh.

India therefore employed strict methods in matters of recruitment, training and logistics towards those who joined the Mukti Bahini.[73] It was not easy for any young man to join the fighting force without proving complete allegiance to and recommendation from the Awami League leaders.[74] India's total reliance on the Awami League raised bitter criticism amongst other nationalist forces, which considered the policy ill conceived. They believed that an independence war of such magnitude could not be confined to one political party and that other political parties and individuals had the right to participate in the war.[75]

In the field, the Indian army in respect of operations conducted by the Bengali freedom fighters assumed same control and authority. This created a lot of strong resentment amongst the Bengali army officers and members of the *Mukti Bahini*. The Indian army's control of war logistics and frequent interference in operational matters were considered unnecessary by the freedom fighters, who gradually developed into an independent group. During the war, they were openly critical of both the Awami League leadership for not taking part in the war and the Indian government for too much interference and high-handedness.

---

[72] When the war broke out, the two pro-Soviet parties, Moni Singh's Communist Party and Muzaffar's National Awami Party, rendered full support to the Awami League. They were members of the consultative committee constituted in India by the government-in-exile during the war period.

[73] Liberation Forces.

[74] For the role and character of the Awami League, see Moudud Ahmed, *Bangladesh: Constitutional Quest for Autonomy*, pp. 272-76.

[75] Although the pro-Soviet NAP and the Communist Party rendered full support to the Awami League, they were not part of the government-in-exile. For the control employed by the Indian government, see *Ibid*.

Thus, while the war had carried the seed of friendship between the government of India and the government of the Awami League, it had also sown the seed of discord from within and outside. This discord was only deepened further by the Indian government's raising of another cadre of freedom fighters under the name of *Mujib Bahini*.[76]

Once the war was over and the Pakistan army had surrendered, the Indian government achieved its twin objectives: a weaker Pakistan, whose military strength had been destroyed; and an increase in India's influence in the region. The people of Bangladesh were grateful for what the Indian army had done for them, and consequently the relationship between the two countries could not have been any better.

The Indian army, technical experts and advisers remained to assist and guide the government of Bangladesh. But for reasons not known, or perhaps because they were the victorious force, soon after the surrender the Indian army started taking arms, ammunition, equipment, machinery and even furniture and household goods in convoy of trucks across the border.[77] Although no formal protest note was sent to India alleging goods taken by the Indian army without the consent of the Bangladesh government, there were a number of heated exchanges by Bangladeshi civil and military officials (particularly those who had actively participated in the Liberation War) with Indian civil and military officials regarding their clandestine activities. A senior army officer and brave freedom fighter was so disgusted with what he was witnessing around Dhaka and the reports he was getting from other parts of the country, that he wrote a piece which was published in a prominent newspaper. This exposure led to his forced resignation and both the country and the army lost an

---

[76] Mujib Bahini was established at the instance of Serajul Alam Khan and Sheikh Moni, who claimed that they had a letter of authority from Mujib and were his real successors, meaning that Mujib trusted them more than he did Tajuddin and others. At the end, both the Bahinis were critical of Tajuddin and they became a threat to the government-in-exile.

[77] According to *Aneek* (Bengali), December 1974, p. 80, the Indian army took away capital goods, industrial raw materials and military hardware worth $1,000 million.

In the *Guardian* of 21 June 1972, Martin Woollacott wrote: 'Systematic Indian army's looting of mills, factories and offices in Khulna area has angered and enraged Bangladesh civil officials here. The looting took place in the first days after the Indian troops arrived in the city on December 17.'

outstanding officer who could soon have occupied the highest position in the army.[78]

Smuggling across the East Pakistan and Indian border was nothing new, but soon after Bangladesh achieved independence the scale of such smuggling increased enormously, as the border between India and Bangladesh remained open for a long time.[79] Moreover, one of the first steps the Bangladesh government took was to withdraw the ban on exporting raw jute and jute goods to India, which helped to increase the volume of smuggling. On the same day, 1 January 1972, the government devalued the Taka, putting the currency on a par with India. Simultaneously, the government declared all foreign sale contracts for raw jute and jute goods entered into by exporters or mills before 16 December 1971 as null and void.[80] When the Bangladesh government once more fixed the price of jute after devaluation, smuggling became more profitable than normal trade.

So jute, the golden fibre and the lifeline of Bangladesh foreign exchange earnings, suffered a great setback in terms of both foreign exchange earnings and domestic production.[81] From independence right through to 1974, for unknown reasons, a series of acts of sabotage took place in Bangladesh, most of which centred round the jute mills and godowns. Widespread outbreaks of fire in jute godowns

---

[78] Major Jalil was the first officer to raise the issue. In November 1972 a Bangladesh Defense Ministry delegation to Delhi raised the question of returning the captured arms but received a cool response. *Holiday*, August 1975.

At a later stage, in reply to a written question in Parliament from an Awami League member, the State Minister for Information and Broadcasting said that India had already returned a substantial quantity of arms and ammunition which it had captured from the occupation forces and that the transfer of those arms and ammunition was still in progress. In reply to another question, however, the minister refused to disclose the full figure of the transfer 'in the interest of the State'. *Bangladesh Observer*, 18 June 1974.

[79] Moulana Bhashani claimed that smuggling and confiscation of goods transferred to India by the Indian army accounted to a total approx. Tk.6,000 cores. According to *Aneek*, December 1974, p. 81, the value of goods smuggled from Bangladesh to India between 1972 and 1975 was estimated to be not less than $2,000 million.

[80] *Bangladesh Observer*, 2 January 1972. According to business and financial experts, all three measures had gone to the advantage of India and it was alleged that these decisions were taken at the instance of the Indian advisers.

[81] For several decades India was able neither to export raw jute nor to produce enough jute to feed its own industries. The position changed dramatically after the birth of Bangladesh. In 1973 India exported 1 million bales of raw jute and by 1974 not only were its existing mills running at full capacity, but it had also started to set up more jute mills. Kamal Uddin Siddiqui, 'The Political Economy of Indo-Bangladesh Relations, 1971-75', University of London thesis, 1975.

became almost a daily occurrence, causing further damage to the jute market.[82] As a result, both the Jute Marketing Corporation and the Jute Trading Corporation incurred heavy losses in 1972-73.

The border agreement signed earlier thus provided no benefits to Bangladesh and consequently was abandoned in October 1972. Bangladesh signed four credit agreements and one bilateral trade agreement with India in May 1972. In 1973 it signed a Tk.500 crore barter agreement with India on a limited repayment basis, but this agreement also failed due to the non-purchase of Bangladesh goods by India. India also printed some currency notes for Bangladesh. But because they could easily be forged or because of leakage it created enormous embarrassment for both governments and caused colossal damage to the economy of Bangladesh.

Soon, effects of all these problems on the Bangladesh economy began accumulating, raising considerable suspicion in the minds of the people. The Pakistan army had already ravaged the country and now the people started to have fears over the presence of the Indian overlords. With the price of essential commodities already soaring and smuggling going unchecked, Bangladesh was gripped with the menace of a flight of capital and inflation. The more the economics of scarcity began to hit the daily life of ordinary people, the more smuggling, hoarding and black marketing became profitable business, causing a serious breach of trust between Bangladeshis and their own government, on the one hand, and Bangladeshis and the government of India on the other.

The transfer of the country's assets by the Indian army, the influence of the Indian bureaucrats in the Bangladesh administration, large-scale smuggling across the border, the removal of the ban on exporting raw jute and jute goods to India, the printing of currency notes in India, the raising of the *Rakkhi Bahini*, the devaluation of currency and the presence of the Indian army — all these combined to increase the distrust of the Bangladesh people. The seed that had been sown during the war, when the Indian government relied on the Awami League government, now began to take root in what was

---

[82] The Jute Minister told Parliament in 1974 that jute worth Tk.139.2 million had been destroyed due to fire incidents since independence.

termed the 'Indian exploitation' of Bangladesh's resources. Due to the carelessness of both governments, no effective measure was taken to remove this element of distrust.

This had far-reaching political and economic consequences as, with the law and order situation fast deteriorating, the confidence of Bangladeshis in the Indian government and army were shaken considerably within the first year of the independence. All the political parties, other than the Awami League, raised criticisms against some or all of the actions of the Bangladesh and Indian governments. The right-wing religious forces, which were banned, were not inactive either. They took the full advantage of the situation and from behind the scenes conducted a vigorous campaign against the domination of 'Hindu India' over Bangladesh, trying to hold India responsible for all the miseries the people were suffering from. Added to this, the Awami League, because of its high-handed behaviour, alienated people who did not cross the border and yet suffered; these people vastly outnumbered those who crossed.

These three factors led to a worsening relationship between the two countries from the very beginning. So while the formal relationship between the two governments remained strong and friendly, as far as the people of Bangladesh were concerned it started to move in the opposite direction from the day the Indian army started taking away the property of Bangladesh and allowed the border to remain open.

The Friendship Treaty

In the first few months, the presence of the Indian army in Bangladesh was an important factor because it raised a lot of misapprehensions both at home and abroad. It constituted a challenge to the new government's ability to run and manage its own people and its capacity to hold the honour and sovereignty of the new state. Pakistan and its allies were claiming that Bangladesh was under the occupation of Indian forces, and that India was forcefully occupying a part of Pakistan. In the international arena, a large number of countries were withholding their recognition of Bangladesh because of the presence of the Indian army. At home, although Mujib had to praise the 'impeccable behaviour of the Indian troops during their brief stay in

Bangladesh',[83] the people became frightened that they were taking away the wealth of the country and were suspicious about their future intentions.

Mujib felt these pressures but was unable to take any quick steps due to his sense of gratitude for what India had done for the creation of Bangladesh and for himself.[84] Once Mujib was released, the Indian government was subjected to embarrassing criticism in the world forums for continuing to have its troops in Bangladesh. India, being a spokesman for non-alignment and the "Panchashila" principles, and in the face of worldwide pressure created by Pakistan and its allies, sought an alternative. Consequently, in the end an arrangement was made to sign a treaty and as a bargain Mujib was able to effect the withdrawal of the Indian army. Accordingly, by prior arrangement, the Indian army was formally withdrawn on 12 March 1972. Mujib's message to departing Indian soldiers in a farewell address was 'to carry love from the people of Bangladesh'.[85]

The relationship that had developed between the two governments during the war of independence led them to follow 'common policies in matters of interest to both the countries', but this understanding, which many alleged had its roots in some secret arrangement made earlier, could not be substantiated until now.[86] In order to formalise the relationship, which was 'cemented through blood and sacrifice',[87] the two governments signed a Treaty of Friendship, Co-operation and Peace for a period of 25 years, with provision for renewal. Sheikh Mujibur Rahman and Mrs Indira Gandhi signed the treaty as part of a Joint Declaration when the latter came to pay her first visit

---

[83] Joint Indo-Bangladesh Declaration, 19 March 1972.

[84] Mujib described how Indira herself requested the heads of states of all the countries of the world to plead for his release.

[85] Mujib's address to the Indian army, 12 March 1972, *Bangabandhu Speaks*, published by the Ministry of Foreign Affairs, Government of Bangladesh, Dhaka, p. 53.

[86] The Awami League government has constantly denied that there was any secret pact with India. The Bangladesh Foreign Minister refused the claim of Moulana Bhashani that there was any secret pact between India and Bangladesh. *Bangladesh Observer*, 14 January 1973. The Indian Foreign Minister, while addressing the press on 23 January 1973 at New Delhi, said that there was no secret document or pact with Bangladesh. He claimed that the treaty was a public document and there was no secret arrangement between the two countries.

[87] Mrs. Indira Gandhi's statement at the Indian Parliament on 20 March 1972. *Bangladesh Documents*, Vol. II, p. 648, published by the Government of India.

to Bangladesh on 17 March 1972. The treaty, 'inspired by the common ideals of peace, secularism, democracy, socialism and nationalism', declared ten objectives in the preamble and included twelve articles in the body of the treaty.[88]

The objectives contained in the preamble made an emphatic assertion about the two countries having struggled together for the realisation of the above ideals. It expressed the determination of the two countries to 'transform their border into a border of eternal peace and friendship', and to safeguard peace, stability and security 'through all possible avenues of mutual co-operation'. Both governments were convinced that further development and co-operation would meet the natural interests of both states as well as the interest of lasting peace in Asia and the world, and that international problems could be solved only through co-operation and not through conflict or confrontation.

Article 1 of the treaty declared that, the two peoples having struggled and made sacrifices together, there would be lasting peace and friendship between them. Each side would respect the independence, sovereignty and territorial integrity of the other and refrain from interfering in its internal affairs. In Article 2 both states condemned colonialism and neo-colonialism in all forms and manifestations, and pledged that they would strive to eliminate them and lend assistance to those who were struggling against colonialism and racial discrimination and for national liberation. In Article 3 the two sides reaffirmed their faith in the policy of non-alignment and peaceful co-existence.

The important items on foreign relations, defence and the economy were contained in Articles 4-10 of the treaty. In Article 4 it was stipulated that both sides 'shall maintain regular contacts with each other on major international problems suffering the interests of both states' and they would hold meetings and exchange views 'at all levels'. Article 5 provided that they 'shall continue to strengthen and widen their mutually advantageous and all-round co-operation in the economic, scientific and technical fields'. The two countries 'shall develop mutual co-operation in the fields of trade, transport and communications between them on the basis of the principle of

---

[88] For the text of the Friendship Treaty, see Appendix E of Moudud Ahmed, *Bangladesh: Era of Sheikh Mujibur Rahman*.

'quality, mutual benefit' and the 'most favoured nation'. By Article 7, it was also stipulated that both countries 'shall promote relations in the fields of art, literature, education, culture, sports and health'.

One of the most significant clauses was contained in Article 6 of the treaty. By this article both sides agreed to make joint studies and 'take joint action in the fields of flood control, river basin development, the development of hydro-electricity, power and irrigation'.

Articles 8, 9 and 10 were of paramount importance as they related to both foreign and defence policies of the countries. Article 8 stipulated that no country 'shall enter into or participate in any military alliance directed against the other party' and each 'shall refrain from any aggression against the other'. Article 9 stipulated that each party 'shall refrain from giving assistance to any third party taking part in an armed conflict against the other party'. In case either party is attacked or threatened with attack, the parties 'shall immediately enter into mutual consultations in order to take appropriate effective measures to eliminate the threat and thus ensure the peace and security of their countries'. Article 10 stipulated that 'no party shall undertake any commitment, secret or open, towards one or more states which may be incompatible with the present Treaty'.

The Indo-Bangladesh treaty was part of a Joint Declaration of the two Prime Ministers and was formally signed on the concluding day of Mrs Gandhi's visit on 19 March 1972.[89] Besides the treaty, the Joint Declaration incorporated certain other significant decisions touching on the relationship between the two countries. The two Prime Ministers declared that the Indian Ocean area would be kept free of great power rivalries and military competition, and they expressed their determination to endeavour to make the Indian Ocean area 'a nuclear-free zone'. In order to strengthen cultural relations between the two countries, concrete steps were to be taken by signing a bilateral agreement of cultural, scientific and technological co-operation.

They took three important decisions. Firstly, transit trade and the agreement on border trade was to be revived. Secondly, they decided that 'in order to strengthen co-operation between the two countries,

---

[89] In the Joint Declaration signed on 19 March, the reason of signing such a treaty was mentioned in paragraph 8 as 'to give concrete expression to the similarity of views, ideals and interest between India and Bangladesh'.

there would be consultation in Foreign Affairs, Defence, Planning Commissions and the Ministries and Departments dealing with economic commercial, cultural and technical affairs of the two governments'. They decided that such consultations would take place periodically 'at least once every six months'. Thirdly, they decided to establish a Joint River Commission 'to carry on a comprehensive survey of the river systems shared by the two countries' and 'formulate projects concerning both the countries in the fields of flood control and to implement them'. They further determined to formulate detailed proposals on advance flood warnings, flood forecasting, the study of flood control and 'irrigation projects on the major river system and examine the feasibility of linking the power grids of Bangladesh with the adjoining areas of India',[90] so that the 'water resources of the region can be utilised on an equitable basis for the mutual benefit of the people of the two countries'.

The Joint Declaration and the Friendship Treaty envisaged the evaluation of an integrated system between the two countries on all vital national and international issues. According to the Indian Prime Minister, the treaty embodied the 'will of the two governments to pursue common policies in matters of interest to both countries' and solemnised 'the close ties of friendship between our two countries and peoples cemented through blood and sacrifice'.[91] With regard to the Joint Declaration, she said: 'it emphasises the importance of close co-ordination and co-operation between the two countries in trade and payments, economic development and transit'. The Indian Prime Minister invited the attention of the members of her Parliament to that portion of the declaration 'which deals with the existing prospect of harnessing the waters of Brahmaputra, Meghna and the Ganges to the benefit of the two peoples'.

Almost all the opposition parties in Bangladesh demanded that the treaty be rescinded, the first person to do so being Moulana Bhashani. He was the leader of the Seven-Party Action Committee,

---

[90] On 4 January 1973 an Indo-Bangladesh Agreement was signed for setting up a Joint Power Co-ordination Board to study the possibility of exchanging surplus power of the two countries. *Bangladesh Observer*, 5 January 1973.

[91] The text of the treaty and the Joint Declaration were placed on the table of the Indian Lok Sabha and Mrs. Gandhi made a statement on the floor of the House on the same day. Mrs. Gandhi's statement in Parliament, *Bangladesh Documents*, Volume II, p. 648.

formed on 29 December 1972, and this was the first of fifteen demands made by the committee. They apprehended that the treaty had been signed not in the interest of Bangladesh, but to guarantee India its influence and domination over the future course of Bangladesh. India had signed the treaty in order to extend and strengthen its sphere of influence over the sub-continent. The Treaty expired in 1997 and was not renewed.

Water Sharing and Farakka

Ganga — the Ganges as the British would call it, the goddess of rivers — carries nearly 2 million cusecs of fresh water originating from the Indo-China border on the mighty Himalayas. It constitutes one of the largest river basins for India, touching seven of its central and northeastern states.[92] This river, some 2,500 kilometres long, provides habitation for 250 million people in the region comprising India, Nepal and Bangladesh. The river originates partly in Indian territory, but the water is supplemented substantially by the three rivers of Nepal,[93] which constitute 40 per cent of the total annual inflow. The river enters Bangladesh in the northwest and flows into the Bay of Bengal after travelling through eight of the country's nineteen districts and one of its two seaports. Altogether 35 million people in Bangladesh live close to the Ganges — one-third of its entire population — and the area affected by its flow covers 51,800 square kilometres, which is more than one-third of the total area of the country. During the monsoons, this international river takes the form of a rough sea flooding the surrounding areas in Bangladesh, helping to drain more than 60,000 square kilometres and carrying millions of tons of silted soil to make the land fertile for agriculture. The flow prevents the saline water of the sea from entering the mainland. In the lean period from January to May, when the impact of the monsoon diminishes, the flow of water falls to a mere 60,000-65,000 cusecs. This is the period when water is required most for the cultivation of land and the production of food grains, upon which depend the life

---

[92] For all technical information the author has relied on the research conducted by Khurshida Begum, *Tension over the Farakka Barrage* (Dhaka: The University Press Limited, 1987).

[93] The Kosi, Gandak and Karnala.

and death of millions of people who have been relying on the same source for thousands of years. Bangladesh is a lower riparian recipient of an international river and is dependent on agriculture as the main source of income for those who live in this area. The people relying on the river need its water during the lean period because this is when the farmers grow their principal rice crop, 'amon'.

When the British colonised India, Calcutta emerged as the most important centre of trade and business for the East India Company and the Hooghly River provided its only outlet to the sea. The value and importance of the port of Calcutta at the mouth of Hooghly River increased day by day. The volume of trade and the amount of profits earned by British merchants depended largely on the flow of water into the Hooghly river and on its navigational capacity. During the period of British rule, Calcutta assumed an important place both for politics and for the exploitation of resources, and eventually it turned into the largest city in India. So since the middle of the nineteenth century, the imperial government had taken steps to resolve the problems of water flow and navigation of the Hooghly river and a number of studies had been conducted by British experts who were opposed to disrupting the natural flow of the Ganges water.

Soon after its independence in 1947, India took a different stance, more because of its political antagonism towards Pakistan than to resolve the problems of the Hooghly river. Experts were engaged to build a barrage over the Ganges to divert its water in order to irrigate the vast region of central and western India as far as Rajasthan. Ignoring all international conventions and practices, and despite opposition from the Pakistan government, India proceeded with its scheme to nourish its own land with the water of others and to integrate the entire water of the Ganges into a national water grid.[94] India needed all the water it could get for its own massive irrigational projects, for which it was building feeder canals up to Rajasthan.[95]

---

[94] K. L. Rao, *India's Water Wealth* (New Delhi: Orient Longman, 1979), pp. 230-37.

[95] The author, as the Co-Chairman of the Joint River Commission, was given to understand by his Indian counterparts that India needed all the water of the Ganges, and that by augmentation India always meant diversion of water from the Brahmaputra to the Ganges by a link canal cutting across from the east to the west of Bangladesh's land mass, destroying the entire ecosystem.

As long ago as 1951 India took the initiative of preparing a grand rrigational scheme that included the Ganga-Kaveri link, connecting the Ganges in the north with Kaveri in the southern state of Madras. The Farakka Barrage was conceived only as part of this scheme for diversion of the Ganges water for irrigational purposes. In October 1951 when this news started to appear in newspapers, the central government of Pakistan demanded that India consult with it before proceeding with the scheme.[96] A series of letters between the two governments gave rise to a formal recognition of the Ganges water dispute, which was taken up in two meetings at the senior level in 1960. Two more meetings were held in 1961 and one in 1962, but after that no formal contact was made for over six years until May 1968. Finally, in December of the same year, a meeting between two Secretaries was held at New Delhi. Two meetings were held in each of the years 1969 and 1970 at the level of Secretary, but without any progress. In the meantime India had gone a long way towards building the barrage. In 1960-61 the design had been finally approved, and construction commenced in 1962. It took more than ten years to complete the work.

There was little that Pakistan could have done except to register a protest with India. Moreover, this issue, involving East Pakistan, was less of a priority for the ruling elite of Pakistan than the dispute with India over the Indus basin. Meanwhile, in order to weaken its principal enemy further, India lent full support to the campaign for the removal of East Pakistan from the sovereign authority of Pakistan.

Once Bangladesh had been born with the active assistance of India; the political circumstances surrounding the Farakka Barrage changed. The barrage had earlier been conceived as a way of irrigating India while at the same time destroying Pakistan economically by withdrawing water from its major rivers. Now it created an embarrassing situation for both India and Bangladesh. While India had to go ahead with the barrage project for its own socio-economic reasons, Bangladesh could not let it proceed as its entire survival depended on the water of the Ganges.

---

[96] See for detail, Khurshida Begum, *Tension over the Farakka Barrage*, pp. 90-95, UPL, Dhaka 1987.

By the time Bangladesh became an independent state, the construction of the barrage had been completed and it was ready for a trial run to test the supply of water to the feeder canals, which had already been built to carry the water away to the irrigational schemes. By that time, flushing of the Hooghly River had already commenced. When this news reached the Bangladesh side, the issue was taken up officially with the Indian government. There was no discussion of the issue when Mujib met Mrs Gandhi at Delhi on his way back to Bangladesh after his captivity in Pakistan. But soon after, B. M. Abbas, an eminent water expert and adviser to the Bangladesh Prime Minister, took up the issue at an official level with the Foreign Minister of India.

In March 1972, when the two countries signed their 25-year Friendship Treaty,[97] Article 6 stated that the countries agreed to make joint studies and take joint action in the fields of flood control, river basin development and the development of hydroelectric power and irrigation. Following this treaty a Joint River Commission (JRC)[98] was formed with one chairman and three members from each country; the chairmanship of the Commission was to rotate annually between the two countries.

The function of the Commission was vague, limited to maintaining 'liaison' between the two countries to maximise the benefits from common river systems, to formulate flood control works 'and to recommend implementation of joint projects'. However, the water of the Ganges and the Farakka Barrage turned out to be its most pressing concern. Although the statute of the Commission did not mention the Farakka Barrage or the Ganges water specifically, the issue was brought within the purview of the Commission with the consent of both sides.

At three meetings of the Commission in 1972, three further meetings in 1973 and a ministerial meeting held in July 1972, both sides agreed that the Farakka Barrage would not start operation

---

[97] The Treaty of Friendship, Co-operation and Peace was signed on 19 March 1972 in Dhaka by Sheikh Mujibur Rahman and Mrs. Gandhi when the latter paid the first official visit. For detailed discussion of the treaty, see Moudud Ahmed, *Era of Sheikh Mujibur Rahman*, pp. 219-25.

[98] See the statute of the Joint River Commission in Khurshida Begum, *Tension over the Farakka Barrage*, Appendix B (Dhaka: The University Press Limited, 1987), p. 255.

unless a mutually acceptable solution was arrived at.[99] However, in the lean period of that year India suddenly opened its feeder canals to withdraw water unilaterally, without any agreement on the sharing of water with Bangladesh. Mujib immediately took up the matter with the Indian Prime Minister and finally, at the summit held in May 1974 between the two leaders, a full discussion took place on the Ganges water and the Farakka Barrage. At this meeting, India emphasised that the barrage had to be commissioned or made operational by the end of 1974, but at the insistence of Mujib it was agreed that an arrangement for water sharing would be made tentatively for an interim period. In the meantime, the Commission would study how best the water resources of the region could be augmented for utilisation of both the countries. It was also decided at the meeting that the composition of the Commission would be raised to ministerial level, thereby demonstrating its importance.

In order to materialise the decision of the summit, and as India was keen to begin operation of the barrage, frequent meetings of the Commission were held — as many as five meetings after the summit in 1974. Finally, at the meetings held in February and April 1975 an ad hoc agreement was reached between the two sides. In the 41-day lean period beginning on 21 April and ending on 31 May, the water would be shared as shown in Table 3.3.

Table 3.3 **Arrangement to share the Ganga as per the *ad hoc* agreement, 1975**[100]

Date of withdrawal	Withdrawal by India (cusecs)	Balance left for Bangladesh (cusecs)
21-30 April	11,000	44,000
1-10 May	12,000	44,500
11-20 May	15,000	44,250
21-30 May	16,000	40,500

Although Bangladesh had been receiving all the available water of the Ganges during the lean period and now was to be deprived of 11,000-16,000 cusecs of water, in the circumstances the arrangement

---

[99] White Paper on the Ganges Water Dispute (Government of Bangladesh), September 1976, p. 5, UPL, Dhaka 1989.

[100] Khurshida Begum, *Tension over the Farakka Barrage*, p. 111, UPL, Dhaka, 1987.

was found to be not a totally unsatisfactory one for Bangladesh, and the agreement was considered as a credit to the efforts of Sheikh Mujib. On the other hand, despite all the goodwill that existed between the two countries and the personality of Sheikh Mujib to lead Bangladesh on this issue, the failure to arrive at a permanent arrangement with India was seen as a great weakness on the part of the Awami League leadership. Moreover, a suspicion that India had made temporary concessions to achieve its immediate goal of commissioning the barrage was substantiated at a later stage when water was withdrawn without any notice. Even during the term of the agreement, India violated its provisions by not allowing a joint team at Farakka to record the discharge of water into the feeder canals and to measure the quantum of the residual water.

Following the death of Sheikh Mujib in August 1975, India took full advantage of the political vacuum in Bangladesh and continued to withdraw water unilaterally. So in 1976 Bangladesh was denied its share of water, and despite repeated attempts made from the Bangladesh side, India remained totally unresponsive. Since Bangladesh was a small neighbour and a lower riparian country, the impact of this action was extremely severe. Added to this, throughout 1976, Bangladesh suffered attacks along its border from India, organised by some of the more ardent followers of Mujib, supported by the Indian Border Security Force (BSF). These attacks, which aimed 'to liberate the country once again', only caused the relationship between the two countries to deteriorate further.

Having found no alternative, Bangladesh decided to take up the water issue in the world forums and made serious efforts to mobilise public opinion, achieving considerable success.[101] Much to the embarrassment of India, the Farakka issue was then raised on the floor of the United Nations.[102] In the General Committee meeting held in September 1976, Bangladesh made a formal request to include the issue of the Farakka Barrage and the Ganges water in the agenda of the General Assembly and also to refer the matter to the

---

[101] Moudud Ahmed, *Democracy and the Challenge of Development* (Dhaka: The University Press Limited, 1995), p. 54.

[102] See A.B.M. Abbas, AT, *The Ganges Water Dispute* White Paper on the Ganges Water Dispute, MOU 1982, MOU 1985.

Special Political Committee of the General Assembly. This request was accepted despite India's vehement opposition and the mobilisation of a counter force aligned to the Soviet bloc. India maintained its stance of bilateralism, arguing that the dispute was between two neighbouring states and as such could be solved by mutual consultation. It also stated that it was willing to negotiate with Bangladesh. In this spirit, effort was made to reach a compromise formula, so that the matter did not roll on any further.

On 24 November 1976 the UN Committee met again, and India and Bangladesh agreed to a consensus text worked out by a group of non-aligned countries. This was adopted by the Committee on the proposal of its Chairman on the same day, and by the General Assembly at its 80th plenary meeting on 26 November 1976. The important portion of the consensus statement, captioned 'Situation arising out of the Unilateral Withdrawal of the Ganges waters at Farakka', read:

> The parties affirmed their adherence to the Declaration on Principles of International Law concerning Friendly Relations and Co-operation among states in accordance with the Charter of the United Nations and stressed, in this regard, their unalterable commitment to strengthen their 'bilateral relation' by applying these principles in the settlement of disputes ... The parties undertook to give due consideration to the most appropriate ways of utilising the capacity of the United Nations system. It is open to either party to report to the General Assembly at the thirty-second session on the progress achieved in the settlement of the problem.[103]

The statement included a clause that the two sides would 'meet urgently at Dhaka at the Ministerial level for negotiation with an aim of arriving at a fair and expeditious settlement'.

Bangladesh did not expect that the issue of sharing water would be resolved at the UN, but it achieved what it wanted. Although it was a humiliation for India, which felt bitter about it, India was relieved to have brought the matter out of the UN system and restrained Bangladesh from going into any kind of multilateral forum

---

[103] Khurshida Begum, *Tension over the Farakka Barrage*, p. 170, UPL, Dhaka 1987.

for a decision that would have affected its ultimate interest in the water. It was able to take Bangladesh back to a bilateral negotiation, leaving the instruments of manoeuvre in its own hands.

Nevertheless the consensus statement, adopted in a world body, had established and recognised the case of Bangladesh and forced India at least to negotiate for a settlement. Once out of the UN, India followed its normal bureaucratic procedure of negotiation, which allowed the lean period of 1977 also to pass by without any water for Bangladesh. After the adoption of the consensus statement, the two sides met four times up to April 1977 at the level of ministers, and three times up to September 1977 at the level of officials. Finally, at a ministerial meeting on 5 November 1977, a formal agreement was signed by both sides for a period of five years, renewable by mutual agreement.[104]

By this agreement, Bangladesh committed itself to co-operating in finding a solution to the long-term problem of augmenting the flow of the Ganges in the dry season. The quantum of water to be received by Bangladesh for the lean period commencing on 1 January and ending on 31 May was specified for each ten days. In addition, the agreement contained a minimum guarantee clause for Bangladesh, providing that at no stage or time would the release of water to Bangladesh shown in column 4 of the schedule of water sharing fall below 80 per cent. According to this agreement, the minimum quantity of water that Bangladesh was to receive in a normal lean period was 34,500 cusecs between 21 and 30 April, and the maximum was 58,500 cusecs between 1 and 10 January. The sharing of water under the agreement is detailed in Table 3.4.

Although in the agreement of 1977 much importance was attached to the role and function of JRC, the record shows that the importance and role of JRC gradually declined, as it could not make any substantial progress in resolving the water issue between the two countries. On the contrary, decisions taken unilaterally at the political level in India went contrary to the spirit and role of JRC. The meetings of JRC turned out to be mere rituals for exchanging views without producing any substantive result. Since the issue of

---

[104] *Ibid.*, Appendix F, pp. 262-68.

Table 3.4 Water sharing under the agreement of November 1977

Period	Flows reaching Farakka (cusecs)[a]	Withdrawal by India at Farakka (cusecs)	Released to Bangladesh (cusecs)
1-10 January	98,500	40,000	58,500
11-20 January	89,750	38,500	51,250
21-31 January	82,500	35,000	47,500
1-10 February	79,250	33,000	46,250
11-20 February	74,000	31,500	42,500
21-28/29 February	70,000	30,750	39,250
1-10 March	65,250	26,750	38,500
11-20 March	63,500	25,500	38,000
21-31 March	61,000	25,000	36,000
1-10 April	59,000	24,000	35,000
11-20 April	55,500	20,750	34,750
21-30 April	55,000	20,500	34,500
1-10 May	56,500	21,500	35,000
11-20 May	59,250	24,000	35,250
21-31 May	65,500	26,750	38,750

Note: [a] Based on 75% availability from observed data, 1948-73.

Farakka became more a matter of political decision, the forum lost its significance and failed to play its due role. In 1980 four meetings of JRC were held, but no decision was ever reached, and at the end of the meeting held in July 1980 only a joint press release was issued.[105]

The agreement of 1977 had bound Bangladesh to find a solution to the problem of augmenting the flows of the Ganges during the dry season. When the JRC meeting in January 1978 decided that each side should submit its proposals for such augmentation, keeping in view a long-term solution of the problem, Bangladesh proposed to build reservoirs upstream. This immediately implied the involvement of Nepal, requiring tripartite regional co-operation — a key strategic approach that Bangladesh adopted throughout. India, in contrast, maintained its fundamental approach of bilateralism, rejecting any proposal involving a third country and insisting on its own proposal for a Ganga-Brahmaputra Link Canal to augment the water of the Ganges.

---

[105] *Ibid.*, p. 258.

As a result, neither proposal was acceptable to the other side nor they continued to reject each other's proposals. At various times, different joint committees were formed at the expert level, but no solution to the problem of augmenting the Ganges water could be found because of the irreconcilable position taken by each side. India continued to build barrages over at least twelve other rivers, but when Bangladesh raised the question of sharing the water of other common rivers, India did not respond. It was busy pursuing its own exclusive interest in utilising the water of the region. While Bangladesh claimed to have 54 common rivers, India claimed to have only nine large rivers, others being only tributaries. So since the signing of the agreement in 1977, each side has taken its own position and the role and function of the JRC has become inoperative in the real sense.

When Mrs Gandhi returned to power in 1980, the Congress government termed the guarantee clause of the 1977 agreement unfair and rejected the involvement of Nepal on the basis of its principle of bilateralism. Consequently, the situation deteriorated further. In the lean period of 1980 — the third year of the implementation of the 1977 agreement — the Joint Committee revealed a shortage of flow caused by India's withdrawal of water upstream through the feeder canals. This activity, in violation of the guarantee clause, was depriving Bangladesh of its due share of water. So when the implementation of the agreement was revised under its own terms at the expiry of three years, no progress towards a long-term solution was recorded. On the contrary, a reduced flow of water in the dry season was giving increased cause for concern. So although the agreement of 1977 subsisted for five years, the guarantee clause ceased to bring any benefit to Bangladesh after the dry season of 1980, and the hope of evolving any long-term solution subsided soon after the review report was submitted in April 1981.

The agreement of 1977 was due to expire on 4 November 1982 and on its expiry there would be no water for Bangladesh, which could put the country into a desperate situation. Since the signing of the agreement with a non-Congress government, the political situation had also changed in India. By the time Mrs Gandhi had returned to power with an added popular mandate, Ziaur Rahman had been killed; Ershad had overthrown an elected BNP government and taken over power in Bangladesh. For his political survival, Ershad followed a safer non-confrontational policy with India. As he took over power from the BNP, Ershad wooed the Awami League for political support. An invisible alliance developed between them[106], which had a direct bearing on Ershad's foreign policy towards India. Despite the fact that Bangladesh had certain disputes with India on issues of vital national importance, Ershad did not play them up or turn them into public issues. As a result, during the nine-year period of his rule, none of the important issues involving the two counties was seriously addressed.

Nevertheless, since the 1977 agreement was about to expire, Ershad took up the issue at his meeting with Mrs Gandhi in October 1982. As a gesture of goodwill towards Ershad, the agreement was extended for a period of eighteen months without the guarantee clause, which Ershad accepted without any protest. A Memorandum of Understanding (MOU) was signed, emphasising the necessity of augmenting the Ganges, which the JRC would examine in order to find a long-term solution. As usual, during the eighteen months the JRC made no progress, but Bangladesh did receive some water during this period. Both sides submitted their respective updated proposals, which were again found to be unacceptable by the other side, and the JRC again failed to make any recommendation.

Although this arrangement for sharing water, based on the agreement of 1977, lost its effectiveness in the absence of the guarantee clause, its extension was necessary for Bangladesh both for domestic political reasons and to assert the right of Bangladesh, as a lower riparian country, to share water under an international agreement. Bangladesh always strove for a permanent arrangement to share the Ganges water, but never succeeded. It only received the guaranteed quantum of water for the first three years of the 1977 agreement and during the lean period of 1975 on the basis of the ad hoc agreement of that year. When the expiry of the MOU of 1982 was approaching, Bangladesh once again made efforts at the JRC level to resolve the issue, but India showed very little interest other

---

[106] For more detail about the political support Ershad received from India and the Awami League after the take-over, see Moudud Ahmed, *Democracy and the Challenge of Development* (Dhaka: The University Press Limited).

than repeating its proposal of building the link canal. Bangladesh has consistently tried to separate the sharing of existing water from the issue of augmentation whereas India has always linked the two.

The MOU of 1982 duly expired in April 1984. At the meeting of Commonwealth Heads of Government held at Nassau in October 1985, Ershad met Rajiv Gandhi. They agreed to extend the sharing arrangement, based on the MOU of 1982 and including no guarantee clause, from the dry season of 1986 for a period of three years.

Again in order to find a long-term solution it was agreed that a joint study would be undertaken at the expert level to locate alternative sources of water from other common rivers for augmentation of the Ganges. The report submitted by the Joint Committee of Experts only revealed the glaring differences between the two sides on the issue, and once more established the failure of the JRC. After considerable pressure and persuasion at the JRC level, an agreement was arrived at on sharing water from the Teesta river. This was an achievement because on the downstream part of the Teesta river Bangladesh has built a barrage of its own which had to be commissioned soon.

As a small and lower riparian country, and one without strong political leadership, Bangladesh continued to remain at the mercy of India with regard to its water supply. Whatever right or recognition it could establish due to the strong leadership of Mujib in 1974-75 and the courage of Ziaur Rahman in taking the issue to the UN in 1976, Bangladesh and India could not come to any permanent arrangement for sharing the Ganges water due to the failure of the political leadership in Bangladesh. For India too, due to its selfishness and the lack of foresight on the part of its leaders, an unresolved Farakka was to continue to be a source of irritation and strain in the relationship between the two countries, which was already bedevilled with suspicion and bad faith.

From 1988 onwards, the whole of the Ganges water came under the total control of India. In the absence of any agreement or understanding, India was withdrawing water unilaterally to suit its own needs and Bangladesh was receiving only what was left over, if anything. In one recent year, 1994, Bangladesh received only 9,000 cusecs of water in the lean period when it was to have received

34,500 cusecs under the 1977 agreement. Having had no meeting at all for several years, the JRC became a dormant organisation, and a proposal to dissolve it came under active consideration. After 1982, when the guarantee clause could no longer be implemented due to a reduced flow of water, India maintained that there was not enough water in the Ganges to share. Given India's priority of fulfilling its own internal commitments, the Ganges could not provide any guaranteed quantum of water for Bangladesh. Whatever amount of water India's feeder canals could not absorb, Bangladesh would be entitled to the residual quantum only.

In 1991 when the democratic government of BNP came to power in Bangladesh, it immediately took up the matter with the Indian government, and the first meeting between the two sides at the Secretary level was held in October 1991. In May 1992, when the Prime Minister of Bangladesh visited India, the matter was discussed at length at the summit level and the Indian Prime Minister gave an assurance that adequate steps would be taken to prevent Bangladesh from suffering a shortage of water. It was decided that the two ministers concerned would meet immediately and that joint action would be taken to monitor water flows in various rivers running through both countries. Accordingly, when the ministers met Bangladesh emphasised the need for a permanent agreement on sharing the Ganges water as well as the water of common rivers.[107] In 1993 another meeting at the Secretary level was held, but because of lack of interest on the part of India the matter did not proceed further.

After nearly two years of silence, the Bangladesh Prime Minister raised the issue with the Indian Prime Minister in May 1995 during the SAARC Summit at New Delhi. As a result, the two Foreign Secretaries held two meetings to discuss the water issue, and after their meeting in Dhaka in June 1995 it was announced in the joint press conference that India had pledged to find a permanent settlement to the question of the Ganges water.[108] In the meantime, Prime Minister Begum Khaleda Zia raised the issue at the General Assembly of the UN and discussed the issue with the Prime Minister of Nepal when she visited that country in 1995.

---

[107] Pani Chukti, *Shuvankarer Faki* (BNP, no date), Dhaka.
[108] *Ibid.*

To summarise, from the time the Farakka Barrage was commissioned for a trial run in 1971-72, the year Bangladesh achieved its independence, until the ad hoc agreement was signed at the initiative of Sheikh Mujib in April 1975, the flow of discharge from the Ganges was totally dependent on India, which had withdrawn water from the river without any agreement. The terms of the *ad hoc* agreement could not be fully implemented because Mujib was killed before the lean period arrived in 1976. After the agreement signed in 1977, commencing from the lean period of 1978, Bangladesh received the allocated quantum of water. However, although the agreement was stipulated to run for five years, Bangladesh received the water for only three years because after the Indian Congress party returned to power, the government of India claimed that there was not enough water at the Farakka. Consequently, it refused to give Bangladesh the water guaranteed by the Agreement of 1977 for the lean periods of 1981 and 1982. From 1982 to 1988 there was no agreement as such, excepting a Memorandum of Understanding signed by Ershad in 1982 and extended in 1985. As this memorandum and its extension were without any guarantee clause, it carried very little importance. From 1988 until 1996 there was no agreement at all. So from 1972 to 1996, except for the four lean periods of 1975, 1978, 1979 and 1980, Bangladesh has been deprived of its share of the Ganges water for 21 years and has been completely at the mercy of India with regard to its availability.

Soon after the Awami League, a party historically aligned to India, was elected to power in Bangladesh in June 1996, India sought to resolve the Farakka issue. The two sides negotiated and reached a settlement of the issue that had strained relations between the two countries for more than two decades. A treaty was concluded between the two governments and was signed by the respective Prime Ministers on 12 December 1996 in New Delhi. The conclusion of the treaty on sharing the Ganges water, within six months of its assuming power, was a historical triumph for the new government.

The treaty[109] to remain in force for 30 years stipulates the quantum of water to be shared by each country for the lean period from

---

[109] See the Water Treaty signed on 12 December 1996.

1 January to 31 May each year. The period is divided into blocks of ten days and there is a provision of 35,000 cusecs of water for each country in alternate ten-day periods between 1 March and 10 May — the leanest time when the water is most needed. The sharing of water and its quantum has been based on the availability of water at Farakka corresponding to average flows of the period from 1949 to 1988, estimated at around 60,000-75,000 cusecs between 1 March and 10 May. The arrangements for the sharing of water are annexed to the treaty and are reproduced in Table 3.5.

Table 3.5 Water sharing under the agreement of December 1996

Annexe I		
Availability at Farakka	Share of India	Share of Bangladesh
70,000 cusecs or less	50%	50%
70,000-75,000 cusecs	Balance of flow	35,000 cusecs
75,000 cusecs or more	40,000 cusecs	Balance of flow

Subject to the condition that India and Bangladesh shall each receive a guaranteed 35,000 cusecs of water in alternate ten-day periods during the period 1 March to 10 May.

Annexe II

Schedule

Sharing of waters at Farakka between 1 January and 31 May every year.
If actual availability corresponds to average flows of the period 1949 to 1988, the implication of the formula in Annexe I for the share of each side is:

Period	Average total flow, 1949–88 (cusecs)	India's share (cusecs)	Bangladesh's share (cusecs)
1-10 January	107,516	40,000	67,516
11-20 January	97,673	40,000	50,154
21-31 January	90,154	40,000	50,154
1-10 February	86,323	40,000	46,323
11-20 February	82,859	40,000	42,859
21-28/29 February	79,106	40,000	39,106
1-10 March	74,419	39,419	35,000
11-20 March	68,931	33,931	35,000
21-31 March	64,688	35,000	29,688
1-10 April	63,180	28,180	35,000
11-20 April	62,633	35,000	27,633
21-30 April	60,992	25,992	35,000
1-10 May	67,351	35,000	32,351
11-20 May	73,590	38,590	35,000
21-31 May	81,854	40,000	41,854

In Article II (iii), the treaty stipulates that if the flow of water at Farakka falls below 50,000 cusecs in any ten-day period, the two governments will enter into immediate consultation to make adjustments on an emergency basis, in accordance with the principles of equity, fair play and no harm to either party.

Article X of the treaty provides for a review of the sharing arrangement by the two governments at five-year intervals or earlier, as required by either party for necessary adjustments. It would, however, be opened to either party to seek the first review after two years to assess the impact and working of the sharing arrangement as contained in the treaty.

In Article XI it is further provided that in the absence of mutual agreement on adjustment following reviews under Article X, India will release downstream of Farakka Barrage water at a rate not less than 90 per cent of the share of Bangladesh according to the formula envisaged in Article II, until such time as mutually agreed flows are decided upon by the parties.

A Joint Committee comprising representatives of both governments will be responsible for the implementation of the arrangement contained in the treaty. If there is any difference of opinion, it will be referred to the Joint River Commission and if the dispute still remains unresolved it will be referred then to the two governments, which will meet regularly at the appropriate level to resolve it by mutual discussion.

Once again the people of Bangladesh did not know the terms of this treaty, which is of national importance, until it was signed. The opposition parties and a vocal section of media within the country came out with sharp reactions. While the spirit of resolving the dispute was welcome, the method of signing the treaty and its basic terms were strongly criticised.

The secrecy maintained in signing the treaty was intriguing. It is not known why the whole nation was kept in the dark. There was no national debate, either in the media or in Parliament. The parties, including the Awami League, had no opportunity of looking at the terms of the treaty. It was negotiated by the Awami League only whose leadership alone knew the terms that were agreed to. The principal opposition party, the BNP, was not consulted, nor was the nation taken into confidence. In a matter involving national sovereignty, where every citizen desires that the issue should be resolved peacefully, a national consensus is essential. In such a complicated international conflict resolution, where the terms of treaties are likely to be arranged on a give-and-take basis, it is wise to take the people into confidence, so that the success or failure of such a treaty and its implementation can be shared by successive governments. Such a treaty could not be a purely partisan affair.

Suspicion surrounded two important questions. The first was why had India, which for more than 22 years[110] deprived Bangladesh of its legitimate share of water and had always played the role of an unresponsive neighbour, suddenly become so enthusiastic about signing a treaty for a period of 30 years? The withdrawal of water at Farakka, unilaterally and most of the time at India's discretion, has already caused colossal damage to the land and people of Bangladesh, the value of which runs into billions of dollars. It has destroyed the agriculture, forestry and fishery industries due to salinity from the sea tides, and also damaged navigation and communications. It has caused floods, drought, erosion, pollution and an ecological imbalance in the entire region affecting a population of nearly 36 million. According to an estimate by the Bangladesh Water Development Board, losses just on certain major items from 1975 to 1988 come to Tk.26,448 million.[111]

Even during the first Awami League government in 1972-75, the Indian government had shown extreme reluctance about coming to any long-term agreement. At the instance of a lofty personality like Sheikh Mujib it agreed only to an ad hoc sharing of water, which in any case did not materialise after Mujib's death. In the last two years of the 1977 Agreement, during the lean period of 1981 and 1982, India in blatant violation of the Agreement did not give the agreed share of water, on the ground that there was not enough water at Farakka. The two MOUs signed during the government of Ershad up to 1988 were nominal, ineffective instruments without any guarantee

---

[110] Other than in the lean period of three years, 1978, 1979 and 1980, Bangladesh did not receive its agreed share of water.

[111] Professor M. Shahjahan, 'Dividing the Ganges', a paper presented in a seminar at Dhaka, March 1997, Table 4.

clause, and from 1988 until 1996 — including the entire five-year period of BNP government — India declined to agree to any water-sharing arrangement. Now, less than six months after the Awami League had returned to power, the Indian government had readily agreed to sign an agreement for 30 years. The reasons for such a change of mind were obviously a matter of some conjecture.

Secondly, the important question at the very heart of the treaty relates to: the availability of water at Farakka during the lean period. The entire sharing arrangement of 1996 is based on a hypothetical availability of a quantum of water calculated on an average of 40 years from 1948 to 1988, showing a greater amount than has ever been available according to the record India had shown in the past. Even in the agreement signed in 1977, based on 75 per cent availability calculated from the recorded flows of the Ganges at Farakka from 1948 to 1973, when hardly any water was withdrawn upstream by India, the flow of water shown in the lean period from 1 March to 20 May was 3,000-14,000 cusecs less than shown in the 1996 agreement.[112] It is common knowledge that the flow was continuously depleting as the Indian states of Uttar Pradesh, Bihar and West Bengal increasingly withdrew thousands of cusecs of water during these years. Moreover, the water flow from 1988 to 1996 was also not taken into the calculation to determine the average flow.

India has persistently maintained in every round of negotiation since 1981 that in the lean period, the amount of water available at Farakka has never been more than 55,000 cusecs,[113] but now, after nearly seventeen years, it is shown at 74,419 cusecs during 1-10 March and 73,590 cusecs during 11-20 May. In the 1977 agreement, the available water shown during 11-20 April was 55,500 cusecs and during 21-30 April was 55,000 cusecs, but for the same period after nearly twenty years the availability of water is shown as 62,633 cusecs and 60,992 cusecs respectively. The experts on both sides of the border have called the inflated amount of water shown to be available and shared by the parties in the treaty imaginary, even fake.

---

[112] See Table 3.6.

[113] As Deputy Prime Minister and Co-Chairman of the Joint River Commission, the author was given this figure repeatedly by his Indian counterparts and the Indian authorities.

According to Devesh Mukherjee, a retired General Manager of Farakka Barrage, since the dam has been commissioned, "Water levels have been steadily falling and there is not as much water for sharing as is projected in the Treaty. The calculations are based on poor arithmetic".[114] He goes on to say 'For instance, the Treaty claims that between April 1 and 10, about 63,180 cusecs of water would be available at Farakka but the average for the past five years has been just 51,000 cusecs. The same problem applies to the figures for May.' What these numbers mean is that India may have worked out a treaty on the basis of outdated figures.[115] According to Sardindu Chattapaddayah of the Center for Research in Indo-Bangladesh Relations, 'Politics has triumphed over logic and reason.'[116] Ashim Das Gupta, the Finance Minister of West Bengal, who was credited with working out the modalities of the treaty, maintained that 'he had no option but to fall back on the 1949-88 figures as there was no joint monitoring of the water level since 1988'. 'The situation has changed considerably since. The last few years have indeed seen a decline in the water level at Farakka. The main reason is that with as many as 400 irrigation points along the Ganga, Uttar Pradesh and Bihar now siphon off anything between 25,000 cusecs and 45,000 cusecs before the river reaches Farakka. 'The old figures simply don't mirror the present.'[117]

Calcutta-based experts were critical of the treaty because they feared that such inflated figures of the amount of water available would affect India more than Bangladesh, and particularly the port of Calcutta, as the Bhagirathi and Hooghly rivers would get less water. The BJP leader, when the party was in opposition, called the treaty a 'bluff'. Bangladesh experts echoed this view with regard to the availability of water, calling it fake and without specific foundation.[118] The treaty suffers from 'Vagueness, inconsistencies, superfluidity and inadequacies', according to Professor Mohammed Moniruzzaman Mia, a water expert and former Vice Chancellor of Dhaka University. He called

---

[114] See *India Today*, 15 January 1997.
[115] *Ibid.*
[116] *Ibid.*
[117] *Ibid.*
[118] *Weekly Holiday*, 14 March 1997.

the treaty 'a cleverly devised mechanism to bleed [Bangladesh] white' and 'unworkable and totally against the legitimate interests of Bangladesh'.[119]

These apprehensions came true as soon as the treaty was put into operation. It is not just that Bangladesh was receiving much less water this time than it received in previous years when there was no treaty.[120] It was also receiving much less than had been allocated in the treaty. On 6 March, Bangladesh received 18,750 cusecs of water at the Hardinge Bridge when it was supposed to be receiving 35,000 cusecs for 1-10 March. On 10 March the amount received went down to 18,000 cusecs. On 27 March the water flow went down to the lowest level of 6,457 cusecs when Bangladesh was supposed to be receiving 29,688 cusecs between 21 and 31 March.[121] Again from 11 to 20 March, Bangladesh received only 21,000 cusecs against the agreed share of 35,000 cusecs and for the next 10-day slot the share was even less.[122]

India tried to defend itself by saying that 'the Treaty has run into rough weather because of insufficient rains during the preceding months'.[123] The Water Minister of India, while admitting that Bangladesh had not received the agreed share, was quoted as saying in their Parliament that the shortage was due to the fact that not enough snow had melted in the Himalayas. The Water Minister of Bangladesh also admitted in his Parliament that Bangladesh had not received the agreed share, but argued that at least there was an agreement. Sardindu Chattaphadhyaya said: 'That the Treaty has gone awry comes as no surprise. It was destined to fail because of its faulty data.'[124] The treaty that was supposed to wash away the 'hate and suspicion' that had divided the two countries was now in 'danger of being reduced to a meaningless document ... it turns out that the Treaty talked about water that just is not there'.

---

[119] Professor Moniruzzaman Miah, *Water Treaty without Water*, p. 21. The Envoy Vol. 1 No. 1, June 15-30, 1997.

[120] See for detail, *Holiday*, 14 March, 1997.

[121] See *Janakantha*, 31 March 97, and the *Independent*, 7 April 1997.

[122] *India Today*, 30 April 1997.

[123] *Ibid.*

[124] *Ibid.*

The treaty has been criticised for being too vague and flexible, completely hypothetical and so unmarketable. It enumerated a great many options, mostly to be exercised by India since the source as well as the discharge of water at Farakka remained completely under its control. In the absence of any guarantee clause — such as the one in 1977 by which Bangladesh was entitled to have at least 80 per cent of the allocated water, whatever the total quantum available — it could now expect only 90 per cent of 50 per cent (i.e. 45 per cent) of whatever water was available in the worst situation. If at any time the water availability was only 6,457 cusecs, as it was on 27 March, and there was no settlement of the issue under Article XI of the treaty, Bangladesh would have to restrain itself to 45 per cent of that amount.

In the treaty there is no provision for arbitration by any third party. If a dispute arises, Bangladesh has to seek a settlement with Delhi, which controls the water. The mechanism provided in Article VII is superficial, as the lean period will already have caused its damage by the time the governments were able to deal with it. Article X, if and when invoked, would only make the 30-year period of the treaty redundant and fruitless, once the terms of the treaty went for review.

The Chief Minister of West Bengal, Jyoti Basu, apprehended that the treaty would not work because of the shortage of water. It is inconceivable that India could ever release water for Bangladesh without fulfilling the requirements of the Hooghly river or at the cost of its own requirements in Bihar and Uttar Pradesh. If such a situation occurs and India needs more water, it can move for a review of the sharing arrangement. So the provisions in Article X and XI to keep the treaty open for review and suspend the sharing arrangement until agreement has been reached is more to the advantage of India than of Bangladesh. Negotiations could go on indefinitely, depending what India wants to do about the dispute and what kind of government Bangladesh has at the time, making the period of 30 years merely an academic number.

The BNP has emphasised how much water Bangladesh will receive under the 1996 treaty compared to the water it received under the agreement signed in 1977 at the instigation of its founder, President Ziaur Rahman. Besides the absence of any guarantee clause, Table 3.6 shows how much less water Bangladesh will receive under the present arrangement than in 1977, even if the latest treaty works. The BNP strongly believed that the treaty serves India's purposes by creating a measure of goodwill in Bangladesh, in order to enable India to accomplish its long-term design in the region.

Table 3.6 Comparison of the quantity of water to be received according to the treaties signed in 1977 and 1996 (cusecs)

Period	Bangladesh			India		
	1977[a]	1996[b]	Increase/decrease	1977[a]	1996[b]	Increase/decrease
1-10 January	58,500	67,516	9,016	40,000	40,000	0
11-20 January	51,250	57,673	6,423	38,500	40,000	1,500
21-31 January	47,500	50,154	2,654	35,000	40,000	5,000
1-10 February	46,250	46,323	73	33,000	40,000	7,000
11-20 February	42,500	42,859	–359	31,500	40,000	8,500
21-28/29 February	39,250	39,106	–144	30,750	40,000	9,250
1-10 March	38,500	35,000	–3,500	26,750	39,419	12,669
11-20 March	38,000	35,000	–3,000	25,500	33,931	8,431
21-31 March	36,000	29,688	–6,312	25,000	35,000	10,000
1-10 April	35,000	35,000	0	24,000	28,180	4,180
11-20 April	34,750	27,633	–7,117	20,750	35,000	14,250
21-30 April	34,500	35,000	500	20,500	25,992	5,492
1-10 May	35,000	32,351	–2,649	21,500	35,000	13,500
11-20 May	35,250	35,000	–250	24,000	38,590	14,590
21-31 May	38,750	41,854	3,104	26,750	40,000	13,250

Notes: [a]Surety of receiving water was 75% during 1977 depending on historical analysis of the flow of water from 1948 to 1973.

[b]Bangladesh is assured of 50% of the total average flow based on the average flow from 1948 to 1988.

Source: Association of Engineers Bangladesh, *Bulletin*, January 1997, Dhaka.

Given the water-flow indicators recorded in the first lean period after the 1996 treaty was signed and repeated in the following years, the credibility of the treaty has fallen apart. But having an agreement is better for Bangladesh than having none, particularly with a large neighbour like India. It means that Bangladesh will always have an instrument at hand to insist upon its rights, and to that extent the Awami League government deserves credit. However, it is widely believed by experts in both countries that the terms of the treaty can never be realised in the way stipulated, and the main issue therefore remains unresolved. The Farakka issue will continue to be a source of strain and irritation in relations between the two countries for a long time to come.

Moreover, Ganga is only one of the 54 rivers that Bangladesh shares with India. In the unlikely event that the treaty is fully implemented, any delay in reaching a long-term arrangement with regard to other rivers, if necessary on a regional basis, will continue to injure the interests of Bangladesh and the relationship between the two countries. It is well known that India is building at least twelve barrages in the upstream sections of the major rivers, on which two-thirds of the population of Bangladesh depend. For example, India proposes to divert 13,000 cusecs of water from Sankosh river in Bhutan, a tributary of the Brahmaputra, to Farakka by digging a 143-kilometre canal. Once the barrages are commissioned and water is unilaterally diverted in violation of international norms and conventions, it will produce an economic crisis in Bangladesh.

Apart from barrages, there are a large number of rivers and tributaries on which India has constructed cross-dams, spurts and weirs, causing considerable damage to the life and property of millions of people. Each of these actions is disrupting the natural flow of rivers, damaging the ecology of the lower riparian areas, and causing floods, drought, salinity, siltation and pollution.

So the issue is a deep-rooted and complicated one. It is not a question of the Ganga alone or the issue of Farakka, which often attracts all the attention. The issue is the availability of the entire water resources of the area, for which a regional, integrated approach is needed. Basin-based development, augmentation and production of hydro-electricity can be used to benefit all the states in the region. Is India in a position to give a lead in this direction?

One should not ignore the situation of India on this issue. It has its own requirements of water. It has impoverished farmers who need water to grow more food for the large Indian population. They have their own irrigation and agricultural schemes. As the rivers flow through their land, they also have the right to use them. So the sharing will have to be fair and equitable, and cause minimum injury to other parties. It should also be remembered that the states in India are not always friendly towards the central government, and as India is a federal democracy, their co-operation is required to implement any treaty. With successive weak coalition governments in India in recent years, the states are getting more powerful, while the power of central government over them is becoming diluted.

The key issue is, once there is a change of the government in Bangladesh, what will be the fate of the treaty? As no government is permanent in a democracy, the test of a treaty or friendship is whether it will survive such changes. As the key to Farakka and, for that matter, the flow of any water from upstream will remain in the hands of India, what will happen if the Awami League is not in power in Bangladesh? As we have seen, India signed the treaty after such a long time only because the Awami League was in power. If the treaty was really based on a principle of sovereign equality between states, why was no treaty signed for so many years? This is not just an agreement or treaty that is important in maintaining good relationship between neighbouring countries; more significant is mutual trust and confidence, notwithstanding which political party is in power in a particular state.

India's motivation for signing the treaty and its expectations of the treaty have been made clear at different stages by different leaders. Jyoti Basu, who was taken into confidence and consulted by the central government before the treaty was finalised, claimed that 'India has earned lot of goodwill'. After the signing of the treaty, at the joint press conference in Delhi the Indian Prime Minister expressed his expectation that the treaty would facilitate the resolution of other problems between the two countries. When asked what these issues were, he said: 'trade and transit; trade, business and transit'.[125] The day the treaty was signed, Bhabani Sengupta, a renowned journalist close to the Indian establishment, told the BBC: 'Now we have to go to the east, i.e. to the north-eastern region. After this, in our journey to the east, Bangladesh will be our land bridge.'[126]

On 30 June 1998, in a seminar in Dhaka, the Indian Prime Minister, I. K. Gujral, who as Foreign Minister was the architect of the treaty,

---

[125] *Daily Inqilab*, 18 December 1996.
[126] *Ibid.*

said: 'In 1996 we saw the ship of Bangladesh-India friendship trapped in the shallow waters of suspicion and mistrust, and we set out to rescue it. Our enthusiasm and the good faith that grew so mutually and so quickly between us, allowed us to successfully tackle a range of issues.' In the seminar, which was organised by the Center for Policy Dialogue to discuss Bangladesh-India relations, Gujral said that if transit facilities were granted, he could see 'Chittagong emerging as the new Hong Kong of South Asia, surviving as the main port, financial centre and entry point to a rich hinterland comprising not only the interior districts of Bangladesh, but also Nepal, Bhutan and the north-eastern states of India'. In connection with a proposal for a regional water grid comprising India, Nepal, Bhutan and Bangladesh, Gujral stated 'you should add to it a gas grid and a power grid'.[127]

So while signing the Water Treaty, India had on its agenda, for a long time, some wider and more significant issues of strategic importance in mind. With the return of the Awami League government to power, India did not want to wait for the bureaucracy to handle the matters in its usual way. These issues had to be settled at the political level. With the goodwill created by the treaty, notwithstanding its merit or substance, India wanted a transit agreement with Bangladesh covering areas of greater significance.

Between 1971 and 1996 India's needs and priorities had changed, and so had its strategy with regard to the entire northeast, where the activities of the insurgents have intensified in recent years. The ethnic tribes in the states of Nagaland, Mizoram, Manipur, Tripura, Assam, Arunachal and Meghalaya are now engaged in secessionist movements. Tribes such as Khasis, the Mizos, the Garokuki, Metheis and Nagas take the lead role in these areas.[128] The collapse of the Soviet Union, the emergence of China as a global power and the USA's enlarged business interests in India and Bangladesh has increased the attention paid to this part of the subcontinent.

The mutual interest of the USA and India in a sub-regional development strategy within the framework of rectangular or a quadruple

---

[127] Ataus Samad, 'The Other Side of the Gujral Doctrine', *Weekly Holiday*, 3 July 1998.

[128] Abdul Hafiz, 'Regional Problems and Prospects of Co-operation in South Asia', paper presented at a seminar held at the University of Colombo, Sri Lanka, 7-9 October 1987.

growth area led them to work from two different dimensions for their respective self-interest and strategic aims. India's principal concern has been the seven northeastern land-locked states, where insurgencies are taking a huge toll in terms of both money and human lives. It now has more than 150,000 soldiers in the rough terrain of the region, but they have been unable to contain the situation, and consequently India has not been able to do much for the development of these states.

The local population is deprived and neglected. Hence the insurgents easily gain public support. The fear of further Communist infiltration from neighbouring countries like China and from fellow armed guerrillas from Burma and Thailand has always been a matter of concern. The policy of bilateralism pursued by the Indian Congress governments is no longer part of the thought process of Indian strategists and policy-makers. For nearly 50 years Bhutan and Nepal were denied access to the sea through the land now known as Bangladesh, as any such transit route needed India's permission.[129] The seven northern states could not develop any trade or business of their own without going all the way through the narrow and inadequate communication routes of the Indian territory.

In order to facilitate dealing with its changed strategic needs, India also had to resolve the problems of Chittagong Hill Tracts. Minority rights being a popular theme in the West, CHT has always attracted international attention. It has been a source of embarrassment for India, which has kept the issue alive by providing sanctuary, training and logistics to the tribal insurgents. A conflict resolution in CHT became essential for India in order to create better understanding with Bangladesh and enhance India's prestige in the international community. India was waiting for an appropriate government in Bangladesh to resolve these issues. It wanted to restore as much harmony and friendship with the Awami League government as they had achieved from 1971 until the death of Sheikh Mujib. India needed a friendly as well as a compliant government in Bangladesh. With Sheikh Hasina, a much weaker personality than her father, in charge of Bangladesh, India was now in a position to take full advantage.

---

[129] Bangladesh and Nepal signed a transit agreement in 1976 but Indian permission was only given in July 1997 (after the Water Treaty was signed) and the agreement is still awaiting full implementation.

Soon after the Water Treaty was signed, India put forward several proposals, both officially and unofficially. They included road, railway and river transit, the use of Chittagong Port, the development of a corridor for India's northeastern states, a water grid and a power grid, a convenient Asian highway and a sub-regional economic unit. As the proposals gave an impression of harnessing broader co-operation and liberalisation, and offered potential for better trade and business opportunities, they enjoyed the support of the USA. This was primarily because of the investment interest of US multinational companies in the gas and oil sectors of the region.[130]

Although many proposals have been raised and discussed, India's pivotal interest remains the containment of insurgencies in its seven northeastern states, primarily from the security and military point of view. One single transit corridor will allow India to cut across Bangladesh to reach Tripura from West Bengal, reducing the distance from 2,200 to only 350 kilometres.[131]

On the other hand, besides developing its business interests, the USA as the only superpower has to keep an eye on China, and from that point of view their presence in the form of extensive business interests in this region has become almost imperative.

The opposition parties in Bangladesh viewed India's proposals with a great deal of suspicion. Sensing the strong adverse public reaction, the Awami League government neither admitted nor denied entering into any discussions on these issues with the Indian government. Although according to the Indian newspapers the two governments started to work out a transit agreement after the Water Treaty was signed, the Bangladesh government preferred to remain silent. Indeed, at times government ministers denied that the issue of transit was ever discussed with India.[132] In the meantime, several unofficial seminars inspired by the government and donor agencies in the country have been held at Dhaka and New Delhi. These were mainly organised through the Center for Policy Dialogue of Dhaka and the Center for Policy Research of Delhi respectively. The idea

---

[130] See Robin Raphel's statement, *Bangladesh Observer*, 29 January 1997.
[131] *India Today*, 30 April 1997.
[132] *Bangladesh Observer*, 2 September 1997.

behind these seminars was to involve the policy-makers and leading citizens of both countries in creating public opinion favourable to a transit agreement. Parliament was not informed about what was going on behind the scenes. In the absence of any official announcement from the government, the opposition parties rejected such proposals, which were based on newspaper reports in both countries.

Finally, without any prior public debate or any reference to Parliament, the Cabinet of Bangladesh approved the proposal of granting transit facilities to India — 'under a hidden arrangement with the Indian authorities', according to the opposition — and made it public.[133] The scheme, in substance, allows India to carry goods across Bangladesh overland from one point to another point of Indian territory, from Benapole of West Bengal to Agartala of Tripura. In response to the outrage created, it was further explained that this arrangement did not involve transit but 'transhipment', meaning that goods would change vehicles and be carried by local transport within Bangladesh. In other words, Indian trucks would not enter Bangladesh at any of the checkpoints. But this idea of "transhipment" was only a make-belief proposal made knowingly that it was unrealistic and costly and was not compliable.

Nevertheless the decision of the Bangladesh government generated a sharp adverse reaction not only by the opposition parties but also in the media and elsewhere. This was not a facility of transit but a corridor given as a special concession to India, from one area to another area of its territory, to facilitate the transportation of unidentified goods, including military hardware and logistics. The concession of a corridor involved India's strategic interests. As it related to the seven belligerent northeastern states of India, the scheme immediately involved Bangladesh in the geopolitics of the region. It raised the question of whether Bangladesh should get involved in the internal conflicts of the Indian states at all. Once such facility has been granted, India may raise the question of its own security if the

---

[133] A large number of people feared that giving facilities of transit or transhipment to India would destroy the sovereign status of Bangladesh. Professor Talukder Maniruzzaman, 'Transit Plan: A Policy for Creeping Annexation of Bangladesh', *New Nation*, 5 August 1999, Dr Md. Mahbub Ullah, 'Transit Economy', *Daily Inqilab*, 18 August 2000, Dr Md. Abdur Rab, 'Transit: Geopolitical Perspective', *Daily Inqilab*, 18 August 1999.

relationship between the two countries becomes strained at a later date. It will therefore result in a permanent sacrifice of Bangladesh sovereignty to Indian interests. Granting such a right to India will entail far-reaching and unpredictable consequences that are not yet calculable or comprehensible.

Then came the question of control and management. Even if the goods were pre-listed and approved and the whole operation was going to be controlled under a strict management structure for years to come, the failure of the custom authorities to check unauthorised imports and realise duties, causing loss of billions of Takas of revenue every year, is already well known. Due to lack of expertise and dedication in management, such new transactions could be turned into a bonanza for the Indian authorities and their merchant class.

Road communication in Bangladesh is already under great strain. It is far from adequate for the country's own needs. Congestion on the highways is outrageous. The roads leading to the border of India in the northeast are just not capable of absorbing any further increase of traffic. So it requires a long-term programme before the scheme can be fully materialised, which will involve a huge investment in Bangladesh. Where will the money come from? Any heavy and strategic investment by a large state in a small neighbouring state will always raise security issues linked to possible interventions of various kinds, including military. It will be a cause of permanent damage to the relationship between the two countries.

So the opposition viewed the corridor proposal as compromising the sovereignty of Bangladesh and suspected that it had been introduced to serve the interests of India. They feared that such a facility would amount to the total surrender of the Bangladesh economy to India. Although India and the Awami League lobby in Bangladesh try to highlight the economic and commercial benefits of the corridor facilities in terms of enhanced earnings, the opposition rejects the argument by asserting that dollars cannot have preference over national sovereignty. These debates had slowed down the progress of the proposed transit agreement for some time. Moreover, the loss of credibility of the Water Treaty has increased concern on all the sides that another treaty might suffer the same fate. This must be one of the reasons why, having proceeded with such speed, the two sides have taken something of a break. A task force has been constituted to look into the details of the proposal and with the assistance of the World Bank several studies on various aspects of the matter have been set in motion.

The discussion of other issues, such as sub-regional co-operation, the Asian highway, international water, gas and power grids and the use of Chittagong Port, continue at various levels. Opposition allegations that the Awami League is selling the vital interests of Bangladesh to India have not had much effect in changing the government's policy. The two governments have moved forward with their mutual commitments to settle matters and achieve consensus on the issues by working out the details and modalities. If the Awami League remains in power, it is widely believed that Bangladesh will enter into a deeper relationship of dependence on India with the two countries increasingly integrated into one economy, which will include the use of Chittagong Port.

Other Conflicting Interests

Water

Bangladesh has conflicting interests with India in areas of sovereign importance.[134] Besides the land boundary issues,[135] the maritime boundary will take a long time to finalise in view of the position taken by each side on the extent of economic zone[136] and territorial waters. The new territories arising in the mouth of the Bay of Bengal have given rise to a new dispute.[137] The most important issue of all,

---

[134] In 1975-76, following the assassination of Sheikh Mujib, India gave sanctuary to a large number of Mujib followers who, with the assistance of the Indian authorities, had been attacking Bangladesh border posts for almost a year. This was clearly a violation by India of Articles 8 and 9 of the treaty.

[135] In 1974 Bangladesh and India signed a border agreement with regard to the demarcation of some disputed areas. Bangladesh ratified the agreement the same year, making it a part of its constitution, but India has not yet ratified the agreement. India's position is that ratification would follow the conclusion of the demarcation, but this is not reconcilable with the terms of the agreement.

[136] Due to the position taken by India on the maritime boundary and economic zone, the Ashland Oil Company — one of the six companies that signed the Production Sharing Contract with the Bangladesh Government in 1973–74 to explore oil offshore — could not do its drilling, although it had paid for it under the contract.

[137] The new island called South Talpatti, rising at the mouth of Haribhanga river, was once taken over forcibly by Indian marines in contravention of an agreement between the two

on which the survival of Bangladesh and 90 per cent of its inhabitants depends, is the question of the water that flows in numerous rivers through the heart of the new country. India's construction of the Farakka Barrage has caused irreparable damage to the life and economy of Bangladesh. The sharing of Ganges water has been most unsatisfactory and with the needs of both countries being so high, the dispute will go on denting the relationship of the two countries.

However, in the absence of any respect for Bangladesh's needs, the relationship could even turn sour. All the major rivers of Bangladesh originating from the Himalayas and the adjacent areas flow through the northeast region of India. The Ganges, the mighty Brahmaputra, the Meghna, Teesta, Jamuna, Gomoti, Muhuri, Surma, Khowai, Kushiara and Padma are essential to the ecological life of people in Bangladesh. India has already constructed the Teesta Barrage and there has, so far, been no agreement on the quantum of water to be shared. Bangladesh will get less water than it was getting before the barrage was commissioned and as a result at least four northern districts will be severely affected. Similarly, India is constructing barrages over the Gomoti, Khowai and at least ten other rivers, which will certainly reduce the flow of water into Bangladesh in the dry season, when the water is most required.

The 'exciting prospect of harnessing', according to the Friendship Treaty, the water of the Brahmaputra, Meghna and Ganga by India includes its proposal to build a link canal to transfer water from the Brahmaputra Basin to the Ganges at the mouth of the Farakka Barrage. On this proposal the Bangladesh government has taken a definite negative stand.

Although the Friendship Treaty had envisaged that the border between the two countries would be transformed into 'a border of eternal peace and friendship', its implication was interpreted in a different way from both military and economic points of view. The Awami League's earlier political commitment that a poor country like Bangladesh should not have a large army coincided 'with the integrated defence objective' of India for its entire northeast region. The best possible way to turn the border into a border of eternal

---

countries that a joint survey would take place before the ownership of the island was determined.

peace and friendship was by 'eliminating all possible means of any military confrontation between the two countries'. This could be ensured if Bangladesh did not have an army, which it would not need in view of the support assured by India through the treaty. It is however, difficult to ascertain the actual import of such an assurance since the real intention of the two governments needed deeper scrutiny. The only position made public was the Awami League's argument for having only a ceremonial army.

Smuggling

There are serious economic implications because, owing to the imbalances that exist between the economies of the two countries and the price difference in many commodities, smuggling across the border has always gone against the interest of Bangladesh.[138] So any 'border of peace and friendship' could not have meant an open border without the Border Security Force or the Bangladesh Rifles. These could only be withdrawn if the two countries had fully integrated into complementary economies. Unfortunately, neither of these conditions exists between the two countries and from the Bangladesh point of view even a liberal border would immediately cause large-scale smuggling, ruining the economy of the country.

Push-in

An issue that has recently gained prominence and has strained the relationship between the two countries is the decision of the Indian government to deport or push into Bangladesh a large number of Muslims alleged to be illegal immigrants. Due to internal political pressure, Indian governments have raised this issue in the past, but they did not press it too hard as long as Congress was in the government. However, the presence of Muslims, who have mostly lived in slums around big cities like Delhi and Mumbai for generations,

---

[138] Tk.45,000 core worth of goods enters into Bangladesh by way of smuggling each year (*Daily Ittefaq*, 8 May 2000). Today India has a market of $3 billion in Bangladesh. It officially exports goods worth $1.2 billion to Bangladesh and another $1.8 billion, if not more, of Indian goods are smuggled into Bangladesh. As against such a figure, Bangladesh exports a mere $60 million Mahfuz Anam, 'How is India as a Neighbour?', *Daily Star*, 6 August 2000.

was made a political issue by Shiv Sena and the BJP, who claimed that they had entered India illegally and therefore must be sent back. In fact the main reason was that this community traditionally votes for Congress against the BJP.

Bangladesh has denied that there had been illegal immigrants to India from Bangladesh, and maintained that it was being subjected to unwarranted pressure for India's internal political reasons.[139] Moreover, Bangladesh has argued that the Muslims were Indian citizens as they had been living there for many decades as voters and residents of India.

Nevertheless, with the return of the BJP to power in the central government in 1997-98, without any consultation the Indian authorities started collecting these poor families from the slums of different cities. In the most inhuman manner, they were taken all the way to the West Bengal border to be forcibly deported. Bangladesh border forces continue to resist such push-ins and try to push them back into India. Although some of the large political parties in India, such as Communist Party of India (M) (CPI(M)), and the West Bengal government itself admit that the Muslims are Indian citizens and have refused to allow their deportation whenever they are handed over to them, Bangladesh in turn accuses the central government of India of violating the Muslims' human rights.[140] The Indian government, on the other hand, claims that there are 11 million such illegal immigrants and is determined to send them back to Bangladesh.[141]

It is not that the conflicting interests of India and Bangladesh should not or cannot be resolved peacefully to mutual benefit. But it requires mature political leadership in both countries. They have to adopt a pragmatic and human approach to the problems — an attitude of domination or deprivation on the part of either will not help resolve the issues. On the contrary, any such attitude will only take the two countries further apart.

---

[139] Successive governments in Bangladesh from 1972 had refused to admit the existence of any illegal immigrants. The BNP government, however, signed a joint statement in May 1992, when Khaleda Zia visited India, allowing India to deport such illegal immigrants.

[140] For detail, see K. M. Sobhan, 'Push back Bandha Karun', *Weekly Khaborer Kajog*, Dhaka, 4-10 October 1992.

[141] *India Today*, India, 10 August 1998.

Chapter 4

Economy: South and South-East Asia

South Asia[1]

With the background of interstate and intra-regional conflicts, rooted in mutual suspicion that has existed historically between India and its major neighbours, as has been outlined South Asia nonetheless today faces a major challenge of survival in the newly emerging economic order. It contains a population of over 1.3 billion in an area of 4.48 million square kilometres and constitutes one of the poorest regions of the world. About half of the world's poor live in this region and it accounts for about 70 per cent of the world's very poorest groups.[2] The region's GNP per capita is $325, real GDP per capita is $1,686, the adult literacy rate is 49.7 per cent, access to sanitation is 35 per cent, access to safe water is 82 per cent, access to health services is 78 per cent and life expectancy is 61.4 years. South Asia's total armed forces stand at 2.5 million and its defence expenditure exceeds $15.5 billion, which is 3 per cent of the region's GDP. It has an external debt of $178 billion with a debt service ratio of 25 per cent and an export/import ratio of 84 per cent. In South Asia, the proportion of people living below the poverty line is 43 per cent[3] and

---

[1] Different figures and tables cited in this chapter are not always consistent because of the variations in the reports and sources mentioned in the footnotes. Figures only indicate the scale of relative development for the purpose of a comparative study.

[2] *World Development Report, 1990* (Oxford: Oxford University Press/World Bank).

[3] Figures quoted are from the *Human Development Report*, 1997, except where stated. As this source includes Afghanistan and Iran, the aggregates will be different when these two countries are excluded.

the fertility rate is 3.5 per cent.[4] With a growth rate of 1.8 per cent its population will double by 2033.

Although it covers only 2.7 per cent of the world's land surface, South Asia is occupied by nearly one-fifth of the world's population. It accounts for only 2 per cent of the world's output, 1 per cent of global exports and 1.5 per cent of global imports. Its per capita income ranges between $170 and $520. The area of forestland in South Asia is less than 2 per cent of the world's total, and it has around only 1 per cent of the world's natural resources.[5] Moreover, 90 per cent of all the major mineral resources of South Asia — coal, crude oil, uranium, iron and copper — are located in India. One-half of the South Asian land is arable and 87 per cent of it belongs to India.[6] Although the share of agriculture in GNP is decreasing in all four major countries in the region, it still ranges from 25 to 50 per cent.

South-East Asia

The South Korean Economy[7]

Korea has a population of 44.5 million with an annual population growth rate of 0.9 per cent. In 1953 the per capita GNP of Korea was $78.90; it rose to $90 in 1961, $125 in 1966, $306 in 1972, $1,741 in 1981 and $10,076 in 1995. In 1961 the growth rate of the Korean economy was only 1.6 per cent; in 1966 it rose to 6.8 per cent, in 1981 to 21.3 per cent and in 1995 to 15.8 per cent. Korea has no natural resources, but its development efforts focused on an early land reform programme along with emphasis being placed on education. Its dependence on agriculture was reduced from 48.9 per cent in 1956 to 7.5 per cent in 1993. At the same time, its industrial output rose from 5.9 per cent in 1953 to 29.4 per cent in 1993, and overall GNP including services changed from 16.1 per cent of GDP in 1953 to 303.2 per cent in 1993.

---

[4] *World Development Report, 1990* (Oxford: Oxford University Press/World Bank).

[5] Figures quoted from Mizanur Rahman Shelley, *South Asia in the Changing Asian Scene*, pp. 12-13. A paper presented at the International Seminar on Changing Global Order, CDRB Dhaka, and 13 August 1992. See also *Weekly Holiday*, 9 June 1992.

[6] *Ibid.*

[7] Dong-Se, Kwang and Dwight, *The Korean Economy 1945-95: Performance and Vision for the 21st Century,* Korean Development Institute, April 1997.

Table 4.1 Economy, wealth and poverty: South Asia

	India	Pakistan	Bangladesh	Nepal	Sri Lanka	Bhutan	Maldives
Total GDP (US$m), 1997	381,000	62,000	41,000	4,900	15,000	200	200
GNP per capita (US$), 1997	370	500	360	220	800	430	1,180
GNP average annual growth rate (%), 1996-97	6.1	0.0	6.3	4.2	7.3	4.9	8.5
Real GDP per capita (PPP$), 1995	1,422	2,209	1,382	1,145	3,408	1,382	3,540
Population below poverty line (%), 1989-94							
$1 a day	53	12	29	53	4	n.a.	n.a.
National poverty line	41	34	48	42	22	n.a.	n.a.
People in poverty (%), 1990							
Urban	38	20	56	19	15	n.a.	n.a.
Rural	49	31	51	43	36	n.a.	n.a.
Public expenditure on education and health (% of GNP), 1990	5.0	4.5	3.7	5.1	5.1	n.a.	7
Gross domestic investment (% of GDP), 1997	24	15	21	21	24	47	n.a.
Gross domestic savings (% of GDP), 1997	20	10	15	10	17	7	n.a.
Tax revenue (% of GDP), 1996	13	19	13	11	21	19	35
Exports (% of GDP), 1995	12	16	14	24	36	28	18
Debt service ratio (debt service as % of exports of goods and services), 1995	28	35	13	8	7	8	4
Total external debt (US$bn), 1997	**94**	**30**	**15**	**2.3**	**8**	**0.1**	**0.2**

Sources: *Human Development in South Asia 1999* (Dhaka: The University Press Limited).

Table 4.2 Social sector: South Asia

	India	Pakistan	Bangladesh	Nepal	Sri Lanka	Bhutan	Maldives
Population without access to health services, 1995							
Number (m)	143	63	68	n.a.	1.3	0.6	0.1
As a % of total population	15	45	55	n.a.	7	35	35
Population without access to safe water, 1995							
Number (m)	178	56	25	11	7.7	n.a.	n.a.
As a % of total population	19	40	21	52	43	n.a.	n.a.
Population without access to sanitation, 1995							
Number (m)	665	98	91	18	6	0.51	n.a.
As a % of total population	71	70	65	80	34	30	34
Adult literacy rate (%), 1995	52	38	38	28	90	42	93
Female literacy rate (%), 1995	58	24	26	14	87	28	93
Infant mortality rate (per 1,000 live births), 1997	71	95	81	75	17	87	53
Illiterate adults, 1995							
Number (m)	291	49	45	9	1.2	0.6	0.01
As a % of total adult population	48	62	62	72	10	58	7.0
Illiterate female adults, 1995							
Number (m)	182	28	26	5.4	0.8	0.3	0.005
As a % of total adult female population	62	76	74	86	13	72	7
Malnourished children under 5, 1996	59	9	8	2	0.06	0.01	n.a.
Number (m)							
As a % of total population	53	38	56	47	38	38	n.a.
Under-5 mortality rate (per 1,000 live births), 1997	136	136	109	104	19	121	74

Sources: *Human Development in South Asia 1999* (Dhaka: The University Press Limited).

Table 4.3 Military spending: South Asia (US$m, 1993 prices)

	India	Pakistan	Bangladesh	Nepal	Sri Lanka	Bhutan	Maldives
Defence expenditure							
1985	7,208	2,088	308	22	214	n.a.	n.a.
1996	9,070	3,000	460	40	700	n.a.	n.a.
Defence expenditure annual % increase, 1985–96	2.1	3.3	3.7	5.5	11	n.a.	n.a.
Defence expenditure as a % of GNP							
1985	2.5	5.1	1.3	0.7	2.6	n.a.	n.a.
1995	2.8	5.2	1.4	0.9	5.3	n.a.	n.a.
Defence expenditure as a % of central government expenditure							
1980	19.8	30.6	9.4	6.7	1.7	n.a.	n.a.
1995	12.7	25.3	9.9	5.8	15.7	n.a.	n.a.
Defence expenditure as a % of education and health expenditure							
1960	68	393	n.a.	67	17	n.a.	n.a.
1995	57	181	46	22	100	n.a.	n.a.

Source: *Human Development in South Asia 1999* (Dhaka: The University Press Limited).

Infant mortality declined from 67 per thousand in 1961 to 17 per thousand in 1993. In the same period, the number of doctors increased from 3 per thousand in 1961 to 1 per thousand in 1993. Korea increased expenditure in the education sector 800-fold between 1961 and 1993, from 12 trillion won to 9,712 trillion won. In the health sector the increase was almost 600-fold from 0.9 trillion won to 504 trillion won; and in housing to more than 10,000-fold, from 0.3 trillion won to 3441 trillion won. The proportion of people living in absolute poverty was reduced from 48.3 per cent in 1961 to 7.6 per cent in 1993, and in 1996 went down to below 5 per cent.

Comparative Economic Performances: South and South-East Region

On the human development index (HDI), Korea is ranked 32, Thailand 59, Malaysia 60, Philippines 98 and Indonesia 99, whereas India is ranked 138, Pakistan 139, Bangladesh 144, Nepal 154 and Bhutan 155. Only Sri Lanka at 91 is placed above the Philippines and Indonesia.

A comparison on the basis of GNP per capita for 1995, shows that while Korea has reached $9,700, Malaysia $3,890, Thailand $2,740, the Philippines $1,050 and Indonesia $980, India achieves only $340, Pakistan $460, Bangladesh $240, Nepal $200 and Sri Lanka $700.[8]

In terms of the percentage of people living in poverty on less than $1 dollar a day (PPP)[9] in 1981–95, while Korea has none, Malaysia has 5.6 per cent, Thailand 0.1 per cent, the Philippines 27.5 per cent and Indonesia 14.5 per cent, whereas India has 52.5 per cent, Nepal 53.1 per cent, Pakistan 11.6 per cent, Bangladesh 46 per cent and Sri Lanka 4 per cent.

In exports of goods and services, Korea raised its value from $22.4 billion in 1980 to $151.8 billion in 1995, Malaysia from $14.8 billion to $84.2 billion, Thailand from $8.5 billion to $74 billion and the Philippines from $7.9 to $52.5 billion. India has raised its value of exports from $12.3 billion in 1980 to $40.9 billion in 1995, Pakistan from $3 billion to $8.4 billion, Bangladesh from $976 million

---

[8] All figures are quoted from *World Development Report, 1997* (Oxford: Oxford University Press/ World Bank). The currency is US$.

[9] Purchasing power parity.

to $4.29 billion, Nepal from $239 million to $1.1 billion and Sri Lanka from $1.3 billion to $4.8 billion.

Korea raised its level of gross internal resources from $3.1 billion in 1980 to $32.8 billion in 1995, Malaysia from $5.7 billion to $24.7 billion, Thailand from $3 billion to $36.9 billion and the Philippines from $3.9 billion to $7.7 billion. India raised its gross internal resources from $12 billion in 1980 to $22.8 billion in 1995, Pakistan from $1.5 billion to $2.5 billion, Bangladesh from $331 million to $2.3 billion and Nepal from $272 million to $646 million.

The average rate of annual GDP growth in Korea in 1980-90 was 9.4 per cent and in 1990-95 was 7.2 per cent. Their growth in gross domestic investment was 11.9 per cent in 1980-90, and 7.2 per cent in 1990-95. In Malaysia the average annual growth rate was 5.2 per cent in 1980-90 and 8.7 per cent in 1990-95 while the growth in investment was 2.6 per cent in 1980-90 and 16 per cent in 1990-95. In Thailand the average annual growth rate was 7.6 per cent in 1980-90 and 8.4 per cent in 1990-95 and its growth in investment was 9.4 per cent in 1980-90 and 10.2 per cent in 1990-95. In the Philippines the average annual growth rate was 1 per cent in 1980-90 and 2.3 per cent in 1990-95; growth in investment was –2.1 per cent in 1980-90 and 3.2 per cent in 1990-95.

In comparison to this for the countries of South Asia the average annual growth rate in India was 5.8 per cent in 1980-90 and 4.6 per cent in 1990-95 while growth in investment was 6.5 per cent in 1980-90 and 5.3 per cent in 1990-95. In Pakistan the average annual growth rate was 6.3 per cent in 1980-90 and 4.6 per cent in 1990-95; growth in investment was 5.9 per cent in 1980-90 and 4 per cent in 1990-95. In Bangladesh the average annual growth rate was 4.3 per cent in 1980-90 and 4.1 per cent in 1990-95; growth in investment was 1.4 per cent in 1980-90 and 8.2 per cent in 1990-95. In Nepal the average annual growth rate was 4.6 per cent in 1980-90 and 5.1 per cent in 1990-95; growth in investment was 1.8 per cent in 1980-90 and 6.3 per cent in 1990-95.

In 1995 gross domestic saving and investment in Korea amounted to 36 and 37 per cent of GDP respectively, and the export of goods and services for 33 per cent. In Malaysia domestic saving, investment and exports were 37 per cent, 41 per cent and 96 per cent of GDP respectively; in Thailand, 36 per cent, 43 per cent and 42 per cent; in the Philippines, 15 per cent, 23 per cent and 36 per cent; in Indonesia, 36 per cent, 38 per cent and 25 per cent; in India, 22 per cent, 25 per cent and 12 per cent; in Pakistan, 16 per cent, 19 per cent and 16 per cent; in Bangladesh, 8 per cent, 17 per cent and 14 per cent; in Nepal, 12 per cent, 23 per cent and 24 per cent; and in Sri Lanka, domestic saving was 14 per cent, investment 25 per cent and exports 16 per cent of GDP.

It appears that every country in southern and eastern Asia has large external debts and that the less developed ones are more dependent on multilateral agencies for their borrowing. In 1995 India had $93.7 billion of external debt, of which 32 per cent was owed to multilateral agencies; Pakistan had $30 billion (40.5 per cent), Bangladesh $16.3 billion (59.7 per cent), Nepal $2.3 billion (81.3 per cent) and Sri Lanka $8.2 billion (34.7 per cent). Indonesia had $107.8 billion of external debt in 1995, of which 18.6 per cent was owed to multilateral agencies; the Philippines had $39.4 billion (21.5 per cent), Thailand $56.7 billion (5.6 per cent) and Malaysia $34.3 billion (4.8 per cent).

In social sectors,[10] the indicators also reflect the level of economic growth and investment, although in some areas South Asia has shown a relatively better result. While in India the proportion of the population having access to healthcare is 85 per cent, in Pakistan it is 55 per cent, in Bangladesh 45 per cent and in Bhutan 65 per cent. In Korea the figure is 100 per cent, in Thailand 90 per cent, in Indonesia 93 per cent and in the Philippines 71 per cent.[11]

The proportion of the population with access to safe drinking water in India is 81 per cent, in Pakistan 74 per cent, in Bangladesh 97 per cent, in Nepal 63 per cent, in Bhutan 58 per cent and in Sri Lanka 57 per cent. In Korea 93 per cent of the population have access to safe drinking water, in Thailand 89 per cent, in Malaysia 78 per cent, in Indonesia 62 per cent and in the Philippines 86 per cent.[12]

Access to sanitation is enjoyed by 29 per cent of the population in India, in Pakistan by 47 per cent, in Bangladesh 48 per cent, in Nepal

---

[10] Figures quoted from *Human Development Report*, 1997 (Oxford: Oxford University Press/UPL), pp. 165-95.

[11] *Ibid.* For the period 1990-95.

[12] *Ibid.* For the period 1990-96.

18 per cent, in Bhutan 70 per cent and in Sri Lanka 63 per cent. In Korea access to sanitation is enjoyed by 100 per cent, in Thailand by 96 per cent, in Malaysia 94 per cent, in Indonesia 51 per cent and in the Philippines 77 per cent.[13]

The daily calorie supply per capita in 1992 was 2,359 in India, 2,326 in Pakistan, 2,019 in Bangladesh, 1,957 in Nepal and 2,275 in Sri Lanka. Calorie supply was 3,298 in Korea, 2,443 in Thailand, 2,884 in Malaysia, 2,755 in Indonesia and 2,258 in the Philippines.

In 1994 the adult literacy rate in India stood at 51.2 per cent, in Pakistan 37.1 per cent, in Bangladesh 37.3 per cent, in Nepal 27 per cent and in Bhutan 41.1 per cent; only Sri Lanka matched the countries of South-East Asia with a literacy rate 90.1 per cent. In Korea the literacy rate in 1994 was 97.9 per cent, in Thailand 93.5 per cent, in Malaysia 83 per cent, in Indonesia 83.2 per cent and in the Philippines 94.4 per cent.

The infant mortality rate per 1,000 live births in 1995 was 68 in India, 90 in Pakistan, 79 in Bangladesh, 91 in Nepal and 16 in Sri Lanka, while in Korea the rate was 10, in Malaysia 12, in Thailand 35, in Indonesia 39 and in the Philippines 30.[14]

Between 1992 and 1994 Korea spent 16 per cent of its total government expenditure on education, Thailand 18.9 per cent and Malaysia 15.5 per cent; India spent 11.5 per cent on education, Bangladesh 8.7 per cent and Nepal 13.2 per cent.[15]

Expenditure on the military is colossal and in almost all the countries of the region it shows the same pattern. In many cases this increase is at the expense of the health and education of the people. In 1995 India spent 2.5 per cent of its GDP on the military, Pakistan 6.5 per cent, Bangladesh 1.8 per cent, Nepal 4.7 and Sri Lanka 4.9 per cent; Korea also spent 3.4 per cent, Thailand 2.5 per cent, Malaysia 4.5 per cent, and Indonesia and the Philippines 1.6 per cent each. At the same time, military expenditure as a percentage of combined education and health expenditure in 1990-91 was 65 per cent in India, in Pakistan 125 per cent, Bangladesh 63 per cent,

---

[13] *Ibid.* For the period 1990-96.

[14] *World Development Report 1994*, Oxford: Oxford University Press/World Bank, p. 224.

[15] *Human Development Report 1994*, Oxford: Oxford University Press/World Bank, pp. 180 and 188.

Nepal 35 per cent and Sri Lanka 107 per cent; in Korea it was 60 per cent, Thailand 71 per cent, Malaysia 38 per cent, Indonesia 49 per cent and the Philippines 41 per cent.

It is interesting to note that in terms of overall economic and social development, despite all the constraints, Sri Lanka has outperformed all the other countries in South Asia. In recent years it is Bangladesh followed by, while Pakistan's performance has been the worst and most disappointing. Similarly, in South-East Asia, Korea has certainly performed the best, with Thailand coming next and the Philippines doing the worst.

Table 4.4 Population, surface area and density: South-East Asia (Group 1)

	Korea	Singapore	Hong Kong	Taiwan
Population (m)	46	3	7	21
Surface area (000 sq. km)	99	1	1	–
Density per sq. km.	470	5,186	6,755	–

Source: *World Development Report*, 1999-2000 (World Bank/Oxford University Press).

Table 4.5 Economy, wealth and poverty: South-East Asia (Group 1)

	Korea	Singapore	Hong Kong	Taiwan
Total GDP (US$m), 1997	62,803	11,718	28,495	–
GNP per capita (US$), 1997	7,970	30,060	23,670	–
GNP average annual growth rate (%), 1997-98	–0.9	–0.4	–7.8	–
GDP growth rate (%), 1998	6.2	8.0	4.4	–
Population below national poverty line (%)	0	0	0	–
Public expenditure on education (% of GNP), 1996	3.7	3.0	2.9	–
Public expenditure on health (% of GNP), 1996	2.3	1.5	2.3	–
Gross domestic investment (% of GDP), 1998	4.3	9.8	8.9	–
Gross domestic savings (% of GDP), 1998	34	51	30	–
Gross international resources (US$m), 1998	52,100	74,928	89,620	–
Tax revenue (as % of GDP), 1997	15.5	15.9	0	–
Exports (US$m), 1997	164,920	156,252	228,877	–

Sources: *Human Development in South Asia* (Dhaka: The University Press Limited, 1999); *World Development Report*, 1999-2000 (Oxford: Oxford University Press/World Bank).

Table 4.6 Social sector: South-East Asia (Group 1)

	Korea	Singapore	Hong Kong	Taiwan
Population, 1994 (m)	46.0	3.3	7.0	21.74
% below poverty ($1/day in ppp$)	n.a.	n.a.	n.a.	n.a.
% adult literacy	97.9	91	92.3	94
% without access to safe water, 1990-95	7	0	0	n.a.
% without access to health service, 1990-96	n.a.	n.a.	0	3.9
Infant mortality	10	5	5	4.8
Life expectancy	71.5	77.1	79	73
Daily calorie supply per capita, 1992	3,298	n.a.	3,144	n.a.

Sources: *Human Development in South Asia* (Dhaka: The University Press Limited, 1999); *World Development Report*, 1999-2000 (Oxford: Oxford University Press/World Bank).

Table 4.7 Economy, wealth and poverty: South-East Asia (Group 2)

	Indonesia	Thailand	Malaysia	Philippines
GDP (US$m), 1994	167,600	129,900	68,700	63,300
Real GDP/capita (US$)	3,740	7,104	8,865	2,681
Population, 1994 (m)	194.5	57.8	19.7	66.4
Population below national poverty line (%), 1989–94	47.0	<2	4.3	6.8
Population without access to sanitation (% of total population), 1995	45	4	6	27
Illiterate adults (% of total adult population), 1995	46	5	14.5	5.5
Illiterate female adults (% of total adult female population), 1995	61	7	19	6
Malnourished children under 5 (% of total population), 1996	53	0	20	30
Under-5 mortality rate (per 1,000 live births), 1997	88	38	14	41

Sources: *Human Development in South Asia* (Dhaka: The University Press Limited, 1999); *World Development Report*, 1999-2000 (Oxford: Oxford University Press/World Bank).

Table 4.8 Social sector: South-East Asia (Group 2)

	Indonesia	Thailand	Malaysia	Philippines
Population, 1994 (m)	194.5	57.8	19.7	66.4
% below poverty ($1/day in ppp$)	15	n.a.	6	28
% adult literacy	83.2	93.5	83	94.4
% without access to safe water, 1990-95	38	11	22	14
% without access to health service, 1990-96	7	10	n.a.	29
Infant mortality	57	29	12	36
Life expectancy	63.5	69.5	71.2	67
Daily calorie supply per capita, 1992	2,755	2,443	2,884	2,258

Sources: *Human Development in South Asia* (Dhaka: The University Press Limited, 1999); *World Development Report*, 1999-2000 (Oxford: Oxford University Press/World Bank).

Table 4.9 Structural change: Korea (% of GDP)

	1953	1961	1966	1972	1981	1987	1993
Agriculture	48.9	47.1	42.5	26.4	16.3	10.9	7.5
Industry[a]	5.9	10.0	13.4	14.2	24.3	29.9	29.4
Social overhead[b]	1.0	2.2	3.5	4.7	7.9	8.3	9.7
Other services	44.2	40.7	40.6	54.7	51.5	50.9	53.4
GNP	16.1	22.0	30.0	55.5	111.9	193.3	303.2

Notes: [a]Industry means mining and manufacturing. [b]Social overhead means transportation, communication, electricity, water and gas.

Sources: BOK, Economic Statistics Yearbook, 1973, 1995 (at 1970 factor cost), BOK, National Accounts, 1994 (at 1975 prices), BOK, National Accounts, 1994 (at 1990 prices). See also The Korean Economy 1945-1995: Performance and Vision of the 21st Century (Korean Development Institute, 1997).

Table 4.10 Average welfare indicators: Korea

	1953	1961	1966	1972	1981	1987	1993	1995
GNP/capita ($)	78.9	90	125	306	1,741	3,218	7,513	10,976
Growth rate (%)	n.a.	1.6	6.8	16.1	21.3	10.7	15.2	15.8
Health								
Infant mortality	67	60	43	27	22	17	n.a.	n.a.
Life expectancy	57	53	59	64	67	70	72	n.a.
Education								
Illiteracy (%)	n.a.	n.a.	n.a.	21	13	10	7	n.a.
Years of schooling	n.a.	n.a.	5	6	8	9	10	10

Sources: BOK, *National Accounts*, 1994; National Statistical Office, *Major Statistics of Korean Economy*, 1981, 1996; and other tables in appendix. See also *The Korean Economy 1945-1995: Performance and Vision of the 21st Century* (Korean Development Institute, 1997).

Table 4.11 Economy, wealth and poverty: South Asia and Korea

	India	Pakistan	Sri Lanka	Bangladesh	Korea
Total GDP (US$m), 1998	383,429	63,895	15,093	42,775	297,900
GNP per capita (US$), 1997	430	480	810	350	7,970
GNP average annual growth rate (%), 1996–97	6.1	5.0	0	5.0	-6.3
GDP growth rate (%), 1998	6.1	4.1	5.3	4.8	-6.2
Public expenditure on education (% of GNP), 1996	3.4	3.0	3.4	2.9	3.7
Public expenditure on health (% of GNP), 1996	0.7	0.8	1.4	1.2	1.9
Gross domestic investment (% of GDP), 1998	5.9	2.7	5.8	7.0	6.3
Gross domestic savings (% of GDP), 1998	18	13	17	15	34
Gross international resources (US$m), 1998	30,647	1,626	1,998	1,936	52,100
Tax revenue (as % of GDP), 1997	10.8	12.9	16.2	0	23.4
Exports (US$m), 1997	44,102	9,956	5,514	5,096	164,920

Sources: *World Development Report, 1999-2000* (Oxford: Oxford University Press/World Bank); *Human Development in South Asia* (Dhaka: The University Press Limited, 1999).

Table 4.12 Social sectors: South Asia and Korea

	India	Pakistan	Sri Lanka	Bangladesh	Korea
Population below poverty line (%)	40.9	34	40.6	42.7	–
Population without access to safe water (% of total population), 1995	15	38	30	16	17
Population without access to sanitation (% of total population), 1995	84	61	25	65	0
Adult literacy rate (%), 1995	52	38	90	38	95+
Illiterate male adults (% of total adult population), 1995	35	50	7	51	less than 5
Illiterate female adults (% of total adult female population), 1995	62	76	13	74	less than 5
Malnourished children under 5 (% of total population), 1996	53	38	38	56	–
Under-5 mortality rate (per 1,000 live births), 1997	71	95	14	75	9

Sources: *Human Development in South Asia* (Dhaka: The University Press Limited, 1999); *World Development Report, 1997* (Oxford: Oxford University Press/World Bank); *World Development Report, 1999-2000* (Oxford: Oxford University Press/World Bank).

Cambodia, Laos and Vietnam

Despite being torn by wars and having doctrinaire communism hanging over their heads, countries like Vietnam, Cambodia and Laos have shown great signs of economic vibrancy, and China, in relative terms, has made remarkable progress economically in the last twenty years. This is a new phenomenon.

Vietnam, with a population of 73.5 million in an area of 332,000 square kilometres and per capita income of $240, has an adult illiteracy rate of only 6 per cent and a life expectancy of 68 years. But it has attained an annual GDP growth rate of 8.3 per cent in 1990–95 with gross domestic saving at 16 per cent, investment at 27 per cent and exports at 36 per cent of GDP while owing virtually nothing to the multilateral agencies. So is the case with Cambodia, a much smaller country with 10 million people in a vast area of 181,000 square kilometres and with per capita income of $270. It attained an average GDP growth rate of 6.4 per cent and a 16 per cent investment rate.

The above figures show that the economic performance of countries like Cambodia and Vietnam,[16] not to mention China, is more commendable than that of the South Asian countries.

India and China

When India exploded its nuclear bombs in May 1998, George Fernandes, the Defence Minister, justified them to the unhappy world community by pointing his finger at China as a security threat. Besides, China was allegedly giving nuclear designs to Pakistan and installing facilities in Myanmar to monitor Indian missiles. India perhaps could still not forget the humiliation it had suffered at the hands of the Chinese in 1962 over a border territory in the northeastern slopes of the Himalayas. So, whether or not China, which is now following a policy of co-operation and not confrontation to achieve its

---

[16]Vietnam, a country that suffered from famines only fifteen years ago, is now one of the world's largest exporters of rice. Although it has a per capita GDP of $330, it has been able to reduce poverty from 58 per cent in 1999 to 37 per cent in 1998, and 90 percent of the population can read. The infant mortality rate is 34 per thousand and 98 per cent of children are fully immunised. The economy is growing by more than 9 per cent a year. By putting the past to the rest, Vietnam has almost forgotten what the USA did to them. It welcomes foreign investment, including from the USA, with great enthusiasm. *Time*, 17 April 2000.

Table 4.13 Economy, wealth and poverty: Cambodia and Vietnam

	Cambodia	Vietnam
Total GDP (US$bn), 1997	3.0	25.6
GNP per capita (US$), 1997	1,240	1,690
GNP average annual growth rate (%), 1996-97	−0.1	−0.4
GDP growth rate (%), 1998	5.5	19.7
Population below national poverty line (%)	39.0	50.9
Public expenditure on education (% of GNP), 1996	2.9	2.6
Public expenditure on health (% of GDP), 1997	0.7	1.1
Gross domestic investment (% of GDP), 1998	16	29
Gross domestic savings (% of GDP), 1998	4	21
Gross international resources (US$bn), 1998	324	1,986
Tax revenue (% of GDP), 1997	0	0
Exports (US$m), 1997	330	8,989
Total external debt (US$bn), 1997	0.2129	2.1629

Sources: *Human Development in South Asia* (Dhaka: The University Press Limited, 1999); *World Development Report*, 1999-2000 (Oxford: Oxford University Press/World Bank).

Table 4.14 Social sector: Cambodia, Laos and Vietnam

	Cambodia	Laos	Vietnam
Population (m), 1994	9.8	4.7	72.4
% below poverty line ($1/day in PPP$)	39	46	51
% adult literacy	35	55.8	93
% without access to safe water, 1990–95	64	48	57
% without access to health service, 1990–96	47	33	10
Infant mortality	112	93	41
Life expectancy	52.4	51.7	66
Daily calorie supply per capita, 1992	2,021	2,259	2,250

Sources: *Human Development in South Asia* (Dhaka: The University Press Limited, 1999); *World Development Report*, 1999-2000 (Oxford: Oxford University Press/World Bank).

Table 4.15 Population, surface area and density: China, India and Korea

	China	India	Korea
Population (m)	1,239	980	46
Surface area (000 sq. km)	9,597	3,288	99
Density per sq. km	133	330	470

Source: *World Development Report*, 1999-2000 (Oxford: Oxford University Press/World Bank).

Table 4.16 Economy, wealth and poverty: China, India and Korea

	China	India	Korea
Total GDP (US$bn), 1997	960.9	381	297.9
GNP per capita (US$), 1997	750	370	7,970
GNP average annual growth rate (%), 1996–97	7.4	6.1	–6.3 (1997-98)
GDP growth rate (%), 1998	11.1	6.1	6.2
Population below national poverty line (%)	8.4	53	Less than 1
Public expenditure on education (% of GNP), 1996	2.3	3.4	3.7
Public expenditure on health (% of GNP), 1996	2.1	0.7	2.3
Gross domestic investment (% of GDP), 1998	39	24	35
Gross domestic savings (% of GDP), 1998	43	20	34
Gross international resources (US$bn), 1998	152.8	30.6	52.1
Tax revenue (% of GDP), 1997	4.9	13	18.6
Exports (US$m), 1997	207,251	44,102	164,920

Sources: *Human Development in South Asia* (Dhaka: The University Press Limited, 1999); *World Development Report*, 1999-2000 (Oxford: Oxford University Press/World Bank).

economic goals, has pointed to India as a threat, India certainly perceived China as a threat to it.

India considers itself as a regional power and would like to play a global role in the coming millennium. This is a dream cherished since its birth as an independent state in 1947. China has already acquired a global position as a permanent member of the UN Security Council and has the potential of developing more as a military and economic power. India cannot afford to underestimate such a nation. Both countries have identical problems of economic growth, underdevelopment and poverty, and face a stupendous task of creating jobs for millions of young people every year to improve the quality of life of their populations.

India, with a current population of over a billion and with a 1.6 per cent population growth rate will double in size by 2036.[17] China with over 1.2 billion people and a growth rate of 0.9 per cent will double in size by 2069. So in ten years' time India's population will exceed that of China, although China is three times larger in area, with 9.5 million square kilometres as against India's 3.28 million.[18]

---

[17] *Human Development Report*, 1997, p.194.

[18] *World Development Report*, 1997, p. 214.

India has a GNP per capita of $370 as against China's $750, an adult illiteracy of 48 per cent as against China's 19 per cent and a life expectancy of 55 years as against China's 69 years. The proportion of India's people living in poverty with less than one dollar a day (PPP) during 1981-95 is 53.5 per cent as against China's 29.4 per cent. Though India raised its real GDP per capita from $617 dollars in 1960 to $1,348 in 1994, China raised its level from $723 in 1960 to $2,604 in 1994.[19] While India reduced its under-5 mortality rate from 236 to 115 per thousand in 1995,[20] China in the same period reduced it from 209 to 47 per thousand. India's total GDP in 1995 stood at $324 billion, whereas China's stood at $697 billion. Even as India's average GDP growth rate during 1980-90 was 5.8 per cent and during 1990-95 was 4.6 per cent, China had an average growth rate of 10.2 per cent and 12.8 per cent during the same periods. Whilst India's average growth in domestic investment during 1990-95 was 5.3 per cent, in China it was 15.5 per cent.[21] India's multilateral debt in 1995 was $32 billion as against China's $13.8 billion. While India's gross domestic saving in 1995 was recorded as 22 per cent and investment as 25 per cent of GDP, in China they are 42 per cent and 40 per cent of GDP respectively. India's exports of goods constituted 12 per cent of GDP as against China's 21 per cent. In the Human Development Index (HDI), India ranks at 135 as against China's ranking of 108.

In India, the proportion of children under the age of 5 suffering from malnutrition is 63 per cent as against China's 17 per cent. India has reduced its total fertility rate to 3.5 per cent, but China has taken it to 1.9 per cent. In providing access to health services, India achievements were closer to China achievements during the period 1990-95 with 85 per cent as against China's 88 per cent. In respect of providing access to safe water and sanitation India has performed slightly better than China with 81 per cent and 29 per cent, as against China's 67 per cent and 24 per cent.

---

[19] *Ibid.* p. 234.
[20] *Human Development Report*, 1997, pp. 49-52.
[21] *World Development Report*, 1997, p. 234.

Table 4.17 Economy, wealth and poverty: India and China

	India	China
Total GDP (US$bn), 1997	381	960.9
GNP per capita (US$), 1997	370	750
GNP average annual growth rate (%), 1996-97	6.1	7.4
GDP growth rate (%), 1998	6.1	11.1
Population below the national poverty line (%)	41	8.4
Public expenditure on education (% of GNP), 1996	3.4	2.3
Public expenditure on health (% of GNP), 1996	0.7	2.1
Gross domestic investment (% of GDP), 1998	24	39
Gross domestic savings (% of GDP), 1998	20	43
Gross international resources (US$bn), 1998	30.6	152.8
Tax revenue (% of GDP), 1997	13	4.9
Exports (US$m), 1997	44,102	207,251

Sources: *Human Development in South Asia* (Dhaka: The University Press Limited, 1999); *World Development Report*, 1999-2000 (Oxford: Oxford University Press/World Bank).

In the military sector,[22] China has total armed forces of 2,840,000 with 8,500 MBTs, 3,740 combat aircraft and 14,500 towed artillery as against India's total armed forces of 1,145,000 with 3,340 MBTs, 777 combat aircraft and 4,175 towed artillery.[23] In 1996 China spent $38 billion or 1.4 per cent of its GDP in military expenditure as against India's $10.4 billion or 2.8 per cent of GDP.

Besides the conventional army and munitions, more important now is nuclear technology, which is the basis of military strength. China started testing nuclear bombs in 1964 and has conducted 45 tests so far. It has 450 operational warheads with an average range of 6,800 miles (11,000 km), 113 land-based missiles, 12 sub-based missiles, 150 bomber-based missiles and 125 non-strategic weapons. Although India first tested a nuclear device in 1974, it was another 24 years before their next tests of five bombs were exploded in May 1998. It has 74 warheads with a range of 1,550 miles to 2,500 km in the Agni and Prithivi missiles it has developed.[24]

---

[22] All figures are based on the data in *Military Balance*, 1997/98.

[23] *Ibid.*

[24] *Time* and *Newsweek Magazine*, 25 May 1998.

Table 4.18 Military spending: India and China

	India[a]	China
Defence expenditure (US$m, 1993 prices), 1995	8,289	31,731
Defence expenditure (% of GNP)		
1985	3.5	4.9
1995	2.4	2.3
Defence expenditure (% of education and health expenditure)		
1960	68	387
1995	65	117

Source: *World Development Report*, 1999-2000 (Oxford: Oxford University Press/World Bank).

Note: [a] In its recent budget (2000/01) India has increased its military spending by 28%, the largest ever annual increase since independence.

Although both countries face problems of extreme poverty, China has comparatively performed better and achieved more. On almost every economic index Chinese indicators are well ahead of India. It is almost universally recognised now that if China maintains the speed of its reforms and keeps its existing political structure, in twenty years it will emerge as a great economic power in the world. In the military field, as well as in nuclear technology, China cannot yet be compared to the USA or even Russia, but it has the potential of being close to them in the future, depending on the future role of Japan and the geopolitics of the Pacific Rim. Compared to India, it is well ahead in this field as well.

India, however, has to its great credit a system of governance based on the tenets of democracy, sustained and nourished by a well-founded civil society, which is totally absent in China. India has earned more respect and prestige in the world community because of the system of governance it has enjoyed since its independence.

But the core challenge of development still has to be addressed. In order to compete with China and establish a global power base, India will need to redefine its role with its neighbours in South Asia and pursue a major structural change in the fields of administration and governance. As discussed earlier, India has to decide its options and determine its policy choice to enable it to play the role it seeks. India has to restructure and reconstitute itself to face the challenge of the new millennium. Otherwise, with or without nuclear warheads, India will lag behind and remain in a state of underdevelopment, maybe for centuries.

If the figures of economic performance are taken into account, the economic development achieved in South-East Asia is stunning compared to that of South Asia.[25] The achievements of Korea and Indonesia, for example, are phenomenal compared to those of India and Pakistan. The People's Republic of China, despite its ideological constraints and a vast population of 1.2 billion — as large as the whole of South Asia — has made a great leap forward in achieving faster growth in recent years than any other country in the region. The four-point modernisation programme initiated by Deng Xiaoping in 1978 has achieved for China, in twenty years, an astonishing annual growth rate of up to 11 per cent and now consistently remains at around 8 per cent. It is now almost universally accepted that China, in 15-20 years, will emerge as a major economic power in the world. Countries like Vietnam, Laos and Cambodia, having gone through the savage repression of bombing and destruction by American military forces, while still remaining under communist regimes, have changed their priorities in recent years to achieve considerable economic growth in many sectors.

Against this background of economic growth in South-East Asian countries, a large number of Indian politicians and economists argue that India has successfully developed and sustained a healthy institutional democratic social order, which these other countries have not. Nor have many of the South East Asian countries practised good governance or developed any civil society. They claim that their sacrifice in terms of development is the price that India has paid for sustaining democracy.[26] How far this argument is logical and sustainable will require a broader study of whether democracy and development can work hand in hand to produce faster economic growth or whether one can be achieved only at the cost of the other.

---

[25] The recent financial setbacks suffered by South-East Asian countries beginning in 1997 should not undermine the growth they have actually achieved. Moreover, the crisis was a temporary phase and the countries' economies have already improved considerably. *The Economist*, 21 August 1999.

[26] Tavlin Singh in her column titled 'A Freedom Failed' argues against such, what she calls 'democracy tax'. *India Today*, 27 May, 2002.

Firstly, it was a matter of choice and, it is the leaders of each country who have chosen their options and priorities. Ordinary people, who clearly want to have a better standard of living, have had no role to play in making this choice. Secondly, the results of experiences in various countries present a wide range of variables and so, on a practical plane, it will be extremely difficult to arrive at any firm conclusion on the issue. There is no doubt that man's eternal urge or desire is to have both freedom and food. He wants to enjoy both his political and his economic rights. But no country has given any specific choice directly to the people as to which path, they would opt for at the cost of the other. When democracy is promised, the right to life, property, employment and food is also promised. In societies like Korea and Indonesia, democracy is also promised, if not practised, but the leaders are allowed to assign priorities for economic growth.

The other argument, which introduces a pertinent philosophical question, is the whole definition of development. In a democratic society, a comprehensive kind of development is sought, from intellectual freedom to the right to participate in the social, cultural, political and economic affairs of the society. In contrast, under an authoritarian rule, which most of the South-East Asian countries have experienced during their core years of development, people have been deprived of their basic political and human rights. Of course, the ideal path is to pursue and achieve both democracy and economic growth at the same time. So while this debate may go on, the basic question remains. In the absence of any clear-cut criterion, whether societies that are still lagging behind can make an economic breakthrough and if so, what their options will be.

It is not always true that authoritarian rules help bring about economic growth faster. Other than a few exceptions, monarchs or dictators have ruled most African, Latin American and Asian countries for decades, but their economies are among the very poorest. Pakistan has had hardly any democracy in the first 24 years of its independence and in the next 28 years it had another spell of military rule for 13 years. Out of 52 years it has had authoritarian rule for nearly 40 years. Bangladesh had 15 years of military rule in its first 25 years, but there has still been no economic breakthrough.

Malaysia, on the other hand, although much smaller in population than India, has set an example of growth and development within a democratic order. So has Sri Lanka, which could have reached a threshold of breakthrough had it not been a victim of Tamil Ellam conflict, and has practised democracy throughout this period. So the argument that India could not produce an economic breakthrough because it practised democracy has very little substance. On the other hand, the authoritarian communist countries should have achieved growth and development much faster, but none of them did.

China sets another kind of example. It was and has remained a communist state. Till the beginning of the modernisation programme, its economy was in a pitiable condition and it appeared to have no future. But today it is different. So the strategies and policies that leaders or governments adopt in achieving economic goals are more important than their systems of government or their society's structure as such. It was therefore up to the Indian leaders and planners to decide the options and priorities of economic growth. They chose to adopt the Fabian concept of a welfare state, a mixed economy in which key economic sectors are in the hands of the state, and pursued this policy until very recently. Although India has adopted some policy reforms, initiated originally by Rajiv Gandhi, it has not moved fast enough and still basically maintains a hide-bound and sheltered economic structure, backward and not sufficiently tuned to the new challenge of a fast-moving economic order.

On the issue of the impact of demography on economic development, again the argument seems to be fallacious. Both China and Indonesia have set new examples to suggest that a large population can be an asset for economic growth. Although such a vast population is certainly difficult to organise and contain, if the policy choice is correct and priorities are in order, development can be achieved within a short period. Of course, South Asian experts will again raise the fact that both China and Indonesia are ruled by authoritarian regimes. The former is a communist one-party state and the latter a nominally democratic one, but the pivotal issue is that of choice. In the case of India, if it is thought that democracy stood in the way of rapid economic expansion and development then, it should have been restructured in such a manner that democracy and development could flourish in tandem. In the Third World context, India could be a unique example of a large functional democracy co-existing with a new economic model to achieve faster growth. Malaysia has achieved both, but it has a much smaller population than India or Indonesia.

These comparisons, however, do not mean that South Asia has not made any progress at all. In spite of being a populous region with so many problems including intra as well as interstate conflicts, some of which are fierce and intractable, it has still made considerable progress in at least some areas. In 50 years, since its decolonization, South Asia has performed well in terms of human development. The institutions of democracy have functioned far better in South Asia than in South-East and East Asia and many other regions of the world. In South Asia, people have enjoyed more individual freedom, the rule of law and a reasonably fair administration of justice through independent courts. They have, despite military interventions in Pakistan and Bangladesh, generally enjoyed a high level of cultural and intellectual liberty and freedom of the press and media. Uninterrupted democratic rule in India and Sri Lanka has certainly added to the quality of life in those countries as compared to most of the nations in South-East and East Asia. In all the major countries in South Asia — India, Pakistan, Bangladesh, Sri Lanka and Nepal — democracy is functioning.[27] Even Bhutan, at the instance of its king, is also going through a democratic transformation, which cannot be said about all the ASEAN nations. On human rights issues too, South Asia enjoys a far better ranking than many of the nations in South-East and East Asia.

In the social and economic fields, progress in some areas is substantial, if not phenomenal. Even with such a large and ever-growing population, South Asia has achieved near self-sufficiency in food production, the most important staple for human survival. Unless natural calamities hit it with special severity, all these populous states grow enough food for themselves and at least two of them have a surplus of produce for export. The number of people who live

---

[27] After thirteen years of democracy, Pakistan has entered into another period of military rule headed by its Army Chief Pervez Musharraf through a coup on 12 October 1999.

below the poverty line has been reduced from 70 per cent to less than 50 per cent, and significant progress has been achieved in infant mortality, child immunisation, securing access to safe water and literacy. In the field of empowerment of women, too, substantial progress has been made in the last two decades. Turning women into an socio-economic force has been one of the principal aims of policy, and NGOs like the Grameen Bank and BRAC have set an example of how to empower millions of assetless women to become a self-reliant, productive force.

However, South Asia is still far away from making an economic breakthrough to achieve a sustainable cycle of rapid growth and bring changes in the quality of life for the masses. It is still besieged with insurmountable problems of deprivation and under-development. It has not achieved what it should have, considering the advantages it enjoyed compared to the nations in the South-East. It has a common heritage of ancient civilisations, a shared history, a contiguous landmass for infrastructural development and a riverine system providing one of the largest fresh water flows in the world. It has the vast Indian Ocean in the south and the mountain ranges of the Himalayas in the north, providing an enormous source of natural wealth for the entire region. When the British left, South Asia inherited a trained bureaucracy, a structured military establishment, institutions of law and justice, a large class of entrepreneurs, a wide infrastructural and communications network, seats of government and Parliament and, above all, English as a language spoken by the elite classes of all the countries in the region. This provided an instant vehicle for international relations, trade and business. It had the good fortune of having articulate and educated political leaders, foreign-trained economists, planners, scientists, intellectuals, writers, authors, poets and painters, and a conscious and agile middle class.

And yet South Asia has remained backward, in a state of underdevelopment for more than five decades now. Why? What has gone wrong? Why has it not been able to escape from this state of underdevelopment and reach a stage of economic breakthrough like some of the South-East and East Asian countries have been able to achieve?

Chapter 5

The South Asian Association for Regional Co-operation (SAARC)

The question why South Asian countries have failed to make an economic breakthrough has haunted the leaders and policy-makers of the region for a long time. While each nation has failed to achieve it desired socio-economic goals, the realisation that conducting a collective effort might be a way of addressing the issue has. This led to the conceptualisation of a forum for mutual co-operation between the countries of the region. Consequently, the South Asian Association for Regional Co-operation (SAARC) was established through a historic summit meeting of the heads of governments of the seven states at Dhaka in 1985[1]. Conceived and initiated by the former assassinated President Ziaur Rahman in 1981, it opened a new horizon for friendship and co-operation amongst the countries involved and promised an end to conflicts and suspicion. While it was understood very clearly that the scale of development of each country would depend on their respective merit, utilisation of resources and leadership. It was also agreed that by mutual co-operation in certain areas they could augment and supplement their respective development efforts to achieve some of their common goals.

It was however not envisaged that the forum would act to solve bilateral problems amongst the member states or take the political issues of the region into its purview. But at the same time, the benefits of such

---

[1] India, Pakistan, Bangladesh, Sri Lanka, Nepal, Bhutan and the Maldives.

a forum of co-operation in international relations are many and varied. A forum of weaker economies will help in making improvements within the structure of their existing economies and is not expected to produce a miracle for the region. However, the laws of economics indicate that an association of economies will bring better results.

Above all, SAARC began its journey promising peace and prosperity for the teeming millions of the region. South Asia is a unique region of diversities. It is a region with hundreds of dialects, subcultures, tribes, castes and classes. Some of the conflicts and contradictions between the states are irreconcilable and, in particular, the ethno-religious conflicts within the states have led to open hostility. Their differences appear to be more striking than the commonalty they exhibit.

SAARC was also inspired by the formation and success of forums like the European Economic Community, the European Free Trade Association, the Latin American Integration Association, the North American Free Trade Agreement and the African Economic Community, and organisations of closer neighbours in South-East Asia, namely ASEAN and the Asian Free Trade Association. The beginning of SAARC was marked by the hope that regional economic co-operation would eventually lead to a system of integrated trade.

Conceptualisation of such an organisation stems from the domination of the South by the North. The developed countries of the North, with their inherent economic strength, dominated the weaker and poorer states of the South not only in directing the terms of trade and markets, but also in international issues of economic and political importance. The arrogance and the overwhelming economic power of the North led the South to develop a strategy for its own development by its own efforts. It was a strategy of self-reliance originally mooted in the Non-aligned Conference held in Cairo in 1962.

At the same time, the Group of 77 (G-77), a coalition of Third World countries within the framework of the United Nations had to evolve an integrated approach to get a fair and equitable deal in international trade and business. The proposals adopted by the G-77 laid the foundation for co-operation among the developing countries in order to achieve the objective of development of the South. The Action Programme, based on two resolutions adopted by the United

Nations General Assembly Special Session VI held in May 1964,[2] though considered as a milestone, was not acceptable to the North. The programme and the recommendations were discussed at United Nations Conference on Trade and Development (UNCTAD) in 1964 following the presentation of the G-77 to develop a consensus on common issues between the developing countries for a new international economic order.

It was argued that the industrialised North, who would manufacture the goods and sell them to the South at a much higher price, was exploiting the South as a source of cheap primary commodities. A process that had operated for decades and indeed still continues. This process of exploitation, termed 'economic imperialism', not only widened the gap between the North and the South, between the world's richest and poorest, but also threatened the peace and stability of the world as a whole. The decline in the purchasing capacity of the South, the rise of terrorism and economic recession, their lack of access to the markets of the North and the gradual determination in the South to resist such exploitation by the North led to the opening of dialogue between the North and South for their mutual benefit. It was in the interests of the North that the South was allowed to develop. However, as the terms stated by the South was not acceptable to the North, the talks mostly failed.

Various international forums of the United Nations eventually worked as a means of achieving solidarity amongst the developing nations. This was to increase their economic strength and to establish a collective bargaining power while negotiating with the North. The recommendations of the G-77, adopted in the meetings at Arusha, also emphasised the need for such co-operation between the developing countries at the regional and sub-regional levels.[3]

All these efforts at the UN level gradually trickled down to the regions. As the changing needs of South Asia were realised, co-operation between the states for their mutual benefit was recognised as an assured path of development. After the European Community's increasing success and ASEAN's emergence as a strong and viable

---

[2] V. Kanesalingam, *Collective Self-reliance of South Asian Countries* (Colombo, Sri Lanka: Marga Institute, Davinsa Development Abstracts, 1994).

[3] *Ibid.*

unit of economic growth, many other such regional organisations came into existence. Although it has taken many years for the South Asian countries to act on such a concept, the fact that despite all their conflicts and differences, they have now established an organisation of their own certainly speaks of their intention to work together to achieve self-reliance.

The objectives of SAARC, as laid down in Article I of its charter, are:

　i. to promote the welfare of the people of South Asia and to improve the quality of their life;

　ii. to accelerate economic growth, social progress and cultural development in the region and to provide all individuals with the opportunity to live in dignity and to realise their full potential;

　iii. to promote and strengthen collective self-reliance among the countries of South Asia;

　iv. to contribute to mutual trust, understanding and appreciation of one another's problems;

　v. to promote collaborative and mutual assistance in the economic, social, cultural, scientific and technical fields;

　vi. to strengthen co-operation with other developing countries;

　vii. to strengthen co-operation among themselves in international for a on matters of common interest; and

　viii. to co-operate with international and regional organisations with similar aims and purposes.

Article II of the charter defines the following principles:

1. Co-operation within the framework of the Association shall be based on respect for the principles of sovereign equality, territorial integrity, political independence, and non-interference in the internal affairs of other states and mutual benefit.

2. Such co-operation shall not be a substitute for bilateral and multilateral co-operation, but shall complement them.

3. Such co-operation shall not be inconsistent with bilateral and multilateral obligations.

In an assessment of the performance of SAARC, it is useful to refer briefly to the motivation and attitudes of South Asian countries towards the association. There are many who believe that SAARC represents an affirmation of faith of these countries in regional co-operation. The seven countries, whose differences are more striking than their commonality, seek to build on what they have in common. They cherish the hope that over time an extended network of economic and technical co-operation will reduce the political differences among them. Although linked by history and culture, these countries have different political systems. The diversity in their economic and military power has been a major cause of mutual suspicion and distrust. These differences and diversities were not lost sight of when the SAARC process was initiated in 1981.

The main thrust of the charter of SAARC has been towards co-operation in the socio-economic sectors, although the scope for extending its operation remains open according to the objectives laid in Articles IV and VII. But SAARC till now has not progressed beyond co-operation in economic issues. Even in that field it has proceeded much too cautiously because of some of its inherent weaknesses.

SAARC has so far been able to make progress in the following areas:[4]

i. Activities in twelve agreed areas of regional co-operation identified in the Integrated Programme of Action (IPA).

ii. Activities delineated by the leaders of the South Asian countries when they met in Bangalore in 1986. These include SAARC Audio Visual Exchange (SAVE), the SAARC Documentation Centre, organised tourism within SAARC countries, fellowships and scholarships and the SAARC Youth Volunteer Programme. These activities aim to promote people-to-people contact and are proof that SAARC leaders realise the significance of increased interaction among different sections of the population of South Asia.

iii. Activities relating to the setting up of SAARC regional institutions (e.g. the SAARC Agricultural Information Centre and the SAARC Meteorological Research Centre).

---

[4] *Ibid.*

iv. Representatives of planning agencies of member states who meet once a year have recommended a group of subjects in which regional co-operation can be promoted (e.g. the South Asian Preferential Trade Arrangement (SAPTA), plan modelling techniques, the establishment of a group on statistics and joint ventures in certain areas.

v. Activities and studies on themes/areas recommended by the Third and Fourth Summits are: (a) causes and consequences of natural disasters and their impact on the environment; (b) the impact on the region of the greenhouse effect; and (c) SAARC 2000 AD.

vi. The establishment of the SAARC Food Security Reserve; ratification of the Regional Convention on Suppression of Terrorism; agreement on the SAARC Travel Document; and agreement on the Draft Convention on Prevention of Narcotic Drugs.

These six categories of SAARC activities, taken together, are proof of the resolve of the seven nations to promote regional co-operation in the areas indicated. True, most of these activities have been in the realm of policy or decision-making. Tangible and result-oriented follow-up actions on these decisions are not to be found and therefore do not match the rhetoric of the summits. To be precise, what has the South Asian region gained over the past seventeen years since the establishment of SAARC? There is no denying the fact that SAARC has completed much preparatory work with regard to the creation of the policy mechanism for promoting intra-regional trade through the South Asian Preferential Trade Arrangement (SAPTA); it has formulated the Regional Convention on the Suppression of Terrorism; it has established the Food Security Reserve; it has established the SAARC Agricultural Information Centre (SAIC); and it has carried out studies on the causes and consequences of natural disasters and their impact on the environment. But none of these has yet made any tangible impact on the problems required to be alleviated.

SAARC's activities until now have focused on non-controversial areas and excluded politically sensitive issues — except the study of trade, manufactures and services, which are the core of any meaningful scheme of regional co-operation. In the political sense, SAARC has still not emerged as a regional community. It is still functioning largely at the government-to-government level and has not engaged broader constituencies. The member nations regard SAARC as a component of their foreign policy, not of their development policy. A judicious blend of both is necessary to sustain the SAARC process and to develop collective self-reliance among South Asian countries. However, an inherent weakness or problem inhibiting efforts to promote regional co-operation in South Asia is the lack of demonstration of a strong will among the member countries to co-operate. This is mainly due to the deterioration in the bilateral relations between some of the countries. The King of Bhutan was conscious of the need for good relations among these countries when he addressed the SAARC Ministerial Meeting in Thimpu (May 1985). He said:

> We are of the view that it is essential to the spirit of SAARC that each of us makes every effort to improve relations between and among ourselves ... unless the individual nations in our region can look to each other with mutual confidence, regional co-operation can rise only to a level of symbolic gestures.

What South Asian nations are not adequately aware of is that every manifestation of regional co-operation has to be founded upon a conscious act of political will undertaken by those concerned. In every case, that act of will, freely entered into, comprises of two recognisable elements: a decision that, notwithstanding disparities and differences, the larger common interest should dictate co-operation; and the recognition that a commitment at the political level to the realisation of this would facilitate its achievement.

Important programmes like the Food Security Reserve, the development of communications, the suppression of terrorism, the Convention on the Prevention of Narcotic Drugs, the Agricultural Information Centre and the Meteorological Research Centre require further development if their benefits are to reach the masses. Although extensive studies have been done on the greenhouse effect, and both the Food Security Reserve and the Agricultural Information Centre have been established, neither has had any real impact due to lack of adequate financial and logistical support, and no active measures have been taken to implement the recommendations made in various studies. At the non-governmental level, organisations like the SAARC Chamber and the Forum of SAARC Lawyers have been formed, but they are still limited to holding occasional meetings or seminars and have yet to take institutional root.

The only major, useful and positive step taken so far is in the trade sector, the most important component of economic co-operation in the region. The proposal of a South Asian Preferential Trade Arrangement (SAPTA) has taken concrete shape in the face of all the difficulties that stand in the way of its ultimate success. Despite all the complexities in business and trade, and the vested interest each country has in respect of its own policy constraints, all the members of SAARC have signed the SAPTA agreement, which promises 'growth and development to eradicate poverty of the common people of the region'.[5] The heads of state and government of the seven member countries, in Dhaka at the Seventh Summit of SAARC, signed this agreement on 11 April 1993. SAPTA has turned into a functional avenue to proceed further in this direction. It provides a framework of rules and modalities for gradually encompassing trade between the member states, which will lead to restructuring the tariff and duty regimes of individual countries and eventually the withdrawal of tariff barriers to open the door to a free trade zone in the region.

South Asia has a very small share of global trade (see Table 5.1). Its total exports in 1992 were only 0.74 per cent of world exports, and its imports only 1.07 per cent, which means that its total trade never exceeded more than 2 per cent of the global trade up to 1992.[6] In 1991 the total trade between SAARC nations (exports plus imports) amounted to $2.13 billion compared to $68.46 billion in trade between SAARC nations and the rest of the world: in other words, only 3.1 per cent of their total trade was within SAARC.[7]

---

[5] Sabbir Ahmed, 'SAARC Preferential Trading Arrangement: A Preliminary Analysis', *BIISS Journal*, vol. 16, no. 2, 1995, p.164.

[6] *Ibid.*, p.12.

[7] Tayyeb Shabbir, *Economic Transformation in South Asia: Nature and Implication for Competitiveness and Interdependence*, a presentation made at the ADIPA Conference, Colombo, October 1993.

Table 5.1 Intra-SAARC trade in relation to world trade

Year	Intra SAARC trade (exports + imports) (US$m)	World trade of SAARC countries (exports + imports) (US$m)	Share of intra-SAARC trade in world trade of SAARC countries (%)
1980	1,210.0	37,885.3	3.2
1981	1,176.8	36,616.2	3.2
1982	1,025.3	39,875.3	2.5
1983	969.0	40,410.1	2.4
1984	1,119.0	44,055.1	2.5
1985	1,088.7	43,759.5	2.5
1986	1,054.5	44,041.8	2.4
1987	1,145.9	49,480.3	2.3
1988	1,731.5	52,669.4	3.3
1989	1,722.8	58,595.1	2.9
1990	1,584.7	65,041.6	2.4
1991	2,136.8	68,462.4	3.1

Source: Estimated from IMF, *Direction of Trade Statistics Yearbook*, 1992.

Almost all SAARC countries largely depend on markets outside the SAARC region for their exports (Table 5.2). India's exports to SAARC countries are only 4.6 per cent of its total exports, compared to its exports to industrial countries of 54.4 per cent; Pakistan's exports are 3.4 per cent within SAARC as against 56 per cent to the industrialised nations. Bangladesh's exports are 4.7 per cent within SAARC compared to 75.8 per cent to the industrialised nations. Sri Lanka exports 2.6 per cent of its total to countries in SAARC but 69.4 per cent to the industrialised nations.

Table 5.2 Major export markets of SAARC member countries, 1991 (%)

	Industrialised countries	Developing countries	Asian countries	SAARC countries	Middle East
Bangladesh	75.8	21.8	10.5	4.7	5.0
Bhutan	n.a.	n.a.	n.a.	n.a.	n.a.
India	54.4	26.9	17.9	4.6	5.4
Maldives	50.9	48.7	44.3	19.2	2.3
Nepal	88.6	11.4	11.2	7.9	n.a.
Pakistan	56.0	42.2	22.7	3.4	12.2
Sri Lanka	69.4	24.7	9.2	2.6	11.2

Source: IMF, *Direction of Trade Statistics Yearbook*, 1992.

It will be seen from Table 5.3 that each nation also depends heavily on the countries outside the SAARC region for its imports. India imports only 5.4 per cent from the SAARC states, Pakistan 1.4 per cent, Bangladesh 7.5 per cent and Sri Lanka 7.2 per cent. Only Nepal and the Maldives exceed 10 per cent in their imports from the SAARC region. However, trading of SAARC nations with other developing countries is quite substantial in both exports and imports.

Table 5.3 Major import markets of SAARC member countries, 1991 (%)

	Industrialised countries	Developing countries	Asian countries	SAARC countries	Middle East
Bangladesh	37.2	42.5	33.5	7.5	5.9
Bhutan	n.a.	n.a.	n.a.	n.a.	n.a.
India	57.0	35.3	13.7	5.4	14.5
Maldives	62.7	36.7	33.7	14.1	0.9
Nepal	48.3	51.7	50.0	13.8	0.5
Pakistan	58.4	39.9	18.7	1.4	14.9
Sri Lanka	36.7	63.1	48.1	7.2	8.6

Source: IMF, *Direction of Trade Statistics Yearbook*, 1992.

South Asian economies still largely depend on agriculture (Table 5.4). Large proportions of the population — between 70 and 85 per cent — who live in rural areas depend directly or indirectly on agriculture. Although the share of agriculture in GDP is decreasing, the manufacturing sector has not made any dramatic improvement.

Table 5.4 Structure of production, 1991 (% share in GDP)

Country	Agriculture 1970	Agriculture 1991	Industry 1970	Industry 1991	Manufacturing 1970	Manufacturing 1991	Services 1970	Services 1991
Pakistan	37	26	22	26	16	17	41	49
India	45	31	22	27	15	18	33	41
Bangladesh	55	36	9	16	6	9	37	48
Sri Lanka	28	27	24	25	17	14	48	48
Nepal	67	59	12	14	4	5	21	27
Maldives	n.a.	n.a.	n.a.	n.a.	n.a.	n.a.	n.a.	n.a.
Bhutan	n.a.	43	n.a.	27	n.a.	10	n.a.	29

Source: *World Development Report 1993* (Oxford: Oxford University Press/World Bank).

While every member state has shown considerable enthusiasm about SAPTA, they have also realised that the scope and potential of SAPTA is limited because, at least for the time being, it covers only those selected items which the members do not compete to export in the international market. The major exports of Bangladesh are jute and jute goods, ready-made garments, leather and leather products, frozen fish, tea, electronics and even computer software. But India exports almost the same items and is itself a strong competitor in the world market. Pakistan and Sri Lanka also fall in the same category in most of these items. Both Pakistan and India export raw cotton and cotton goods, and in these and other items they have conflicting interests in exports. So the process of identifying the items that can be traded intra-regionally is being completed in phases. Another crucial issue is a mutually exclusive tariff barrier, which is hindering the flow of trade. After the identification of agreed items, member states will have to rationalise their tariff and duty structures to facilitate trade. Some progress has been made in identifying items that are complementary in nature and removing tariff barriers, but the full implementation of the programme will obviously take time.

In the last summit, keeping in line with the ASEAN Free Trade Agreement, the heads of government have decided to turn SAPTA into the South Asian Free Trade Agreement (SAFTA), which has been put into operation in the year 2001.

Both the value and volume of intra-regional trade, at least in the foreseeable future, will remain relatively small and its economic benefits will be insignificant compared to the need. It is also feared that due to interstate conflicts and hostile bilateral relationships, the objectives of SAPTA or SAFTA may not be achieved as desired.

In the absence of major political conflicts between their members, ASEAN, the EU, NAFTA and other regional trade facilities, have successfully worked through their differences. Whereas the divergence between SAARC states — at least between the major states — cast doubt over the measures to institutionalise trade in the region. Suspicion and mistrust still dominate the relationships between India and its smaller neighbours.

In addition to conflicts of political nature, there are also some economic and psychological factors that stand in the way of progress.

India is much larger and stronger, both geographically and economically, than its neighbours. It accounts for 76 per cent of the region's population, 59 per cent of its imports, 62 per cent of its exports, 41 per cent of its external resources, 79 per cent of its manufacturing value added and 68 per cent of the region's manufacturing exports.[8] The unequal size of the market and the fear of Indian domination over the economies of the smaller nations have both real and psychological impacts on the entire spectrum of SAARC. The trade imbalances that exist between India and the rest of the states, excepting Pakistan, are so wide and disproportionate that the smaller neighbours will never be able to catch up, even if India grants some radical concessions in the field of tariff reform.

In 1992 India exported to Bangladesh goods worth $283.9 million and imported from Bangladesh goods worth $4.2 million.[9] Also in 1992 it exported to Nepal goods worth $85 million and imported goods worth $21 million; and in the same year it exported to Sri Lanka goods worth $192 million and imported goods worth $13 million.[10]

Excessive dependence on the industrialised countries for trade, lack of financial and monetary co-operation, informal trade and smuggling between bordering states and weak infrastructure are other obstacles to the development of trade in the region.[11] In order to achieve their respective economic goals, which would help strengthen SAARC as well, each country has adopted some significant policy reforms in various fields, ranging from the financial sector to the labour market. Although some progress has been achieved in certain areas, but reforms of any nature always take time to yield results. Moreover, in the absence of adequate and proper institutions, many such reforms fail to achieve the desired goal and the people who expect benefits from them get quickly frustrated. If the bureaucracy, a key element in the implementation of reform, is not competent and

---

[8] Rehman Sobhan, 'The Logic of Planning Economic Co-operation on the SAARC Agenda', in Imtiaz Ahmed and Meghnath Guha Thakurta (eds), *SAARC: Beyond State Centric Co-operation* (Dhaka: Centre for Social Studies, 1992), pp. 43-44.

[9] Iftekharuzzaman, *Regional Economic Treaty and South Asian Security* (Dhaka: The University Press Limited, 1997), p. 83.

[10] Quoted from Sabbir Ahmed BIISS, Vol. 16, No. 2, 1995, p. 186.

[11] Sabbir Ahmed, 'SAARC Preferential Trading Arrangement', BIISS journal, Vol. 16 No. 2, 1995, pp. 185-92.

dynamic, many reforms may lead to disaster, inviting social unrest and convulsions. The success of some of the reforms also depends on foreign private capital inflow, but only a healthy economic and socio-political environment in the countries involved can attract such foreign investment. Compared to China and some of the South-East Asian states, direct foreign investment in South Asia has been so far insignificant.

In substance, SAARC has achieved only a meagre success in tangible terms. Based on all the work SAARC has performed so far and all the reports, studies, books and articles published in the capitals of SAARC nations, the general assessment is that SAARC has not been a success so far, either in political or in economic terms. Apprehension, suspicion, distrust and respective security perceptions have been the dominant factors affecting its growth. Political issues and conflicts between some of the states, particularly between Pakistan and India, and some of the intra-state conflicts still stand in the way of harmonising SAARC as an effective organisation. In the seventeen years of its existence, the Integrated Programme of Action (IPA) could not be implemented in any substantial form in any of the six categories of activities identified earlier. The objective of collective self-reliance has remained confined to rhetoric and statements, seminars and conferences. There was no room in the review of SAARC for discussion of bilateral or other conflicts. In the absence of a strong political will on the part of individual states to bury their ideological or political differences to achieve economic goals, the future of SAARC remains uncertain. The dominance of India in economic and military matters, and its relations with its neighbours, places a great burden on the growth of SAARC as an economic unit. The testing of nuclear bombs by India and Pakistan in May 1998 has further worsened the conditions for any collective effort to enhance the cause of peace and prosperity. Indeed, some argue that it has destroyed the very objectives and spirit of SAARC as enshrined in its charter.

One may say, however, that the greatest success of SAARC has been that it has survived. Despite the nuclear bombs exploded by India and Pakistan, the two principal members of SAARC, the summit was held peacefully in Sri Lanka in 1998. Although SAARC is not a forum to discuss or decide political or bilateral issues, or any interstate conflict, it has at times of bilateral tension at least worked to bring normality between the states concerned. It has also certainly contributed to creating a better understanding between the governments and their leaders. The annual summits of the heads of governments have undoubtedly created opportunities for politicians to meet privately to resolve bilateral issues through negotiation and peaceful means. When relationship between India and Sri Lanka turned sour over the refusal by India to withdraw its troops from Sri Lanka in 1987-89, SAARC leaders had a role to play in bringing the two countries together. Similarly, despite the strain caused by the nuclear test of India and Pakistan, the SAARC summit in Sri Lanka provided an opportunity for the leaders of both countries to meet and facilitated the immediate beginning of a dialogue. Moreover, SAARC has survived despite the volatile dispute over Kashmir. Some would even argue that, since SAARC was established in full knowledge of the divisive and conflicting relations between its members, it has a better chance of survival.

But is the survival of SAARC, without any success in achieving its objectives, well enough for South Asia? What then is the future of South Asia? In answer to this question most scholars, experts, economists, diplomats, analysts and politicians have expressed pessimism, although they have also made countless suggestions in the hope that SAARC will survive. Such recommendations are always tied to mostly philosophical and hypothetical conditions that are not attainable in the face of some problematical geo-political realities.

Chapter 6

Politics and State Management in South Asia: Some Characteristics

Assassination and Killing of Leaders

Political assassination figures as one of the characteristics of South Asian politics. Soon after the independence of India, Nathuram Godse shot the man who created a thematic non-violent movement in the subcontinent against British rule, Mahatma Mohandas Karamchand Gandhi, on 30 January 1948.[1] In Pakistan a similar assassination took place on 16 October 1951 when Liaquat Ali Khan, the first Prime Minister of Pakistan and a close associate of Mohammad Ali Jinnah, was shot dead while addressing a public meeting. In India again, after a strong rule of nearly eighteen years as Prime Minister, Mrs Indira Gandhi was assassinated by bullet shots from her own Sikh body guard on 31 October 1984. Seven years later her son and successor Prime Minister Rajiv Gandhi was assassinated by a suicide bomb while attending a public meeting at Sriperumbuder in Tamil Nadu on 21 May 1991. In Pakistan, Zulfiqar Ali Bhutto the flamboyant elected Prime Minister although not assassinated but was hanged, on 4 April 1979 by a military Junta on a charge of murder. On 17 August, 1988, General Ziaul Huq, who ruled Pakistan for nearly 11 years after removing and later hanging Bhutto, was killed in a plane crash. It is alleged that a bomb had been planted in a fruit basket, which had been carried into the aircraft.[2]

---

[1] For more detail, see Chapter 2.
[2] General Pervez Musharraf removed Nawaz Sharif, an elected Prime Minister, unceremoniously in a coup on 12 October 1999. He was charged with treason and hijacking the plane that was carrying the General from Colombo to Karachi. On his conviction, he was imprisoned for life by a Karachi court on 6 April 2000 and later on sent to Saudi Arabia on exile.

In Sri Lanka, S. W. R. D. Bandernaike, the popular Prime Minister who led their independence movement, was assassinated in 1959. His political opponents killed later President Premadasa, on 1 May 1993. Every President and Prime Minister acting as the Chief Executive of Sri Lanka has faced the threat of assassination.[3] In Bangladesh, Sheikh Mujibur Rahman, the founding father, was savagely killed along with some members of his family, including an 8-year-old son, on 15 August 1975 by a group of disgruntled army officers. On 30 May 1981, while visiting the port city of Chittagong, some army officers brutally killed President Ziaur Rahman, a charismatic and popular military ruler who had in March 1971 declared independence and led the war against Pakistan.

Every unnatural death of a political leader hanged or otherwise assassinated, had a serious political impact with far-reaching multidimensional consequences. These deaths not only affected the existing leadership and the party the person belonged to, but changed the course of political history of the societies concerned. They led to the birth of dynastic politics in South Asia, retarding the growth of real democracy and democratic institutions. After the assassination of Mahatma Gandhi, the Nehru family dominated politics in India for nearly 40 years. The assassination of Mrs Gandhi led to the induction of her son Rajiv, a commercial airline pilot by profession, into politics to become the next Prime Minister of India. After the killing of Rajiv, his Italian-born wife Sonia was under tremendous pressure to take an active role in national politics. But when she resisted, Narshima Rao, a Congress leader who was not a member of the Nehru family, led the government for a five-year term. But as the Congress weakened further in 1998, the situation forced Sonia to enter politics and assume the office of the President of All India Congress and the Leader of the Opposition in the Parliament.

In Pakistan after the hanging of Zulfiqar Ali Bhutto, his wife Nusrat Bhutto carried the flag of the Pakistan People's Party. His

---

[3] In May 2000 an attempt was made to assassinate President Kumaratunga, the daughter of Sirimavo Bandernaike and the assassinated President S. W. R. D. Bandernaike. In the seventeen-year conflict, Tigers have killed one Sri Lankan President and more than 50 prominent Lankans, including Cabinet ministers and lawmakers. Prabhakaran, the leader of the Tamil Tigers, argues that the Tamils, who comprise 12.5 per cent of Sri Lanka's 19 million people, and the majority Sinhalese, cannot live together in peace. So a separate state is necessary. *Time*, 29 May 2000.

daughter Benazir Bhutto eventually took up the mantle and was elected as the first female Muslim Prime Minister in the world. As the head of the party and now as a Leader of the Opposition, she still dominates politics in Pakistan.

The Bandernaike family in Sri Lanka has dominated the political scene in that country for nearly 50 years now. Sirimavo Bandernaike, wife of the assassinated President, assumed the executive office of Prime Minister in 1960 and their daughter, Chandrika Kumaratunga, became the present President of Sri Lanka, after the elections of 1996.[4]

In Bangladesh the two assassinations led to two ladies emerging as the contenders for power. Begum Khaleda Zia, a housewife assumed the post of chairperson of the party soon after the assassination of her husband, President Ziaur Rahman. She led a national movement for the restoration of democracy against military rule and took over the office of Prime Minister after winning a general election in 1991. In 1996 she lost the general election and spent five years as the Leader of the Opposition in Parliament. Only after the general elections of 2001 was she returned to power again as Prime Minister. Similarly, Sheikh Hasina is the daughter of the assassinated President Sheikh Mujibur Rahman. Very soon afterwards she emerged as the President of the Awami League, a party that struggled for the independence of Bangladesh under the leadership of her father. She also provided leadership for the restoration of democracy in the country and an end to military rule. In 1996, having won the general election she became the Prime Minister. Five years later, in 2001 she lost the next general election and is the present Leader of the Opposition in Parliament.

Democracy within Parties

The rise to power of almost all the contemporary leaders of South Asia has been by heredity rather than through any democratic process, thus establishing a dynastic political order. This is largely due to lack of institutionalised development of political parties in all four countries in South Asia: India, Pakistan, Sri Lanka and Bangladesh. In each of these countries a political vacuum occurred soon after the

---

[4] The Constitution was amended to return the country to a presidential system.

death or killings of their respective leaders and the rank and file of their parties looked to the family members of their leader to rescue them in order to keep their political entities united. Because of the great charisma and popularity of the assassinated leaders who enjoyed a very strong mass based support in their own countries, no other personality of the party outside the family could be accepted as someone who would command the respect and emotional attachment of the millions of followers they had left behind.

So in each case this pattern of dynastic 'democratic' leadership emerged. In India it led to the emergence of Indira Gandhi after the death of her father Jawaharlal Nehru and then of Rajiv Gandhi after the killing of his mother; in Sri Lanka of Sirimavo Bandernaike after the killing of her husband and later of Chandrika Kumaratunga, their daughter. In Pakistan Nusrat Bhutto, the wife of Zulfiqar Ali Bhutto, assumed the mantle after Bhutto's killing and then their daughter, Benazir Bhutto. While in Bangladesh Sheikh Hasina Wazed, on her return home from a self imposed exile of nearly five years after the killing of her father Sheikh Mujibur Rahman, assumed leadership of their political party. So too did Begum Khaleda Zia, soon after the killing of her husband President Ziaur Rahman, assume a similar position of leadership of the party her husband had founded. Historical necessities at a given time in their respective societies have led to such situations. Each of the present leaders — Khaleda Zia, Sheikh Hasina, Sonia Gandhi, Chandrika Kumaratunga and Benazir Bhutto, now stand on their own merit as leaders democratically elected both by the people and the parties they represent. So democracy has assumed a different dimension in South Asia. In the context of modern democracy this form of leadership changes is now a reality. It exists even in some countries beyond South Asia. So there is nothing wrong in a dynastic democratic order as long as the leaders are elected by the people and their parties.

A healthy growth of political parties is an essential pre-condition to developing good democratic institutions. On the other hand lack of democratic practices within the political parties may give rise to democratic authoritarianism. Although the party's constitution and structure in all the major political parties in South Asia tend to concentrate too much of power in the hands of an individual, it is seen as a transitional phase only which will in time lead the party towards further democratisation. There is of course the need for developing a culture to consolidate a functional democratic order at all levels and the initiative of moving the party towards a more democratic order has to come, in the first instance, from the leaders themselves.

The most pertinent and relevant issue therefore is to see how the leaders of these countries decide to strengthen the party system and develop the practice of democracy within their respective parties. The constitution of every one of the major political parties of South Asia do provide for a democratic process at all the levels of the party structure but fulfilment of such practice is limited to only a few. Since democracy is in a nascent stage and these societies are in a transition, the practice of democracy within the parties is yet to take roots in South Asia.

Corruption and Patronage

In each of the South Asian societies, like many others all over the world, corruption is widespread and embedded in the very roots of the social fabric. It is not poverty or deprivation that causes corruption; rather, corrupt practices are endemic and go on unabated as part of the system. The whole social contract is based on patronage. In the distribution of state largess, favours, contracts, jobs and businesses, the client-patron relationship plays the most important role. There is a barrier between those with power and influence in the government, on the one hand, and the rest of the people on the other, and this barrier cannot be removed without patronage.

It is difficult to evolve a natural or institutional mechanism to reduce the conflict between the citizens and the state. Nothing happens or yields without *tadbir*[5] or persuasion. A letter written to the government, the bureaucracy or government agencies on a simple routine matter will remain unanswered for months — perhaps forever — unless it is pursued by way of a *tadbir*. So the general grievances of the public remain unattended. Meanwhile, in every

---

[5] A Bengali word with an element of graft included.

government contract or business, big or small, from the top to the bottom, patronage plays the key role. The higher up in the hierarchy, the bigger the price one has to pay for any favour. In recruitment, posting and promotion of citizens in public service, the same forces operate and patronage is the most effective vehicle for advancement in government departments. All this happens because individuals in these societies assume more importance than institutions.

In the absence of any strong institutional system of accountability and transparency, political corruption has become a common phenomenon in all the countries of South Asia. Crimes perpetrated in the political arena are increasing with the rise of the new moneyed class who have accumulated wealth by dubious and illegal means. With the rise of social crimes in all societies, the character of politics and of politicians is also changing fast. The state being the largest repository of wealth, greed for power to dominate and distribute that wealth has made politics a gainful profession. Rather than being driven by the cause of the people and their well-being, politics tend to become motivated by individual selfish interest.

The Rule of Law

In order to guarantee the rule of law, all the countries in South Asia have historically relied on written constitutions. They have opted for and maintained constitutional rule, except when military interventions have taken place in countries like Pakistan and Bangladesh and the constitutions have been suspended. Besides these short periods of rule under martial law, all the countries of South Asia have exercised constitutional rule based on the British principles of governance. The constitutions of India, Pakistan, Bangladesh, Sri Lanka and even Nepal have common objectives as principles of state — the primary one being to nourish and sustain democracy and a democratic order.

India, by an uninterrupted constitutional rule, has given a lead in practising democracy in South Asia. So has Sri Lanka, except for a very brief period of military rule. Bangladesh and Pakistan, although ruled for varying periods under martial law, returned to constitutional rule as soon as it was possible. In Nepal, the monarchy dominated the political structure till the mid-1980s with the king enjoying executive powers, but it has since gone through a great transformation. The monarchy has been retained, but the executive powers have been transferred to the elected representatives and the constitution has been reframed in line with other countries in South Asia.

The characteristics of the South Asian constitutions are that the fundamental objectives of each state are enshrined in the Principles of State Policy with a guarantee of fundamental human rights enforceable by the highest court of law. In each constitution, the independence of judiciary is guaranteed and Parliament has been made sovereign to represent the will of the people, with control over the executive branch of the state. The main features of the constitutions are almost identical and the basic structure of the constitutions is also similar. The system of government practised is of a parliamentary form, maintaining the tradition of the British system.

In the Indian Constitution, the directive principles of state policy are contained in Part IV (Articles 36-51). In Pakistan, they are contained in Chapter II (Articles 29-40). In Bangladesh, they are in Part II (Articles 8-25). In Sri Lanka they are contained in Articles 27-29 and in Nepal they are incorporated in Part IV (Articles 24-26). The fundamental rights guaranteed in each constitution also look very similar. In the Indian constitution, the fundamental rights are contained in Articles 12-30; in Pakistan, Articles 8-28; in Bangladesh, Articles 26-44; in Sri Lanka, Articles 10-14; and in Nepal the fundamental rights are guaranteed in Articles 11-23. All these fundamental rights, based on the human rights charter of the UN, are almost identical in nature and content.

It is not the making of law but the enforcement of law that is crucial to sustaining a healthy civil society. South Asia has been used to the concept of rule of law for a long time. Historically, and more so during the last century of British rule, the concept of rights and obligations of citizens regulated by the law was advanced in order to contain the rising aspirations of the people of the Indian subcontinent for freedom. The election at the *Panchayat* or village level (the grass-roots unit of local bodies), introduced towards the end of the nineteenth century, set the trend for the democratic principle of rule by the people. This developed into a fuller concept of a democratic order where every citizen was to be considered equal in the eye of law and every citizen was to be treated equally without any discrimination. This awareness also helped develop the idea of the independence of judiciary in order to enforce the equality concept. Adherence to these two concepts turned out to be the most essential pre-condition for the attainment of a democratic order.

In simple terms, the rule of law implies that every citizen is subject to the law and no one is above the law. This basic concept and its acceptance are considered to be a standard norm of civilisation in the modern context. Democracy and the concept of the rule of law go hand in hand. Laws are made for the welfare of the people, to bring a balance in society — a harmony between the conflicting forces in society. Laws affecting individuals and regulating their behaviour are of great importance in maintaining social equilibrium and tranquillity. Another important objective of making laws is to maintain order in society, a peaceful environment for the progress of the people. Subordinate legislation, by-laws, rules, regulations, policy guidelines and executive orders, which create rights and obligations and have the force of laws, are equally important in achieving the social and economic objectives of society.

The concept of the rule of law alongside tradition, usages, practices, values and heritage also leads to the creation of institutions. Laws alone cannot fulfil all the basic demands of society, but where law is absent its functions can be fulfilled by general practices based on traditions, values, usages and practices. If institutions are to be honoured and valued, individuals need to subject themselves to the authority of such institutions. But in an emerging civil society like those in Asia, Africa or Latin America, where doctrinaire rule has been abandoned and a democratic order is practised, the culture of the rule of law is faced with a hard challenge. In these transitional societies, political and governmental power immediately tends to produce authoritarianism, and in exercising power, elements of arbitrariness, discrimination and patronage become prominent. Individuals exercising power or authority easily forget that such an exercise of power is also subject to law and institutions. The tendency to misuse or abuse the law is common. Those who are in authority talk of the rule of law but in practice they do not abide by the principles of the rule of law. In the political sphere, pressure from the rank and file, and from sycophants and cronies, personal greed and an authoritarian mentality lead those in power to undermine the law and the institutions. In the process, they install themselves above the law and conduct themselves in a regressive manner.

Gunnar Myrdal, the Swedish scholar and a Nobel laureate[6] identified these countries, where he had found any rule of law difficult to sustain, as 'soft societies'. He found in these societies that rule-makers were the principal agents of rule-breakers and that the lack of the rule of law was a major cause of poverty and vice versa. Those in authority very frequently break the law when exercising power. They do not hesitate to do so because in the process of enjoying power their arrogance keeps growing. The elite and the privileged use laws to their advantage, while the majority of people remain in the dark and deprived of the advantages of law. Law is enforced more rigorously against the poor and helpless, and certain laws are used as instruments of repression against the weaker sections of society. Mutual accommodation, compromise and patronage play a dominant role in social conflicts. The powerful and influential members of society exploit the system to their own advantage.

The social fabric breaks down once it is found that the essential ingredients of the rule of law and equality are being ignored and undermined by those who govern the society. If the country's rulers i.e. politicians, bureaucrats and those who are powerful and privileged, do not subject themselves to the law and institutions, the effect is contagious and it cannot be expected that their subordinates or the common citizens will have respect for law and institutions either.

So when measuring the extent or the existence of the rule of law in a given society, the crucial issue for consideration is the degree of enforcement of law. The level, extent and quality of such enforcement will determine how far a society guarantees its citizens an equal status in life. The right to life and liberty and the right to equal opportunity and employment, guaranteed in all the constitutions of the South Asian states, can be cherished and fulfilled only when all are treated equally before the law.

---

[6] See *Asian Drama* (Vols. I-III). *An Inquiry into the Poverty of Nations*, Kalyani Publishers, New Delhi, 1985.

One of the major weaknesses of administration and governance in these societies lies in their failure to enforce the law strictly, without any fear on the part of those who are responsible for such enforcement. The agencies of law enforcement are always under pressure from the higher authorities as to where and how and to what extent a particular provision or weapon of law ought to be applied. The prevalence of any such weakness only corrodes the very basic foundation of discipline in society. The client-patron relationship that dominates the dynamics of interactions between the state and the citizens in South Asian societies takes away the essence of the rule of law or the principle of equality before law. Whether to favour a relative or a friend or a party man, or whether one is motivated by one's own greed and personal gain, becomes more important than the serenity of the law and its application. The same deficiency prevails in the economic field, in the decision-making process for approving a project, in a business proposal, in foreign investment and in granting loans or licences. If a society is run in such a manner that a person feels that, however heinous a crime he commits, he can get away with it unpunished because he enjoys the patronage of those who matter in politics or society, social order is bound to lose its moorings. This is not an exceptional situation any longer — it has become a general rule, a common scenario in many of the societies of South Asia.

In societies where the practice of the rule of law is weak and dominated by the client-patron relationship, widespread corruption and discrimination take deep root to retard progress and development. This could be one of the reasons why South Asia lags behind the South-East Asian countries, where discipline and the rule of law are more vigorously enforced, whether the government or the country is democratic or authoritarian.

The Bureaucracy and Governance: Policy Planning and the Policy-making Process

Bureaucracy, an institution inherited from British rule in India, plays an important role in the decision-making process in South Asia. The administrative system set up by the British was designed to suit their own colonial needs — primarily to maintain law and order, to ensure the collection of revenue and the exploitation of resources. Headed by an elite class of civil servants, trained to govern and administer the subcontinent, the bureaucracy developed into a permanent institution in the various countries of the region. Although the British left almost 55 years ago, the system has remained the same. Paper and file-oriented administrative work still continues in all the South Asian societies, controlled by a bureaucracy that is still perceived to be a different class from the rest of the people.

Despite political convulsions, radical changes and certain reforms in the administration of the governments, in most countries, the basic structure, style and management pattern has remained essentially unchanged. Indeed, in the early years after independence, each government adopted the system they had inherited, as they did not have any better system to introduce.

As a result, although attempts have been made to bring changes in the system, which politicians have frequently promised, the basic structure has remained the same to the present day. Any major attempt at reform to suit the changing needs of the time has been strongly resisted by the incompetent civil servants. As a result, the bureaucracies in almost all the South Asian states remain generally indifferent, slow, non-committal and largely alienated from the people. As an institution, the bureaucracy is still considered a secluded class, distant from the people, yet in every aspect of people's daily lives the bureaucracy plays a dominant role. From the grass roots of union organisation up to the level of central government, bureaucracy is omnipresent. The bureaucracy being large, its power and influence in the running of governments is overwhelming. Poverty, the influence of public expenditure, the restrictive rules and regulations, and the scarcity of jobs make the bureaucracy even more important for common people. From factories to paddy fields, from ecology to electricity, from roads to rivers, in every arena people become dependent on the government and the bureaucracy.

However routine or ordinary it may be, any application for any kind of approval addressed to a Secretary will go to the Additional Secretary, then to the Joint Secretary, then to the Deputy Secretary and then to the Assistant Secretary or to the clerk below him to initiate a file on the application submitted. The file will then move upwards through the same stages to the Secretary before any final decision can be given. By that time 3-6 months might have elapsed, but still the decision will not be forthcoming. If the matter is something important, it may have to travel upwards to the office of the Prime Minister before any final decision can be given.

In formulating policies and making decisions, the bureaucracy plays a crucial role. Most of the policies relating to any vital issue, even if initiated by ministers or the Prime Minister, will go through the same process and the bureaucracy from the rank of a Deputy Secretary or a Joint Secretary will prepare the actual articulation of the policy. Every such proposal, after being approved by the minister concerned, is sent to the Cabinet Division to place it before the Cabinet. Once the Cabinet approves the matter, it travels back to the relevant ministry and then goes to the lowest rung of the bureaucracy to pass the necessary order thereby giving effect to the cabinet decision.

The preparation of an annual development plan or a three-year rolling plan or a long-term perspective plan is left with the Planning Commission, which is mostly staffed by civil servants, a set-up common to all the major countries in South Asia. The Planning Commission prepares the development plan and its budget under the overall direction of the Cabinet on some of the basic matters only. Neither the Prime Minister nor the other ministers have time to go through all the details and to see what is really being developed or prepared by the bureaucracy. The role of the Cabinet or the minister or the head of the government is superficial in most cases, as they do not have the time, knowledge, expertise or patience to undertake the arduous task of determining the plan.

These Planning Commissions follow more or less the same system in each country, preparing plans or projects and then having the relevant ministries negotiate with donor countries and multilateral agencies for loans and grants under various heads. The World Bank and the International Monetary Fund (IMF) play an important role in all the South Asian countries, in formulating and developing plans and projects. Almost all the governments of South

Asia are heavily dependent on foreign agencies for funds, technical know-how and the supply of arms and ammunition for military institutions.

Attempts are being made to introduce administrative reforms in order to increase efficiency, accountability and transparency, and to speed up decision making, policy formulation and policy implementation. A section of people in all the South Asian countries is arguing very strongly that, in the absence of any effective accountability, the system of administration left by the British is not suitable for coping with the challenges of the new millennium and is an important reason why the nations of South Asia are lagging behind those of South-East Asia. Dynamism, openness and a new orientation are difficult to infuse in a bureaucracy that is traditionally conservative and resistant to any innovation needed to keep pace with the needs of growth in the economy. It is still old fashioned, incompetent and highly corrupt. Fast economic growth is considered as one of the principal goals in achieving a change in people's quality of life, but the present system of administration by a bureaucracy established almost 100 years ago cannot help in improving the present state of the economy in South Asia. On the other hand, neither the politicians nor the government, whether democratic or authoritarian, has been able to bring any basic change in the system of administration in these countries. In the present age of globalisation and fast-moving technology, reforms are essential to improve the lives of the millions of people living below the poverty level.

The same crisis surrounds the judiciary and the administration of justice originally established by the British. It is still considered as one of the model systems for maintaining a balance between the principal organs of the state. The judiciary plays a central role in protecting the rights of citizens against the illegalities committed by the executive branch of the state. In each constitution of the South Asian countries, except during the occasions when they were modified by martial law — particularly in Pakistan and Bangladesh — the independence of the judiciary and the structure and management of justice under the overall supervision of a Supreme Court are more or less guaranteed. In the constitutions of India, Pakistan, Bangladesh, Sri Lanka and Nepal, the judiciary — particularly the Supreme

Court—enjoys a unique position in interpreting the law and enforcing the fundamental rights guaranteed by the constitution.

Yet the justice system in the present context is considered archaic, old fashioned, indifferent, slow and corrupt. Although Law Commissions have been established and efforts made to improve the quality of the judicial system and to recommend new laws in all the societies in South Asia, progress has been slow and disappointing. The number of cases pending in all the courts of South Asia is phenomenally large.[7] There is a lack of court rooms, trained judges and efficient staff, working and living conditions are poor, and the process of law left behind by the British rulers is generally inefficient and complex. In the absence of some radical changes in the laws relating to investment and production, local investors, not to mention foreign investors, face enormous difficulties in putting their money to use. So entrepreneurs blame the judiciary and bureaucracy for standing in the way of growth and investment. The judicial system and laws need to be reformed urgently to deal with the new challenge South Asia faces today.

The question of good governance in South Asia has been another challenging issue. Besides the issue of accountability and transparency in decision-making and implementation, the administration as a whole needs to undergo serious scrutiny. The utilisation of the wealth of the state and how the government and its administration manage is a particular priority. The criterion of good governance is no longer limited to the fact of having an elected government. The quality of the electoral process and the existence of an effective participatory Parliament are considered as essential pre-conditions for good governance. The Standing Committees of Parliament are equally crucial in ensuring the accountability of each ministry of the government. An objective media, an active civil society, effective local government, non-governmental organisations, the private sector, trade unions and bipartisan politics at all levels can achieve a desired

---

[7] Professor Bibek Dedbroy in his assessment published in the *New York Times* mentioned that in India 25 million cases remain untried. It would, according to him, take 324 years to clear the backlog of cases in Indian courts without any addition of new cases (*India Today*, 19 June 2000). See also the articles by Tavleen Singh on the slow-moving judicial system in India (*India Today*, 13 December 1999 and 23 October 2000).

quality of governance, with a modern, independent and effective judiciary in hand. The issues of governance are now assuming more importance in determining the quality of a state in achieving the desired growth rate for its people. Although the level and quality of governance vary in each of the states in South Asia, the basic issues remain the same.

Chapter 7

Bangladesh as a Test Case: Some Special Features

Besides the regional and global issues, interstate conflicts and nuclearization, there are other reasons why South Asia has fallen behind the economies of South-East Asia. It is necessary to examine whether the political systems practised in South Asia, their political cultures and behaviour, the existing institutions of policy planning and instruments of policy making, the role of the government and the opposition parties, the intra-party decision-making process, the bureaucracy, the Parliament and the whole range of issues relating to governance and administration have hindered the development of South Asia. What role have they played in the advancement of society and what have been the successes and failures? There is no short-cut to development and it is not expected that such development can be achieved overnight, but an objective assessment of 50 years of performance will help the countries to move towards a better future.

While examining these common issues, a comprehensive study taking Bangladesh as a test case may have significant relevance. If democracy and development have to go hand in hand and if it is believed that fast economic growth can also be achieved under a democratic political order, then the level and quality of democracy are issues of great importance.

Quality of Elections

Free and fair elections are fundamental to democracy. Governance by the representatives of the people cannot be effective unless these representatives are truly elected, reflecting the wishes of the people. If the election itself is not fair, the authority of the representatives will always be questioned, which will weaken the government when it needs to take important or bold decisions. Only truly elected representatives can enjoy the authority to introduce strong reforms and implement them even though they may be unpopular. In a democratic order, the electoral process and the political system as a whole are vitally important. One of the main reasons why faster growth cannot be achieved or structural reforms cannot be adopted or implemented in the South Asian context and among the developing countries in general, is the weakness of the representatives and their political leadership. They prefer to adopt soft options, although people expect hard decisions. If a party wins in a questionable election through unfair means, it loses the moral authority to govern effectively or take strong decisions.

If the election is good and fair and the people are free to exercise their right of franchise without intimidation or undue influence, and if the Election Commission is independent of political authority and in full control of the entire machinery of the election, including the mainstream bureaucracy, Parliament will emerge as an institution that represents the sovereignty of people. On the other hand, any distortion or deviation from these basic requirements is not likely to produce a Parliament that represents the will of the people. So the effective participation of the people in an electoral process where the right of franchise is unfettered can be the only guarantee of establishing democracy at the national level.

The struggle for the right of franchise in Bangladesh was the cornerstone of all democratic movements. This very elementary prerequisite of a civil democratic order was found to be lacking both because of political interference as well as military interventions in the electoral process thus retarding the development of democracy in the country. As a consequence, whenever a Parliament was established either by political actions or when established under military regimes, it was not able to fulfil the aspirations of the people. Constitutional rule was disrupted again and again and democracy could not blossom among a people who had fought a war to achieve it. Beginning with Mujib's one-party rule and ending with

Ershad's debased Parliaments, democracy could not take root. The power of the people, the will of the people and the effective participation of the people in choosing their representatives in the administration of the country were the objectives written into the constitution but they found no practical expression.

At no time was the Election Commission able to make any mark as an independent institution to ensure free and fair elections. In the general elections of 1973, 1979, 1986 and 1988, it was the government rather than the Election Commission that controlled the electoral process. On 7 March 1973, the first election was held under the new constitution of an independent Bangladesh. The Awami League and particularly Sheikh Mujib were at the peak of their popularity. Mujib's charisma and personality dominated the election, and the fact that the Awami League would win with a large majority was not in doubt. Although the public in general was disappointed over the way the Awami League was ruling the country, they were willing to give Mujib a chance to retrieve the nation from the existing chaos.

Yet the Awami League resorted to intrigue and intimidation. The leaders of the Awami League plunged into a competition to prove their popularity and impress their 'leader'. An attitude of arrogance dominated their thoughts and an element of intolerance crept into their minds as they maintained that they alone had the right to rule the country. So when the election strategy was worked out, democratic practices and norms were disregarded and sometimes deliberately violated for petty personal reasons. There was a general notion that there was actually no opposition in the country but this was erroneous. With the entire administrative machinery on its side, the government utilised daily newspapers, radio and television, transport, patronage and other facilities to advance its cause. It became irritable, intolerant and arrogant, despite all the advantages it had on its side, for securing a certain and decisive victory.

The first conflict between the ruling party and the parties in opposition arose when the time came for submitting nomination papers. Election of a person unopposed or uncontested is considered a prestigious matter in the subcontinent. If someone is returned in an election uncontested an extra point is added to his credentials for holding office in the government or party. On 5 February, when the nomination papers were received, the Awami League candidates had no opposition in six seats. Furthermore, on the date of withdrawal of candidature, five more Awami League candidates were found to be without contestants.[1]

A reign of terror prevailed in some of these areas. In order to compete with some of their colleagues who had earlier been declared elected unopposed; others now set out to prove their popularity in their own constituencies. The method applied was the same — in most cases; nomination papers of all opposition candidates were forcibly withdrawn.

The same attitude was maintained throughout the election campaign and it reached its climax on election day. Despite all the constraints and disadvantages that the opposition faced, in about two dozen constituencies, the opposition leaders and candidates showed a solid advantage at the polls over the Awami League candidates and when the counting of votes ended they were unofficially declared elected by the local officials. They claimed that they had won the election, but the polls result announcement had been later rigged in their constituencies and the Awami League had adopted unfair methods.[2]

The central leadership of the Awami League made it an issue that prominent opposition leaders should not be allowed to win in the election. The party stalwarts argued that victory for people like Ataur Rahman Khan, Mashiur Rahman,[3] M. A. Jalil, Shahjahan Siraj, Rashed Khan Menon, Dr Alim Al-Razee, Muzaffar Ahmed and Suranjit Sen would cast direct aspersions not only on the party but also on the 'Father of the Nation'. How could these people win when Bangabandhu was still alive and was the chief of the party and the government? The election of such persons would confirm the decline

---

[1] See Moudud Ahmed, *Bangladesh: Era of Sheikh Mujibur Rahman* (Dhaka: The University Press Limited, 1983), pp. 168-69.

[2] Some opposition names were even declared elected over television and radio. See for more detail Moudud Ahmed, *Era of Sheikh Mujibur Rahman*, pp. 169-70.

[3] Mashiur Rahman (Jadu Mia) of NAP-B contested the election from prison, where he was detained on political grounds and was not allowed to come out even on election day. He secured 28,870 votes against his nearest rival Abdur Rouf of the Awami League, who secured 39,056 votes. Jadu Mia claimed that he would have won even from prison if the Awami League candidate had not adopted unfair means.

of the Awami League's popularity and would mean victory for the opposition. With these personalities in the opposition, the Awami League feared that it would be difficult to manage the Parliament. Moreover, many of them were considered 'unpatriotic' people who, according to the Awami League, were opposed to the independence of Bangladesh. If they had won in the election, it would have undermined the whole spirit of the independence movement. The election of a few people who were not politically known was of less concern than that of the key personalities from the opposition. The loss of seats by two senior ministers, Abdul Mannan and Abdus Samad Azad (in one of the two constituencies) would have been disastrous — or at least this is how the Awami League leadership viewed the outcome.

It is true that the Awami League would have won the election with an overwhelming majority in any case. If the central leadership of the Awami League had not intervened and the state machinery had not been misused, the opposition would have won an additional twenty seats or so only over the nine they actually won. What ultimately happened was that it raised a serious question of credibility. It sowed the seed of a deeper resentment and distrust between the parties in opposition and the ruling party. It created a genuine suspicion in the minds of the people about the bonafide of the whole election result.[4]

With the death of Sheikh Mujib in 1975 there was a great political vacuum in the country. The Awami League took time to recover from the loss of their leader, and the JSD was in a shattered condition. Zia, although a military general, had a great deal of charisma and popularity, and was in a position to go for a general election without much fear of losing it. Although the election of 1979 was held under martial law, it was far more credible than the one held in 1973.

For his own consolidation, Zia and his ruling party the Bangladesh Nationalist Party (BNP), established at his own initiative on September 1st, 1978, played a different role in this election to the one played by the Awami League in the previous election. The government

---

[4] A conservative estimate in the government newspapers suggested that the opposition could secure at least 30 seats. A political correspondent of the government-owned English daily made this assessment based on views gathered from different quarters. See his account in *The Bangladesh Observer*, 4 March 1973.

encouraged the political parties to take part in the election and restrained its party men from interfering in the electoral process. Moreover, Zia ensured that in all the constituencies where opposition leaders were contesting, there were no disturbances and the administration played a neutral role.[5]

The election campaign was fierce and generated a lot of emotion and tension; although compared to previous election it was peaceful. Unlike the 1973 election, no candidate was kidnapped or forced to withdraw their nomination paper to enable another candidate to win the election unopposed. Neither were there reports of ballot boxes being hijacked, as had occurred in 1973. In most constituencies, the contest was between the BNP and the Awami League, and in many places the winning margin of each party was very narrow. Out of 300 seats, the BNP won 207 seats with 44 per cent of the total votes cast, whereas the Awami League won 39 seats with 25 per cent of the votes cast in their favour. This showed that the Awami League had lost many seats by a small margin, and had fewer seats relative to the number of votes they secured. The ML-IDL alliance secured 20 seats with 8 per cent of the votes cast and the JSD secured 8 seats with 6 per cent of the votes cast. Clearly the JSD also had relatively few seats compared to the percentage of votes they secured. The independents won 16 seats, securing 9 per cent of the votes cast. The AL Mizan Group secured 2 seats and other political parties together won 8 seats, securing 6 per cent of the total votes cast.

As a result of the liberal policy adopted by Zia towards the opposition, which he could afford because of his personal popularity, the new Parliament contained a galaxy of opposition leaders. Other than Abdul Malek Ukil, almost all the opposition leaders were elected many of them representing a one-man party and becoming a single-member party in Parliament. Prominent among those leaders were Md. Toaha, Professor Muzaffar Ahmed, Rashed Khan Menon, Suranjit Sen Gupta, Mizanur Rahman Chowdhury, Ataur Rahman Khan, Abdus Sabur Khan and Moulana Abdur Rahim. Normally the leaders of minor parties find it difficult to win seats, but in this

---

[5] For detail, see Moudud Ahmed, *Democracy and the Challenge of Development* (Dhaka: The University Press Limited, 1995), pp. 103-08.

election most of them were elected because of their individual popularity in their respective constituencies.

The results of this election went very much in Zia's favour. Although he secured a two-thirds majority, Parliament had the strongest ever opposition in the history of Bangladesh. In every election since 1946 a particular party or alliance had swept into power, while the number of the opposition members elected was so low that it made democracy unworkable. The arrogance of brute majority crippled the value and function of Parliament. Now for the first time about 90 members had been elected from the opposition. Moreover, the principal objective of subjecting the political parties to democratic rules within the four walls of Parliament was now achieved. The attempt to turn Parliament into a centre of national politics was successful — however inadequate its capacity to exercise any authority over the executive.

Although the elections in 1979 were held in a completely different environment and they were better conducted than before, the fact that they were held under martial law with Ziaur Rahman as the President and the Chief Martial Law Administrator presiding over the country as the Chief Executive posed a serious question as to the institutional legalities of the electoral process as a whole.

Zia's rise to power was an astounding event in Bangladesh history. In the background of Awami League politics and the killing of the founding father, Sheikh Mujibur Rahman, Zia filled the vacuum by changing the entire course of politics in the country. Because of his personal image as a war hero and the populist politics he pursued, he remained close to the people till the last day of his rule. Zia was more a conformist than a reformist and the main task he performed was that of consolidating the newly independent country with a 'politics of unity', maintaining the status quo of social forces in the administration of the country. Having survived seventeen coup attempts, Zia ultimately fell victim to one at Chittagong, where he went to settle a dispute between two contending leaders of his own party. The army that he had built up, from a shattered and undisciplined force of 26,500 to 77,000, equipped and modernised, took his life when he was at the peak of his glory.[6] His sudden

---

[6] See *Ibid.*, pp. 146-59.

assassination created unprecedented despair, anger and shock in the country. He was the second elected President to be killed by members of the armed forces.

After a second major military intervention in 1982, led by H. M. Ershad as the Chief of Army Staff, which overthrew the elected civilian government, the third general election was held in 1986. As the public mood was hostile to military rule from the day the army took over, Ershad had a long, hard road to travel. Unlike Zia, Ershad had great difficulty in reaching an understanding with the political parties with regard to their participation in a general election. As Ershad's personal credibility was frequently questioned and his political opponents had very little trust in him, his desperate attempts to be accepted by them failed at every step. The need to be accepted by the people was linked to the legitimacy to govern and this was possible only by holding meaningful national elections where the people could vote freely.

In response to his call for a dialogue, 360 leaders from 75 political parties joined the discussion session with Ershad at Bangabhaban in January-February 1984. Almost all prominent leaders and parties participated, putting forward their respective demands and suggestions. Begum Zia began the dialogue by voicing her refusal to sit with some members of Ershad's government, including his Prime Minister, Ataur Rahman Khan. She then held a dramatic meeting with Ershad at Bangabhaban by herself, without the knowledge of many of her colleagues. However, the dialogue did not produce any concrete results, for the major political parties held common views on the subject — views that did not serve the interest of the regime. Ershad's aim was to bring the political parties round to his terms so that he could claim legitimacy for his rule, whereas the parties refused to change their own stated demands.

The essential and common demand of the major political parties was not so much concerned with the election as such; rather they believed that no election held under the cover of martial law and with Ershad in office could be regarded as free and fair. Ershad, on the other hand, was interested only in the election and in winning it for himself. Thus the views, intentions and interests of the parties were so conflicting that the dialogue broke down. But Ershad, while buying time for himself, could show the world how serious he was about a transition to democracy. The party leaders did not gain anything except the release of some political prisoners and funds that had previously been confiscated by the government.

Ershad tried in many ways to bring the political parties to elections, for without them he could neither legalise the actions of his regime, including his take-over, nor gain the sanction to govern the country legitimately. This was precisely what the major political parties were unwilling to grant him. They considered Ershad to be a usurper, heading an illegal government, who had no right to govern the country. The conflict and struggle centred round this issue of legitimacy and it haunted Ershad till the last day of his rule.

At this point he decided to consolidate his own position in politics and the government by announcing the Upazila elections and a referendum for himself. Under the strict cover of martial law and military supervision, the Upazila elections were held in February 1985 without the participation of the opposition parties. In the face of their silent protest, the regime manipulated the election. Although officially it was an election on a non-party basis, in effect the newly elected chairmen turned out to be an adjunct to the regime's central authority. At the same time, the offices of the zonal, sub-zonal and district martial law administrators, which were earlier withdrawn to induce the political parties to take part in the political process he initiated, were swiftly re-established along with all the Summary and Special Courts.

With the situation thus under control, Ershad went on to obtain his sanction to govern by holding a national referendum on 21 March 1985 in the same way as Zia had done. He argued that the referendum was necessary in view of the fact that the national elections could not be held, and he blamed the opposition parties for not taking part in the elections previously announced. He deplored the fact that, despite his sincere and relentless efforts, the opposition parties were not responsible enough to facilitate the transition to democracy.

In the absence of any opposition, the people obviously gave the regime what it desired: 86 per cent of the voters said 'yes' to Ershad continuing in office. Once the Upazila election and the referendum were completed, he had some breathing space to contemplate his future.

In early 1986 Ershad began to prepare for the parliamentary elections. His primary objective remained the same, which was to make the opposition agree to take part in the election despite their avowed stance of not taking part as long as martial law was in force. But their resistance gathered strength and they were in no mood to come to any kind of rapprochement. On 2 March 1986, Ershad put forward further concessions in an address to the nation in which he agreed to hold the parliamentary elections first. The concession was more suited to the Awami League's line of thought than the BNP's. It was also announced that ministers intending to stand in the election would resign from office and that the offices of the Martial Law Administrator from the zonal level and below would be closed and the martial law courts dissolved. These concessions would be effective only if the opposition agreed to take part in the election. Protracted behind-the-scene negotiations were launched with the opposition to ensure that they agreed to participate. They were also assured of equal media coverage and other facilities for conducting the campaign.

Subsequently, this declaration led some minor political parties to announce that they would take part in the election. Even so, the major alliances were still reluctant to take part; on the contrary, they were threatening to resist the election. However, discussions with the opposition alliances continued, particularly with the Awami League, on the assumption that if they joined the poll the BNP would not want to be left out. Ershad assured the Awami League that in addition to his earlier commitments to Hasina, he would himself refrain from campaigning in the election. The BNP was still organisationally weak, and some of its leaders who had been convicted by martial law courts were not eligible to take part in the election, so they were less enthusiastic about the polls.

On 21 March, Ershad addressed the nation again and gave further concessions. Reaffirming his earlier announcement of 2 March, he declared that the Upazila chairmen, or anyone connected with the administration, would be debarred from associating or campaigning in favour of any party or candidate. He made a commitment that the election would be free and fair and that the administration would play a completely neutral role. By this time, Ershad was desperate to hold the elections, for he realised that four years was already too long a period for martial law to be in operation. He therefore concentrated on the Awami League, with which he had already built up a rapport, and directly negotiated with its leaders, agreeing to almost all of Hasina's demands in order to persuade the party to participate. Simultaneously, he threatened that if the opposition did not agree to participate in the elections, he would reimpose all the rigours of martial law.

In a late night manoeuvre, the Awami League agreed to take part in the election and announced its intention only hours before the Election Commission's schedule was fixed for submitting nominations. The earlier calculation that, once the Awami League joined the election, political compulsion would force the BNP to also take part in these elections proved wrong. A section of the regime did not want the BNP to take part in the election, fearing that if it did so the ruling party would have no chance to win a majority. The BNP publicly condemned the Awami League for betraying the movement and made serious insinuations about its motives. It alleged that the Awami League had entered into an unholy alliance with the regime to enable Ershad to survive in power and legitimise his rule. The Awami League, on the other hand, attacked the BNP for betraying the cause of the people by backing out of the understanding to contest the election on a combined list of candidates. It claimed that if the BNP had participated on this basis, Ershad could have been thrown out of power. On this same issue, the fifteen-party alliance had also split; the five parties of the alliance led by Rashed Khan Menon decided not to take part in the election for the same reasons as the BNP, and this led to the birth of a new five-party alliance. Ershad had achieved exactly what he needed to stay in power.

While Ershad promised to hold a free, fair and neutral election, he also needed the support of a two-thirds majority in Parliament to pass an amendment to the constitution — commonly known as a Ratification Bill — to post facto legalise his martial law rule, as Zia had done in 1979. This necessitated single-party nomination under the banner of his newly formed political platform — Jatiyo Party (JP) which was launched on January 1st, 1986 — and winning as many seats as possible in order to have the necessary support in Parliament to pass this bill. Only thereafter could martial law be lifted. Besides, Ershad knew that the Awami League would not support the bill in Parliament and that it would then be virtually impossible to mobilise the support of 220 members out of 330. He therefore financed not only his own party but also other parties and independent candidates in order to win their support after the election.

On 7 May 1986 the parliamentary elections were held, boycotted by the BNP and contested by the Awami League, in the midst of allegations of widespread violence and vote-rigging. As the party in power, JP obviously had advantages over the Awami League and other parties. In a large number of constituencies, voters either remained disillusioned or were not allowed to vote for the candidate of their choice. The Election Commission was not strong enough to play the role of a watchdog, as it did not have sufficient power and authority to ensure a fair poll. The flow of election results was interrupted on several occasions on the TV and radio. Delays in announcing the results of a large number of constituencies raised a great deal of suspicion about the validity and credibility of the election. After several days, the results finally showed the JP winning 153 and the Awami League 76 seats. Questions were immediately raised in all quarters as to whether the elections really reflected the wishes of the people. Moreover, Ershad had not kept his promise to refrain from campaigning, so he could not claim that his office had remained neutral.

Hasina immediately rejected the election result and claimed that widespread ballot rigging, manipulation of results and biased media coverage had resulted in the declaration that she had won only 76 seats. The Awami League accused Ershad of violating all his pre-election promises; it boycotted the Parliament for months, held parallel and mock assemblies outside the Parliament building and refrained from taking part in the deliberation on the Ratification Bill (Seventh Amendment), allowing it to be passed without the Awami League's participation. However, the fact that the Awami League had taken part in the election undermined its public support and their movement against the government never got off the ground.

The BNP now renewed its attempt to justify why it had not taken part in the election, and made vicious attacks on Hasina and the Awami League for betraying the cause of the people. It alleged that this was an election where votes were not cast, but seats were divided between the JP and the Awami League led eight-party alliance on an agreed formula. Khaleda directly accused Hasina of granting Ershad a further lease of life in power. According to the Awami League, the BNP had backed out of the election because its deal with Ershad had failed; but according to the BNP, the decision of Hasina had legalised Ershad's regime and so enabled Parliament to pass the 'Ratification' law.

Eventually Hasina assumed the role of the Leader of the Opposition and the eight-party alliance joined the Parliament. She succeeded in establishing that the Awami League was the only alternative political force in the country and that she had the effective support of the people. As the official and recognised Leader of the Opposition, she started using the flag-car, office and other facilities, and in this capacity travelled to Washington and gave the clear impression that she was enjoying her role in the opposition. This heightened profile and exposure of Hasina pushed Khaleda out of the limelight.

But the election served Ershad's purpose very well. He had a Parliament that would ratify a bill legalising the martial law regime, permit the withdrawal of martial law and make him a constitutional ruler. At the same time, he was able to widen the gap between the Awami League and BNP and between Hasina and Khaleda Zia in particular. Although the JP won a bare majority of 153 seats, it also garnered the 30 women's seats. Soon, a large number of independents joined the bandwagon and MPs from smaller parties joined the JP to further the cause of 'democracy'. In this way the government managed to get the 220 votes required to pass the Seventh Amendment Bill which led to the lifting of martial law and ratified all that Ershad did under the cover of martial law.

Promptly after the parliamentary election and before any session of Parliament was summoned, Ershad decided to hold the presidential election so that he could assume the office of an elected President under Article 48 of the constitution. However, he had a difficult task persuading the opposition to take part in this election. Hasina was already taking up a strong position against the government on vote rigging and was particularly annoyed with Ershad for not honouring the various commitments he had made to her privately. Moreover, the Awami League and the eight-party alliance were not in favour of the presidential system as such. Khaleda Zia favoured a presidential system, but remained firmly against taking part in any election under the government of Ershad. In the end, Ershad was unable to find any viable candidate to contest the election when it was held on 15 October 1986. In the face of the boycott and hartal called by the opposition, and in the absence of any real opponent, no one showed any interest. Without the participation of any major political party or contestant, it turned out to be a total farce.

Moral issues apart, legally and constitutionally the country now had an elected Parliament and a President to carry out the functions of government. The process of civilianization of the military government was now complete as far as Ershad was concerned. Nonetheless, he was perfectly aware that his authority to govern continued to be seriously questioned by his opponents. Despite their differences, the dynamics of politics and social conditions led the alliances again to take up a common stand against the regime and they relentlessly pursued the course of agitation to overthrow the government.

So the legitimacy of the elections held in 1986 was under serious challenge both by the party that boycotted them (the BNP) and the party that took part in them (the Awami League). In less than six months after the elections, the opposition led by the BNP took to the streets demanding Ershad's resignation and a fresh election.

By October 1987 a united movement was beginning to take root. With the support of students and youths, Khaleda continued to mobilise public opinion against the regime and the so-called Parliament. Hasina could see that Parliament was no longer regarded as the focal point of national politics. Rather it was Ershad who was the issue in the eyes of the nation. The demand for his removal and the holding of a free and fair election began to gather momentum. In a Joint Declaration, the two major alliances organised a massive demonstration of around a million people scheduled for 10 November in the capital. This created enormous enthusiasm amongst the public and it was predicted that the fall of the government was now imminent.

This was the acid test of Ershad's survival. He proclaimed an emergency, banned assemblies and public meetings, tightened the administration, arrested and interned political leaders and workers, stopped movements of trains and launches so that protestors from the rural areas could not reach the capital, and deployed the army along with the BDR and other regular law-enforcing agencies to contain the situation. The opposition could not muster sufficient public support to overcome the measures taken by the government. As a result, the meeting held in Dhaka was larger than before, but not as large as was expected by the opposition.

Although the 10 November demonstration was almost an anticlimax in the eyes of the administration, the wave of opposition to Ershad's regime did not seem to have diminished. On the contrary, it took a more serious turn. Demands for the dissolution of Parliament and agitation for the resignation of the opposition members in Parliament were putting serious pressure on those parties that had participated in the 1986 election. Resolutions passed to this effect by various parties, including the members of the eight-party alliance, caused serious anxiety to the government. If all the members of the opposition resigned, Parliament would become almost *functus officio*.

At this stage of the anti-government movement, the Jamaat-e-Islami announced the resignation of all ten of their members in Parliament, and some independent members followed them. Although Hasina was under house arrest, the Presidium members of the Awami League held a meeting and passed a resolution asking their members to resign from Parliament. Once again Ershad had to fight for his survival. In order to contain the prevailing mood and retain the political initiative, Ershad decided on 8 December 1987, even before all the opposition MPs had formally resigned, to dissolve Parliament.

Under the constitution, the elections had to be held within 90 days. For Ershad, the purpose of the election was to save the constitution and himself. The only alternative left to the opposition, both the BNP and the Awami League was to ensure that the election did not take place and thus push Ershad into a constitutional vacuum. They therefore decided to boycott the election.

Without the participation of the major political parties, the election held in February 1988 was nothing but a farce. There was no enthusiasm amongst the people and the turnout all over the country was negligible. Foreign reporters and observers estimated that voting was below 10 per cent. Here again, in an election where Ershad's party had a free ride, polling boxes were stuffed with ballot papers in almost every constituency to show a higher turnout, and the election was totally rigged by the ruling party's workers in the absence of any control from the administration or the Election Commission. Inspired and financed by Ershad, some small political parties and lesser politicians were taken into the election process. A government sponsored combined opposition led by A.S.M.A Rab of the JSD secured 35 seats and now became the major opposition in Parliament; the ruling party had 252 seats and the rest 13 seats. Although the election had fulfilled the requirements of the constitution, in effect it had disfranchised the entire nation.

The two elections held under Ershad in 1986 and 1988 vitiated the entire electoral process and led the two major political alliances to unite on one single demand — the holding of a free and fair election under a 'neutral caretaker government'. The two leaders, both Khaleda and Hasina, now agreed that they would not take part in any election under Ershad and that he must quit his office.

With the disfranchised elections held in 1988, the institutions of democracy in the true sense no longer existed. The challenge now facing the opposition was to restructure those institutions. The first task they considered was to restore the right of franchise to the people, who had not been able to exercise their right to vote for more than a decade now. The tendency to corrupt the electoral process started in 1973 but it reached its climax during the Ershad regime when the same distortions prevailed from the Upazila down to the Union level.

The political vacuum created by the election of a hollow Parliament in 1988 made the country more volatile, and the movement in the streets moved very fast against the government. The removal of Ershad was the prime target, since it was alleged that as long as Ershad was in power the country would never have a free and fair election. But to achieve such a goal within the framework of the existing constitution was difficult and the opposition took time to make any concrete suggestion in this direction.

Finally, on 19 November, prior to their 48-hour *hartal* programme, the three alliances, one led by the Awami League, the second by the BNP and the third by the Workers' Party, forged a closer understanding through their respective liaison committees, and evolved a common formula for the transfer of power to an interim government with some well-defined guidelines. On the due day, Jamaat-e-Islami also gave its support to this 'caretaker government' formula proposed by the three alliances.

The substance of this formula was that the President would dissolve his Cabinet and Parliament under Article 58(5) and Article 72(1) of the Constitution. The incumbent Vice-President would resign under Article 55(A)(3) and the President would appoint a person acceptable to the opposition as the Vice-President under Article 55A(1). The President would then resign under Article 51(3) and immediately thereafter the new Vice-President would take over as the Acting President under Article 51(1) of the Constitution. The Acting President would then form his own Council of Ministers under Article 58 and no member of the 'caretaker government' would take any part in the presidential or parliamentary elections. Under Article 118(1) the Acting President would reconstitute the Election Commission, recast its powers and functions, and hold elections to Parliament within 90 days of its dissolution under Article 123(3) of the Constitution.

The declaration of the three alliances also included the following demands and pledges:

1. The state-run media, including radio and television, would become independent and autonomous bodies and would give equal publicity to the contesting political parties.
2. The interim government would hand over power to a sovereign Parliament, to which the government would be responsible.
3. A provision would be made to maintain the continuity of the constitutional government and to ensure that under no circumstances could an elected government be removed without a due process of election under the constitution.

4. Protection of the fundamental rights of citizens, the independence and neutrality of the judiciary and the rule of law would be guaranteed.
5. Any law inconsistent with fundamental rights would be repealed.

In a situation where politics takes to the streets, the niceties and literal meanings of the constitution lose their significance and the constitution becomes less important than the demands of the people. When questions were raised with regard to the validity of such a transfer of power to a caretaker government outside the constitution, the answer came from the opposition that events would take care of any technicalities. Since the power of the people was to be recognised as supreme, the new Parliament would be able to resolve the issue. In other words, the new Parliament would enact a constitutional amendment legalising such a transfer of power with retrospective effect in order to maintain the continuity of the constitution. This process would be similar to that followed for the Fifth and Seventh Amendments except that those amendments were made to legalise the martial law regimes. But the principle was the same: the new Parliament would by law ratify or legalise any constitutional violation caused by the transfer of power under the formula suggested by the opposition alliance.

So the entire struggle of the opposition from 1982 to 1990 was for the restoration of democracy and was opposed to the autocracy of Ershad, for the restoration of people's power and for the restoration of the right of franchise. The continuous erosion of the people's power and the marginalisation of the will of the people in the administration of the country from 1975 onwards ultimately culminated in 1988 in a state of total disfranchisement, when elections were boycotted by all the major political parties and were held without any effective participation of the people. Parliament, without the opposition, although technically meeting the requirements of the constitution, in effect failed to represent the will of the people, the supreme source of power under the constitution.

The formula for the transfer of power put forward by the opposition now became the rallying point of the movement, which was joined by people from all walks of life. Teachers, lawyers, doctors, engineers and all other professionals raised the same demand. The movement in the streets took the shape of a violent upheaval that the law-enforcing agencies were no longer in a position to cope with.

In the face of such a situation Ershad proclaimed a state of emergency, suspending all fundamental rights and banning public meetings and demonstrations. But this did not work either. The demonstrations continued, the curfew imposed was openly violated and the proclamation of a state of emergency became totally ineffective. As the situation went out of control, Ershad started the process of surrendering power.

On the night of 4 December, Ershad decided to resign as soon as the opposition could nominate a person to take charge of the caretaker government, and Parliament was dissolved. On 5 December, the opposition alliances decided to nominate Justice Shahabuddin Ahmed, the Chief Justice of the Supreme Court, as Vice-President to enable him to become the Acting President of the interim government. The next day, the Vice-President resigned[7] at 3 p.m. and Ershad appointed Justice Shahabuddin Ahmed as the Vice-President while continuing in the post of the Chief Justice. Immediately thereafter, Ershad himself resigned and the new Vice-President assumed the office of Acting President to lead the nation on a new journey in search of democracy.

On 27 February 1991 a free and fair election under a neutral caretaker administration was held in Bangladesh for the first time since its independence and a government duly elected by the people took charge of the nation. The right of franchise was restored and the electoral process was re-established once again.

The emergence of Begum Zia in politics is a unique phenomenon. A pretty bride to a young army officer, a helpless prisoner in the hands of the Pakistan army while her husband joined the war to liberate the country, a housewife rearing two sons with all the affection of a loving mother — it was impossible to conceive that Khaleda Zia would one day make a charismatic, formidable popular leader and on three occasions become the Prime Minister of the country. She had roots in

---

[7] The author was the Vice-President at the time.

Noakhali but was born in Jalpaiguri,[8] India, where her father had migrated in 1919. After the partition in 1947, when she was only two they moved to Dinajpur. Khaleda Zia, slim and attractive, used to love singing and dancing. More for her beauty than her education, she attracted eligible bachelors at an early age. Her affectionate parents having found it difficult to keep her at home she was soon given away as a bride to a young army officer before she could finish her higher education. When her husband, Ziaur Rahman, the valiant leader of the freedom war who had declared independence over the radio at Chittagong, returned home with the glory of victory, it was a great reunion for the family. The suffering she had endured during the war instilled in her a power of determination to survive with honour and dignity.

From the day of her marriage until the day Zia was killed, Khaleda lived an obscure domesticated life. Even after independence, when Zia assumed a prominent role in the army, becoming the Deputy Chief of the Army Staff, Khaleda pursued the role of a housewife. When Zia was finally installed in power, in a dramatic upheaval jointly staged by the troops and the public, Khaleda had no visible role to play. Later on, when Zia became a charismatic and highly popular leader, Khaleda refused to assume any public role. During the entire tenure of Zia's rule, Khaleda hardly appeared in public except on ceremonial occasions or foreign visits. In six years of Zia's rule, Khaleda was not seen in the drawing rooms of their residence, where late night meetings were held, food was served and debates took place on various national issues. She never took part in any political discussion throughout that regime. And yet she was, no doubt, the single source of inspiration for Zia to lead the nation into a new chapter of Bangladesh history.

Khaleda must have been a constant source of solace and courage to Zia, who had a tumultuous life both as a soldier and as a ruler. Like Zia, Khaleda was an introvert by nature. While in power, Zia lived a highly insecure life. There were about seventeen attempted coups either to remove him from power or to kill him, and Khaleda must have shared the strain from behind the scenes. She must have

---

[8] Syed Abdal Ahmed and Syed Mesbahuddin, *Nandito Netri Khaleda Zia*, Inqilab Publication Group, Dhaka, 1991, p. 1.

seen from close proximity how Zia handled the army and administered the country at a very critical time.[9]

After the formation of the new government under the existing constitution, the Acting President continued to be the Chief Executive under a presidential system of government. A historic amendment — the 12th Amendment — was passed unanimously by Parliament in September 1991 to return Bangladesh to a parliamentary system of government and virtually restore the original Constitution of 1972. A long cherished goal of the people was achieved by changing the basic structure of the Constitution back to its original form. Prior to this, the 11th Amendment was passed to legalise the appointment of the Chief Justice as the Vice President of the Republic while continuing as the head of the judiciary.[10]

It was a moment of great triumph for democracy in Bangladesh. On 19 September 1991, Begum Khaleda Zia, widow of the assassinated President Ziaur Rahman, took the oath to assume the office of Prime Minister, vested with all the executive powers of the state.[11] It happened, after nearly eighteen years, when a civilian politician elected by the people became the Chief Executive to govern and lead the country once again under a parliamentary system of government. For the people of Bangladesh, a country born in a war twenty years ago, it was indeed a victory, a restoration of people's power and their universal right of franchise — for which they had struggled, sacrificed and achieved their freedom from the colonial rule.

Movement for a Non-party Caretaker Government

But hardly three years had expired with the BNP at the helm of government[12] when the opposition parties in Parliament, led by the

---

[9] For detail, see Moudud Ahmed, *Democracy and the Challenge of Development*, Dhaka: The University Press Limited, pp. 66-72.

[10] The Chief Justice holding an office of profit could not be appointed to run the political office of Vice President or Acting President; nor he could hold two posts at the same time under the Constitution.

[11] Earlier, all the executive powers were vested in the President. The Prime Minister would carry out only those functions assigned by the President, which the author did as the Prime Minister under Ershad.

[12] Hasina could not accept defeat in the election, which she thought BNP had won by subtle rigging. Soon after the BNP's installation in power, Hasina warned that the new government would not be allowed to live in peace even for a day.

Awami League, started to raise the demand that all general elections in future should also be held under a neutral caretaker government and that the constitution should be amended to make it a permanent feature. As the demand intensified, it led to a deadlock between the ruling government and the opposition. As a result of which the entire energy of the government shifted from concentrating on the economic priorities to containing the opposition in Parliament.

The role of Parliament and the opposition in consolidating a democratic political order in Bangladesh faced a new challenge. The behaviour of the opposition both inside and outside Parliament and the ruling party's treatment of the opposition and failure in pursuing the norms and principles of bipartisanism were crucial to good governance, transparency and accountability in administration, all of which depended on the effective functioning of Parliament. If Parliament failed to serve its purpose or was not effective in its major task of controlling the executive, democracy would obviously falter and the development efforts would suffer.

The Parliament elected in 1991, after the victory of democracy following a struggle of nine long years, was almost paralysed by the demand raised by the opposition and the ruling party's failure to come to any settlement with them. For two years Parliament was run without any opposition, and laws were made and budgets passed without any scrutiny and debate. No issue of economic or social policy was discussed. More tragic was that the ruling party thought that the participation of the opposition was not necessary, and with their boycotting of Parliament it was easier for the ruling party to pass laws and run Parliament and the government.

So it is not only the resource constraints, overpopulation, intra-regional and interstate conflicts, high military spending and nuclearization that have caused the slow growth in the economy of the region. The practice of democracy, the quality of leadership and governance, the party system, the intra-party relationship, the role of the ruling party, opposition and Parliament, the assassination of political leaders and rise of family leadership, policy planning processes, decision-making procedures and their implementation, the role of the bureaucracy and the competency of administration are all linked to the issues raised in this study. The experience of Bangladesh in these areas will in substance reflect the overall situation in South Asia with some variations in experience, degree and quality.

The crisis of Parliament in 1994 started with a rather innocuous statement made by the Information Minister on the massacre at Hebron, a city South of Jerusalem where a towering marble fortress in the Judean hills stands as Abraham's tomb. It is considered to be holy both by Muslims and Jews. The Jews, who consider Abraham as their father, call it the cave of the Patriarch, and the Muslims, who consider Abraham a prophet, call it Ibrahim's mosque.[13] Like the city, the structure is now divided with separate entrances and separate praying areas. One day in February 1994 when the Muslims were praying in the early morning congregation, a Jewish settler, Barauch Goldstein, walked into the mosque and shot them in the back killing 29 of them. He used an automatic rifle issued by the Israeli government and this aroused strong and bitter reactions all over the world.

The people of Bangladesh also reacted sharply. The Awami League, known to be more secular than some other opposition parties, reacted with considerable enthusiasm in condemning the incident. Its President, the Leader of the Opposition, demanded that a resolution be passed in the Parliament condemning the incident. The Information Minister, Nazmul Huda, one of the key spokesmen of the government, refused by saying that such action might encourage people to go for communal disorder. He was sarcastic about the Awami League, saying that he was surprised that such a strong demand was coming from the 'newly converted Muslims' in Parliament. He added that they were trying to do politics in the name of Islam, which they had always opposed in the past. The Awami League, supported by other opposition parties, reacted sharply to this statement and demanded the withdrawal of the comments with an unconditional apology. When the Information Minister refused to do so, the opposition walked out of Parliament *en masse*.

No one expected that such a small and trivial matter, which happens in almost every Parliament, would turn into a serious issue. The opposition decided to continue with their boycott until the

---

[13]*New York Times*, 15 October 1998.

minister had withdrawn the statement and tendered an unconditional apology on the floor of the Parliament. In subsequent days, the minister, feeling guilty for creating a deadlock, made a statement of regret and requested the Speaker to expunge his earlier comments. But this did not satisfy the opposition and they continued to boycott the proceedings of Parliament.

While this deadlock was continuing, the opposition intensified its demand for holding all future elections under a neutral caretaker government. The ruling party rejected the demand outright on the ground that such a proposition was neither democratic nor within the purview of the constitution. The opposition argued that if necessary the constitution ought to be amended and they would support such an amendment if it were placed before Parliament. The issue led to a national debate outside Parliament and the opposition continued to boycott not only the sittings but also the sessions of the Parliament.

As a result, the authority and importance of Parliament continued to erode and it turned into a one-party Parliament. When the opposition demanded a discussion of the subject as a formal agenda in Parliament, the treasury bench was not willing to do that either. The crisis deepened in spite of conciliatory mediation by various professional leaders and groups. Finally some diplomats led by the US Ambassador, tried to bring the two sides together. A series of informal discussions and meetings outside Parliament began with intermediaries shuttling between the ruling party and the opposition leaders.

Despite all these efforts, the impasse continued. In order to make the government agree to discuss the matter in Parliament, three similar amendment bills, one from the Awami League, the second from the JP and the third from the Jamaat-e-Islami, were submitted in Parliament. However, the government ignored them and refused to hold any discussion on the subject, fearing that such a discussion would amount to giving recognition to the demand of the opposition.

In 1994 when the budget was passed in the absence of the opposition, the ruling party realised that the opposition should return to Parliament. Until this point the opposition had maintained that they would return to Parliament only if the government agreed to discuss the issue of a caretaker government in Parliament. The Speaker, at the instance of the ruling party, met with the leaders of the opposition. It was agreed that the Prime Minister would make a statement in Parliament inviting a discussion of the subject and on receiving that assurance the opposition would return to Parliament, which was then running for its fourth month without them.

For some unknown reason the Prime Minister did not make any such statement in Parliament, and the opposition saw this as an act of retraction. The opposition argued that the present government, having itself been elected under a neutral caretaker government in 1991, should not be reluctant to accept the demand of the opposition. In any case, the refusal of the Prime Minister to make the statement, which the Speaker had assured the opposition, they continued to boycott the Parliament. The budget of 1994/95 was finally passed without any debate or participation by the opposition.

In the meantime the opposition put forward a suggestion that an amendment bill from the government be placed before Parliament by 26 June so that they could still join the final stage of passing the budget. Since the government declined to respond, the opposition leaders in a press conference held on 27 June presented their own proposal in the form of a framework or 'Ruprekha' for holding future parliamentary elections under a neutral, non-partisan caretaker government.[14] The framework envisaged that in order to hold such an election, on the dissolution of Parliament by the President:

1. The Prime Minister shall resign.
2. To run the government during the interim period until the election of Parliament and the formation of a new government, the President shall appoint, in consultation with the opposition, an acceptable person as the Prime Minister, who during that period will administer the country as the Chief Executive under Article 55 of the Constitution.
3. The Prime Minister of the interim government and his ministers shall not be candidates in the ensuing election, nor they can be members of any political party.
4. The main responsibility of the interim government shall be to ensure a free, fair and neutral election and to carry on the

---

[14] The author prepared the first draft of this framework and has retained a copy.

day-to-day affairs of the state and matters of national emergency.
5. The interim government shall stand dissolved as soon as the new Prime Minister is administered the oath of office under Article 56 of the Constitution.

Further, in order to ensure a free and fair election:
1. The Election Commission was to be reconstituted and re-established in such a manner that it could function as a fully independent body.
2. A self-contained code of conduct for the election was to be framed and its implementation ensured.
3. In order to implement the above two proposals, laws were to be enacted, if necessary.

The government reacted very sharply to these proposals and rejected them right away. They attacked the opposition, accusing them of harbouring autocratic motives by suggesting the replacement of an elected Prime Minister by an appointed one, and maintaining that the proposal, being both undemocratic and unconstitutional, could not be acceptable to the nation.

Both the government and the opposition remained unrelenting for several months, causing a great amount of uncertainty in the political arena, and making the existence of an elected Parliament irrelevant. The widespread vote rigging by the ruling party in the by-elections held at Mirpur-Mohammadpur and particularly at Magura weakened the government position and bolstered the claim of the opposition that no election could be free and fair under a political government in future.

At the same time, the government and the opposition exchanged letters[15] for the purpose of holding a discussion by the Deputy Leaders of the BNP and the Awami League. In his last letter, on 8 October 1994, Samad Azad, the Deputy Leader of the Opposition, proposed that on the basis of all the letters written between them, discussions could now start in the committee room of the Parliament.

---

[15]The author has copies of all the correspondence mentioned here.

It appeared that common ground had been identified for discussing the issues and the two sides deliberated upon them. However, these discussions did not produce any result as the government was not agreeable to the core demand of the opposition that there should be a neutral caretaker government.

In the meantime, amid concern that democracy was being threatened by the strong stand taken by both the government and the opposition in Bangladesh, some western countries sympathetic to Bangladesh initiated efforts to resolve the crisis. The Secretary General of the Commonwealth Secretariat, Chief Emeka Anyaoku, visited Bangladesh in the third week of September and entered into mediation between the government and the opposition. He visited both the Prime Minister and the Leader of the Opposition more than once and offered his good offices to bring the matter to an amicable settlement. For both political and diplomatic reasons both agreed to accept the mediation. According to the Secretary General, 'there existed sufficient common ground between the parties which allows for a meaningful dialogue between them'.[16] He had put forward a three-point plan for the talks, which according to him both the Prime Minister and the Leader of the Opposition had agreed upon.[17] The three points were as follows:

1. The governing party and the principal opposition party agreed to commence a dialogue in good faith and on the basis of an open agenda, which would include any topics raised by either side such as the strengthening of the Election Commission, the question of a caretaker government, and proposals for an overall code of conduct to guide political activity.

2. On the commencement of such talks and given the intensity of the feelings on the matter and as a confidence building measure, the parties agreed that at the conclusion of each session of their talks they should issue to the press and public an agreed joint statement only, with the participants otherwise refraining from further public comment.

---

[16] See the press release dated 26 September 1994, issued by the Commonwealth Secretariat.
[17] Letter of the Leader of the Opposition to the Secretary General on 21 September 1984.

3. An envoy would be despatched by the Secretary General who would be available to facilitate discussion between the parties in any way that might be necessary.

Sir Ninian Martin Stephen, an eminent barrister and judge and the former Governor General of Australia, arrived in Dhaka on 13 October 1994 as the envoy of the Secretary General of the Commonwealth Secretariat to facilitate the dialogue between the government and the opposition over the issues mentioned in the three-point plan. On the day of his arrival Sir Ninian told the press that he hoped 'by means of discussions between the parties the prevailing atmosphere of confrontation and tension can be dispelled and normal political activity restored, as well as confidence in the institutions of democracy in Bangladesh being consolidated'.[18]

The dialogue between the two sides was conducted, facilitated and for all practical purposes mediated by Sir Ninian for nearly six weeks, each side making its stand clear and communicating the same to the other through Sir Ninian. He was in constant touch with both sides, sometimes sitting with government leaders, sometimes with opposition leaders and sometimes with both of them. While the BNP accepted the concept of having a caretaker government, it insisted that it had to be within the framework of the constitution. On the question of the earlier precedent of a caretaker government in 1990, the ruling party argued that Ershad had seized power illegally by military force from an elected government, and that neither his Parliament nor his government was legitimate or elected by the people. They cited other democracies where governments that are elected by the people remain in office at the time of the election, and argued that there was a lot of difference between Ershad's government and the present one. The government side submitted its reaction to the opposition's proposals to Sir Ninian, who in turn passed it on to the opposition.[19]

On 31 October the BNP submitted the outline for an interim government within the framework of the Constitution. While consenting

---

[18] See the Commonwealth News Release dated 13 October 1994.

[19] See the letter dated 7 November 1994 from Sir Ninian to S.A.M.S. Kibria, Political Adviser to the Leader of the Opposition.

to having a caretaker government, it was not willing to go beyond the constitution. However, it agreed that the ministers in the interim government would not hold any specific portfolios and in the Cabinet of ten members, five would be from the BNP and four from the opposition; the incumbent Prime Minister would head the Cabinet.[20] The question of whether the incumbent Prime Minister should stay on to head the interim government became the central issue. The opposition, knowing very well that, if the charismatic Begum Zia continued as the Prime Minister, the BNP would enjoy an enormous advantage over the opposition, was adamant that she must go. For precisely the same reason the ruling party stuck to the constitutional position that the Prime Minister should head the interim government. Since the strategy of the opposition was to pull down the Prime Minister by any means and it was not ready to compromise on this, the dialogue finally broke down.

Sir Ninian was at least able to persuade the BNP to make the Prime Minister agree to have members of the opposition in the Cabinet as a compromise. The constitution did not debar such a situation. The opposition, however, thought this compromise would not meet its demand of having a non-partisan neutral caretaker government. So all the international efforts to break the impasse came to an end without any result. Sir Ninian, disappointed by the outcome, left Dhaka on 10 November 1994. He was deeply disheartened that no agreement arising out of this dialogue had proved possible. He noted that, although 'suspicion and mistrust' were both deep and strong between the parties, he was happy that at least the parties had come together and conducted a rational debate. He hoped that the leaders would still find a way to 'secure a future of peace, prosperity and true democracy for the people of Bangladesh'.[21]

In political terms, although the dialogue failed, the internationalisation of its demand for a neutral caretaker government had benefited the opposition enormously. It had helped force the government to recognise the concept of a caretaker government, which weakened the government further. Taking advantage of this

---

[20] Letter from Sir Ninian to S.A.M.S. Kibria, 7 November 1994.

[21] Commonwealth News Release, 20 November 1994.

situation, the opposition now intensified its campaign further, concentrating on involving the masses in its political programmes. It warned the government that all members of the opposition parties in Parliament would be forced to resign if the government failed to place an amendment bill incorporating the opposition proposal in the constitution by 6 December, later extended to 27 December. In the meantime all 147 Members of Parliament belonging to opposition, had already submitted their individual resignation letters to their respective leaders.

With the resignation letters already signed, the situation became extremely grave, making a national crisis imminent. The ruling party, having failed to comprehend the seriousness of the situation, remained oblivious of its implications. The Prime Minister was continuously given to understand that the opposition would not go to the extent of actually resigning from Parliament and that their resignations were only political threats. The deadline given by the opposition passed without any serious initiative from the BNP to defuse the situation.

On 28 December 1994 the Members of Parliament, led by their respective leaders, went to the Speaker to submit their resignations from Parliament. While they were waiting in the lounge for the Speaker to arrive to receive the resignation letters, a message was conveyed that senior government leaders were coming to meet the opposition leaders in search of a compromise. On their arrival[22] the government leaders did not have any specific proposal but indicated that they were willing to negotiate the issue of the caretaker government on the condition that all the political programmes of the opposition were withdrawn forthwith. This infuriated the opposition further and, considering it to be only a delaying tactic to destroy their credibility, the opposition decided to go ahead with the resignations. On that very night at about 9.30, the leaders of all the opposition political parties in the presence of all the Members of Parliament handed over their resignation letters to the Speaker.

The matter did not end there. It was expected that the Speaker in accordance with the provisions of the constitution would accept the resignations and that the matter would be referred to the Election

---

[22]Professor B. Chowdhury, Abdus Salam Talukder and Col. (Rtd) Oli Ahmed represented the government.

Commission so that by-elections could be held for the vacant seats, unless the government advised the President to dissolve the Parliament and hold a general election. The government, having failed to take any decision, did not go for either option. Article 67(2) of the Constitution provides that a Member of Parliament may 'resign his seat by writing under his hand addressed to the Speaker and the seat shall become vacant when the writing is received by the Speaker'. So as soon as the Speaker received the resignation letters, the seats stood vacant. All that the Speaker had to do was to communicate to the Election Commission through the Secretary of his Secretariat that such seats had fallen vacant and the Election Commission would proceed to fill the seats within 90 days of the occurrence of vacancy. Under Rules 177 and 178 of the Rules of Procedure, the Speaker was only obliged to inform the Parliament about the resignation.

Obviously an *en masse* resignation of all the Members of Parliament belonging to the opposition, fifteen months prior to the expiry of their term, had put the political situation into a serious crisis. The government, however, either due to lack of experience or lack of foresight failed to comprehend the impact of such a resignation would have on the functioning of the government and Parliament and on the constitutional rule in the country as a whole. It appeared that the common-sense approach to politics was outweighed by the unrealistic perceptions of some leaders within the government.

Due to this state of political flux within the government, actions taken by the ruling party were not only divisive but also self-contradictory. The government was not willing to recognise that the resignations had actually taken place and that, by the operation of Article 67(2) of the Constitution, the seats immediately fell vacant. As a result, the government's attitude was to ignore the new realities by taking the view that there had been no resignation and that opposition members continued to be Members of Parliament. News of the resignation of so many Members of Parliament was not allowed to be broadcast over the radio and television.[23]

---

[23] Although a committee of inquiry was constituted on 31 December to investigate why the news of the resignations was not broadcast, it had no significance any more in the light of the political developments that had taken place by that time.

Instead of following the mandate of the constitution as contained in Article 67(2), the Speaker tried to withhold the resignation letters. Under Article 123(4) the Election Commission was required to complete the by-elections to fill the vacant seats within 90 days of the date when the resignation letters had been received, i.e. 28 December. Each Member of Parliament signed the resignation letters submitted individually.[24] Once the resignation letters were submitted and received by the Speaker, there was no scope for any reconsideration or withdrawal of such letters and none of the members who had resigned expressed any desire to do so. So the only option for the Speaker should have been to follow the Constitution. Instead, for obviously political reasons and under pressure from his own party, the Speaker ignored the Constitution and took a partisan view, toeing the line taken by the government, which was to avoid any kind of election.

Three days later, on 1 January 1995, the Prime Minister addressed the nation over the radio and television, explaining her position *vis-à-vis* the demand of the opposition. However, her address did not contain anything new — it was more or less a regular address, saying positive things about the government and declaring that her government would like to uphold the constitution and the democratic order at any cost. She rejected the demand of the opposition for an interim non-party government as being outside the purview of the constitution. Although she called upon the opposition to uphold the constitutional and democratic process, she did not invite the opposition for any dialogue, nor did she show interest in any kind of compromise. So her address to the nation had very little impact in political circles.

On the other hand, the opposition movement, so far confined within the four walls of Parliament, was now gradually taking to the streets. The *en masse* resignation of the Members of Parliament aimed to compel the government to hold a general election, which the ruling party was not willing to accede to. The three-day hartal called by the opposition on 2, 3 and 4 January ended in the throwing

---

[24] The author drafted the letters of resignation and had them signed individually by each Member of Parliament through their respective leaders.

of bombs, brick batting and violence. The opposition further declared a blockade of river ways and railways on 19 January and continued to adopt agitational programmes for the whole of January.

The Speaker, instead of accepting the resignation letters, adopted a passive role and reported sick at a hospital on 30 December where he remained for a week. When contacted he said that he was still considering the resignation letters received by him from the Members of Parliament.

On 19 January, the Speaker announced that he would give a ruling in Parliament within a day or two. He claimed that he was working very hard to scrutinise the resignation letters from various legal perspectives. He took the view that he had to examine various laws, including those of Britain and India, and the general parliamentary practices with regard to such resignations before he could take a decision.

The government took the position that even if the Members had resigned and a general election was called there was no scope for a neutral, non-partisan government within the framework of the Constitution. The Prime Minister in her speeches and public statements invited the opposition to work within the framework of the Constitution, to withdraw their resignations and return to Parliament to maintain the democratic framework of the constitution, but she refused to open any dialogue with the opposition. In any case, the Speaker continued to refrain from giving a decision.[25] He had fallen ill for the second time and stayed at home to avoid the media.

So there was no serious effort on the part of the ruling party to settle the matter with the opposition by any kind of negotiation. On the contrary, a well-wisher of the government in the High Court Division filed a writ petition to have the continuous boycott declared illegal and to direct the opposition to rejoin Parliament. The High Court did indeed direct the Members to attend Parliament,[26] but the

---

[25]Unfortunately in every Parliament in Bangladesh, the Speaker has played a partisan role, which is one of the reasons why Parliament has not functioned effectively.

[26]In this writ petition the Leader of the Opposition, Sheikh Hasina, the author as the leader of the Jatiyo Party and Moulana Motiur Rahman Nizami as the leader of Jamaat-e-Islami were made respondents and they contested the case reported in 47 Dhaka Law Reports (DLR), p. 42. The judgement was delivered on 11 December 1994.

Appellate Division stayed the decision. Two more writ petitions were filed before the High Court Division.[27] One was to declare why the resignations submitted by the 147 Members of Parliament should not be declared illegal and the other one was to declare why the non-acceptance of the resignation letters by the Speaker should not be declared illegal. All these petitions were filed only to divert the attention of the public and delay the constitutional process. These writ petitions gave the Speaker the opportunity to delay his decision further,[28] leading to an assumption that he had in effect rejected the resignations submitted by the Members of Parliament, which power he did not have under the constitution. Obviously this was a political move to keep the matter hanging as long as possible, although there was no rationale for doing so on such an important issue.

Finally on 23 February, the Speaker gave his decision on the *en masse* resignation of the Members of Parliament in a lengthy ruling delivered in Parliament. It was no less than a judgement, as if delivered by a court, where the Speaker gave his own interpretation of the Constitution. He held the view that the resignation letters could not be deemed to have been received by him as contemplated by Article 67(2) of the Constitution. Since the ruling was delivered in Parliament and was a part of its proceedings, the ruling's validity could not be challenged in any court.[29] As a result, according to the Speaker, those who had resigned continued to be Members of Parliament, although they remained absent from the sittings and sessions of Parliament.

This dichotomy and conflict continued between the opposition on the one hand and the Speaker and the ruling party on the other, creating a further vacuum in the politics of the country. Parliament continued to function without the opposition. Laws were made without any debate and Parliament lost its significance when the budget for 1995-96 was also passed without the opposition.[30]

---

[27] See 47 DLR, p. 361. The judgement was delivered on 23 February 1995. The High Court Division discharged both the rules on grounds of maintainability.

[28] The Speaker postponed his decision on the ground that the matter of resignation was now pending before the High Court Division. *The Daily Inqilab*, 6 February 1995.

[29] 46 DLR, p. 555.

[30] The budget for the year 1994-95 was also passed without the opposition due to the boycott.

Due to the long absence of such a large number of Members belonging to the opposition, the question now arose as to whether such a boycott ought to be construed as 'absence' from Parliament under Article 67(1)(b) of the Constitution. This article, if read in conjunction with Article 152(1) of the constitution, provides that those Members who have been absent for more than 90 consecutive sitting days without the leave of Parliament shall vacate their seats. The government and the Speaker were now faced with another constitutional obligation. If the seats of the Members of Parliament who had been absent now stood vacated under the law, the government had no alternative but to decide whether to hold by-elections in these seats or go for a general election, as demanded by the opposition. In order to gain more time, on 4 July the President, under Article 106 of the Constitution and on the advice of the Prime Minister, made a reference to the Appellate Division of the Supreme Court to report to him its opinion on the following:

1. Could the walk-out and consequent period of non-return by all the opposition parties, taking exception to a remark of a ruling party minister, be construed as 'absent' from Parliament without leave of Parliament under Article 67(1)(b) of the constitution, resulting in vacation of their seats in Parliament?

2. Did the boycott of Parliament by all Members of the opposition parties mean 'absent' from the Parliament without leave of Parliament within the meaning of Article 67(1)(b) of the constitution, resulting in vacation of their seats in Parliament?

3. Had 90 consecutive sitting days had been completed, excluding or including the period between two sessions intervened by the prorogation of Parliament within the meaning of Article 67(1)(b), using the definition of 'sessions' and 'sittings' in Article 152(1) of the Constitution?

4. Should the Speaker or Parliament compute and determine the period of absence?

The Supreme Court delivered its judgement on 24 July, answering all the questions raised in the reference. The substance of the long judgement was that the seats of the Members who had resigned and absented themselves from Parliament for 90 consecutive sitting days without the leave of Parliament had indeed been vacated.[31]

On 28 July the Speaker, while addressing the press, announced that in the view of the judgement of the Supreme Court, under Article 67(1)(b) the seats of the opposition Members had been vacated due to their absence from Parliament with effect from 20 June 1995. Accordingly the vacant seats of 87 Members of Parliament were published in the Gazette Notification. The Parliament Secretariat sent a letter to 55 Members seeking some clarifications, but the opposition considered this to be another delaying tactic and the Members did not reply.

Under Article 123(4), the Election Commission was required to hold the by-elections within 90 days, i.e. by 18 September. Demands from various quarters, including professional groups, were raised for a general election and various individuals and parties to open dialogue between the ruling party and the opposition to resolve the crisis. In the meantime, however, a total of 142 seats were declared vacated and only 42 days now remained for holding the by-elections. At last, due to pressure from the government and the general political stalemate, the Election Commission used the 'floods', which had by that time submerged a large portion of the country as a reason to invoke the provision "Act of God" in Article 123(4) of the Constitution. So the time for holding the by-elections was extended for another 90 days, until 16 December 1995. The opposition alleged that the Chief of the Election Commission was not acting independently and that he had extended the time for holding the by-elections only to suit the political needs of the government.

On 28 October, Begum Zia addressed a letter to Sheikh Hasina, the Leader of the Opposition, inviting her to a discussion of the issues relating to the holding of elections.[32] In her reply on 30 October, Hasina suggested that the government should first accept in principle that the election would be held under a non-party caretaker government and requested the Prime Minister to create a congenial atmosphere for a dialogue. On 2 November, Begum Zia wrote

---

[31] See 47 DLR (AD) 1995, p. 111.
[32] See *Bhorer Kagoj*, Dhaka, 29 October 1995.

another letter, to which Hasina replied on 4 November asserting that unless the concept of a non-party caretaker government was accepted in principle, no dialogue would be fruitful. In her third letter, dated 12 November 1995, Begum Zia reiterated that the government was prepared to discuss any matter relating to holding a free and fair election, but she would still not concede a non-party caretaker government as long as there was an elected government in office. So these letters, basically exchanged for public consumption, did not produce any result; each side only reiterated its own position, which only deepened the crisis further. It was now obvious that the government no longer intended to hold the by-elections as it was at the very end of its tenure.

In a statement on 21 November, the Prime Minister declared that if the opposition were not going to take part in the by-elections, she would advise the President to dissolve the Parliament. She argued that, since the time for the general election was also not far away, holding the by-elections and soon thereafter the general election would be too costly for the state. However, she indicated for the first time that she was willing to discuss the formation of an interim national government for the period when the general election would be held.

Almost at the same time the Election Commission, in order to maintain the continuity of the constitution, announced a schedule to hold the by-elections on 15 December 1995. As soon as the opposition rejected the schedule announced by the Election Commission for the by-elections,[33] the government decided to hold the general election. The Prime Minister addressed the nation, announcing that she had advised the President to dissolve the Parliament and that the Election Commission was to make the necessary arrangements for holding a general election for the 6th National Parliament.

However, the address of the Prime Minister did not resolve the core issue between the government and the opposition. In a dramatic move on 26 November, the Leader of the Opposition phoned the Prime Minister, but she was not available. After three hours the

---

[33] See the *Daily Ittefaq*, Dhaka, 23 November 1995.

Prime Minister called back. They talked on the telephone for 16 minutes. The Leader of the Opposition requested the Prime Minister to create history by advising the President to form a non-party, neutral caretaker government. In reply the Prime Minister invited the Leader of the Opposition to sit with her to discuss whatever she had to say, but at the same time said that she did not understand what a caretaker government meant. Nothing substantive emerged from this telephone conversation; nor was there any follow-up from either side as no one was ready to make any concessions on the stand they had already taken.

The tension mounted in all the branches of the state and each day witnessed events of great significance. There was no sign of the political crisis being resolved. As the stand-off position between the ruling party and the opposition continued, the rumours started spreading that there could be a military intervention and no one could predict in which direction the situation was going. In a press briefing, the US State Department indicated that it would not support any military intervention against an elected government. The diplomatic corps in Dhaka, led by the Ambassador of the United States, David Merrill, tried their best to bring the two sides together. They were in frequent touch with both the Prime Minister and the Leader of the Opposition and tried to negotiate a peaceful settlement between the two, but these efforts did not work. The Prime Minister confined herself to the constitutional position and the opposition demanded an immediate general election and the formation of an interim caretaker government headed by the President. In other words, the opposition wanted the Prime Minister to step down and a neutral government to be formed by the President in order that the Election Commission could hold the general election.

The opposition movement then took a more violent turn.[34] On 29 November, bombs were thrown at the residence of two ministers — the Flood Control and Water Resources Minister, and the Finance Minister — and at the hostel of the Members of Parliament at Nakhal Para. In the meantime, on 3 December the Election Commission

---

[34] See also *The Independent*, Dhaka, 7 October 1995 and the *Daily Ittefaq*, Dhaka, 25 October 1995 and 1 January 1996.

announced the election schedule for a general election, the date of polling originally having been fixed on 18 January 1996 but subsequently shifted to 16 February. This timetable was rejected outright by all the major opposition parties, which called upon the people to resist the election. The opposition adopted various political programmes to mobilise the people, including a 72-hour *hartal* on 9, 10 and 11 December and the encirclement of the Office of the Prime Minister.

The Election Commission went ahead with all the official election preparations,[35] including the recovery of illegal arms. The BNP, as the ruling party, decided to participate in the election to fulfil the constitutional requirements. They argued that if the elections were not held, the constitution would fail causing a great vacuum in politics and a disruption to the democratic process. The Election Commission called upon the armed forces to assist in conducting the election. As far as the opposition was concerned, the crisis could only be resolved if the Prime Minister resigned, which she was determined not to do.

The whole year of 1995 passed in a traumatic way.[36] The opposition took full advantage of the government's indecision and adopted various political programmes to strengthen their movement. Parliament hardly functioned as a sovereign body and the government operated without any kind of scrutiny or accountability. The opposition now escalated the agitational movement with a series of *hartals*, *gheroas*, meetings and demonstrations. With rising inflation and the price of essential commodities sharply increased, it became easier to mobilise public opinion against the government.[37]

General Election, February 1996

The BNP leadership made efforts to come to a compromise with the opposition on 12 December 1995. The government offered a package

---

[35] On the same day (3 December) an ordinance was made to make provisions for a Code of Conduct for the election. This increased the election expenses to Tk. 3 lakhs and disqualified candidates who were bank defaulters from contesting the election.

[36] *Janakantha* described the year of 1995 as a year of hartals, revolt by farmers against corruption in distribution of urea fertiliser and repression of women (see *Janakantha*, Dhaka, 31 December 1995).

[37] *Daily Ittefaq*, Dhaka, 10 August 1995.

of proposals to break the political impasse. The three options offered[38] were as follows:

1. An interim government to be headed by a Prime Minister from the ruling party, chosen by the opposition after the resignation of the Prime Minister.
2. The new Prime Minister would not participate in the next election.
3. The opposition would prepare a proposal for an interim government within the framework of the existing constitution.

There was an exchange of letters between the Prime Minister and the Leader of the Opposition, but in the end no tangible result could be achieved because of the adamant position taken by the opposition. They maintained that no meeting could be held with the Prime Minister unless she had decided to resign and the only agenda that could be discussed was for a neutral non-party caretaker government. They also wanted the meeting to be broadcast live by the government-controlled electronic media.[39] As a result, while the opposition boycotted the election, the BNP continued to announce the name of its candidates.

The ruling party ignored the terms of the opposition for the resignation of Begum Zia and the formation of a neutral caretaker government. The President also ignored the demand of the opposition to cancel the election, for which the opposition had written to the Election Commission. Sheikh Hasina then announced, at a public meeting on 21 January, that what she considered to be the farcical election should be cancelled by 23 January, otherwise she warned that the confrontational agitation would be escalated further to bring about the fall of the government. Following the statement

---

[38] Due to an obsession that it must stick to power for its full tenure of five years, the BNP government ignored the ground realities. In the pretext of seeking solution within the framework of the Constitution or their attempt to "save the Constitution" the concessions they offered at later stages were too late for the opposition to accept in the prevailing dynamics of the movement.

[39] See *The Independent* and the *Daily Ittefaq*, Dhaka, 15 and 25 December 1995. In 1994-95 the opposition called hartal for 171 days (see the *Inqilab*, Dhaka, 3 January 1996, the *Morning Sun*, Dhaka, 5 January 1996). Two thousand people were murdered in 1995.

made by Hasina, more than a hundred vehicles were set on fire and destroyed in the streets of Dhaka.

The Prime Minister addressed the nation on 23 January and rejected the opposition proposal on the ground that an unelected person could not be the head of the caretaker government. Although she called upon the opposition to come forward to reach a settlement,[40] Begum Zia asserted that the general election would have to be held in order to save the constitution and democratic process. However, she indicated that if there was an election before the expiry of 90 days from the dissolution of the Parliament, there would be no constitutional crisis. Once Parliament was elected it would be able to take the necessary decisions to enable all political parties to take part in future elections and if necessary provide for an interim government in the Constitution. Since there was no provision for such a non-party caretaker government in the present Constitution, a change in the basic structure of the Constitution was required.

Obviously the election was going to be a one-party poll. Although 1,500 candidates submitted nomination papers in 300 seats, the contest was only between different members of the BNP itself and 44 candidates were declared uncontested.[41] In the face of the resistance put up by the opposition in the constituencies, BNP candidates were not able to campaign freely.[42] Terrorists attacked the Sonargaon, the only five-star hotel in the capital. Bombs were hurled at a meeting of ministers and BNP candidates, and a state of total anarchy prevailed in the country.[43]

In order to resist the general election, the opposition announced a six-day programme and a hartal was declared for 14 and 15 February. The following day, Sheikh Hasina called for a people's curfew on polling day.[44] Opposition workers attacked and encircled the Prime Minister's Secretariat, television and radio centre. The situation was

---

[40] See the *Daily Ittefaq*, 24 January 1996.

[41] See the *Inqilab*, 25 January 1996.

[42] See the *Daily Ittefaq*, 25 January 1996; *Sangbad*, 27 January; and *Janakantha*, 31 January 1996.

[43] See the *Daily Ittefaq*, 7 February 1996; *Janakantha*, *Sangbad* and *Inqilab*, 8 February 1996; *Janakantha*, *Sangbad* and *Inqilab*, 10 February 1996; and *The Independent*, *Inqilab*, *Ittefaq* and *Sangbad*, 11 February 1996.

[44] See the *Daily Ittefaq*, 16 February 1996.

beyond the control of the government and law and order collapsed. In the midst of a *hartal*, the general election was held on 15 February, boycotted by all the opposition political parties. In the absence of voters and any strong contestants, BNP candidates rigged the election and filled up the boxes with ballot papers to show a higher turnout.[45] Due to the violence and ballot rigging, the Election Commission had to suspend the election in 119 constituencies.[46]

The Election Commission took a long time to declare the results and the broadcasting of the election results over the government-controlled radio and television was stopped. Although the Prime Minister claimed that the elections were free and fair and blamed the opposition for creating disruption, the *New York Times* and other foreign reports estimated the turnout of voters at less than 10 per cent and said that the election was not credible. On 18 February 1996, out of 205 seats declared, the BNP secured 203 seats; in 90 constituencies repolling was needed.[47]

The farcical election held on 15 February 1996 was a death knell for the BNP. The election caused widespread damage to people and property all over the country. It had also once again disfranchised the nation, since the voters did not go to vote. It caused an intensification of the movement against the government and assured the participation of the general public in the movement. On 16 February the opposition called for a non-co-operation movement beginning with a three-day programme from 24 to 26 February in all government and semi-government offices, the barricade of roads, rivers and railways, and the closure of Chittagong and Chalna Ports. Six national political leaders[48] were arrested by the police in a midnight raid before the non-co-operation movement was started, which only aggravated the mounting public protest. Seventeen days later they were released under political pressure. The non-co-operation movement took an extremely violent turn and paralysed the major port city of Chittagong, where the army was called in to contain the situation. Upheaval and

---

[45] *Daily Ittefaq*, 15 and 16 February 1996; *Sangbad, Inqilab* and *Banglabazar Patrika*, 16 February 1996.

[46] *Daily Ittefaq*, 17 February 1996.

[47] *The Independent*, 19 and 24 February 1996.

[48] Including the author.

confrontation, culminating in non-stop non-co-operation marked the whole month of March 1996.

The crisis only deepened as the days passed by. On 3 March 1996, Begum Zia addressed the nation and declared that a constitutional amendment bill would be introduced in the first session of the new Parliament aiming to provide for a non-party caretaker government for all future general elections. A general election for the 7th Parliament would be arranged in the shortest possible time. She called upon the opposition for a dialogue. The opposition responded that such discussion could only take place at the initiative of the President.

The President invited the leaders of all the political parties separately on 10 March. The demands put before him were common, such as the election held on 15 February ought to be cancelled, the government to resign and fresh general elections be held during May. Begum Zia agreed to the formation of the caretaker government and a fresh election in May, and her position was communicated to the President on 11 March. As soon as the government conceded to the demands of the opposition, Begum Zia lost the strength to govern the country for long. The public perception was that the government has lost politically to the opposition, and the rank and file of the opposition, now further boosted, went all out against the government.

Due to the closure of the Chittagong port by opposition activists and the volatile political situation prevailing in the country, not only did exports start declining but also the whole economy came to a standstill. The volume of investment had started decreasing and the prices of essential commodities continued to rise. The law and order situation worsened further. Added to this was a crisis of urea fertiliser, now aggravated to such a scale that the offices of the Thana Nirbahi officers were gheraoed by farmers all over the country, demanding supply of fertiliser at a fair price. In some areas the farmers raided the godowns.[49] Meanwhile, almost all sections of the population were gradually joining the non-co-operation movement and campaigning for the resignation of the government. On 19 March, 23 professional groups, comprising teachers, doctors, engineers, lawyers, journalists, poets, writers, artists, agriculturists, etc., held a

---

[49] *Daily Ittefaq*, 19 March 1996.

massive rally in front of the Press Club to express their solidarity with the opposition.[50] The leading chambers representing the business community of the country had also taken the same stand against the government.

On 23 March, at the initiative of the Mayor of Dhaka City Corporation, an Awami League leader built a huge people's platform in front of the Press Club, known as *Janatar-mancha* or peoples platform. People from all walks of life, particularly the government and semi-government employees along with their trade unions, started joining the movement by way of lending support to the Janatar-mancha. The senior government officials, led by the Secretaries, called on the President on 27 March to express their concern over the law and order and economic situation of the country. They submitted a six-point proposal to the President and communicated their decision not to attend the offices until the President had formed a caretaker government. This unprecedented stand taken by the civil servants totally shattered the moral authority of the government to hold on to power. The government employees held a demonstration within the Secretariat, violating magisterial orders not to do so. On 30 March the senior civil servants, led by Dr Mohiuddin Khan Alamgir[51] and the Government Employees Solidarity Council, walked out of the Secretariat in a long procession and joined the Janatar-mancha.[52] The same support continued to come from all the sector corporations and semi-government agencies and organisations.

In the meantime, on 19 March, a new 47-member Cabinet had taken a fresh oath of office with Begum Khaleda Zia as the Prime Minister. In an address to the first session of Parliament on the same day, the President announced that a suitable amendment would be made to the constitution so that the next general election would be held under a non-party caretaker government. The sitting of Parliament sparked further violence and turned the entire area surrounding the building into a battlefield.[53] Dhaka was in a rage.

---

[50] *Inqilab, Independent*, 19 February 1996.

[51] Once Sheikh Hasina formed the government the officer was made a state minister.

[52] By this time the movement had been completely taken over by the Awami League.

[53] For detail, see the *Inqilab*, 20 March 1996.

People had set fire to vehicles, petrol pumps, shops, government buildings and buses.

The government hurriedly introduced a bill, the 13th Constitutional Amendment Bill, and had it passed in Parliament on 27 March. What the opposition had demanded twenty months ago the government was at last forced to concede but at a huge cost to the government, the people and Parliament. Soon afterwards, Begum Zia resigned as the Prime Minister on 30 March and advised the President to dissolve Parliament. She addressed a huge mass meeting from a public platform called *Ganatantra Mancha* ('platform for democracy'), claiming that she had no alternative but to hold the election on 15 February because there was no provision in the constitution for an interim government. Begum Zia claimed that it was her commitment to the people that such an arrangement could not be made without amending the constitution, so she had no other recourse but to hold the election and have the 13th Amendment passed by Parliament. Now she was ready to go for the election under the non-party caretaker government.

On the same evening, under the 13th Amendment the last retired Chief Justice, Habibur Rahman, took the oath of office as the Chief Adviser and head of a non-party caretaker government at Bangabhaban, where both Begum Khaleda Zia and Sheikh Hasina were present. This also brought to an end the 21 days of the non-co-operation movement.

Constitutional Recognition of an Interim Government

In order to make provision for an interim government, the basic structure of the constitution had to be changed. In a parliamentary system of government, the Prime Minister having the confidence of the majority of Members of Parliament continues to hold office until a new Prime Minister enters into that office. Even with Parliament dissolved, the Prime Minister still continues running the day-to-day affairs of the government. This has been the practice all over the world. The replacement of an elected Prime Minister by an unelected person was not conceived by the constitution of Bangladesh, but the country had to adopt a different course due to the prevailing socio-political conditions.

A new chapter (Chapter IIA in Part IV) has been incorporated under Article 58 of the Constitution. Articles 58A-C contain the basic changes made to incorporate the provisions for a non-party caretaker government. The head of the caretaker government was designated as the Chief Adviser. He or she enters office after Parliament is dissolved and holds the same until the day a new Prime Minister takes office after Parliament is constituted. The Chief Adviser exercises the executive power of the republic during the period he is in office (Article 58B). The composition of the interim government consists of the Chief Adviser as its head and not more than ten other Advisers to be appointed by the President (Article 58C(1)). The caretaker government is collectively responsible to the President (Article 58B(2)) and is to be appointed within fifteen days of the Chief Adviser's appointment.

The President will appoint a person as the Chief Adviser who is the last retired Chief Justice of Bangladesh, and if the retired Chief Justice is not available or is not willing to hold the office of Chief Adviser, the President will appoint the person who retired immediately before the last retired Chief Justice. If no retired Chief Justice is available, the President will appoint the person who among the retired judges of the Appellate Division retired last, and if he is not available or willing to hold the office, the judge who retired before him will be appointed. If no retired judge of the Appellate Division is available or willing to hold the office of Chief Adviser, the President after consultation, as far as practicable, with the major political parties will appoint the Chief Adviser from among the citizens of Bangladesh who are qualified to be appointed as Chief Adviser (Article 58C(3), (4) and (5)). If, however, none of the provisions in Clauses 3, 4 and 5 of the new Article 58C can be given effect, the President can assume the function of the Chief Adviser in addition to his own functions assigned in the Constitution.

As to the qualifications of the Advisers including the Chief Adviser, the important feature is that such an Adviser will not be a member of any political party or associated with any organisation affiliated to a political party (Article 58C(7)(b). Such an Adviser will not be a candidate for the ensuing election for Members of Parliament

(Article 58C(7)(c). The President will appoint the Advisers on the advice of the Chief Adviser.

The non-party caretaker government will discharge the duties as an interim government and carry out routine functions of such a government with the aid and assistance of persons in the service of the republic and will not take any policy decision except when it is absolutely necessary (Article 58D(1)). The interim government will render all possible aid and assistance to the Election Commission to hold the election for Members of Parliament peacefully, fairly and impartially (Article 58D(2)).

Amendments made in the Constitution relating to Articles 99, 123, 147 and 152 and the 3rd schedule are all consequential amendments made only to safeguard the provisions for the formation of a non-party caretaker government. Some of the more significant features of this new arrangement are that during the period when the non-party caretaker government is functioning, provisions in the constitution requiring the President to act on the advice of the Prime Minister or upon his prior countersignature will not be effective (Article 58E). There is no significant difference between the earlier proposal made by the opposition and the final constitutional position, except that under the 13th Amendment the President has been empowered to exercise certain executive powers at his own discretion without being advised by the Chief Adviser.[54] The President could even, without the advice of the Chief Adviser, proclaim an emergency under Article 141A(1) and suspend the fundamental rights under Article 141C(1) of the Constitution.

Equally important was the amendment of Article 61 of the Constitution regarding the administration of the Defence Services. In the present constitution, although the supreme command of the Defence Services was vested in the President, the exercise of that command was regulated by law and exercised by the executive authority of the Prime Minister. In the amendment, the administration of the Defence Services was given to the President for the period of the non-party caretaker government. In other words, during the time when there is a caretaker government, the President has been given

---

[54] See Articles 48(3), 141A(1) and 141C(2) of the Constitution, under which the President is to act on the advice of the Prime Minister.

wider power in matters of both administration of government[55] and the Defence Services.

Role of the Speaker

Another distinctive feature in Bangladesh politics is the role of the Speaker. Unlike in India, and other more developed countries, the Speakers in Bangladesh have played a blatantly partisan role. In both the Parliaments, under the BNP and the Awami League, the Speaker functioned under the influence of the respective political governments. This is one of the reasons why politics in Parliament failed to grow. There was very little difference in the behaviour and approach towards the opposition between the Speaker under the BNP government (1991-96) and the Speaker under the Awami League government (1996-2001). Each of them was under constant political pressure of the party they belonged to and failed to act independently.

On all issues and not just the crucial ones, they only fulfilled the desire of the ruling party. Even in matters like the allocation of time and allowing notices and adjournment motions, the political interest of the ruling party would be the prime consideration. Although the Speaker in the BNP Parliament was more balanced and tolerant and performed far better than the Speaker of the Awami League Parliament,[56] they essentially behaved in the same manner. The behaviour of the first Speaker in dealing with the resignation of the Members of the opposition[57] and that of the second Speaker when two BNP MPs, Mohammad Hasibur Rahman Swapan and Dr Mohammad Alauddin,[58] crossed the floor was identical. In both cases the matter had to be resolved by the Supreme Court instead of the Speaker. The Court found both Speakers to be at fault as they had only served the political interests of the respective ruling party, ignoring the clear mandate of the Constitution.

---

[55] See the new Article 58B(2), whereby the caretaker government has been made collectively responsible to the President.

[56] In the first session of the 5th Parliament the Speaker turned off the microphone of the Leader of the Opposition in the middle of her statements, which was outrageous and against parliamentary practice.

[57] See 47 DLR (AD), p. 111.

[58] 51 DLR, p. 1, upheld by the Appellate Division in 4 BLC (AD) 1999, p. 273.

Role of the Election Commission

The Election Commission, an institution of great significance in Bangladesh, has again been a victim of political influence. The electoral process has become corrupt largely because the Commission has not been able to play its constitutional role in ensuring free and fair elections when there has been a political government. Only when there has been a non-party caretaker government has the Election Commission been able to play a relatively neutral role. During by-elections when a political government runs the country, the Election Commission has failed to maintain a neutral position in conducting the elections in a free and fair manner.[59]

The irony is that soon after the fall of the Ershad government and the formation of an interim government headed by the Chief Justice Shahabuddin Ahmed, the Election Commission was reconstituted and Justice M. A. Rouf, a sitting judge of the High Court Division, and a consensus nominee was appointed as the Chief Election Commissioner. In the same manner, after the fall of BNP government and formation of a caretaker government headed by the last retired Chief Justice Habibur Rahman, the post of the Chief Election Commissioner was filled by appointing a consensus nominee of all the major political parties, Abu Hena, who was a retired civil servant. But both met with the same fate. As long as there was a non-party caretaker government during the election period, the Election Commission was able to function fairly independently; but as soon as the political government was installed, the role of the same Commission became subservient to the ruling government.

Although the law places all the functionaries of the election process, including the mainstream bureaucracy, under the control and command of the Election Commission, in practice it was not sufficient to make the functionaries adequately accountable to the Election Commission. Yet the mainstream bureaucracy and the police administration play a vital role in ensuring free and fair elections at the grass-roots level. The Deputy Commissioners of the

---

[59] See the reports on the Magura by-election during the BNP regime and the Luxmipur by-election during the Awami League regime. The worst happened under the first Awami League government in 1973.

districts act as the Returning Officers and the Thana Nirbahi Officers (TNOs) as the Assistant Returning Officers. In most of the constituencies at the Thana level, the Returning Officers select the Presiding Officers, Assistant Presiding Officers and other Polling Officers for polling day. These officers or functionaries are generally drawn from the civil servants at the Thana level and schoolteachers of the area concerned. In the absence of any strong institutional control and supervision, in many cases these officers and functionaries do not follow the rules or can easily be influenced by any of the contesting parties. At the field level they may fail to implement the constitutional mandate of holding a free and fair election.

An election on a free and fair basis does not depend only on having a non-party caretaker government at the central level and an Election Commission supervising the conduct of elections. Both bodies sit in the capital without a sufficiently effective system for monitoring and controlling the functionaries in the field. So it is difficult to implement the code of conduct prepared by the Election Commission, and violation of the code in most cases goes unpunished. The cost and nature of elections have also changed. Money and muscle power play a key role over which the Election Commission has hardly any control. Although election expenses are restricted to Tk. 300,000 for all constituencies, some candidates particularly in the south-east spend up to Tk. 5 crore (Tk.50 million). There is no way that the Election Commission can play any role in enforcing restrictions on expenses. When sophisticated arms are used to occupy polling centres, the security personnel with one or two World War II vintage 303 rifles in their hands look helpless. There are some inherent weaknesses in the election laws that demand urgent reforms.

But of all the predicaments the most pertinent one is the behaviour of the political parties themselves in the electoral process. There is neither hardly any serious commitment on the part of the major political parties nor any orientation amongst the candidates to follow and implement the code of conduct in the electoral process. Holding a free, fair and peaceful election does not solely depend on the election laws or the code of conduct or the role of the Election Commission, or on having a non-party caretaker government. These can only play an important and effective role if the political parties follow the rules and democratic norms and are tolerant towards each other. People at large in Bangladesh are conscious of their right to vote and they have always exercised their franchise whenever they have had the opportunity of doing so. Furthermore, on every occasion they have given a correct verdict. So the conduct of a meaningful election ultimately depends on the behaviour and attitude of the major political parties, their candidates and party leaders at the local level.

The credibility of the Election Commission during the rule of the BNP declined dramatically when by-elections were held at Mirpur (Dhaka) and later at Magura. At the conclusion of the latter election Justice M. A. Rouf had to leave the Election Commission and return to the Supreme Court as a judge in order to save his honour. With that experience in mind — that even a judge could not play an effective role in the event of political pressure — Abu Hena, a bureaucrat, was appointed. The expectation was that as a civil servant he would assert his position and perform his functions independently, keeping in mind, as a role model, the part played by Mr. Seesan of India[60]. But here, too, as soon as the political government of the Awami League was installed, the Chief Election Commissioner failed, right from the beginning, to play a neutral role in the by-elections, as the election at Luxmipur showed. In the end, Abu Hena also had to leave the office, ostensibly on health grounds, in an unceremonious way.

Despite the difficulties they faced under the pressure of the respective political governments, none of the Chief Election Commissioners of the different democratic regimes had the courage to assert his position. The Chief Election Commissioner and other Election Commissioners are appointed under Article 118 of the constitution. Since theirs was a constitutional post with tenure of five years and they were removable only by the same lengthy process applicable for judges of the Supreme Court, they had nothing to fear. But unfortunately on each occasion they failed to rise to the occasion to perform their duties properly and conscientiously under the constitution.

---

[60] Seesan, a veteran civil servant, as the Chief Election Commissioner of India earned a great respect and reputation for his independent and creative role.

Politics of Boycott and Resignation

Although the Parliaments of 1991 and 1996, were elected under a non-party caretaker government and embodied great hopes of the people, they were not able to function meaningfully. The Parliament elected in 1991, when Khaleda Zia was the Prime Minister, lost its significance when the opposition, led by Sheikh Hasina, boycotted not only the sittings of Parliament but the sessions as well, first for eleven months and then for another thirteen months after the 147 opposition Members of Parliament had resigned. So the Parliament elected in 1991 functioned without any participation by the opposition for almost two years, As a result the very purpose of having a Parliament was lost.[61] Accountability, transparency and good governance became non-existent as the functions of Parliament as an effective national sovereign body became defiled.

The same experience was repeated in the Parliament elected in 1996. Sheikh Hasina, now the Prime Minister, received the same treatment from her opponent, the Leader of the Opposition and former Prime Minister. The politics of boycott and resignation from Parliament made the very existence of Parliament ineffective, meaningless and *functus officio*. Apart from making laws by simple majority, no fruitful purpose has been achieved in either of the two Parliaments elected by the people.

In the Parliament elected in 1996, the Awami League took an aggressive stand from the beginning, although they were now in the Treasury Bench. The League behaved as if it was still in the opposition, while the BNP behaved as if it was in the government. It took time for them to adjust to their respective new positions. So right from the first day there was intolerance by the ruling party towards the opposition, and with the BNP not being able to effectively assume its role as an opposition in Parliament, a great deal of damage occurred in the functioning of Parliament.

The first dispute arose when the Speaker, having had no experience in running Parliament, took an extremely partisan role against the opposition, which prevented it operating effectively in Parliament.

---

[61] For more detail on the background to the boycott and the events leading to the resignation of all the opposition MPs from the Parliament, see pp. 269-279.

For instance, Khaleda Zia was denied the opportunity to speak when the Speaker turned off the microphone on three occasions in the first session. The entire attitude of the Awami League was to shut down the opposition in Parliament.

The next major issue arose with regard to the formation of Standing Committees under Chapter XVII of the Rules of Procedure of Parliament. The BNP's demand for proportional representation in all the committees, which would not have reduced the majority representation of the ruling party at all, was refused. This created a stalemate that continued for almost a year and a half. Parliament therefore continued without the functioning of the committees — the basic forums to establish the accountability of the executive to Parliament. The government's political repression and violation of human rights, instituting false cases against opposition leaders and workers all over the country, was an issue that the BNP had to strongly vindicate in the Parliament. The other issue raised by the opposition was the biased broadcasting of the state-controlled media in favour of the ruling party.

In less than six months the relationship between the ruling party and the opposition had deteriorated to the point at which there was a long boycott of the Parliament by the opposition. Later an agreement was signed between the parties on 14 January 1997 on four points raised by the opposition. The BNP then returned to Parliament, but the agreement was not implemented, each side accusing the other of not fulfilling its obligations.

When the opposition again threatened to boycott Parliament, negotiations were held and the two parties signed a second agreement on 2 March 1998. It was agreed that false cases against the leaders and workers would be withdrawn, and that all the MPs belonging to the BNP would be included in the Parliamentary Committees. Furthermore, the proceedings of Parliament would be broadcast in a neutral and objective manner, giving equal time to the opposition members.

Once the opposition returned to Parliament on 8 March, however, the government did not show much interest in implementing all the terms of the agreement. Only the Standing Committees were formed as agreed by the end of 1998. Despite all the pressures exerted, no effective measures were taken by the government side to mitigate the situation. More false cases were initiated against the opposition, and one-sided broadcasts by radio and television continued without any change.

Finally the boycott started by the opposition in April 1999 took a serious turn, resulting in a boycott of the sessions of Parliament for nearly two years. In the meantime, out of considerable frustration, Members of Parliament belonging to the BNP submitted their resignation letters to the Leader of the Opposition, for her to hand over to the Speaker whenever she decided to do so.

Political Victimisation and Repression of Opposition

Victimisation of political opponents, when a government falls or a new government is formed, has long been a part of the political culture in Bangladesh.[62] The Martial Law Courts convicted, mainly on charges of corruption, a large number of former ministers of the Awami League government of 1972-75. But some of the same politicians were used by the regime in various ways to serve their own political interests after they were released. When the elected government of the BNP, headed by Sattar, was removed by the new martial law regime of Ershad, they imprisoned all the former ministers of the BNP government on charges of corruption and had many of them convicted by the martial law courts. Later when they were released, Ershad inducted many of them as his ministers, thus proving how false these cases were.[63]

It is not uncommon that when the military rulers take over power by removing elected governments, they launch their first attack on the civil politicians. This has happened not only in Pakistan and Bangladesh, but also in almost every country where military interventions have taken place. However, this culture and practice is no longer limited to military regimes. In the last two democratic regimes, the same victimisation of the opponents has taken place once a new

---

[62] The same, in varying degrees, is true of all the major countries in South Asia.

[63] For detail, see Moudud Ahmed, *Democracy and the Challenge of Development* (Dhaka: The University Press Limited). Ershad had the author convicted in a Martial Law Court. He then set aside this conviction on review and inducted the author as a Minister. Later Ershad made him the Prime Minister and a few months afterwards the Vice President of Bangladesh.

government has been installed in power.[64] When the BNP returned to power in 1991, the first crusade was launched against Ershad and his former ministers. Almost all of them were sent to prison on charges of corruption. Except Ershad, who was imprisoned for more than five years, none was convicted of any offence. Subsequently, when the BNP fell from power, it joined hands with the same Ershad to form an alliance against the Awami League government. And when the AL government returned to power in 1996, they not only instituted cases against Begum Zia, her family members and former ministers on charges of corruption, but also made extensive use of the Special Powers Act and the provisions of the Penal Code to institute thousands of cases against BNP workers and activists all over the country.[65]

Instituting such large numbers of criminal cases, ranging from murder to treason, against political opponents under the provisions of Penal Code is a new trend in Bangladesh.[66] It is an effective method for repressing the opposition, harassing them for life without conducting any trial or securing any conviction. Most of the cases are false and fabricated, but the process of the criminal law is such that cases can continue indefinitely unless they are finally resolved either by way of an acquittal or a conviction or through a final report being submitted by police. This method is one of the worst forms of human rights violation. A political leader or worker accused in several cases at the same time can hardly be free to take part in politics. Firstly he may or may not get a bail, but if he does so, he must then regularly present himself at the court without been able to attend to his normal

---

[64]In Sri Lanka, after the general election held on 10 October 2000 resulted in a hung Parliament, the ruling People's Alliance and the main opposition, the United National Party, reached an agreement to resolve some of the outstanding problems. They have agreed to introduce legislation to set up an independent Election Commission and an independent Public Service Commission. They have also agreed to introduce media reforms and bring an end to political victimisation and harassment. The aim is to introduce a new political culture in Sri Lanka. They have also decided to discuss constitutional changes necessary to resolve politically the long ethnic civil war in Sri Lanka. *Daily Star*, 23 October 2000.

[65]See the petition filed by the BNP before the High Court Division, Writ Petition No. 1216, 1999.

[66]See the petition filed by the BNP before the High Court Division, Criminal Miscellaneous Case No. 668, 1999.

socio-political life.[67] All such actions are largely politically motivated and have not helped either to eliminate corruption nor the other crimes for which the cases are allegedly instituted.

Polarisation and the Political Divide

Bangladesh has a highly politicised culture. The polarisation in politics has gone so deep that it has divided the country into almost two nations. The Awami League, perceived to be a pro-Indian political party having strong links with India's economy and politics, claims to represent those who were in favour of the independence of Bangladesh from the colonial rule of Pakistan. The BNP, formed by Ziaur Rahman, the person who declared the War of Independence against Pakistan and was the nation's most celebrated freedom fighter, represents all the forces opposed to the Awami League and any kind of Indian domination.

Having returned to power after 21 years, the Awami League took a truly petty and vengeful stand in all aspects of the country's social, political and economic life. In pursuing this attitude they have sharply divided civil society itself. Every organised section of Bangladesh society, including the professional organisations, is divided into two major streams that are totally polarised and adamant about retaining their own political position. No civil society can develop without a strong group of citizens who pursue and promote objective and balanced views on important issues in society. But those who are neutral and non-partisan amongst the professional groups have become a very marginal force, unable to play an effective role in Bangladesh.

The same is true of the administration and governance of the Awami League government. Political loyalty and background have been given precedence over merit and competence in appointing, posting and promoting civil servants, police officers, teachers in the school and universities, officers and workers in government-controlled

---

[67]Up to May 1999, 86 criminal cases had been filed against Sadek Hossain Khoka, MP, President of Dhaka City BNP and the party's mayoral candidate for the City Corporation, all in connection with his political activities; 29 cases against Amanullah Aman, MP; 117 cases against Md. Mohan, Secretary, Kotwali Thana BNP; and 79 cases against Nasiruddin Pintu, General Secretary of the Student Wing of the BNP. See the affidavit filed in Writ Petition No. 1216, 1999, High Court Division, Bangladesh Supreme Court.

television and radio and in every other branch of the state. The Awami League has patronised only those who would support it and has disgraced others who are opposed to the League. As a result, in the police and civil administration, the institutions of governance have failed to function. Partisanship is also reflected in awards of land, government contracts, businesses and licences. Distribution of state largess is based primarily on the party line, notwithstanding the government's rules and procedures.

Chapter 8

The Future of South Asia: Issues and Options
The Case of Bangladesh

Is South Asia then going to sit back and be only an onlooker as the rest of the world makes progress in the new millennium? Has India decided to stay as backward as it is today?[1] Does it want its billion people, set to double in 35 years, to remain in a state of underdevelopment for no fault of their own? Does it not want to lead South Asia and win support from its neighbours by being good to them?

Many would argue that the political and economic structure of South Asia today is unlikely to bring an economic breakthrough in the near future. SAARC cannot achieve miracles either. The authority of the central government of India, under coalition governments for many years to come, will weaken further and the rise of Hindu fundamentalism will not work to keep India together. India, too large and now too weak in central planning, is unable to present a model for rapid economic growth either for itself or for its neighbours.

The nuclear tests have also altered security perceptions and made the future of South Asia more uncertain. India and Pakistan may sign the Comprehensive Test Ban Treaty, but they will not roll back their nuclear programmes and the threat of war will always be there. Pakistan will continue to be ruled by the Punjab backed by the military elite, and their obsession about Kashmir and neglect and repression of Sind, Baluchistan and the North-West Frontier Province will continue

---

[1] India is showing signs of a faster pace of development with about 6 per cent growth rate for the last five years. It has already made a mark in information technology and software and will soon occupy a significant place in the world market.

to keep the country unstable. The economic collapse of Pakistan will be hard to contain. The recent military take-over and the situation arisen out of the Afghan issue will not make any difference — it may make the situation even worse.[2] Meanwhile, India's hegemonistic policy towards its smaller neighbours will continue to hinder the socio-economic and political progress of the region as a whole.

But despite all the present predicaments South Asia cannot go on the way it is going. It must survive and to survive with dignity it must change. It has the potential to turn itself into a region of prosperity, but it has to look for alternatives in-terms of both geopolitics and economy. The future of South Asia is largely linked with the future of India, so one must think about India first. The strategic importance of South Asia in the global context is an undeniable fact. It is destined to play a dominant role not only in Asia, but also on the world stage. The emergence of China increases the importance of South Asia as a balancing force for world peace and security.

In its present structure India is too large and too slow to cope with the soothing breeze of development blowing over the Asian horizon. What are the alternatives for change then? The first option for South Asia is to continue with the system and structure that it has now, and to allow progress to come in an evolutionary way; to let the traditional administration move at its own pace, not to try to move faster than it can. To let democracy take root in society rather than pursuing the material well being achieved by some of the South-East Asian countries. In essence, therefore, the first option is to maintain the status quo. With insubstantial changes and occasional incorporation of reform programmes, the conventional annual budgets, annual development plans and the mis-allocation of resources would continue in the same format as today. Food scarcity, environmental calamities, malnutrition, hunger, poverty, illiteracy, lack of health care, unemployment and poor sanitation would receive no more than the usual attention. Foreign relations and conflicts with neighbours would continue as usual.

If this is the course pursued, it will mean that India and South Asia have withdrawn from the challenge of the millennium. This

---

[2] In Pakistan, the military took over state power on 12 October 1999 by removing an elected government.

choice may not affect the elite classes who govern the countries of South Asia today, but it will have a bearing on over a billion people who live with the hope of a better future for themselves and their children. To be poor and poverty-stricken is an experience that cannot be shared by those who are not in the same condition. Historically nations in a state of under-development have remained so for centuries, and in the process their civilisation has suffered and perished. But the dynamism of the people of South Asia cannot accept the status quo as their destiny. People want a change and so do their governments and leaders. But to wish for a change and not to act for it will be disastrous.

On the other hand, as a second option, one may look at South Asia as a region with the potential to blossom in prosperity. Instead of retracing the past, it is possible to look forward and adopt a pragmatic programme for collective self-reliance. India has to change its role in the region in order to assume a bigger role in world politics. It must take a broader view to realise its dream of taking a place on the global stage. Instead of looking at Pakistan as only a 'breakaway territory',[3] Sri Lanka as an 'off-shore island of India' separated by the little waterway of the Palk Strait, at Nepal as a 'land-locked Hindu state' ethnically tied to India, Bangladesh as a state 'created by the blood of the Indian soldiers' and Bhutan as virtually a 'protectorate', India could open its heart and adopt a much larger vision, considering itself as an entity beyond the political boundaries of India. It should feel proud of being the representative of an ancient civilisation comparable to any in Europe or the West, an heir to the heritage of Samudra Gupta, Ashoka, Prithviraj, Babar, Akbar, Shahjahan and Aurangazeb.[4] Let India think that its neighbours are assets for development rather than threats to its security.

India did not need nuclear bombs to establish its presence in the world. Some, like I. K. Gujral, advocated and tried to justify the tests by saying that one 'either had to be rich or needed many a bomb to be globally important, and as India was not rich it opted for the bombs'. The former Prime Minister of India must have taken a very

---

[3] Mizanur Rahman Shelley, 'The Ulysses Syndrome', *Weekly Friday*, Dhaka, 28 July 1989.
[4] *Ibid.*

narrow view of the country's vastness and potential to have adopted this perspective. Such phrases are used only to cover the failures that have kept India in a state of backwardness and impoverishment, and depriving its one billion people of their right to a better future.

Against whom is India going to use the nuclear bombs and for what purpose? No one in India is in a position to give a straight answer to this question. Then why have them? Everyone ignored the Indian Defence Minister's explanation of the Chinese threat to justify the testing of the nuclear bombs. China is too far away for this to be realistic, and for next twenty years or so China will be too busy in tackling the poverty and problems of its own people. China is seeking co-operation and not confrontation. India has managed the main valley of Kashmir for about 50 years now. India does not need a bomb to keep Kashmir under its control. The only fear is a pre-emptive attack from Pakistan, which suggests that the bombs might be useful as a deterrent. But it is extremely difficult to establish any reason why Pakistan should launch such an attack. Pakistan is way behind India in both military power and technology, and has neither the capability nor the realistic offensive means to attack India first. From the viewpoint of war analysts, Pakistan's military preparations are for defensive purposes.

The current situation will keep pushing the countries of the region, including China, into an unnecessary arms race, and will increase defence spending at the cost of human development. Emotion should not lead one to invoke illogical approaches in national policy making particularly in matters of such enormous importance. Let India be a rich democratic country rather than a country that has 1 billion poor people but the bombs to establish its presence in the world. India should take the initiative in rolling back its nuclear programme along with Pakistan. It should take the lead in putting pressure on others who have the weapons to do the same at an early date. This is the leadership role that the world demands of India, and that will enhance its image and prestige more than the possession of nuclear weapons.

On Kashmir, Pakistan has to be realistic. After the end of the Cold War and the withdrawal of Soviet troops from Afghanistan, Pakistan's strategic importance to the USA in counteracting communism has substantially diminished. It will not now receive much international support for its cause in Kashmir.[5] Nor will China fight a war on Pakistan's behalf. In both national and international context, a Pakistani solution of the Kashmir issue will be extremely difficult to achieve, as the matter has now become more complex than ever before.

Moreover, the threat of wars over Kashmir is ultimately not going to hold Pakistan together. It has to contain the demand for greater autonomy in Sind, Baluchistan and North-West Frontier Province. With its shattered national economy and the burden of having nuclear bombs, Pakistan's own viability as a state has now come under close scrutiny. The ethnic and tribal conflicts, family feuds among the upper class, and dominant feudal and military influences in politics do not show much promise unless Pakistan undertakes a radical geopolitical reconstruction. On the other hand, India will gain in Central Asia and the Gulf Region by having a good relationship with Pakistan. If India wants to play a global role, it cannot ignore the increasing importance of Central Asia.

Full autonomy for the whole of Kashmir, agreed by both India and Pakistan within the framework of their respective constitutions, could be a viable solution. It would make the Kashmiris, who have entered into an armed conflict for a land of their own, happy too. If Pakistan were taken into confidence and given due importance in arriving at such a conclusion, it might feel that it had a role to play in achieving something substantial for Kashmir. If India does not desire any third party involvement in this matter, it should take the initiative itself and resolve the issue bilaterally.[6]

If the issue of the Kashmiris is resolved, or at least if a process begins at the voluntary initiative of India, it will create goodwill both in Kashmir and in the outside world and diffuse the tension considerably. No one expects that these issues can be resolved overnight, but intentions and good faith will matter a great deal and will create a better environment for a harmonious collective growth in

---

[5] Although the recent US military offensive on Afghanistan, following the terrorist attack on the Twin Towers in New York on September 11, 2001, has increased the strategic importance of Pakistan once again and the issue of Kashmir is highlighted, the basic conflict between the two States over the valley remains unchanged.

[6] See the Article suggesting Plebiscite as one of the options to resolve the Kashmir Dispute. *India Today*, August 26, 2002, p. 56-57.

the region. This will immediately justify a reduction in military spending, enabling each country to divert its resources to the more urgent tasks of alleviating poverty and improving human productivity.

Pandit Jawaharlal Nehru wrote in 1946, 'Self interest itself should drive every nation to wider co-operation in order to escape disaster in the future and build its own free life on the basis of others' freedom.'[7] General K.M Arif, Pakistan's former Vice-Chief of the Army, stated: 'To resort to war is a poor option to establish peace or even hegemony. It is counter-productive to build up the security of one country on the insecurity of her neighbours. To achieve peace in South Asia, efforts should be made to win over hearts. And hearts cannot be won through conflict.'[8] General K. Sunderji, India's former Chief of Army Staff, echoed the same spirit when he said, 'to work towards a loose South Asian Federation based on the South Asian Regional Co-operation by 2010, we must carry Pakistan along as a major and honoured partner in the enterprise'.[9] He further suggested that 'we must wholeheartedly support Pakistan's right to develop a minimum nuclear deterrent'.

As far as China is concerned, India has nothing to fear. India should take advantage of the present Chinese policy of non-confrontation and devote more time to its own economic development. The testing of bombs will invariably, and quite unnecessarily, engage China in taking reciprocal defensive measures and the installation of Agni missiles in Assam by India will only provoke China to take counter-measures. Instead, India should continue to strengthen its policy of *rapprochement* with China and improve the relationship further. Chinese transfer of nuclear designs to Pakistan and equipping a naval base in Myanmar to monitor Indian missile tests may have caused genuine concern to India, but these irritations can be eased only by improving bilateral relations with China.

---

[7] Pandit Jawaharlal Nehru, *Discovery of India* (Signet, 1946), p. 539.

[8] 'The Roots of Conflict: A Pakistan Perspective', in Bharat Karnad (ed.), *Future Imperilled: India's Security in the 1990s and Beyond* (New Delhi: 1994), pp. 159-75. Quoted from Anirudha Gupta, 'Issues in South Asia: Geopolitics or Geoeconomics', *International Studies*, 34, 1997, Sage Publications, New Delhi.

[9] 'Indian Military Compulsion' in Canrad N. 5 pp. 144-45, quoted from Anirudha Gupta, 'Issues in South Asia'.

The USA, the world's only superpower, can also help by encouraging India to resolve these issues. India can no longer be viewed as an ally of the Soviet Union. In view of the end of the Cold War, India should be considered as a major force on its own merits. The USA should encourage India to have a place along with China and Russia in world affairs. Pakistan should also be assisted and encouraged to strengthen and consolidate its position as a viable state and to play an important role in Central Asia. Pakistan still has an immense strategic importance in view of the situation in Iran, Afghanistan and the Gulf States. A weaker Pakistan will not serve the US interests in the region.

If India fails to lead South Asia or if its leadership cannot rise to the occasion, then India will only have itself to blame. Pran Chopra, a well-respected author and journalist, described South Asia as a 'region of mistrust'. In one of his papers he summed up the situation thus: 'far from facilitating regional co-operation the over-hang of history has cast a shadow upon South Asia, creating a fog of mistrust in which the problems of centrality of India and the disparity between India and its neighbours loom even larger than life'.[10]

Pran Chopra said this in 1989, more than a decade ago. The situation still remains the same; nothing much has changed. India has continued to pursue the same policy. It has picked on its neighbours only because it has failed to become an economically advanced nation. In effect, India has underestimated its ability to realise its dream by taking a wrong approach from its inception. Over the years India has deviated from what Mahatma Gandhi and Jawaharlal Nehru envisaged for the nation.

The other task for India is to undertake restructuring and reform of the Indian system of governance. India is in a serious political crisis and is having considerable difficulty in holding the nation together. The central government of India will continue to lack any coherent vision or authority and command as long as it is a coalition with regional parties. In the absence of any nation-wide, broad-based political party or leadership to lead the nation through a cohesive central government, the present style of administration will continue

---

[10] Quoted from Mizanur Rahman Shelley, 'The Ulysses Syndrome', *Weekly Friday*, Dhaka, 28 July 1989.

to erode the hope that India will be taken seriously as a market for investment and as a major player in international affairs.

In order to overcome this, one may argue that India could go for a presidential system of government. Such a system could be as democratic and accountable as that of the USA, and India has the necessary institutions to develop it. But it is unlikely that political leaders in India will have the courage to introduce such a change. They have become too used to the present parliamentary system. The rise of and support for Hindu fundamentalism as a means of holding the nation together is also not going to last long. Fundamentalism may work for the time being as a cushion in politics. Eventually because of pressure from diverse forces and the middle-class political culture developed in the last 50 years, it will have to give way to global liberalisation, not only in the economy but also in politics and culture.

In this process, the states or provinces who are already demanding more autonomy and authority will assume more control over issues that would otherwise have been handled by the central government. Provincial leaders and politicians already resent the central government's power to appoint governors. They would like to have the Governors elected by the state assembly. They also resent the motivated dismissals of state governments and the imposition of President's rule in the provinces to suit the political purpose of those who run the central government. Issues such as the distribution of tax revenues between the centre and the provinces, the tenure of Lok Sabha, the lower house of the Parliament, and state assemblies, and judicial accountability are frequently debated in India.[11] Corruption in the electoral system and the criminalization of politics has already gone beyond the control of central government.

So because of the demands of the changing times, India has no alternative but to go for devolution of power to the states, which will turn India into a loose federation.[12] To cope with the present trends

---

[11] For the recent controversy over review of the present constitution of India, raised by the Prime Minister himself and disputed by the President of the Republic, see *India Today*, 14 February 2000.

[12] See the special interview given by Prafulla Mohante, Chief Minister of Assam. He has categorically warned that if the demand for autonomy for Assam is rejected, the territorial

of globalisation and economic integration, if the provinces have more freedom to achieve their own economic goals; they may opt to form common markets or economic units among themselves or with neighbouring countries. These smaller units are likely to be more effective than the whole country in achieving faster growth. For example, the southern provinces of India, which have already performed better than the northern provinces,[13] may prefer to join Sri Lanka to form potentially one of the most prosperous regions of South Asia. Kashmir as an autonomous state may also decide to form an economic unit with the adjacent states of Pakistan and India.

It is true that what can be said cannot always be done, particularly in the highly complex and sensitive situation of sovereign states, where nationalism plays a very emotional role. But at a time when electronic and knowledge-based technology is coming to dominate the world, the traditional concept of nationalism is undergoing a radical change and needs to be redefined. Due to the forces of technology and market liberalisation, the economic boundaries between states will hardly exist. In other words, trade will flow more freely than

---

integrity of India will be in danger. In this long interview, the Chief Minister narrated the grievances of the people not only of Assam, but of six sister states: namely, Arunachal, Meghalaya, Manipur, Nagaland, Mizoram and Tripura. He describes how Assam and other states are exploited by the central government of India and how badly the central government treats the state governments. He also mentions that the Chief Ministers of all 7 states held a meeting at Gauhati about the question of autonomy and how to contain the rising insurgencies in the respective states. *The Daily Ittefaq*, 23 September 2000.

A resolution for the autonomy of Jammu and Kashmir was recently passed unanimously in a special session of the state assembly. The resolution, steered through by Farooq Abdullah, the Chief Minister of Jammu and Kashmir, arose from a report of the Autonomy Committee. In many ways they reflected the demands made by his late father Sheikh Abdullah as early as 1953, for which Abdullah had to spend almost two decades of his life in gaol. However, the resolution was rejected by the central government in New Delhi. *India Today*, 10 and 17 July 2000.

See the article by Jairam Ramesh on greater fiscal autonomy for the states of India. *India Today*, 17 July 2000.

The central government of India set up the Sarkaria Commission on Centre–State Relations in March 1983. Its report was submitted in the middle of 1987. The government also constituted a State Finance Commission for decentralisation and a Constitution Review Commission to prepare a new fiscal framework for reforming the structure of interstate governmental economic relations. *India Today*, 17 July 2000.

[13]The southern part of India is surging ahead of other states. Tamil Nadu, Karnatak and Andhra Pradesh account for one-third of the total investment of India and provide 60 per cent of India's software exports. The combined purchasing power of Tamil Nadu and Andhra Pradesh is 50 per cent more than that of Gujarat and Punjab. *India Today*, 20 May 2000.

human beings in every region of the world. Competition and the well being of consumers, not the protection of geopolitical frontiers, will determine the region's economy. Prosperity and growth will be the new objectives for a 'progressive nationalism'. Nationalism as an emotional instinct will be needed to keep the people united and inspired to achieve their common economic goals, while the quest for prosperity will require people to forge links with others outside their own territorial boundary to achieve common objectives. Any kind of parochial thinking in the name of nationalism will not work in this millennium. Only a redefined nationalism aimed at achieving a faster economic growth will enable a nation to embrace change and face the challenge of survival with honour and dignity.

Role of Bangladesh

Bangladesh stands in a unique position, notwithstanding all the internal problems. One of its significant features is that it is a homogeneous, small and compact state, unitary in all connotation, which puts the country ahead of all the others in South Asia. It does not have the problems of India or Pakistan, either internally or externally. It is also in a much better position than Sri Lanka, a country torn apart by the Tamil ethnic conflicts in the north. Other than the Chittagong Hill Tracts issue, which has to a great extent been resolved, although not to the entire satisfaction of all the involved parties, Bangladesh has no internal problems on the scale of other major states in the region, and it can safely be said to be the most peaceful state in South Asia.

Politically, despite having had one period of single-party rule and two under military regimes it has now considerably matured. Three successive governments have been democratically elected and state power has been transferred peacefully from one party to the other. Teething troubles apart, democracy is now taking firm root in Bangladesh and civil society has been activated to grow in strength in years to come.

Economically, although Bangladesh lost some valuable years in the anarchy created by the political regime soon after independence, it has not done too badly compared to other states in the region. It has a well-defined Constitution, the fundamental structure of which is democracy, guaranteeing freedom of press, fundamental rights and independence of judiciary. Despite all the predicaments, it has been able to reduce its population growth rate from 3% to around 1.4%, increase food production to the level of self sufficiency for a population of 130 million, reach drinking water to more than 95% of its population and immunise more than 90% of the children. It has reduced the number of people below poverty line from 80% to 50%.

Geographically also, Bangladesh stands in an advantageous position. It has the wide-open sea on one side and the landmass on the others. In the north it has India's seven land-locked states and then the kingdoms of Nepal and Bhutan, both land-locked. Bangladesh is the only country which can provide them with easy access to the sea and the outside world.

And yet, having had many more advantages than others, it has lagged behind and failed to take the opportunities that the world has offered in the last two decades. Although it has implemented reforms more vigorously than other nations, the achievements could have been more substantial. When the USA withdrew the Generalised System of Preference (GSP) from the four Asian Tigers, Bangladesh failed to fill the vacuum. When the economies of the South-East Asian countries boomed and their wages rose high, Bangladesh still could neither keep pace nor take over the markets with its abundance of cheap labour.

The reasons for these failures have deep roots linked with the backwardness of South Asia as a whole. In economic terms, business proceeded as usual: annual budgets and plans, dependence on foreign aid, World Bank and IMF performance reports, high growth targets fixed but not achieved, a rise in military spending and too much rhetoric and emotion dominated the economic scene. Budget and fiscal deficits, low savings and investment and the level of foreign exchange reserves were the indicators that donors examined to determine whether or not to give more aid. Preoccupied with all these issues, neither the planners nor the politicians had sufficient time to take a broader view of the future of Bangladesh. So the country has remained basically as backward as the other nations of the region.

Bangladesh has seemed poor in terms of resources with a per capita income of $340 dollars and a population density that is one of the highest in the world: 850 persons in every square kilometre. But it has remained poor partly because it has failed in its policy choices and partly because it has not been able to utilise its resources, both physical and human. In addition to the vast human resources, it is endowed with enormous natural resources of fresh water, coal, hard rock, high-quality gas and probably oil too. With the discoveries of an abundance of gas, the question of its utilisation has become highly pertinent. The ever-growing demand for energy and urea fertiliser, both for home consumption and for export, is presenting the country with new economic issues. Once the drilling has been successful, the newly engaged multinationals allowed to operate in the energy sector would like to export their share of gas to other countries, particularly India, which is the nearest market. The use of water to generate electricity in the upstream rivers in Nepal and Bhutan can also be seen as a great source of wealth.

In exchange for the Water Treaty, India has demanded transit and port facilities for its land-locked states in the Northeast. On the other hand Bhutan, Nepal and the northeastern states, all land-locked, want to have stronger economic ties with Bangladesh. None of them is happy with its business terms with India and all of them continue to suffer economically from this relationship, resulting in insurgencies and social unrest. Moreover, because of its own internal complexities and economic chaos, India is no longer able to meet their needs and offer them the facilities they deserve.

A number of ideas have been floated since 1994 highlighting all these issues, when the first US oil and gas multinational company entered into a production-sharing contract with Bangladesh. The US government took a great interest in developing the concept of a sub-regional unit with Bangladesh as the main component.[14] With the coming to power of the Awami League in 1996, the Indian government came closer to Bangladesh to discuss issues of 'mutual interest'. Their interest was primarily in being able to gain transit and port facilities. During this time, one of the ideas discussed was the creation of a Triangular Sub-regional Economic Development unit in the Ganga-Brahmaputra-Meghna region, comprising Bangladesh,

---

[14] Mr Frank Wisner, the first US Ambassador to India ever to visit Bangladesh, mooted the idea in Dhaka.

Nepal, Bhutan and the north-eastern states of India. This was subsequently renamed as the South Asian Growth Quadrangle (SAGQ).

Almost at the same time, ideas for more multinational forums for economic co-operation were advanced, such as the one comprising Bangladesh, India, Sri Lanka and Thailand, formally launched at Bangkok to forge co-operation between South Asian and South-East Asian nations. This forum, named the Bangladesh India Sri Lanka Thailand Economic Council (BISTEC), was set up in June 1997 with Myanmar as an observer state. Another forum, Developing Eight Block D-8, conceived by Turkey and including Iran, Pakistan, Bangladesh, Malaysia, Indonesia, Egypt and Nigeria was launched in Islamabad, also in June 1997. In November 1993, a forum called the Indian Ocean Rim Association (IOR-ARC), comprising 24 counties, was formally launched in Mauritius. Both Bangladesh and Pakistan have since sought membership of the association.

The idea of a sub-regional growth quadrangle in South Asia became a matter of particular concern to Bangladesh. This concept, together with the issue of the proposed route of the Asian Highway, the transportation of Indian goods primarily for military operations in the Northeast and the use of Chittagong Port to this end, created serious controversy. Various research organisations held a series of meetings, seminars and workshops in both Dhaka and Delhi to identify and promote areas of co-operation. They were encouraged by the USA[15] and other donor agencies serving the business interests of the foreign multinationals. The USA was mainly concerned with the marketing of gas or gas-based industries in which US multinationals had made substantial investments. Although Indian and US interests coincided to the extent of supporting the idea of sub-regional co-operation, India's perception of its security needs could not accept any substantial presence of the USA in Bangladesh as it was considered a potential threat to its own regional interests.

So the process of awarding the blocks for exploration of gas and oil was slowed down and the terms of bidding and procedure of evaluation were changed, much to the annoyance of big multinationals like Mobil, Shell, Enron and Chevron. In order to accommodate

---

[15] *The Bangladesh Observer*, 29 January 1997.

Tallow,[16] a hitherto unknown Irish company, the Bangladesh government deviated from its earlier commitment in awarding these blocks. After taking more than two years to decide, it awarded contracts for only five blocks, retaining the most coveted ones for itself. The whole idea was to discourage the US companies from investing in Bangladesh and the unusual delay did indeed force some of the companies to withdraw. This was exactly what was desired by India and by a section of the Bangladesh government that was tied strongly to the Indian interests.

The idea of a sub-regional grouping for granting transit facilities disguised in the name of economic development brought bitter criticism from the opposition, primarily for three reasons. First, the government tried to maintain secrecy in the matter. The Prime Minister did not make any formal statement in Parliament about the government's position; nor did the government ever offered any elaboration on highly sensitive issues such as the terms and conditionalities of the transit and port facilities sought to be granted. Other than the reports in newspapers in India and Bangladesh and the occasional seminars of known pro-Indian organisations held in collaboration with their Delhi counterparts, it was difficult to deduce what was going on behind the scenes between the two governments. This obviously aroused a great deal of suspicion in the minds of the opposition and the people at large.

Secondly, the opposition looked at these schemes as a total surrender to Indian hegemony. To the opposition it seemed that every concession given was only for the strategic benefit of India, which would ultimately lead to the colonisation of the Bangladesh economy by a giant neighbouring country.

Thirdly, the creation of a sub-regional unit of co-operation was seen as a direct threat to the spirit and purpose of SAARC. According to the opposition, it was intended to undermine the objectives of SAARC and thereby alienate Pakistan and Sri Lanka, which could cause the demise of SAARC as a whole. While the Leader of the Opposition called the sub-regional grouping a conspiracy to make Bangladesh into a province of India and a sell-out of its independence and

---

[16] Backed by a powerful lobby within the government.

sovereignty,[17] the Prime Minister tried to defend the concept by saying that such a grouping would not be contrary to the spirit of SAARC.[18]

In order to remove any doubt about this aspect of SAARC, the Bangladesh Prime Minister, at the instance of India, invited the Pakistan Prime Minister to a three-member business summit at Dhaka in January 1998.[19] The widespread and pungent criticism by the opposition had put the government on the defensive. The delay and irregularities in awarding the gas blocks to the multinationals had also caused considerable annoyance and discouraged the USA from taking an active stand on the issue. Although India pushed strongly to obtain the transit and other strategic facilities and the Bangladesh government kept negotiating on these issues in secret, the overall enthusiasm for formalising the growth quadrangular had lost its initial momentum and no formal structure has yet taken shape.

Notwithstanding the way in which the whole issue has been handled by the Indian authorities and the AL government, the fact is that Bangladesh today has emerged for the first time as a centre for strategic development in the area. For those who have always believed in the potential of Bangladesh as a vibrant state, as opposed to those who predict that the country will remain economically stagnant and in a state of perpetual under-development, the time has arrived to put this challenge to test.

The case of Bangladesh stands on its own merit. It should prepare itself to face the challenges of the millennium on the basis of its own strategies and policy options. Today, whatever will be good for Bangladesh ought to be done with courage and conviction, based on the principle of enlightened self-interest. Bangladesh now stands a better chance not only of survival but also of playing a leading role in using the geo-political situation and the new opportunities to achieve fast economic growth. Economics cannot be driven by emotion; nor can growth be achieved by rhetoric and undefined nationalism. First, it must be realised that in this age of globalisation and rapid

---

[17] *The Bangladesh Observer*, 1 January 1997.
[18] *Ibid.*
[19] *Ibid.* 16 August 1988.

technological advancements, it is inconceivable to think that Bangladesh can survive on its own. It has resource constraints and it is heavily dependent on foreign assistance and the global economy. Secondly, however hateful or friendly the Indian government is, Bangladesh has to live with India, as the borders between the two countries will always remain to bind them.

Keeping these two conditions in mind, Bangladesh has to achieve a breakthrough in its economy and come out of the vicious circle of poverty. It should adopt strategies and formulate policies with this objective as the single most important goal. It should not look at India; it should look at itself for its own development. Nor it should be afraid of India on any account; it should do what is best for Bangladesh.

Bangladesh is today the most advantaged country in the area for development. It has a democratic political order, a trained bureaucracy, a well-structured army, a thriving community of entrepreneurs, engineers, scientists and economists, a high class of managerial personnel and a trained workforce. It is much more organised than any of the northeastern states of India and countries like Nepal and Bhutan. Besides its human assets, it has an abundance of fresh water, fertile land, an enormous quantity of natural gas, a reasonable infrastructure and access to sea.

So the proposition is that Bangladesh should establish itself in the leadership position and take the initiative to implement its own policy for growth and development. Instead of looking at India with suspicion on every issue, it should develop its programs with confidence. If India fails to rise to the occasion, it will go through a tumultuous structural change in ten to fifteen years' time. If Bangladesh gains economic strength that will be the best safeguard for its own security. If it fails, it will be more likely to surrender to India.

As India is now willing to co-operate and the USA is interested in lending support to develop a concept of sub-regional co-operation, Bangladesh should take full advantage of this opportunity. By whatever name the new organisation is called, Bangladesh should take the lead in formalising its structure by negotiating directly with the north-eastern states of India, and with Nepal and Bhutan, and if need be, with West Bengal and Myanmar. If the central government of India refuses such direct negotiations, Bangladesh should still pursue it. The use of transit and port facilities by the northeastern states, and by Nepal and Bhutan for purely commercial purposes will benefit Bangladesh both economically and politically. Building the Asian Highway is only a part of the process of global integration. Bangladesh ought to take this opportunity to determine its routes within Bangladesh territory to the country's own advantage, but the quicker the issue is resolved, the better.

As far as water is concerned, Bangladesh suffers from the disadvantage of being a lower riparian country. It will be to its own benefit to obtain, as soon as possible, an agreement to implement a programme for integrated regional water resource management. By this means, not only will the supply of hydroelectric energy be ensured, but the share of water of all the major rivers will be determined and economic development in agriculture and fisheries achieved.

Bangladesh suffers from severe resource constraints at the moment. The development projects are largely financed by multilateral agencies. Only 40 per cent of resources are mobilised from internal resources.[20] In the development structure, the public sector investment so far for education, health and the empowerment of women is extremely limited due to scarcity of resources. So within the present framework, the limited allocation to the sectors from where the nation could gain substantially means that progress will be invariably slow and mostly discouraging. It is obvious that if Bangladesh is to take-off and make its economy vibrant, it will need additional resources to supplement its present efforts to achieve rapid growth. A nation will obviously have more freedom to pursue its own priorities if it has surplus funds at its disposal.

There are two basic approaches to dealing with a nation's surplus resources. If Bangladesh obtains additional resources or income from its gas surplus, the choice is either to hold it unutilised for an uncertain future or sell the surplus gas now in order to have additional funds in hand to invest for quicker growth. In the next 20-25 years, the commercial value of gas may change radically and Bangladesh may not find its reserved gas to be of much use or value because of

---

[20] In 2002-2003 budget, the figure is estimated at 55%.

changes in technology or market. Of the two options, most experts today tend to suggest that surplus resources should be utilised now to achieve immediate faster economic growth. The return on investment made today will certainly help to increase the speed of economic growth and will achieve better results than investing it in 25 years' time. If Bangladesh can be sure of having a surplus reserve beyond its potential need based on the demand of consumption and growth in discovery on a 10-year rolling projection, it should sell the gas now and invest this surplus fund in priority areas of its own choice. In this regard, commercial and business considerations should guide the sale, no matter which country is the buyer.

So with regard to the export of gas and electricity, business principles must apply. The multinationals have been allowed blocks of the gas field under contracts with the Bangladesh government. Once they discover gas, they will own a portion of it, which they would like to sell to others including Bangladesh. If Bangladesh does not require or is not willing to purchase the gas, what should the multinationals do? Anything done against market principles will only be counter-productive. If they want to sell it to India, why should the Bangladesh government stop it? Although the government may decide not to export its own share of discovered gas but the share of gas that the foreign companies own is not the property of the government and so the government can not deny them of their right to sell their own gas. If the government takes a conscious decision not to allow the export of gas, foreign investors should be told of this before they start investing.

Establishing the leadership of Bangladesh in South Asia will require courage and vision on the part of its political leaders and parties. This can only be achieved by way of a national consensus on the country's core objectives, and all the major political parties, the people and the nation are taken into confidence. Neither the Awami League nor the BNP alone can evolve this consensus. It requires a multiparty approach to arrive at a consensus for achieving the ultimate goal of an economic breakthrough for Bangladesh. Bangladesh should look to the east (South-East Asia) and not to the west (India or Pakistan) for its own growth model. It should open up new doors and new strategies for its own development.

The alternatives for Bangladesh are stark. One is to maintain the status quo, the conventional and archaic way of achieving growth, which has so far not been able to attain the desired goal in any of the countries in South Asia. Bangladesh in that case will have to live in a shell that will keep the nation under-developed for an indefinite period of time, where millions will continue to die from malnutrition, shortage of food, lack of health care and education, and general poverty. The population of Bangladesh, which will double in another 33 years, will then enter into the future with no hope of prosperity. With occasional pressure for reform from the donor agencies, and with its existing political culture, it will only face a deeper crisis of survival.

The alternative is to face the millennium with courage: demolish all the barriers standing in the way of progress, aspire to and work for an economic breakthrough, and help lead South Asia to prosperity.

Conclusion

Despite the interstate conflicts and numerous internal problems in each state, South Asia has made substantial progress in the last five decades, and yet it has lagged behind the South-East Asian countries. The issues basically centre on the development of individual states and then of the region as a whole. There are some commendable aspects of South Asian development in terms of sustaining democracy, human rights, the independence of judiciary, the freedom of press and civil societies. But to overcome the present state of under-development, a stupendous task lies ahead for South Asia. The options open to South Asian states are as follows:

1. To adopt a combined effort for development through mutual co-operation within the framework of SAARC.
2. To re-arrange the South Asian zone into economic blocks on a regional or sub-regional basis, comprising areas across the geographical boundaries, driven by a common concept of growth under a federal structure, leading to a kind of confederation.
3. For each individual state to evolve its own strategy of development either on its own or in combination with other states

or parts of other states that are geographically contiguous and economically harmonious.

Inter-state rivalry and political conflicts apart, the target of growth can be pursued. As the first option will yield only very limited benefits, SAARC is not going to serve the purpose. If the second option is pursued, it will be difficult to evolve any workable formula to develop a confederal structure and growth will take a long time to materialise. The third option remains the only answer, particularly for Bangladesh.

India as a model of development should be discarded. Pakistan has so far failed to emerge as a modern state. It will neither be able to harness democracy nor achieve development as long as Kashmir remains its core issue with India.[21] So Bangladesh should not look either to India or to Pakistan to develop its socio-economic growth model. Fear of India must not be allowed to stand in the way of Bangladesh formulating its own strategy and building its own self-confidence. In the geo-political context, Bangladesh cannot survive all by itself; nor it will be able to make any substantial economic progress on its own. In the context of the present process of globalisation and the integration of trade and economy, any active hostility with a large and powerful neighbour like India is not going to help. Keeping this in view, Bangladesh should develop its own strategy for growth and offer strong leadership not only to its own people but to all the neighbouring states — the north-eastern states of Tripura, Assam, Meghalaya, Arunachal, Manipur, Mizoram, Nagaland, and Kingdoms of Nepal and Bhutan. The most impoverished region of the world can then be turned into a prosperous zone for about 300 million people.

For sustaining a democratic order Bangladesh should not look to the West. While the philosophy and value of democracy is well recognised, the model and practice of democracy in less developed societies cannot be the same as in developed societies. What has been attained in the course of hundreds of years in other countries cannot be achieved in Bangladesh overnight. Democracy is an evolutionary socio-political process and there is no model that can be

---

[21] It is argued that Pakistan can only survive as long as the Kashmir issue is alive.

said to be perfect. In most of the developing countries where democracy is practised, they have developed their own model based on their own culture, education, economy and social habits. In fact, democracy as practised in South-East Asia may be a more suitable model than the western democracies for Bangladesh to follow. As it is a new state, Bangladesh has the advantage of being able to create a system of its own. Every country has its own peculiar conditions to which a democratic order has to be integrated.

Bangladesh has already developed certain distinctive features in its democratic system. The concept of having a non-party caretaker government replacing an elected government 90 days prior to a general election is unique to Bangladesh. This change to the basic structure of the Bangladesh Constitution has not happened in any other constitution where democracy is the political order. A second feature that Bangladesh has adopted, which is now being followed by one or two other countries including India, is to restrict MPs' behaviour and voting rights inside Parliament. The provisions made in Article 70 of the Constitution are to discipline Members of Parliament so that they cannot vote against the party decision without losing their seats. Thirdly, the provision made under Article 65 to have 30 seats reserved in Parliament exclusively for women designed to provide opportunities for women to take part in the affairs of state at the highest level.[22] All these special provisions incorporated in the constitution of Bangladesh may be undemocratic in character, but all of them are justified by the needs of the country in the context of its own socio-political conditions.

Bangladesh needs a kind of democracy where human rights will be guaranteed — a kind of democracy where the rule of law will be strictly followed without any compromise. Every citizen, no matter how powerful, and no matter which party he belongs to, must be subject to law. In order to achieve this, whatever kind of restrictive measures are necessary should be incorporated into a system in which institutions will have precedence over individuals. The

---

[22] Although this provision has expired but soon a new provision for reserved seats with a larger number, now to be directly elected is expected to be incorporated into the Constitution.

political leaders in the government or in the opposition, the senior civil and military officers and big business houses must come under constant scrutiny from strong independent institutions run by people who have the reputation of being courageous, competent and utterly honest. Along with an independent judiciary that already exists, Ombudsman-like offices, Independent Human Rights Commission and Anti-corruption Commission are the institutions to be established without any political bias. If there is no corruption amongst the high-level politicians and civil-military bureaucrats, corruption at all levels can be reduced and be controlled.

Once the rule of law has been established and its practice and implementation have been institutionalised, and the political leadership is free of corruption, then the focus on the goal of faster growth can be effectively materialised and an economic breakthrough for ordinary people will be achievable. People will forgive the mistakes of their political leaders provided they see that such mistakes are bonafide, that the government is committed to the rule of law, that they have not adopted any corrupt practice or made any personal gains, and that they have not been discriminatory in their treatment of citizens. In order to achieve this goal, if necessary, appropriate laws ought to be made irrespective of whether they are contrary to some democratic rights.

Bangladesh should be a democracy where an elected government is able to take some drastic measures to streamline the country, establishing the rule of law and social justice as two essential preconditions to development. If economic development and the welfare of the people are considered to be the supreme priority of the nation, then for a certain period of time some restrictive laws will have to be enacted, if possible by consensus voting in Parliament, if necessary, by amending the constitution.[23] Some of these are:

1. Ban the students' and workers' frontal organisations of all the political parties.
2. Suspend trade unions in nationalised banks, sea ports, airports and energy sectors for fifteen years.

---

[23] The present 4-Party Alliance Government installed in October 2001 has the requisite two-thirds majority to amend the Constitution.

3. Ban *hartals* of any kind throughout the country.
4. Political parties should be required by law to register themselves with the office of the Election Commission and to submit their annual income and expenditure statements duly audited by qualified auditors.
5. Provide state allocation of funds to the political parties in proportion to their representation in the Parliament or votes received in general elections. Any political party, which secures less than 7% of votes cast in a general election will not be entitled to any state fund and will lose its status as a political party.
6. Adopt a legally enforceable Code of Conduct for media and newspapers in consultation with the owners, editors and journalists' associations for giving emphasis on national priorities and to avoid negative and 'yellow' journalism.
7. Make every citizen earning above Tk. 100,000 a year subject to taxation. Any evasion of tax should be promptly and strictly dealt with rigorous punishment irrespective of the position of the person concerned.
8. All political leaders must submit income-tax returns and fully disclose their sources of income and make these available for public scrutiny.
9. Amend the University laws to change the present system of election of the Vice Chancellors. Introduce legal provisions for the accountability of the teachers for their academic performance by an independent body. Provide more incentives to reward the teachers for their professional dedication so that they remain involved in academic pursuits rather than petty group or party oriented university politics.
10. Recruit and promote public servants only on the basis of merit without any quota.

Besides what has been stated, one of the most crucial issues that divide the nation today needs to be resolved urgently. It relates to the recognition of Sheikh Mujibur Rahman as the Father of the Nation, as demanded by the Awami League and the recognition of Ziaur

Rahman as the Leader who declared the Independence of the country and led the war of liberation as demanded by the Bangladesh Nationalist Party. Considering that the well being of the people and the future of the country is of utmost importance to everyone, this issue can be resolved by mutual recognition of the respective roles the two great assassinated leaders have played in achieving our independence. If need be, the Constitution ought to be amended to incorporate such a recognition thus settling the matter forever.

To lead the people of South Asia in the context of the issues discussed in this study, the present structure and character of the political parties will need to be redefined. How to achieve the required leadership level is a challenge that needs to be discussed dispassionately. While the emergence of two major political parties, led by two strong leaders, commanding unique position in their respective parties has a positive side, it also bestows on them an enormous responsibility to demonstrate the vision, courage, commitment and confidence that the nation so desperately needs.

If Bangladesh can provide the desired leadership by creating mutual trust between the two leaders, agree on the ten minimum points as mentioned above and resolve the status of the two great leaders of the past, it has tremendous potential not only to alleviate the poverty of its own people, but also to bring greater prosperity to the region. Establishing leadership for the same goals on both sides of the current divide is an immediate task to undertake and it can only be achieved by the efforts of the major parties and their leaders under strong pressure from an active civil society, including the media.

If for my reason, it is not possible to establish any mutual understanding between the two leaders or one party goes on rejecting the other or refuses to co-operate with each other, then the party which is elected to form the government at a given time, should proceed on its own by taking the people into confidence. To this end, it should lay before the nation a clear programme covering the points and issues discussed above and have it approved by the people by way of a referendum, followed by enactment of necessary laws in the Parliament.

Otherwise, while the millennium ushers in the hope of greater prosperity for most of the countries in Asia, Bangladesh like many other countries will not be able to overcome the gap that new technology will create between those having the knowledge and those without it and will continue to lag behind, resulting in misery for millions of people for an indefinite period. If the political leadership of Bangladesh fails to take up this challenge, regardless of the kind of government it has, the country will plunge into social disorder, chaos, anarchy and criminalization, civil strife, political instability, geographical divisiveness and ultimate disintegration, leading to a subjugated statehood. Must Bangladesh accept this position?

Index

A'chick Liberation Front (ALF), 22
Abbas, A.B.M., 160, 162
Abdullah, Farooq, 313
Abdullah, Sheikh Mohammad, 96-101, 104-5, 107, 313
administration
of the governments, 241; accountability of, 36, 236, 243-4, 268, 285, 299, 312, 327
Advani, L.K., 26
Afghan refugees, 103
Afghanistan, 2, 36-8, 91, 103, 125, 191, 309, 311
Afzal, Justice A.T.M., 83
Agni, 117, 120, 127, 130, 137, 209, 310
agreements (between Nepal and India), 43
Ahmed, Chief Justice Shahabuddin, 54, 84, 87, 265, 295
Ahmed, Col. (Rtd) Oli, 72, 276
Ahmed, Imtiaz, 228
Ahmed, Khandaker Moshtaque, 52
Ahmed, Moudud, iii, xv, 31, 33, 50-4, 108, 146, 148, 154, 160, 162, 167, 250, 252, 267, 300
Ahmed, Muzaffar, 250, 252
Ahmed, Sabbir, 19, 43, 224, 228
Ahmed, Syed Abdal, 266
Akbar, Mughal Emperor, 3-4, 307
Akhanda Bharat, 24
Al Beruni, 2
Alamgir, Mohiuddin Khan, 290
Alauddin, Mohammad, 294
Alexander, The Great, 2
All India National Congress, 7
All Jammu and Kashmir Muslim Conference, 96

All Tripura Tribal Force (ATTF), 22
All-India Muslim League, 9
Al-Razee, Alim, 250
Aman, Amanullah, 302
Amritsar, 95, 97
Annan, Kofi, 121
Ansar, 81
Anyaoku, Chief Emeka, 273
Apsara, 115
Arab-Israeli conflicts, 120
Arif, General K.M., 310
arms race (between India and Pakistan), 130
Arunachal, 22, 47, 181, 313, 324
Aryans, 7
ASEAN Free Trade Agreement, 227
Ashoka, Emperor, 3, 24, 307
Asia Centre at Harvard, xiv
Asian Highway, 183, 186, 317, 321
Asian Tigers, 315
Assam, 7, 11, 15-6, 22, 47, 127, 130, 181, 310, 312, 324
Association of South East Asian Nations (ASEAN), xiv, 19, 41, 214, 218-9, 227
Atlee, Prime Minister, 15
Aurangzeb, Mughal Emperor, 3
authoritarian regimes, 213
Awami League (AL), 32-3, 50-7, 72-3, 76, 82, 87, 89-91, 147-53, 162, 167, 170, 172-3, 178, 180-3, 185-7, 233, 249-53, 256-61, 263, 268-70, 272, 290, 294-5, 297-302, 316, 322, 327; Mizan Group, 252
Ayodha, 27
Azad, Abdus Samad, 251

Babar, Mughal Emperor, 4, 307
Babri Mosque, 27, 69

Baluchistan, 11, 33, 38, 117, 125, 305, 309
Bandarban, ix, 64-6, 71, 89
Bandernaike, S.W.R.D., 232
Bandernaike, Srimavo, 232, 234
Bangabandhu, 153, 250
Bangabhaban, 53, 254, 291
Bangladesh
army, 58, 62; economy, 57, 59, 151, 185, 318; government-in-exile, 33, 50, 147-9; road communication in, 185; Role of, viii, 314
Bangladesh India Sri Lanka Thailand Economic Council (BISTEC), 317
Bangladesh Krishak Sramik Awami League (BAKSAL), 51
Bangladesh Nationalist Party (BNP), 53-5, 57-8, 72, 75-6, 166, 169, 172, 174, 177, 189, 251-2, 256-61, 263, 267, 272, 274-6, 285-8, 294-5, 297-302, 322, 328; leads 4 Party Alliance, 55
Bangladesh Rifles (BDR), 188, 261
Bangladesh Rural Advancement Committee (BRAC), 58, 215
Bangladesh Water Development Board (BWDB), 173
Basu, Jyoti, 28, 177, 180
Batuta, Ibn, 2
Belarus, 113, 136
Bengal Muslim League, 12
Bhagabat Gita, The, 6, 24
Bharatyia Janata Party (BJP), 8, 23, 26-8, 142, 175, 189
Bhutan, vii, 1, 20, 42-3, 46-8, 93, 132, 144-5, 179, 181-2, 193-6, 198-9, 214, 217, 223, 225-6, 307, 315-7, 320, 324; Bhutanese of Nepali origin, 145; signed a treaty with India, 48; trade route for, 144; United Front for Democracy in, 47
Bhutto, Benazir, 34, 233-4
Bhutto, Nusrat, 232, 234
Bhutto, Zulfikar Ali, 32-3, 106, 116, 231-2
Bihari, 28, 115, 122, 146
Black, Eugene, 106
Bodo Security Force, Assam, 22
Bombay High Court, 25, 27

Border Security Force (BSF) 162, 188
Boundary Commission, 15, 16
Brahmans, 6, 8
British East India Company, 3
British rule, 1, 3-4, 7-8, 13, 16, 49, 97, 116, 158, 231, 237, 240, 244
Buddhism, 2, 4, 46
bureaucracy, viii, 29-31, 56, 122, 181, 215, 228, 235, 240-4, 247-8, 268, 295, 320

Cabinet Mission, 10-1, 14
Calcutta Port, 144
Calcutta, 3, 15-6, 33, 50, 144, 146, 158, 175
Cambodia, viii, ix, xiv, 205-6, 211
Caretaker Government, 55-6, 262-5, 267-8, 270-1, 273-6, 282, 284, 286-7, 289-96, 298, 325
Centre for Policy Dialogue (CPD), 181, 183
Center for Policy Research, Delhi, 183
Central Asia, 2, 36, 309, 311
Central Intelligence Agency (CIA), 121
Central Treaty Organisation (CENTO), 36, 102
Chagai Hills, 117, 125, 131
Chakma, 60-1, 66, 68, 71, 88
Chakma, Upendra Lal, 72
Chalna Port, 288
Chattaphadhyaya, Sardindu, 176
Chevron, 317
Chief Adviser, 291-3
Chief Election Commissioner (CEC), 295, 297
China, India and Pakistan, 137
China, viii-x, 18, 42-3, 45-6, 48, 52, 82, 94, 100, 102-3, 109, 112, 114, 116, 118-21, 124, 127-30, 132, 134, 137-8, 143-4, 181-3, 205-11, 213, 229, 306, 308-11; testing nuclear bombs in 1964, 209
Chinese
scholars, 2; threat, 308
Chittagong Hill Tracts (CHT), vii, ix, 59-64, 67-8, 70-1, 73-83, 87-91, 182, 314; agreement signed with Jana Sanghati on, 73-4; Bengali settlers of, 60, 88-90;

demilitarisation of, 88; laws were identical for three districts of, 66; people of, 69; security of, 68; special Five Year Development Plan was undertaken for, 64

Chittagong Hill Tracts Commission, 88

Chittagong Hill Tracts Regional Council Act, 79

Chittagong Hill Tracts Regional Council Bill, 75

Chittagong Hill Tracts Regulations, 67

Chittagong Port, 183, 186, 289

Chittagong, 60, 232, 288

Chopra, Pran, 311

Chowdhury, Justice Badrul Haider, 83

Chowdhury, Mizanur Rahman, 252

Chowdhury, Professor B., 276

Christian Tamils, 139

Christianity, 4-5

civil
democratic order, 248; servants, 12, 51, 241-2, 290, 295-7, 302; societies, 21, 28, 33, 35, 38, 48, 210-1, 237-8, 244, 302, 314, 323, 328

client-patron relationship, 235, 240

Clinton, President Bill, 108, 121, 129, 134

Cold War, 30, 35, 37, 56, 103, 111, 117, 120, 308, 311

collaborators, 52

Communist Party of India (M) (CPI(M)), 189

Comprehensive Test Ban Treaty (CTBT), 111-2, 128, 130-1, 133-6, 305

Constituent Assembly of Bangladesh, 50, 61

Constituent Assembly of India, 21, 99

Constituent Assembly of Pakistan, 14

Constitution of 1972, 267

Constitution, 9-10, 21, 28-9, 31, 33, 35, 38, 40, 42-5, 49-51, 53, 55-6, 61-2, 69, 71-2, 74, 76-88, 99-100, 186, 233-5, 237, 243, 249, 257, 259, 261-4, 267-8, 270-2, 274-83, 285-7, 290-4, 297, 312-4, 325-6, 328; 7th Amendment Bill, 259, 264; Ratification Bill (7th Amendment), 257-8; 8th Amendment, 82, 87; 12th Amendment, 55, 267; 13th Amendment Bill, 291, 293

Convention on the Prevention of Narcotic Drugs, 223

Co-operative Threat Reduction Programme, 130

corruption, 33-7, 47, 235-6, 240, 285, 300-2, 326; causes of, 235

Cripps Mission, 10, 14

cultures, xiv, 1-3, 5-7, 12, 17, 19, 31, 42-3, 46, 49, 59, 61-2, 64-5, 67-8, 70, 74, 84, 115, 138, 155, 221, 235, 238, 300, 302, 312, 325

Cunningham, Joseph, 7

Dedbroy, Professor Bibek, 244

defence
expenditure, 37, 191; services, 293

Delhi Agreement of 1952, 99

demand for self-rule by the indigenous people, 61

democracy, 20, 30, 32-5, 38, 47, 51, 54, 56, 85, 94, 114, 154, 180, 210-4, 232-6, 247-8, 253, 255, 259, 262, 264-5, 267-8, 273-5, 306, 314-5, 323-6; practice of, 234-5, 268, 324; within parties, viii, 233, 235

Developing Eight Block D-8, 317

Dhaka Law Reports (DLR), 72, 85, 87, 279-80, 282, 294

Dhaka Race Course, 33, 50

Direct Action Day, 15

discipline in society, 240

Dorji, King Jigme Singye, 46

Dravidians, 5, 7

East Bengal, 11-2, 15-6, 49

East Pakistan, xiv, 17, 49, 85, 117, 150, 159

East Punjab, 16

economic growth, xiv, 19, 30, 39, 111, 127, 198, 207, 211-3, 220, 243, 247, 305, 314, 319, 322; in South-East Asian countries, 211

economy
of South Asia (Table), 193; of South-East Asia (Table), 200, 201; of intra-SAARC trade (Table), 225; of major export market of SAARC (Table), 225; of major import market of SAARC (Table), 226

Eelam National Democratic Liberation Front, 141

Eelam People's Revolutionary Liberation Front (EPRLF), 40
eight-party alliance, 259-61
Election Commission (EC), 21, 100, 248-9, 257-8, 262-3, 272-3, 277-8, 282-6, 288, 293, 295-7, 301, 327
election
by-election in September 1996, xiii; framework or 'Ruprekha' for holding future parliamentary elections, 271; free, fair and peaceful election, 247, 249, 260, 262, 265, 272, 283, 295-6; general elections, February 1996, 285; 288; of 1973, 252; parliamentary elections 1986, 258
Elliott School of International Affairs, xi, xiv
empowerment of women, 58, 215, 321
Enron, 317
environmental calamities, 306
Ershad, General H.M., 53-5, 57-8, 63-4, 69, 80, 82, 166-8, 170, 173, 249, 254-62, 264-5, 267, 274, 295, 300, 301; decided to resign, 265; into a constitutional vacuum, 261; over thrown, 54; proclaimed a state of emergency, 265
ethnic and religious conflicts, vii, 39, 47, 60, 87, 91, 140, 142, 314
European Union (EU), 227
export of gas, 322

Fa-Hsien, 2
Falklands War, 112, 119
Farakka Barrage, 157, 159-60, 162-3, 170, 172, 175, 187
Fernandez, George, 129
fertilizer, 285, 289, 316
fissioning uranium, 126
Five Year Plan, 56-7
food
production, 58, 214; security reserve, 222-3, 306
foreign
invaders, 2, 96; investors, 244, 322
Friendship and Co-operation Treaty signed, 103
fundamental rights, 21, 44, 51-2, 69, 72, 78, 99, 237, 244, 264-5, 293, 315

Gama, Vasco da, 3
Ganatantra Mancha ('platform for democracy'), 291
Gandhi, Indira, 17, 20-2, 104, 106, 116, 153, 155-6, 160, 166-7, 231, 234
Gandhi, Mahatma Mohandas Karamchand, 231
Gandhi, Mahatma, 7-8, 13-4, 24-7, 120, 129, 231-2, 311
Gandhi, Rajiv, 22-3, 105, 139-40, 142, 168, 213, 234
Gandhi, Sonia, 232, 234
Ganga-Brahmaputra Link Canal, 165
Ganga-Kavery link, 159
Ganges river, 25
Ganges water, 94, 158-62, 167-70, 187; arrangement to share of (Table), 161; augmenting the waters, 166; Treaty, 170; unilateral withdrawal of, 163
Garokuki, 181
Gayum, Abdul Mamun, 48
Generalized System of Preference (GSP), 315
George Washington University, xi, xiv
globalisation, 46, 243, 313, 319, 324
Goa, 93, 104, 116
Godse, Gopal, 24-6
Godse, Nathuram, 24-6, 231
Golden Temple, 17, 21
good governance, 211, 244, 268, 298
Gouhri missile, 120
Government Employees Solidarity Council, 290
Government of India Act, 13, 16
Grameen Bank, 58, 215
Group of 77 (G-77), 218-9
growth
model, xiv, 322, 324; pattern, xiv
guerrilla training, 62
Gujarat, 4, 28, 313
Gujral, I.K., 180-1, 307
Gulf Region, 309
Gulf States, 311
Gupta, Anirudha, 310

Gupta, Suranjit Sen, 250, 252
Gurkhas of Nepal, 5, 45

Harappa culture, 6
hartal (general strike), 260, 263, 278, 285-7
Hasina, Sheikh, 55, 58, 182, 233-4, 279, 286-7, 290-1, 298
Hastings, Warren, 3
health services, 59, 191, 194, 201-2, 206, 208
Heidelberg University, xi, xiii
Hena, Md. Abu, 295, 297
High Court Division, 82, 279-80, 295, 301-2
High Court of Bhutan, 46
Highly Enriched Uranium (HEU), 118, 126
Hill Women's Federation, 88
Himalayas, The, 1, 18, 42, 45-6, 104, 107, 109, 114, 131-2, 157, 176, 187, 205, 215
Himar People's Convention (HPC), 22
Hindu
community, 14; exploitation, 12; fundamentalism, 23, 26, 120, 305, 312; India, 8-9, 13, 116, 152; nationalist, 26, 115; religion, 6-7, 139
Hinduism, 5-8, 24
Hindustan, 24-5
Hiroshima, 111, 119, 126
Hizbul Mujahidin, 109
Hooghly River, 158, 160
Hossain, Dr. Kamal, 53
House of Commons, 13
House of Representatives, 44-5
human
development, 196, 214, 308; rights, 21-2, 85, 89, 189, 212, 214, 237, 299, 301, 323, 325
Humayun, Mughal Emperor, 4
Huq, A.K. Fazlul, 9
Huq, General Ziaul, 33-4, 36, 231
Hyderabad, 17, 93, 116
hydroelectric power, 160
Hyunitrep Volunteers Council, 22

Iftekharuzzaman, 228
illegal immigrants, 188-9
illiteracy, 59, 205, 208, 306
Imamuddin, Sheikh, 95
India, vii, viii, ix, x, xiii, xiv, 1-5, 7-30, 33-8, 41-50, 58, 60, 62-3, 68-70, 72-3, 77, 81-2, 87, 90-1, 93-110, 113-45, 147-53, 155-89, 191-9, 203-11, 213-4, 217, 225-9, 231-4, 236, 240, 243-4, 266, 279, 294, 297, 302, 305-20, 322, 324-5; first tested a nuclear device in 1974, 209; governance of, 2; has a GNP per capita of $370, 208; history of, 2
Indian Independence Act, 16, 49
Indian National Congress, 8-9, 13-5, 23-8, 45, 96-7, 100, 105, 113, 136, 142-3, 166, 170, 182, 188, 232
Indian Ocean Rim Association (IOR-ARC), 317
Indian Ocean, 1, 48, 138, 145, 155, 215, 317
Indian Peace Keeping Force (IPKF), 40-1, 139-42
Indian
army, 17, 110, 127, 139, 141, 148-53; constitution, 99-100, 101, 237; Empire, 2, 7, 16; history, 6; missile tests, 310; politics, 8, 23; psychosis of policy-makers, 93; strategists, 115, 182; Tamils, 39; threats, 123; violations of human rights by Indian troops, 108
Indo-Aryan Hinduism, 5
Indo-Aryan history, 6
Indo-Bangladesh treaty, 155
Indonesia, 4, 196, 198-9, 201-2, 211-3, 317
inflation, 151, 285
insurgents
dissenting, 89; Maoist, 45; surrendered, 71
International Atomic Energy Agency (IAEA), 119
International Monetary Fund (IMF), 59, 122, 135, 225-6, 242, 315; performance reports, 315; prescriptions, 59
Iqbal, Allama, 96
Iran, 38, 113, 130, 146, 191, 311, 317
Iraq, 113, 130
Islam, 4-5, 7, 31, 38, 69, 269

Islamic
  bomb, 110, 116; militancy, 38; rule, 4; Summit, 146; zealots, 5
Israel, 113, 120, 130

Jahangir, Mughal Emperor, 4
Jalil, M.A., 250
Jamaat-e-Islami, 261, 263, 270, 279
Jammu and Kashmir Liberation Front (JKLF), 109
Jammu and Kashmir National Conference, 96
Jana Sangha, 26, 61-2, 70, 72, 74, 81, 88-9
Jana Sanghati, 61-2, 70, 72, 74, 81, 88-9
Janatarmancha, 290
Japan, 109, 114, 116, 121-2, 210
Jatiyo Party (JP), 257-9, 270, 279
Jatiyo Samajtantric Dal (JSD), 251-2, 262
jhoom, 62, 68, 74
Jinnah, Mohammad Ali, 11, 15-6, 31, 97, 231
Joint Declaration, 153, 155-6, 260
Joint River Commission (JRC), 156, 158, 160, 164-9, 172, 174
judiciary, 20-1, 35, 38, 44, 47, 51-2, 83, 237-8, 243-5, 264, 267, 315, 323, 326
Junagadh, 17, 93, 116
justice system, 244
Jute Marketing Corporation, 151
Jute Trading Corporation, 151
jute, 57, 150-1, 227
Janatha Vimukthi Peramuna (JVP), 141

Kanesalingam, V., 219
Karachi, 3, 35, 38, 56, 137, 231
Kargil, 35, 109, 110; incursion, 35; war, 109-10
Karkare, Vishnu, 24
Kashmir Students League, 109
Kashmir, vii, 16-8, 22, 24, 36, 91, 94-110, 112, 115-6, 122-4, 132, 230, 305, 308-9, 313, 324; ceasefire in, 99; dream of, 96; issue, 102, 104, 106, 109, 123, 309, 324; liberation forces, 132

Kazakhstan, 113, 136
Kangleipak Communist Party (KCP), 22
Kennedy, President, 106
Khagrachari, ix, 64-6, 71
Khalistan, 17, 21
Khan, Abdul Quader, 123
Khan, Abdus Sabur, 252
Khan, Ataur Rahman, 250, 252, 254
Khan, Ayub, 32, 36, 100-1, 106
Khan, Ghulam Ishaq, 34
Khan, Liaquat Ali, 231
Khan, Yahya, 32
Khandakar, Air Vice Marshal (Rtd.) A.K., 64
Khasis, 181
Khoka, Sadek Hossain, 302
Khosla, Justice G.D., 25
Kibria, S.A.M.S., 274
Koran, The, 5
Korea, ix, xiv, 114, 130, 192, 196-204, 206-7, 211-2
Krishna, 2
Krishna, Justice B.N. Sri, 27-8
Khasi Students Union-Federation of Khasi Jaintia Garo Parties (KSU-FKJGP), 22
Kumaratunga, Chandrika, 42, 232-4

Lahore Resolution, 9-13, 31, 97
Lama, Dalai, 133
languages, xiii, 2-4, 6-8, 17, 31, 49, 59, 84, 138, 139, 215
Laos, viii-ix, xiv, 205-6, 211
Larma, Jotirinda Bodhpriya, 73
Larma, Manabendra Narayan, 61
Law Commissions, 244
Lawrence, Lord Pethwick, 14
Legal Framework Order, 32
Leghari, Sardar Farook Ahmad Khan, 34
Liberation Tigers of Tamil Eelam (LTTE), 40-2, 141-2
Liberation War, 48, 149
Libya, 113, 130
Limited Test Ban Treaty (LTBT), 119

Line of Control, 101, 105-6, 109-10
Local Government Councils, 69

Mahabharata, The, 6-8, 24
Maharashtra, 27
Malaysia, 196-9, 201-2, 213-4, 317
Maldives, The, vii, 1, 20, 48, 132, 145, 193-5, 217, 225-6
malnutrition, 20, 29, 37, 208, 306, 323
Manipur, 22, 181, 313, 324
Mannan, Abdul, 251
Manzur, General, 63
market economy, 57-8
martial law, 32, 54, 253, 256, 300; administrators, 255; courts, 256, 300
massacres in Logang, 89
Mauritius, 317
Mauryas, 2
Megasthenis, 3
Meghalaya, The, 22, 181, 313, 324
Menon, Rashed Khan, 250, 257
Merill, David, 284
Mesbahuddin, Syed, 266
Mia, Mohammed Moniruzzaman, 175
military
  intervention, 55-6, 145, 214, 236, 248, 254, 284, 300; officials, 51, 149; rule, 34-6, 49, 52, 54, 56, 212, 214, 232-3, 236, 254, 300; spending, 19, 22, 37, 131, 210, 268, 310, 315; spending for South Asia (Table), 195, 210; strength, ix, 137
Ministry of Special Affairs, 70
Mizoram, 22, 181, 313, 324
Mizos, 181
Mobil, 317
Modi, Narendra, 28
Mohammad, Bakshi Ghulam, 100
Mohan, Mohammad, 302
Mohante, Prafulla, 312
Mongolian institutions, 5
Mosharraf, General Pervez, 231
MOU of 1982, 167, 168

Mountbatten, Lord, 13, 15-6, 98
Mughals, 4, 27, 95
Muhajir Quami Mahaz (MQM), 38
Muhammad of Ghor, 4
Mujib Bahini, 149
Mukti Bahini, 148
multinationals, 20, 183, 316-7, 319, 322
Murma, 71
Muslim United Front, 105, 107, 109
Muslim
  businessmen, 12; Conference, 97; conquerors, 4; landlords, 12; leaders, 10, 97, 145; League, 10-5, 31, 34, 49, 96-7; rule, 4, 7, 17; rulers, 7, 17; Tamils, 39; in Bihar, 15; of Bengal, 9, 12
Myanmar, 60, 205, 310, 317
Myrdal, Gunnar, 239

Nagaland, 22, 181, 313, 324
Nagas, 181
Naniarchar, 89
Narvada, 2
National Assembly, 31, 32, 34, 44, 46-7
National Iquition Facility, 112
national referendum, 255
National Security Council, 34
nationalism, 14, 24, 27-8, 121, 154, 313, 319
Nehru, Pandit Jawaharlal, 8, 13, 15-6, 20-1, 23-4, 27, 30, 96, 98, 100, 106, 232, 234, 310-1
Nepal Communist Party, 45
Nepal Congress Party, 44
Nepal, vii, 1, 5, 20, 42-5, 47-8, 94, 125, 132, 143, 144-5, 157, 165, 166, 169, 181-2, 193-9, 214, 217, 225-6, 228, 236-7, 243, 307, 315-7, 320, 324; Boundary Treaty with India, 143; to develop effective democratic institutions, 45
Nepalese monarchy, 45
Nepalese of Indian origin, 45, 144
New York Times, The, 41, 136, 244, 269, 288
Nikata, Selukas, 3
Nizam, 18

Nizami, Moulana Motiur Rahman, 279
Non-aligned Conference in Cairo, 1962, 218
Non-aligned Movement, 102, 129, 133
non-cooperation movement, 288-9, 291
Non-Governmental Organisations (NGOs), 58, 215
non-tribal citizens, 71, 77
North American Free Trade Agreement (NAFTA), 227
North Korea, 113, 127, 130
North-West Frontier Province (NWFP), 11, 33, 38, 305, 309
Nuclear Non-Proliferation Treaty (NPT), 111, 113-4, 118-20, 128, 130-1, 133
nuclear
devices, 118, 121, 124-5, 127-31, 133-4; explosions, 112, 116-7, 124, 126, 131; threshold countries, 119; weapons, 111-21, 124-5, 128-30, 132-4, 136, 308
nuclearization, vii, 110, 131, 247, 268; delivering nuclear weapons, 127

one-party Parliament, 270
opposition parties, 40, 55, 156, 172, 183-4, 247, 255, 267, 269, 273, 276, 281, 285
Oxford History of India, The, 2, 8

Pahari Chatra Parishad (Hill Students Forum), 88
Pahari Gono Parishad, 88
Pahva, Madanlal, 24
Pakistan army, 33, 35, 50, 108-9, 145, 147, 149, 151, 265; defeat of, 117
Pakistan International Airlines, 35
Pakistan People's Party, 32, 232
Pakistan, vii, ix, xiv, 1, 8, 11-2, 14-20, 24, 26, 30-8, 42, 48-50, 52, 56-7, 91, 93-5, 98, 100-3, 105-10, 113-4, 116-38, 145-7, 149, 151-3, 158-60, 193-200, 203-5, 211-2, 214, 217, 225-9, 231-4, 236-7, 243, 265, 300, 302, 305-11, 313-4, 317-9, 322, 324; break-up of, 32-3, 36, 49-50, 107; creation of, 11-2, 15, 49, 93, 117; military strength (with China and India) (Table), 137; population of, 37
Palk Strait, 138, 307

Panchayat, 44, 237
Parbattya Chattagram Jana Sanghati Sangha (PCJSS), 61, 82
Parliament (Jatiyo Sangsad)
boycott the proceedings of, 270; brute majority in, 253; election boycott, 261; *en masse* resignation from, 276-8, 280; issue of a caretaker government in, 270
Parliamentary Committees, 72-3, 299
Partition of India, vii, 8, 14, 21, 24, 69, 115
Patel, Sarder, 98
patronage, 235-6, 238-40, 249
Peace Accord with India, 40-1
Peace Accord, 40-1
Peoples Liberation Army (PLA), 22
Peoples Revolutionary Party of Kangkleipak (PREPAK), 22
Persian civilisation, 4
petrochemicals, 30
Pintu, Nasiruddin, 302
Planning Commissions, 56, 156, 242
plutonium, 115-6, 118, 126-7; weapons-grade, 126
Pokhran, 117, 121, 131
polarization in politics, 302
policy planning processes, 268
political
assassination, 231; cultures, 247, 300-1, 312, 323; leaders, xiii, 31, 36, 48, 56, 90, 96, 168, 189, 215, 232, 248, 261, 268, 288, 301, 312, 322, 326-7, 329; repression, 299
politics
criminalization of, 312; of boycott and resignation, 298
population, ix, xiv, 1, 4, 8, 18, 20-1, 31-2, 37, 39-40, 42, 44, 46, 48-9, 58-60, 62-5, 69, 71, 82, 93-4, 114, 117, 138, 139, 144, 157, 173, 179, 182, 191-2, 194, 198, 201, 204-5, 207, 211, 213-4, 221, 226, 228, 289, 315, 323; density, 315; density of South Asian countries (Table), 1; ethnic distribution of (Table), 60; of Bangladesh, 179, 323
poverty, ix, 20, 29, 36-7, 44, 59, 114, 191, 193, 196, 200-10, 215, 224, 235, 239, 241, 243, 306, 308, 310, 315, 320, 323, 328

power reactors, 115-6, 118
Premadasa, President Ranasinghe, 140, 232
Press Club, 290
Pressler Amendment, 117, 120, 123
Prithvi missile, 117, 120, 127
privatisation, 56, 58
professional groups, 76, 282, 289, 302
prosperity, 314
public expenditure, 241
Punjab, 11-6, 21, 24, 31, 33, 91, 115, 136, 137, 305, 313
push in, 188

Quasim, Mohammad bin, 4
Quit Kashmir, 97
Qureshi, Moinuddin Ahmad, 34

Rab, A.S.M.A., 262
Rahim, Moulana Abdur, 252
Rahman, Justice Mohammad Habibur, 84, 295
Rahman, Mashiur (Jadu Mia), 250
Rahman, President Ziaur, 52-3, 55-6, 58, 63, 166, 168, 177, 217, 232-4, 251-5, 257, 266-7, 302, 328; charismatic general, 52
Rahman, Sheikh Mujibur, 50-2, 55, 61, 108, 145-6, 148, 153-4, 160, 162, 170, 173, 182, 186, 232-4, 249-51, 253, 327
Rakkhi Bahini, 151
Ramayana, 6, 8, 24
Rangamati Communist Party, 61
Rangamati, ix, 61, 64-6, 71
Rao, Narshima, 23, 27, 72, 232
Regional Council, 79-82, 85, 87, 89
religion, 3-7, 9, 17, 19, 43-4, 69
Returning Officers, 296
Revolutionary Front of the Talu Party, 109
right of franchise, 248, 262, 264-5, 267
Rigveda, 6
Rishis, 5
rival nuclear arsenals, ix, 137
Rouf, Abdur, 250

Rouf, Justice M.A., 295, 297
rule of law, 214, 236-40, 264, 325-6; concept of, 238
Russia, 18, 114, 116, 123-4, 129, 210, 311

SAARC Agricultural Information Centre, 221-3
SAARC Meteorological Research Centre, 221, 223
Sadiq, Ghulam Mohammad, 100
Salam, General Abdus, 64
Sanskrit, 6-8
Sattar, Justice Abdus, 53, 55, 300
Saudi Arabia, 52
Second World War, 13, 102, 111
Sengupta, Bhabani, 180
Shabbir, Tayyeb, 224
Shahjahan, Mughal Emperor, 4
Shahjahan, Professor M., 173
Shamsuddin, Khaja, 100
Shanti Bahini, 61-2, 70, 72-3
Sharif, Mohammad Nawaz, 34-5, 56, 109-10, 123, 125, 134, 136, 231
Shastri, Lal Bahadur, 100-1, 106
Shell, 317
Shelley, Mizanur Rahman, 61, 70, 192, 307, 311
Shia and Sunni communities, 38
Shiv Sena, 23, 25-8, 123, 189
Sikhs, 7, 15-6, 21, 95
Sikkim, 93, 104, 116, 144
Simla Agreement, 106, 109, 145
Sind, 4, 11, 33, 38, 305, 309
Sindhu, 25
Singh, Baldev, 15
Singh, Maharaja Hari, 95, 98-9
Singh, Master Tara, 16
Singh, Tavleen, 244
Sinhalese Buddhist, 41
Sinhalese, 39-41, 139, 141, 232
Siraj, Shahjahan, 250
Smith, Vincent A., 2, 8

smuggling, 150-1, 188, 228
Sobhan, Rehman, 189, 228
social sector (Table), 202
South Africa, 113, 136
South Asia, vii-ix, xi, xiii-xv, 1, 8, 19-20, 30, 36-42, 45-6, 48, 50, 59, 93-5, 98-9, 101-3, 114-7, 121, 128-9, 131-2, 134, 136-7, 181, 191-5, 197-8, 200-7, 209-11, 213-5, 217-24, 226-37, 239-44, 247-8, 269, 300, 305-7, 310-1, 313-5, 317, 322-3, 328; challenge of survival for, 191, 314; future of, 8, 95, 230, 305-6; options open to, 323
South Asian Association for Regional Cooperation (SAARC), viii, x, xiv, 19, 94, 116, 131-2, 138, 139-40, 169, 217-8, 221-30, 305, 318-9, 323-4; Chamber, 224; into great uncertainty, 131; lawyers, 224; objectives of, 220, 318
South Asian Free Trade Agreement (SAFTA), 227
South Asian Growth Quadrangle (SAGQ), 317
South Asian Preferential Trade Arrangement (SAPTA), 222, 224, 227
South East Asian countries, xiii, xiv, 211
South-East Asia Treaty Organisation (SEATO), 36, 102
Soviet Union, 30, 35, 50, 101-4, 106, 108, 112-4, 116-7, 120, 130, 181, 311
Soviet withdrawal, 37, 308
Speaker, 75, 270-1, 276, 278-82, 294, 298, 300
Sri Lanka, vii, xiv, 1-2, 20-1, 38-42, 56, 77, 91, 125, 132, 138, 139-43, 145, 181, 193-200, 203-4, 213-4, 217, 219, 225-9, 232-4, 236-7, 243, 301, 307, 313-4, 317-8; literacy rate of, 42; a multi-ethnic society, 39
Sri Lankan government, 41-2, 139, 141-2
Sri Lankan Tamils, 39
Standing Committees, 244, 299
state of under-development, 131, 305, 307, 323
Stephen, Sir Ninian Martin, 274, 275
Stiftung, Frederick Ebert, xi, xiii
strategic highway, 109
sub-continent, xiii, 1, 4, 157

Sufis, 4
Sultan Mahmud of Ghazni, 4
Sunderji, General K., 310
Supreme Court of Bangladesh, 84
Supreme Court of India, 21
surface-to-surface Missiles, 127
Swapan, Mohammad Hasibur Rahman, 294
Sylhet, 16, 82

tadbir, 235
Tallow, 318
Talukder, Abdus Salam, 276
Tamil Nadu, 39, 138, 231, 313
Tamil Tigers, 91, 141-2, 232
Tamils, 2-3, 21-2, 39-42, 91, 138, 139-43, 213, 231-2, 313-4
Tashkent Declaration, 101
Teesta Barrage, 187
Tengubhadra rivers, 2
Thackaray, Balasaheb, 26-7, 123
Thailand, 182, 196-202, 317
Thakurta, Meghnath Guha, 228
Thana Nirbahi Officer (TNO), 296
Tibetan, 5
Toaha, Mohammad, 252
Trade and Transit Agreement with Bangladesh, 43
Transit of Nepali goods through India to Bhutan, 43
transparency, 36, 236, 243-4, 268, 298
Treaty of Friendship, viii, 45, 143, 152, 153, 154, 156, 160, 187
trial of 195 prisoners of war, 145
Triangular Sub-regional Economic Development, 316
tribal
  conflicts in Pakistan, 38; guerrilla, 22; leaders, 61-2, 69, 70, 72-3; population, 64-6, 68-9, 88
Tripura, 22, 60, 71, 181, 183-4, 313, 324
tritium-production technology, 118
Tsang, Hse-iüan, 2

Ukil, Abdul Malek, 252

Ukraine, 113, 136

United Liberation Front of Assam (ULFA), 22

United Nations Conference on Trade and Development (UNCTAD), 219

unemployment, 42, 306

United Nations Commission for India and Pakistan (UNCIP), 98-9, 105

United Nations General Assembly, 136, 219

United Nations resolutions, 101

United Nations Security Council, 98, 101

United Provinces, 15

United States of America (USA), 20, 35, 56, 91, 98, 102-4, 108-9, 111-7, 121-5, 129-30, 135-6, 181, 183, 205, 210, 308, 311-2, 315, 317, 319-20; policy, 117; wants India and Pakistan to sign and ratify the CTBT, 136

Upanishads, 6

upazila, 54, 58, 64, 255-6, 262

Urdu, 49

URENCO, 118

US State Department, 284

Vajpayee, Atal Behari, 23, 28, 115, 122, 129, 134-5, 142

Vedas, 5, 8, 24

Vedic literature, 5-6

Vietnam, viii-ix, xiv, 205-6, 211

Village Defense Party, 81

Washington, xi, 110, 116, 118, 126, 135, 259

water
available at Farakka, 174; flow indicators, 178; sharing and Farakka, viii, 157; sharing under the agreement of December 1996, ix, 171

Wavel, Lord, 15

West Pakistan, 12, 31-3, 49

West Punjab, 16

Wisner, Frank, 316

World Bank, 34, 59, 106, 135, 186, 196, 200-4, 206-7, 209-10, 242, 315

Xiaoping, Deng, 127, 211

Zia, Begum Khaleda, 55, 58, 72, 75, 80, 169, 189, 233-4, 254, 259, 265-7, 275, 282, 286-7, 289-91, 298-9, 301; accused Hasina, 259; addressed a letter to Sheikh Hasina, 282; an introvert, 266; favoured a presidential system, 260; in politics, 265